UNDERSTANDING
ASTROLOGY

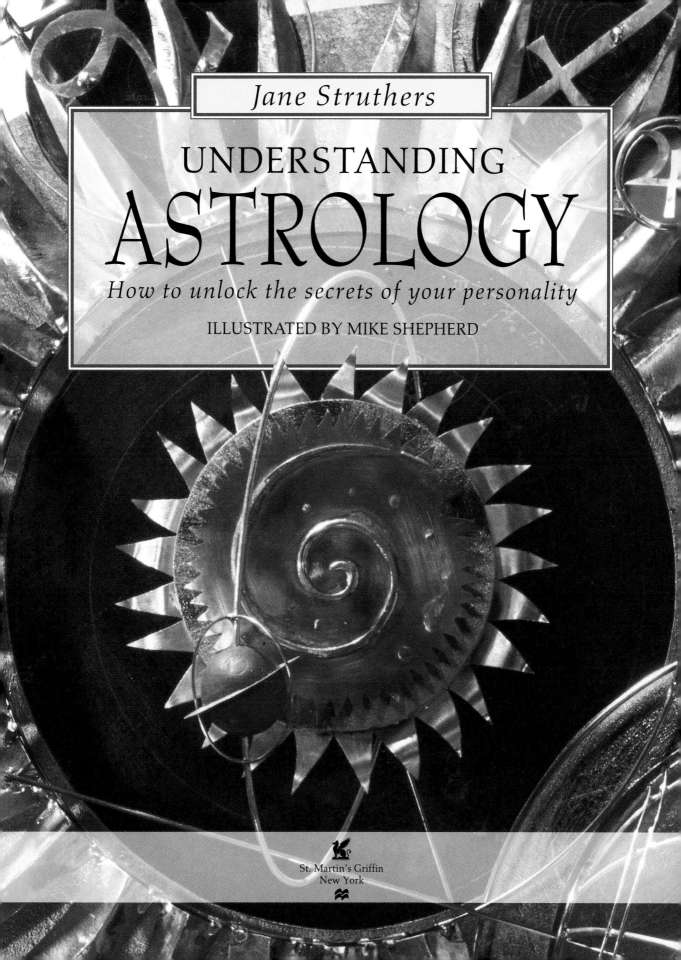

Jane Struthers

UNDERSTANDING
ASTROLOGY

How to unlock the secrets of your personality

ILLUSTRATED BY MIKE SHEPHERD

St. Martin's Griffin
New York

*I often joke that my interests range from A to Z – from astrology to Zen Buddhism.
I have studied astrology for almost thirty years while Zen is a comparatively new addition
to my life. They have both introduced me to some wonderful friends and it is to all of them
that I dedicate this book, with love and gratitude. Thanks, everyone!*

Library of Congress Cataloging-in-Publication Data available on request.

ISBN: 0-312-27709-1

First St. Martin's Griffin Edition: 2001

1 3 5 7 9 10 8 6 4 2

AN EDDISON•SADD EDITION
Edited, designed and produced by
Eddison Sadd Editions Limited
St Chad's House, 148 King's Cross Road
London WC1X 9DH

Phototypeset in Aldus and Bernhard Modern BT using QuarkXPress on Apple Macintosh
Origination by Pixel Graphics, Singapore
Printed by C & C Offset Printing Co. Ltd, Hong Kong

CONTENTS

INTRODUCTION

When seekers after the truth visited the Delphic oracle in ancient Greece they were greeted by a profound message: 'Know thyself.' This sounds like a very simple piece of advice, yet knowing oneself can be a lifetime's work if you have no techniques or methods to guide you through the intricacies of your personality. So where do you begin?

Astrology is one of the keys that can help you to unlock the secrets of your character, both good and bad. It can describe your inner self, your secret longings, your potential and your capacity to love, plus many other things including your family history. It can help to explain mysteries in your character and can also pinpoint your contradictory personality traits. It may not solve all your problems in an instant, but it certainly helps you to see why and how they have arisen, and perhaps what you can do about them. And it can set you on the path to knowing yourself, at your worst but also at your best.

If you have ever wondered why you get on so well with some people but have problems with others, astrology can provide the answers. Just as you can learn a lot about your own personality through astrology, it can also provide insights into the characters of the people around you – your boss, partner, parents, children, friends and enemies.

Calculating and reading a birth chart takes time and practice, but the techniques given in this book are easily mastered and will give you a good introduction to the world of astrology. Once you have read about your own personality you can discover what makes the people in your life tick.

ABOUT THIS BOOK

The astrology in this book consists of nineteen basic ingredients: twelve signs and seven planets. The signs are the twelve signs of the zodiac that will already be familiar to you if you enjoy reading your horoscope in a newspaper or magazine. They are Aries, Taurus, Gemini, Cancer, Leo, Virgo, Libra, Scorpio, Sagittarius, Capricorn, Aquarius and Pisces. The seven planets that are described in this book are the Sun, the Moon, Mercury, Venus, Mars, Jupiter and Saturn. Of course, the Sun and Moon are not really planets but are a star and a satellite respectively, yet that does not matter in astrology. It is their function that we are concerned with, and both the Sun and Moon have very important effects on our personalities.

All seven planets move relatively quickly through the Solar System: the Sun takes four weeks to move through a sign; the Moon takes two and a half days; Mercury can never be more than 28° away from the Sun so follows its orbit closely; Venus can never be more than 48° away from the Sun so also follows its orbit; Mars usually takes slightly

under two months to move through a sign; Jupiter spends just under one year in each sign; and Saturn spends a little over two years in each sign.

These seven planets were all that was known of the Solar System until Uranus was discovered by accident in 1781. This was followed by Neptune in 1846 and Pluto in 1930. Together, these three planets are known as the 'transpersonal' planets and affect whole generations because they move very slowly through the heavens. On average, Uranus takes seven years to move through a sign, Neptune takes just under fourteen years and Pluto spends an average of twenty years in each sign. Detailed readings for these planets are therefore omitted from this book because their sign placings do not affect the personality in the same way as the faster-moving planets. They are, however, listed as the modern rulers of Aquarius, Pisces and Scorpio, respectively, as these are the most widely used rulerships today.

The Influence of the Planets

Each of the planets rules a particular aspect of our personalities as well as a particular Sun sign *(see right)*. The Sun describes our essential self, our creativity and how we express ourselves. Our Sun, or star, sign is the sign that the Sun occupied at the time of our birth and this is the sign that you read in horoscope columns. The Moon describes our instinctive reactions and the things that make us feel safe. These can sometimes be in sharp contrast to the message that the Sun is giving us. Mercury describes the way we communicate with others. Venus describes our need for harmony, and shows what and how we love. Mars describes our energy levels and what we desire in life. Jupiter describes where we seek to expand our experiences, both physically and intellectually. Saturn shows where our limitations lie and how we can learn through experience. Together, the positions of these seven planets make up a detailed picture of our personalities, as you are about to discover.

SUN SIGN RULERSHIPS	
PLANET	SIGNS
Sun	*Leo*
Moon	*Cancer*
Mercury	*Gemini, Virgo*
Venus	*Taurus, Libra*
Mars	*Aries*
Jupiter	*Sagittarius*
Saturn	*Capricorn*
Uranus	*Aquarius*
Neptune	*Pisces*
Pluto	*Scorpio*

Sun

Moon

Mercury

Venus

Mars

Jupiter

Saturn

THE PLANETS

HOW TO DRAW UP YOUR OWN
PLANETARY PICTURE

It is easy to draw up a planetary picture of the time you were born. If you are not familiar with astrology the completed picture may look rather complicated at first, but if you follow the simple instructions you will soon be able to create your own chart – and you can then get to work on the birth data of your family and friends.

1 WHAT YOU NEED

There are only two essential pieces of information you need to create your planetary picture. These are:

- Your date of birth • Your place of birth

If you also know your time of birth this will give you a more accurate picture, as a planet might have moved signs on the day of your birth. Even if you only know that you were born in the morning, for example, this may be useful information. If you don't know your birth time, and you find that a planet did move signs on your birthday, read the interpretations for both sign placings (for example, Moon in Leo or Virgo) and see which one sounds most like you. Alternatively, you can create a chart based on a birth time of noon, which is what many professional astrologers do when the time of birth is not known.

2 WORKING OUT YOUR GMT BIRTH DETAILS

Write down your date and place of birth, plus the time if you know it, on a sheet of paper. You must now convert the date and time to GMT, or Greenwich Mean Time. GMT is used by all astrologers, because it is the time on which every world time zone is based. If you were born in the UK, you must discover if British Summer Time (BST) or Double Summer Time was operating at the time of birth. Look at the chart on page 103 to see whether you were born during either of these time zones. If you were born at the very start or end of a day, you may find that converting your birthday to GMT moves your astrological birth time into the day before or the day after your birthday.

If you were born in a different time zone, in a different part of the world, you will have to convert your birth time to GMT. Consult the world-time-zone diagram on page 102 to find the country in which you were born, and check how many hours ahead or behind GMT it is. For instance, if you were born in Tasmania, you will see on the diagram that it is ten hours ahead of GMT – so when it is 22:00 in Tasmania, it is noon in GMT. To convert your birth time to GMT, you must therefore deduct ten hours. If you were born

in San Francisco, however, you will see that it is eight hours behind GMT, and you must therefore add eight hours to your birth time to convert it to GMT. You also need to check whether a local summer time was operating at the time of your birth. If so, you must deduct one more hour from your birth time.

3 FINDING YOUR PLANETARY POSITIONS

When you have done this, double-check your calculations to make sure they are correct. Write down your GMT birth time and birth date. You now need to consult the charts at the back of the book *(see pages 104–127)*. Firstly, see which sign the Sun occupied at the time of your birth. If you were born on a day when the Sun moved from one sign to another, and you know your birth time, compare the time of its move with your GMT birth time. For example, if you were born at 08:00 GMT on 21 January 1952, your Sun is in Aquarius because it moved into this sign at 02:39, but if you were born at 02:10, your Sun is in

Capricorn. Write down your Sun sign on the piece of paper. Now look at the charts to see which sign the Moon occupied at your GMT birth time, and write this down. Continue this process to discover the positions of Mercury, Venus, Mars, Jupiter and Saturn at the GMT time of your birth. Double-check your calculations to make sure they are accurate.

4 COMPLETING YOUR CHART

You are now ready to complete the planetary picture of your birth time. Photocopy the blank chart on page 128, then write your name, date and time of birth (if known) in the middle of the chart. Start by writing the symbol for the Sun in the correct segment. For instance, if your Sun is in Aquarius, write the symbol for the Sun in the segment of the chart corresponding with Aquarius. Now write in the symbol for the Moon in the correct segment, followed by the symbols for Mercury, Venus, Mars, Jupiter and Saturn in the appropriate segments *(see sample chart below)*.

Isabella was born in December in the UK, when GMT was operating. This chart shows the planetary picture at the time of her birth.

ISABELLA

28 DECEMBER 1997
17:56 BRIGHTON,
ENGLAND

Pisces

THE SIGNS

TAKING THE NEXT STEP

Studying the signs that the seven planets occupied at the time of your birth will help you to build up a well-rounded picture of your personality. You will be able to see how you relate to other people on an emotional level, you might understand why you always react instinctively in a certain way and you could realize that you have many potentials that are waiting to be tapped.

If you want to add another subtle layer to the picture of yourself you are building up, you can explore a further realm of astrology – what are known as the elements and qualities. These will show whether you have a good balance of energies or whether you lean heavily in one or two directions.

ELEMENTS

Astrology recognizes that four elements make up the world: Fire, Earth, Air and Water. Each element rules three signs and it describes the way these signs express themselves. The Fire signs – Aries, Leo and Sagittarius – are energetic, enthusiastic and open. The Earth signs

ELEMENT	SIGN
Fire	*Aries, Leo, Sagittarius*
Earth	*Taurus, Virgo, Capricorn*
Air	*Gemini, Libra, Aquarius*
Water	*Cancer, Scorpio, Pisces*

– Taurus, Virgo and Capricorn – are stable, security-conscious and practical. The Air signs – Gemini, Libra and Aquarius – are detached, intellectual and rational. The Water signs – Cancer, Scorpio and Pisces – are emotional, empathic and sensitive.

QUALITIES

In addition to the elements, each sign is also ruled by one of three qualities. These are cardinal, fixed and mutable, and they describe the form that each element's energy takes. The cardinal signs – Aries, Cancer, Libra and Capricorn – like to take action and are outgoing. The fixed signs – Taurus, Leo, Scorpio and Aquarius – have firm opinions and enjoy some form of stability. The mutable signs – Gemini, Virgo, Sagittarius and Pisces – are flexible and changeable.

QUALITY	SIGN
Cardinal	*Aries, Cancer, Libra, Capricorn*
Fixed	*Taurus, Leo, Scorpio, Aquarius*
Mutable	*Gemini, Virgo, Sagittarius, Pisces*

PUTTING IT ALL TOGETHER

When you have calculated the positions that the planets occupied when you were born *(see pages 8–9 for details about how to do this)*, you can begin to collate all the information

that you have amassed. First of all, you need to see whether there is a good balance of elements and qualities among your planetary placings. Then you can see whether any planets are placed in signs in which they perform particularly well.

On page 9, there is a chart for Isabella, who was born at 17:56 GMT on 28 December 1997 in Brighton, England. This shows that she has the Sun in Capricorn, the Moon and Mercury in Sagittarius, Venus, Mars and Jupiter in Aquarius, and Saturn in Aries. If we count up the balance of elements and qualities, we get the following result:

Fire signs	3	(Moon, Mercury and Saturn)
Earth signs	1	(Sun)
Air signs	3	(Venus, Mars and Jupiter)
Water signs	0	
Cardinal signs	2	(Sun and Saturn)
Fixed signs	3	(Venus, Mars and Jupiter)
Mutable signs	2	(Moon and Mercury)

Isabella's birth data shows a strong emphasis on Fire and Air signs, so she is enthusiastic and intellectual. She only has one Earth sign, suggesting that it may be difficult for her to feel grounded, and she has no Water signs at all. When there are no planets in a particular element, the person may compensate for this with behaviour that overemphasizes the missing element. So Isabella may be extremely sensitive or emotional or she may attract people who behave this way.

There is a good balance between the qualities. If there were an imbalance, however, the person would lean in the direction of whichever quality rules the most planets. The lack of a quality would be compensated for in the same way as the lack of an element.

When you have calculated your own planetary picture, you can begin to work with the birth data of your partner, family, colleagues and friends. You may make some exciting discoveries, such as realizing that you have an instinctive rapport with people who share your Moon sign or that you adore the sense of humour of people whose Jupiter is in the same sign as one of your own planets. You may also begin to understand why some people annoy you or argue with you. Rather than dwell on your differences, you may be able to find ways to create some form of harmony with them, and this could have a very beneficial effect on your most challenging relationships.

Planets, qualities, elements and signs.

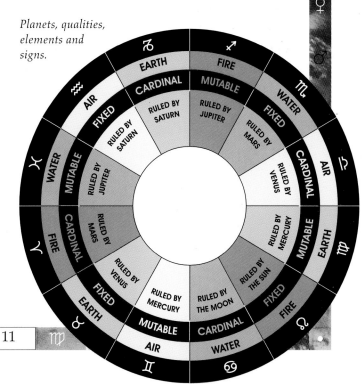

PART ONE

THE TWELVE SUN SIGNS

Even if someone knows nothing else about astrology, they are usually familiar with their Sun, or star, sign. This is the sign that the Sun occupied at the time of birth. So if your Sun sign is Aries, this means you were born during the four weeks when the Sun was moving through the sign of Aries.

Your Sun sign describes your essential self, whatever it is that makes you the person you are. It also indicates areas of life in which you can shine and be at your very best. Your Sun sign may be predominantly practical, it could have a strong creative flavour or it might operate on an emotional level. Whichever attitudes and activities it describes, these are areas in which you will feel particularly at home.

The description of each Sun sign on the following pages gives a general interpretation of the main characteristics, then goes on to reveal how that sign is affected by relationships, money, health and career. The quality, element and ruling planet are also listed, so you can start adding to the knowledge you already have about your Sun sign straight away.

ARIES

21 MARCH – 20 APRIL

You love to lead the way through life. The idea of being a follower doesn't appeal to you at all – you need to be at the forefront of whatever is happening. That is because Aries is the first sign of the zodiac and, therefore, you need to come first as well.

This can make you very competitive, whether you are taking part in something sporty or fighting your way up the promotion ladder at work. As far as you are concerned, life is a series of races and you are determined to be a winner every time. Besides, this helps to keep life exciting because you have a low boredom threshold and can quickly become fed up if you think things are becoming stale or stuck in a rut.

Your ruler, Mars, can make you fearless. You have an endearing love of adventure that means even if you get hurt doing something daring, you will have another go once the cuts and bruises have mended. It is difficult for you to learn

QUALITY: *Cardinal*
ELEMENT: *Fire*
RULING PLANET: *Mars*

from experience because you have a tendency to repeat mistakes. You instinctively hope that things will be better second, third or fourth time around, and can feel bewildered when this doesn't happen. You may even leap out of the frying pan into the fire sometimes. At least it keeps life interesting for you!

The Fire element to which you belong fills you with enthusiasm and energy, so you are always eager to get involved in the next escapade that comes along. Even when you are old, you will still be eager to know what is round the corner. If infirmity or other circumstances prevent you from throwing yourself heart and soul into life, you can feel frustrated and angry.

RELATIONSHIPS

Life is one long adventure for you, and the same is true of love. You are blessed with a very big heart and a tremendous capacity to show affection for the special people in your life. They are left in no doubt about the way you feel because it is almost impossible for you to disguise your emotions. You are very honest, sometimes to the point of bluntness, so people usually know all about it if you don't like them!

When it comes to romance, your heart has probably been broken more times than you care to remember. Metaphorically speaking, it is covered with pieces of sticking plaster, yet you may find it hard to learn from your mistakes. The phrase 'once bitten, twice shy' rarely applies to you. It is more likely to be 'once bitten, twice bitten, thrice bitten' and so on. Yet this is one of the reasons why people love to be with you – you are so open and receptive to whatever may come along.

Sex is an important part of a romantic relationship for most Ariens. You can be very lusty and you need to express this with a willing partner. Sometimes, however, you may confuse lust with love, which can cause problems if your partner feels that you don't appreciate their brain as much as you obviously enjoy their body.

As far as you are concerned, the main purpose of money is to have fun with it. Whenever you are feeling flush the last thing you will want to do is stash away all that money for a rainy day. The entire concept of planning for the future at the expense of the present is completely foreign to you. Instead, you will want to spend money in the most exciting and imaginative way you can possibly think of. If you are an especially daredevil Arien, most of your spare cash may well go on fast cars and motorbikes, as well as other exciting ways of laughing in the face of danger. It may take a prudent partner to dissuade you from spending all your money as soon as you get it.

Your impulsive generosity means that you can also spend a lot of money on loved ones. You will gladly treat them to holidays, take them out for meals or stand them a round of drinks, according to what you can afford. It gives you great pleasure to give your loved ones gifts, but you probably always tend to shop for these at the last minute. It's not that you've forgotten – it's simply that you have had other things to do in the meantime. Besides, looking for presents at the eleventh hour concentrates your mind wonderfully.

MONEY

HEALTH

If you managed to survive childhood without sustaining at least one dramatic injury to your head, it is a miracle. Aries rules the head and, given your tendency to hurl yourself at life (sometimes literally), your face probably carries several small scars that are permanent reminders of various exciting adventures.

Everyone needs to take exercise but it is especially important for you. You are blessed with so much natural energy, impetus and drive that they have to find positive outlets. If circumstances mean you can't work off this energy, you can quickly become fractious, irritable or just plain angry. You are especially suited to athletics and sports, plus any other activities that rely on muscle power. Martial arts may also appeal – you can daydream about being a fearsome adversary even if tears do come to your eyes every time you break a fingernail.

Many Ariens have a naturally lithe, muscular build, but you can easily put on weight if your life is too sedentary. You will dislike this because it means you can't move about as quickly as you would wish. Headaches can be a problem if you are forced to spend too long indoors rather than out in the fresh air. You enjoy getting together with friends for drinks and meals, but too much of the good life can occasionally lead to kidney ailments.

As with so many other areas of your life, one of the most important requirements for your career is that it should be exciting. You don't like the idea of doing a job that is boring, unadventurous or which involves taking too many orders from other people. It is very important for you to have some independence and autonomy in your career, otherwise you will quickly lose interest in it.

The more energy you are able to use in your career, the happier you will be. You need to keep active, so sitting in one place all day will not appeal at all. Ideal jobs get you out into the fresh air and include professional athletics or sports, the armed services, the building trade, mechanics and engineering.

It is important for you to know that you have the chance to make it to the top of your chosen profession; if not, your natural competitiveness will be stifled. This means it is much easier for you to give orders than to carry them out. Teamwork is enjoyable but you need plenty of praise and recognition, otherwise you may feel that you are being taken for granted or overlooked. You excel at coming up with brilliant ideas but you may lack the stamina to see them through to completion. You prefer to let someone else do all the donkey work!

CAREER

TAURUS

21 APRIL – 21 MAY

*L*ife can be a serious business for you. Even though you may have a wonderful sense of humour, your emotions go very deep. You have a strong conventional streak and a healthy respect for tradition. This means that you appreciate rituals and the need to do things in a certain way. However, occasionally this can spill over into a reluctance to introduce change into your life and an over-conservative attitude that clings to the status quo even when it has obviously outlived its usefulness.

You have an instinctive need for material and physical security, and this can make you fearful of anything that threatens your comfort or happiness. You may want to shy away from any form of innovation or new idea because you are frightened of what it might mean for you. Your natural determination can turn into obstinacy and stubbornness. This is something you need to guard against,

QUALITY: *Fixed*
ELEMENT: *Earth*
RULING PLANET: *Venus*

because it can make you become stuck in
ruts and bogged down in a way of life that no
longer has anything to offer you.

Your greatest strengths include your loyalty and fidelity.
People can count on you because they know you will do your best for
them. You are practical, reliable and comfortingly matter-of-fact – the
sort of person anyone can turn to in a crisis. This means you have many
devoted friends and loved ones because they know they can count on
you when the chips are down.

Venus, the planet of beauty and love, is your ruler and it is therefore no surprise that you are said to belong to one of the most
attractive signs of the zodiac. You may well have a beautiful voice and
a tremendous appreciation for music and all the good things in life.

RELATIONSHIPS

Relationships are of utmost importance to you. You can feel unsettled if you don't have a permanent partner, just as you can feel like a fish out of water if other areas of your life lack a sense of permanence. Although you may play the field when you are young, you will quickly look for a partner you can stay with for the rest of your life. You strongly believe in the power of love and, with your instinctive suspicion of change, you are only interested in relationships that will stand the test of time. The thought of ending a relationship can bring you out in a cold sweat.

Ideally, your partner should be able to satisfy your powerful need for emotional security while encouraging you to be more adventurous in the rest of your life. They should also match your sensual nature, because you can be one of the great lovers of the zodiac.

Although you can be a wonderfully loving and affectionate partner, you have a tendency to become possessive when you think your security is being threatened by outside forces. You may secretly want to keep tabs on your partner, reassure yourself that they belong to you, body and soul. But this attitude can gradually erode your relationship, making your partner feel like nothing more than a valued possession.

This is an area in which you feel completely at home. As a Taurean you have an innate understanding and appreciation of the power of money. As far as you are concerned, it can make or break your life so you treat it with caution and respect.

Some signs are happy to live in rented accommodation but you will only feel truly settled when you own your home. You may even buy your first property at a much earlier age than most of your friends, and you could also take out pensions and other financial provisions for the future long before your contemporaries. This is your natural prudence at work, and it may guide you into some very good investments over the years. However, you may have to guard against a slight tendency to be so careful with your money that you become tight-fisted or count every penny you spend. This is especially likely if life has been tough for you.

When you do spend money, you prefer to buy things that are made to last. Your furniture will probably be sturdy and large, even when this goes against the latest style. You hate the thought of wasting money on items that will soon break or go out of fashion. You would rather be thought of as a traditionalist than a spendthrift. Wasting money is an alien concept to you.

MONEY

HEALTH

One of your biggest health problems is your love of the good life. Many Taureans battle with their weight and may even spend years switching from one diet to another, trying to find a magic formula that will keep them svelte and trim. Unfortunately, the only answer may be to restrict your intake of all those foods you love so much. Moderate exercise will also help you to keep one step ahead of the scales. If you are unhappy or insecure, your instincts tell you to take refuge in comfort food or too much alcohol, both of which exact a hefty price around the waistline.

Taurus rules the throat, so this may be a vulnerable area for you, especially when you are under pressure or feeling miserable. Getting out into the fresh air is one of the best ways to keep healthy. Because you belong to an Earth sign, it is very important for you to enjoy the great outdoors. Gardening is a hobby that literally suits you down to the ground – not only will you enjoy growing your own flowers and vegetables (think of the money you can save!), but it will do you good to connect with nature through your hands and feet. Long walks in beautiful surroundings will also help you to keep fit, and can be very restorative when life gets you down.

Your sense of responsibility makes you want to contribute something to the world and you will take pride in doing your best in your job. You are a hard and dogged worker, and will willingly put in extra hours if that's what is needed to complete a project on time. However, beware of letting this become a habit – otherwise your spare time will gradually become eroded by work.

Ideally, you should have a career that makes the most of your practical, down-to-earth nature. You will feel at home in any career connected with finance, such as banking, investment advice, pensions and insurance. Careers connected with property will also do well for you. Professions that allow you to work with nature, such as gardening, agriculture, ecological concerns, horticulture and floristry, will be very good for you. You have a natural artistic ability, so may enjoy working in the decorative arts. You could also be an excellent masseur, aromatherapist, perfumier or beautician.

Unlike many other signs, you may choose a career and stick to it, come what may. You might even work in the same office or factory for the whole of your working life. This will give you a much-needed sense of permanence. However, it may also mean that you feel incapable of changing jobs if you are unhappy.

CAREER

GEMINI

22 MAY – 21 JUNE

If you are a typical Gemini you have bright, alert eyes that take in everything that is going on around you. You may look younger than your years and you have an abiding interest in all sorts of ideas and activities. This is partly because you are ruled by Mercury, the planet of communication, and partly because you belong to the Air element, which makes you operate on a primarily intellectual level. You are far more comfortable with the realm of ideas than what you regard as murky emotions.

Geminis are clever, lively and spirited. You are good company, provided you stop talking long enough to let others get a word in edgeways every now and then! You love puns and other jokes that play with language. You are also an insatiable communicator who can run up massive phone bills because you can't resist keeping in touch with your friends, whether they live round the

QUALITY: *Mutable*
ELEMENT: *Air*
RULING PLANET: *Mercury*

corner or on the other side of the world. The advent of the internet and e-mail has been a blessing for you because it means you can send instant messages around the globe. You also enjoy reading and like to keep up to date with the latest news, whether you do it through television or radio, or burying yourself in a newspaper or magazine. You would even read the back of a cereal packet if nothing else were available.

This is the sign of versatility, making you very adaptable and flexible. You like to lead a busy life and can cope with a hectic schedule that would exhaust some of the other Sun signs. However, you have a low boredom threshold and can have trouble concentrating on one project for long enough to finish it. As a result, you may need to develop more staying power.

RELATIONSHIPS

Geminis can function on two levels at once, so you can give the appearance of being the life and soul of the party while deep down you feel absolutely wretched. However, it makes you feel uncomfortable to explore your innermost feelings. You would prefer to make light of everything or discuss it on a purely intellectual level. The same is true of your sex life – intense, passionate encounters make you uneasy.

This is the sign of the twins, and all Geminis spend their lives searching for their twin. You may be lucky enough to find a long list of soulmates over the years – and you are rarely short of friends because you are so popular. Yet something is usually missing in the relationship and you may decide to go your own sweet way and find someone else. It can take you years to understand that your other twin was there all the time, within yourself.

When you do find a partner, it has to be someone who is as bright and mentally sharp as you. Dunderheads, even if they are so beautiful they can stop traffic at fifty paces, need not apply. Most Geminis are simply naturally flirtatious – you instinctively like to bring out the best in your companions – but you may need to guard against a slight tendency to be unfaithful.

If someone gives you some money, you will immediately wonder how to spend it. The concept of saving money for saving's sake can be completely foreign to you. It doesn't occur to you to jealously guard every penny and stash away most of your money for a rainy day. You reason that life is short and it is meant to be enjoyed, so you should live now and pay later. Your favourite shops are probably always overjoyed to see you because, even though you spend a long time browsing, you usually stagger out weighed down with purchases that you simply had to have.

You also enjoy spending money on items that will help you to keep in contact with others. You may regularly update all your computer equipment because it genuinely pains you if you can't use the latest software programs. You enjoy going on short trips and weekend breaks, and you may also spend a lot of money on cars and motorbikes.

The only time you become interested in making your money grow is when you view it as an intellectual exercise, perhaps following the markets to see how they will perform and keeping up to date with the latest monetary theories. Otherwise, you will have periodic blitzes on your finances to get things back in some sort of order.

MONEY

HEALTH

Living, as you do, in your mind, it is important for you to get plenty of exercise. Not only does this help to keep your body working properly, but it can also act as an antidote to all the thinking you do. However, you will avoid exercise if it is boring or repetitive; ideally it should offer an opportunity for socializing afterwards. Team games appeal, and tennis is a big favourite. You excel at hand and eye coordination, so you may wipe the floor with your opponents.

However, you do not have as much stamina as you like to imagine. Your tendency to live on your nerves can exhaust you, leaving you vulnerable to colds and other respiratory ailments. Yet, if life becomes too restful, predictable or sedentary for you, that can make you ill as well! You need to find a balance between hectic activity and complete indolence. It can also be difficult for you to get a good night's sleep because your mind rarely stops chattering away. Relaxation techniques can help you considerably.

Gemini rules the hands, arms and lungs, making these vulnerable areas of the body for you. You can also be accident-prone because you are so busy talking or thinking that you forget to pay attention to what you are doing. Your hands usually carry at least one minor cut or bruise.

Your tremendous ability to communicate with others means you excel in the media. You might be a marvellous broadcaster, journalist, writer or translator. You also enjoy working in the communications industry, perhaps selling computer equipment or telephones. You have great selling techniques, so can go far when working in the retail trade or real estate. You also excel at ideas, and can come up with the kind of plans and concepts that are ideally suited to the advertising profession.

The most important criterion for you when you look for a new job is that it should be interesting and lively. You would prefer to work in a busy, open-plan office than to be locked away in an office by yourself, and you can become depressed if you work from home and also live alone. You need plenty of contact with others, especially if that means getting together over some coffee for a good gossip.

Ideally, if you are to avoid the ever-present threat of boredom, you need to have at least two projects or two jobs on the go at the same time. The thought of only doing one thing can appal you after a while because you need to stay flexible. Something else that may be flexible is your time-keeping – you can lead such a busy life that you often arrive late for appointments.

CAREER

CANCER

22 JUNE – 22 JULY

Cancer is the first of the Water signs, so you operate on a predominantly emotional level. You are happiest when dealing with the realm of the emotions and may struggle to view life from any other angle. This means you can be extremely sensitive and are easily hurt. You may even become quite defensive, often primed for someone to launch an attack on you. When threatened by the prospect of being hurt or confronted by someone, you may long to anticipate trouble and strike the first blow. You can also disguise your acute sensitivity by cultivating a slightly tough outer persona, in exactly the same way that your crustacean namesake protects its soft body.

Emotional security is of paramount importance to you. You need to be surrounded by people you love, whether they are family or friends. In fact, if you don't have a family of your own, or you

QUALITY: *Cardinal*
ELEMENT: *Water*
RULING PLANET: *Moon*

don't like your own relatives, you will create a circle of unofficial kith and kin instead. You have a natural talent for gathering people around you.

You find it very hard to forget things. Like elephants, you have a very long memory. You may become a kind of family historian, instinctively recording important events by taking photographs and stashing away various mementos.

Hearth and home figure greatly in your life. You will be very unhappy if you are forced to live somewhere that you don't like or don't own. Your home is a refuge from the rest of the world, which can be a frightening place for you. If you invite someone into your home, they should take it as a compliment because you won't let just anyone into what you see as your inner sanctum.

RELATIONSHIPS

You place such a strong emphasis on your emotional security that you closely guard your relationships and will do your utmost to ensure that they continue. Any form of emotional change is anathema to you because it threatens your stability, so you will cling on to your partner like grim death if you think they might leave you. You can even continue a relationship long after everyone else can see that it's dead on its feet. You would rather be unhappy living with your partner than unhappy living alone.

Cancerians are wonderfully affectionate and demonstrative. You will delight in giving your loved ones lots of hugs and kisses, and you will also go out of your way to cook them delicious food – especially if you think they need a little tender loving care or some home comforts. Being loved by you is like lying back in a warm bath – reassuring and safe. However, your loved ones may have to beware of metaphorically sitting on the nail brush – upsetting you so that you go on the attack.

Sex is an important emotional outlet for you but you need to be wooed and to know that you are truly appreciated and loved by your partner. You can have love without sex but you may become very unhappy if you have sex without love.

If there is one thing you understand, it is the power of money. You see it as a way of ensuring your emotional and physical security, such as providing a roof over your head and putting plenty of food on the table. The majority of your budget may be spent on your home and family, because these are your two main priorities in life. You will buy items for your home that are built to last – you like the permanence implied in such objects. You may also enjoy buying antiques, which can be a very good investment for you, because you take pleasure in being surrounded by objects with a long history. Silver, which is the Cancerian metal, can be another good investment for you.

You aren't exactly mean, but you can be careful with your money. You certainly don't throw it about in all directions or splash out on fripperies and passing fancies. Instead, you want to get value for money. One way to increase your sense of security is to start a regular savings scheme. You take great comfort from knowing you have a supply of emergency money if you need it, and also from knowing that you are being prudent in planning for the future. Even so, you should avoid high-risk investments because these could bring you a great deal of anxiety.

MONEY

HEALTH

Worry is a state of mind that you are very familiar with and if this goes unchecked it can play havoc with your health. You can lose sleep worrying about things that may never happen and you will wear yourself out fretting about problems from the past. Ideally, you need to practise relaxation techniques that will help you to deal with the stresses and strains of everyday life. It will also be beneficial if you can confide in someone who you know will listen to your problems.

The breasts and stomach are the two areas of the body ruled by your sign. If worries take con-trol of you, you can be plagued by stomach complaints such as indigestion or even stomach ulcers. You can also encounter difficulties with your stomach for another reason – when the going gets tough, many Cancerians head straight for the cake tin. Comfort eating can lead to weight problems.

This is a Water sign, so one excellent way for you to unwind is when you are near water. You enjoy swimming, which helps you to keep fit while also ensuring that you are literally in your element. Gentle water sports can also appeal, although you may draw the line at dangerous pursuits such as jet-skiing. Even strolling by the bank of a river or relaxing in a scented bath can help you to relax.

It is very impor-tant for you to know that you are earning enough money to keep the home fires burning. You enjoy providing for your nearest and dearest, even if it means working very long hours. With your instinctive need for security, you will be unhappy in any job that seems impermanent because you'll worry about what you will do when it finishes. As a result, you may not be suited to self-employment because you will feel very anxious about having enough work.

Whatever your job, you will try your hardest to create a happy, safe environment for your col-leagues. You may even bring them home-cooked treats and will always want to hear the latest news about their families. Your ideal is to work in such a safe environment it feels like a home from home.

With so much accent on home comforts, it is hardly surprising that you excel in jobs that revolve around the home. Cooking is another profession you enjoy. You can be an inspired cook, although you prefer creating traditional food to following the latest foodie fad. You will also enjoy jobs connected with the sea and water in general.

Whatever your sex, your lunar ruler makes you strongly maternal, so you like working with children. You could be a good obstetrician, paedi-atrician, midwife, nanny or teacher.

CAREER

LEO

23 JULY – 23 AUGUST

The key to your Leo character is to remember that your sign is ruled by the Sun. Without the Sun, our solar system would not exist and there would be no life on Earth. Thus, as a Leo, you have an instinctive sense of your own importance in life. This may not necessarily mean that you are big-headed, but it does mean you are blessed with self-confidence, dignity and a strong belief in yourself. You could hardly be described as a shrinking violet, and you bring gaiety, vibrancy and fun to any gathering.

Just as the Sun is the centre of our solar system, you are happiest when you are in the limelight. You don't mind taking a back seat every now and then, provided it is not for long. However, you don't like being ignored and there may well be times when you have to steel yourself to let others have their say.

You have a very regal quality, which is hardly surprising since Leo is the sign

QUALITY: *Fixed*
ELEMENT: *Fire*
RULING PLANET: *Sun*

of royalty. Although you may not walk around wearing an ermine-trimmed robe, you do take a lot of care over your appearance and you always like to look your best. Instead of a crown, your hair may be your crowning glory, especially if it is typically thick and glossy. It may even resemble a mane.

Pride is very important to you. You like to feel proud of your achievements and you want everyone else to appreciate them too. Sometimes this can spill over into arrogance, making you believe that you are automatically in the right or the only person who can do things properly. Although most Leos shy away from such attitudes, one or two may believe they are a cut above everyone else, and can act accordingly. This is the sign of the snob!

RELATIONSHIPS

Leos have huge hearts and a tremendous capacity for love. You are warm-hearted, affectionate and effusive, and you are very generous in showing your love. One of your greatest gifts is your ability to let others shine in your presence – you bring out the best in them because you have such faith in their qualities and talents. You can boost their confidence and make them feel that your life would be poorer without them.

You are a Fire sign so you need to express your emotions, and one way you like to do this is through sex. You are an enthusiastic and generous lover, although you also like to be treated properly and with due respect, both in and out of bed. Whether you are male or female, your partner may secretly believe that you are the one who calls the shots in your relationship.

Your family mean a lot to you and you can be very protective of them. You enjoy having children around, whether they are yours or not. Friends also have an important place in your life and you may view them as an extended family.

You are capable of great loyalty and fidelity, and thus are bewildered and hurt if a partner lets you down in some way. You will also become very angry if you think someone has betrayed your trust.

That famous Leo love of luxury and enjoyment of all the good things in life can cause havoc with your finances if you are not careful. You have such a strong sense of your own self-worth that you may stop short of getting into massive debt, but you can still overspend. Creating a good impression is very important to you, so you will do your best to look well-groomed and stylish. This, of course, costs money! You certainly have expensive tastes and, if you can afford it, would rather pay over the odds for a designer label than save money on its cut-price, high-street equivalent. After all, you do have certain standards to maintain! Loved ones also benefit from your good taste and enjoyment of luxury. You will spend time tracking down special gifts for them and are also a very generous host.

So how do you pay for all this? Ideally, you need a well-paid job that will take care of all the bills. You may even aspire to having a private income, but not every Leo is this fortunate. You take pride in choosing good investments and making sure that your future is provided for through pension schemes and the like. Investing money in jewellery, gold and other precious items will also appeal to you and give you much more pleasure than looking at a healthy bank statement.

MONEY

HEALTH

With your love of the good life, it is no wonder that you can struggle to maintain your ideal weight. Although your Fire element gives you abundant energy and stamina, your liking for delicious food and drink may mean that the weight eventually starts to accumulate. You therefore need to take regular exercise to keep yourself fit. One very enjoyable way to do this is to attend a dance class, or even to work up a sweat at home to the sound of your favourite music. If you attend a gym, you should take great care of your back, which is one of your vulnerable areas.

Make sure you don't jar it or put too much strain on it. This is also important in every other area of your life, and you may well benefit from sitting in a chair specially designed to support your back. You should also make sure that you lift items properly, while keeping your back straight. Look after it!

The heart is also ruled by Leo, and this is another part of the body that you need to look after. Once again, regular exercise will help to keep your heart healthy although you should consult your doctor first if you already have heart problems. Children will help to keep you young, and you will enjoy playing with them and making a fuss of them.

You excel in any job that makes the most of your tremendous organizational skills. Your natural authority ensures that other people will listen to what you tell them and carry out your instructions. However, you must make sure that this does not tip over into bossiness or the conviction that you are the only person who knows how to do things properly.

Creative and artistic pursuits were made for you, and you will enjoy working on anything that showcases your many talents. Many Leos are instinctively drawn to the stage and screen, making successful actors, dancers, producers,

directors and show-business personalities. You love basking in the limelight! You are less happy about taking a back seat while someone else enjoys all the glory, and if this happens over a long period you will become resentful and angry.

It is a matter of pride for you to work to the very best of your ability. Anything less simply won't do, because it is not worthy of you. You are a loyal employee, provided you are treated well and do not feel that you are being exploited.

You might also enjoy working in the beauty trade, in which case you will be a good advertisement for your products or skills. The more luxurious the field in which you work, the more you like it!

CAREER

VIRGO

24 AUGUST – 22 SEPTEMBER

If you ask a Virgo what their Sun sign is, they will usually apologize for belonging to such a boring sign! They can feel embarrassed about having the reputation for being so practical, reliable and responsible. Yet the world would fall apart without them, because how else would we get things done?

If you are a Virgo who squirms whenever the subject comes up in conversation, you are probably also typically modest about your abilities and talents. You like to underplay your achievements and may well find strategies for avoiding compliments simply because you find them so embarrassing. You're not that special, you protest. But you are!

Virgos have a reputation for being very neat and house-proud, yet you think you are just as untidy as other signs. However, you have far higher standards than most people, so you might find that you worry about having a messy underwear

QUALITY: *Mutable*
ELEMENT: *Earth*
RULING PLANET: *Mercury*

drawer or not sorting your spare change into neat piles.

One of your biggest qualities is your ability to be of service to others. This is central to your happiness and you like to be a useful member of the community in whichever way is most appropriate. However, this helpful attitude can sometimes mean that people take advantage of your good nature and expect you to do more than your fair share of the chores. This isn't helped by the fact that you probably carry them out much better than anyone else, so it isn't really in anyone's interests to stop you.

You are ruled by the planet Mercury, which gives you a natural ability to communicate and a very enquiring mind. You operate on a much more intellectual level than your fellow Earth signs, yet you still like to keep your feet on the ground.

RELATIONSHIPS

Many Virgos feel much happier living by themselves. It doesn't mean you are incapable of deep, lasting relationships but it can show that you are self-sufficient and you enjoy your own company.

It is very difficult for you to reveal your true feelings. You hate extravagant emotional displays and hope that loved ones will interpret your brief hugs and quick kisses as heartfelt expressions of your affection. Although you are a skilled communicator, you can become quite tongue-tied when it comes to telling someone how you feel. You need a partner who will encourage you to be more forthcoming and demonstrative.

Sex appeals to your earthy nature but your natural Virgo fastidiousness may find the whole business rather messy. Some Virgos even avoid sexual relationships completely because they find them too difficult to cope with. Other Virgos are wholehearted enthusiasts!

One Virgo trait that can cause you difficulties is your tendency to criticize others when things go wrong. You are very conscientious and this can make you critical of people whose standards are not as high as yours. In fact, you may not hesitate to point out someone's faults to them. Yet you are far tougher on yourself, often believing that you never do things as well as you should.

This is an area where you really come into your own. Your Earth element gives you a natural ability to deal with the material side of life. You have an appreciation of the power that money can give you and the things it can buy, yet you would never dream of flaunting your wealth or being a spendthrift. It simply isn't in your nature. In fact, you are far more likely to be an assiduous saver who slowly builds up a solid portfolio of investments. You may also be very careful about not wasting food.

You are very practical and resourceful, so you are more likely to give other people financial advice than to ask for it yourself. You like to keep track of your outgoings and probably balance your cheque book each month. Even though you may not exactly enjoy such tasks, you are even less keen on the alternative option – not knowing how much money you have to your name!

When you do spend money, you like to make sure that you buy things that will last for a long time or are a bargain. You are never tempted by status symbols or designer labels unless you can genuinely afford them. And even then you may still avoid them: they are simply not your style because you are too modest for such displays of wealth.

MONEY

HEALTH

The sign of Virgo rules health and it is a favourite hobby for many Virgos. You may simply take care of your body, making sure that you have plenty of exercise and you eat a well-balanced diet. You might swallow the contents of your medicine cabinet at the first sign of a cold or you may be such a frequent visitor to your doctor's surgery that you almost have your own chair in the waiting room. There is definitely a tendency for Virgos to become hypochondriacs, and you can scare yourself silly reading medical dictionaries and symptom-sorters. You will convince yourself that your headache is an incipient brain tumour or that your hangnail will eventually lead to the amputation of your finger.

Worry is one of your biggest health problems, so you can get caught up in a vicious circle of worrying about your health and then feeling wretched as a result, which in turn leads to more worry. The digestive system is ruled by Virgo and if you become very anxious over a long period you can develop stomach upsets or even such embarrassing conditions as irritable bowel syndrome.

You are very sensitive to the food you eat and you may even be prone to food allergies. A vegetarian or vegan diet might suit you, or you may try your hardest to eat mainly organic food.

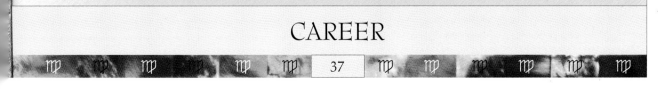

This is another area of life in which you excel. You are so practical, conscientious and methodical that you are a valuable member of any team. Colleagues admire you and bosses rely on you. You may even be the central pivot at work, because without your input everything would soon grind to a halt. You are an inspired inventor of organizational systems and strategies that ensure everything runs smoothly. You are happiest working behind the scenes or in a supportive capacity rather than on the front line. Occupations that are ideal for your many talents include secretarial and clerical work, the service industries, accountancy and working as an agent on behalf of other people. The medical profession is also good for you. With your innate need to be of service to others and your interest in health, you make a caring nurse, dedicated doctor or skilled surgeon. Your patience may also make you a good psychotherapist.

Whatever you do for a living, you have to guard against a tendency to take your work home with you. It can be very difficult for you to stop work at the end of each day because you are so aware of all the jobs you have yet to achieve. As a result, people can take advantage of your willingness to do overtime or you may make a rod for your own back.

CAREER

LIBRA

23 SEPTEMBER – 23 OCTOBER

Harmony is essential if you are to feel happy and fulfilled. You have a particular need for harmonious relationships but you also need to feel that every other area of your life is balanced and stable. This entails quite a juggling act and, although you may give the appearance of being serene and calm, you are always busy trying to keep all the elements of your life in balance. Like the scales after which your sign is named, there is always one part of your life that is in the ascendant and one that is on the way down.

Libra is the peacemaker of the zodiac. You loathe the thought of conflict and argument, and you will do your utmost to smooth over any rough patches in your dealings with other people. Your great weapon in all this is your tremendous charm. You can win people over and have them eating out of your hand in no time at all. You are able to choose your words carefully, and know exactly

QUALITY: *Cardinal*
ELEMENT: *Air*
RULING PLANET: *Venus*

*how to handle people to get the best out of
them. Although this is a natural gift and you may
therefore not always be aware of what you are doing, you
can also turn on the charm at full force when you want to. This
can sometimes have the ring of insincerity because you can seem too
good to be true.*

*You belong to the second of the Air signs, meaning that you adopt
an intellectual approach to life. You like to think and talk about
things rather than get violently involved emotionally. Venus, your
ruler, gives you the enviable reputation of belonging to one of the
most attractive signs in the zodiac. You take great trouble over your
appearance and you hate the thought of wearing clothes that are
tatty, grubby or in colours that clash.*

RELATIONSHIPS

If you are a typical Libran, relationships are the most important area of your life. You can't help it – you simply need to have other people around you. Primarily, this means a loving partner who understands you, but you also need close relationships with friends, family and colleagues. Your Air element means you are attracted to people who are blessed with more than their fair share of brains – you might become infatuated by someone who is drop-dead gorgeous but love will soon die if they turn out to be a lamebrain. Yet being ruled by Venus means that your potential partners have got to look good. So you need someone who has brains and beauty. After all, you manage it OK, don't you?

You will soon feel that you are only half alive if you have to spend too long by yourself. It is particularly difficult for you to live alone because this is a completely unnatural state for you. Although you may enjoy your own company, you need to share your life with someone, whether they are a relative, friend or partner. This reluctance to be on your own may mean that you hold on to relationships long after they should have ended, simply because you can't bear the thought of being alone again.

This is a sore point for most Librans! Money has a funny knack of slipping through your fingers, for several reasons. You truly appreciate beautiful things and it is very hard to resist temptation when you see something you want to buy, no matter how much it costs. You also have an innate reluctance to face up to unpleasant facts, such as checking to see how much money is in your bank account. You would rather bury your head in the sand and hope for the best! This *laissez-faire* attitude can lead to worry because you are no fool and you will know deep down when you are heading for financial disaster.

You enjoy buying the best that you can afford. This has nothing to do with snobbism or elitism – it is simply because you have great artistic taste and would rather go without than buy an object that you think is ugly. You take tremendous care over your clothes, and these may be a great weakness of yours. You also enjoy buying perfumes, luxurious cosmetics and anything else that will pamper you. And, because you can be indecisive, rather than have the bother of choosing between two objects you may buy them both! But at least you can comfort yourself with the knowledge that you always look – and smell – fantastic!

MONEY

HEALTH

As Oscar Wilde (another Libran) once said, you can resist everything except temptation. This means that, faced with a plate of delicious food, you can't help but eat it. Well, it would be a waste not to, wouldn't it? Besides, you might offend someone and that would be terrible. Your ruler, Venus, gives you a sweet tooth and an innate appreciation of food and drink. She also lowers your willpower, so you may struggle to keep your weight in check. One way around this problem may be to continue to eat your favourite foods but in smaller quantities than before.

Unfortunately, any form of strenuous exercise is probably your idea of hell. You are far happier reclining elegantly on a sofa or walking around your favourite shops. Try to find enjoyable ways of keeping fit – otherwise you will soon go off the whole idea and be back to square one. Ideally, you should combine exercise with beautiful surroundings and the chance to be sociable, such as joining a luxurious fitness club. You would also love the idea of a few days in a top-notch health farm.

Libra rules the kidneys, so you need to make sure you drink plenty of fluids and keep your alcohol intake moderate. You may also suffer from headaches, especially when you have been enjoying the high life too much.

Ideally, you need to earn enough money to be able to live in the style to which you would like to be accustomed! You certainly have many talents and skills, including a wonderful ability to get on well with other people. This makes you ideally suited to jobs that involve diplomacy and social skills, because even if you don't like someone you will still give the impression that they are your best buddy. You make a good intermediary, so would do well as some form of agent or representative.

Your ruler, Venus, gives you tremendous artistic and creative talents, which you enjoy putting to good use. Music is an abiding passion for many Librans, whether you are writing, recording, playing or singing it. You may also do well in the beauty business because you understand the need to look good and you will take pleasure in helping other people to achieve this.

Whatever you do for a living, you excel at being part of a team. You work much better when you can bounce your ideas off other people and feel that you are part of a unit than if you are isolated from your colleagues. Self-employment may not suit you because it can be difficult to motivate yourself to get on with your work and, if you work from home, you may miss chatting to colleagues.

CAREER

SCORPIO

24 OCTOBER – 22 NOVEMBER

You belong to the most intense and passionate sign of the zodiac. You take things very seriously, despite having a great sense of humour. You believe that you have to put a lot into life in order to get a lot out of it, and this involves handling the tricky moments as well as the enjoyable times. In fact, if you are a typical Scorpio you may have endured many more difficult encounters and experiences than most other people. There is a saying that what doesn't destroy you makes you stronger, and this certainly applies to you. Looking back on your life so far, you may even realize that you have lived it in distinctly separate chapters, with definite boundaries between one episode and the next.

Your Water element means you adopt an emotional approach to life. These emotions go very deep indeed. You may be reluctant to examine your feelings because some of them are painful to

QUALITY: *Fixed*
ELEMENT: *Water*
RULING PLANET: *Pluto*

*say the least, and so you may prefer
to bury them rather than bring them
out into the cold light of day. This
means you have an enigmatic, mys-
terious quality that is very seductive
to others. They long to penetrate
your defences and get to know the
real you. What they may not realize
is that you are a very private individual who can be quite secretive about
your innermost thoughts and feelings.*

*Once you have made up your mind
about something, you can show formidable
willpower and resolution. If you think you are in
the right you can stand your ground, come what may. You might see
this as knowing your own mind, but sometimes other people may
experience such a powerful conviction as stubbornness and obstinacy.*

RELATIONSHIPS

It takes a lot for you to be able to trust someone implicitly and this can cause a sense of reserve in your relationships. It is as if you are always one step removed from other people, watching them and checking that they will not let you down or go back on their word. You may have learned this behaviour as a result of bitter experience, making you suspicious of some people's motives and reluctant to be hurt ever again. As a result, you may try to keep control of your partner, perhaps by making sure you know what they are doing when they are out of your sight. Jealousy is an emotion that is very familiar to many Scorpios, even if they dislike it in themselves. You can also be possessive when the mood takes you. In fact, you may find that people are much more willing to stay with you if you give them more freedom. When someone lets you down, you will brood and may even plan your revenge.

Despite all this, you are a rewarding partner. You are capable of intense, profound love, and you may even have loving relationships that change your life in some way. Scorpio has the reputation for being the sexiest sign of the zodiac, and you can also be extremely tactile and passionate.

You have a great respect for money and what it can buy. It is important for you to be in a good position financially, not only because you hate the thought of not paying your way but also because you enjoy the power and emotional security that money can bring. You feel very anxious if you have to juggle your budget every month because you worry how you will manage if there is an emergency – like the roof falling in. Even so, you will do your utmost to own your home because you can see no point in wasting money on rented accommodation when you could be investing in bricks and mortar. You may also have several savings accounts and you will enjoy playing the stock market, although you will steer clear of anything too risky. It is important for you to make financial provision for your future.

When it comes to spending money, you prefer to err on the side of caution. It's not that you are mean – you simply want to make sure you are making good investments. Rather than walk into a shop and be sweet-talked into buying something that the salesperson recommends, you will prefer to do some behind-the-scenes research first. Most Scorpios enjoy fine wines and you might take pleasure in collecting your own small cellar.

MONEY

HEALTH

Most Scorpios tend to bottle up their feelings, brooding on them and chewing them over at great length. As a result, you may be no stranger to worry, depression and anxiety, even though you might be reluctant to admit to such feelings. This can become a vicious circle because the more you mull over your emotions, the worse they seem and the more unlikely it is that you will be able to tell anyone about them.

The two areas ruled by Scorpio are the genitals and the bowels. Scorpio is the sign that rules taboo subjects, so it is quite fitting that it also rules two areas of the body that usually aren't talked about in polite society!

It is very important for you to take regular exercise because it gives you a physical outlet for your emotions. If you don't do this, or you can't release your feelings through sex, you can become very irritable or depressed. However, you have to take things gently because you can have a tendency to throw yourself into life at full tilt. You believe that if you don't do things with passion and intensity, you might as well not bother. So you won't do yourself any favours if you suddenly take up a vigorous exercise regime after a long time of doing nothing. Moderation in all things!

As with every other area of your life, you need a career or job that fulfils you emotionally. If this is not possible, you will soon feel frustrated and as though you are wasting your time, which will make you miserable, especially if you feel there is nothing you can do to change matters. You are happiest if your job offers you some power and authority, and you certainly won't like being at someone's beck and call the whole time. You need to be able to call the shots, even if only every now and then.

Careers that involve plenty of concentration or input are ideal for you. With your ability to see what is going on behind the scenes, you are a natural researcher who will enjoy getting to the bottom of whatever you are studying. Your ability to sniff out double-dealing and intrigue means you would excel at detection and police work, especially if you had to go undercover or work in some underground capacity. For instance, you would delight in being a spy or double agent!

Many Scorpios make good scientists, especially when carrying out research. You are interested in life-and-death issues, so you might feel at home working in the funeral industry or in a hospice. You might also enjoy being a forensic scientist because Scorpios are rarely squeamish!

CAREER

SAGITTARIUS

23 NOVEMBER – 21 DECEMBER

A boundless sense of optimism is your greatest strength – you can't help viewing life in the best possible light. Even when things seem bleak, you soon regain your good humour and innate sense of resilience because you will find something to be positive about. No wonder you are said to be the luckiest sign in the zodiac.

This admirable attitude to life is thanks to your planetary ruler, Jupiter. This is the planet of good fortune and optimism, so you always look on the bright side. You view life as one long adventure and you love rising to challenges, even when they seem insurmountable. When things don't work out, you simply shrug and focus on the next big adventure that is coming over the horizon.

Sagittarius is the third of the Fire signs, making you expansive, enthusiastic and always keen to take the initiative and make things happen. You like to keep on the move

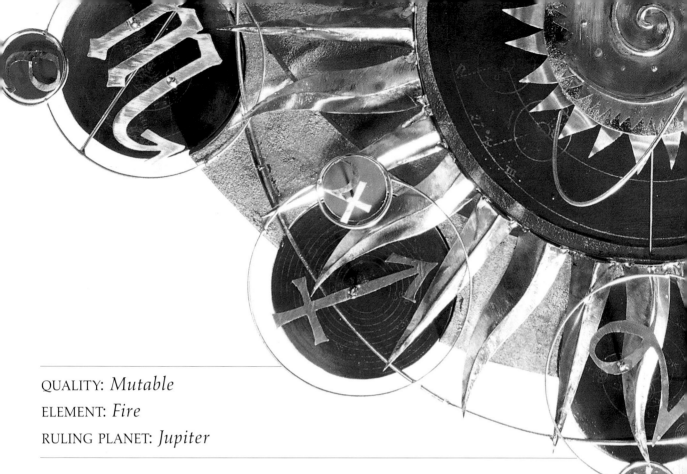

QUALITY: *Mutable*
ELEMENT: *Fire*
RULING PLANET: *Jupiter*

and you adopt a very flexible approach to life. This is also the third of the Mutable signs, making you open, versatile and eager for new experiences.

Life is always lively when you're around. You enjoy discussing ideas with friends and loved ones, especially if they involve a favourite topic or have philosophical, spiritual, historical or religious overtones. Despite your happy-go-lucky attitude, you have a very serious side and a strong intellectual curiosity about the world. You enjoy stretching your mind, so you probably have a home full of books and an extremely broad range of knowledge. You have a tremendous respect for education and you spend your life learning more about people and the world around you, even if you do it in very informal ways.

RELATIONSHIPS

You thoroughly enjoy getting to know people and discovering what makes them tick, so you have many friends from different walks of life. People appreciate your open and straightforward manner because, even though you can sometimes put your foot in your mouth, at least they know where they stand with you. The last thing you could be accused of is being insincere. Of course, this means you will never win any awards for tact but at least you can be relied upon to be honest.

Something that you find very difficult is feeling tied down or hemmed in by your partner. You have a strong sense of independence and a deep need for emotional freedom, so you need to be able to live your life without feeling that someone is peering over your shoulder or keeping you tied to their apron strings. If this happens too often, you will probably disappear into the sunset before they know what is going on.

Although sex means a lot to you because it allows you to express your emotions, your number one priority when looking for a partner is someone who will be a friend as well as a lover. They must also be able to match your own high intellectual standards, otherwise you will bid them a fond farewell and move on to pastures new.

You love money because it represents fun and freedom. When you get fed up at work you can always remind yourself of all the things you could buy with your earnings – a book, dinner at a favourite restaurant, or even a plane ticket. In fact, you are much better at spending money than saving it, and the thought of keeping a close eye on the performance of your bank balance is enough to bring on a fit of yawning. As far as you are concerned, there are far more important things to do in life than worry about whether your standing orders have been paid on time. This rather happy-go-lucky approach to money can lead to the odd financial crisis when you discover too late that you have overspent or you are faced with an unexpected bill that you can't pay. To encourage you to save money, it might be better to tell yourself that you are saving up for a massive treat rather than your old age.

Books and travel come high on your list of priorities, and you may spend more money than most on them. You also enjoy the odd gamble, so you could be drawn to card games or horse-racing. You don't see much point in buying lots of status symbols – unless they happen to be expensive sports cars!

MONEY

HEALTH

You are lucky enough to belong to one of the most active signs of the zodiac, so keeping fit may come naturally to you. You enjoy walking, you love being in the wide open spaces and you may also be keen on sports. All of these activities help to keep you in peak condition. However, problems can arise if your hectic schedule means you spend more time in the car or behind a desk than doing something energetic. Not only do you start to feel sluggish and confined, but you can also begin to put on weight. Since the natural Sagittarian build is tall and lean, you can feel very distressed when you realize that your clothes are becoming too small for you. They must have shrunk in the wardrobe!

Among the activities that appeal to you are horse-riding, motor-racing, squash and any other sport that requires stamina and nerves of steel. You may also enjoy archery, because you belong to the sign of the Archer.

The areas of the body ruled by Sagittarius are the hips and liver. Both can suffer if you regularly eat and drink too much – the weight will collect on your hips and your liver will be put under a strain. Even though you may not enjoy the idea, you will benefit from exercising a little moderation every now and then.

You are blessed with a good brain so you need a career that will put it to the test. Ideally, your job should offer you some exciting opportunities and challenges, otherwise you might quickly tire of it and look around for something else. It should also give you the chance to learn more about the world – something that you will continue to do throughout your life. You loathe the idea of having a job that is tedious, predictable or so monotonous that you can switch off while you do it.

You have a great respect for knowledge and education, so are an instinctive teacher. You are an eternal student of life but you may also enjoy studying subjects in formal ways, such as taking various university courses long after your contemporaries have given up. A job connected with the travel industry is right up your street, especially if you get the chance to see something of the world. You also excel at writing, publishing, religion, philosophy, the law and ecology. Working in a library or bookshop would appeal because you have an abiding love of books.

Colleagues and superiors enjoy your company and like working with you as part of a team. Your independent nature means you are ideally suited to self-employment and you will relish the challenge of chasing up new contacts.

CAREER

CAPRICORN

22 DECEMBER – 20 JANUARY

*E*ven though you can appear rather serious when you are young, you have the advantage over every other sign. As you get older, you become more youthful. You seem to live your life in reverse, starting off with an old head on young shoulders and ending up much more lively and sprightly than your friends.

You can thank your ruling planet, Saturn, for this strange phenomenon. Saturn is the planet of restrictions and responsibilities, and these can weigh very heavily on you in your younger years. Yet, as you grow older, life becomes much easier. Many Capricorns find that they really start to enjoy life after the age of thirty and that they don't look back once they reach forty. You can be a slow starter but you finish on great form!

Your Earth element makes you reliable, sensible and grounded in reality. It is a rare Capricorn who allows themselves to be carried away for long – you usually like to have

QUALITY: *Cardinal*
ELEMENT: *Earth*
RULING PLANET: *Saturn*

your feet firmly on the ground. This can mean you are rather conservative and you may also be firmly wedded to tradition – you like to know that there is a certain way of doing things. Sometimes this may make you resistant to change as you can worry that the new idea won't be as successful as the one it is replacing. You subscribe to the belief that if it ain't broke, don't fix it. However, if you carry this attitude too far it can mean that you miss out on lots of exciting and innovative things.

One of your greatest strengths is your wonderful ability to laugh at yourself. Capricorns can seem very buttoned down and reserved at first, but once something tickles your funny bone you will reveal a very dry, often satirical sense of humour that endears you to everyone around you.

RELATIONSHIPS

If there is one thing that partners have to understand about you, it's that you loathe public demonstrations of affection. You will give them a quick kiss on the cheek, possibly even a hug in exceptional circumstances, but that's it. You will blush, feel uncomfortable and look around to make sure no one has noticed. But when you get behind closed doors … that's quite another matter! Even though you may give the impression that butter wouldn't melt in your mouth, you can be really hot stuff when with the right person.

You are naturally shy and reserved with other people, so it can take a lot of courage to make the first move with someone you fancy. You may wonder what they see in you because you can lack confidence, especially when it comes to matters of the heart. You might even feel this way in a committed relationship, and this can mean that loved ones misinterpret your actions, thinking you are being offhand or remote instead of shy.

It is important for you to be affectionate and open about your feelings, otherwise your reserved air can give the wrong impression. Nevertheless, you are dedicated to looking after your family and you will do your utmost to provide them with material and physical support, even if it is a little more difficult to open up emotionally.

Capricorns have the reputation for being very careful with their money. You don't like throwing it around and you make sure that what you do buy is good value for money. You also know, often through bitter experience, that life has a way of kicking you on the shins every now and then so you like to set some money aside for a rainy day – perhaps even a rainy month. As a result, you can sometimes be accused of being tight-fisted or mean.

You have a healthy respect for money and an innate fear of what might happen if you don't have enough of it. You are one of the signs that likes to invest in bricks and mortar at an early age because you may find it almost physically painful to pay out money on renting accommodation. Other forms of investment also appeal to you, yet you are wary of risking your shirt on the stock exchange unless you know exactly what you are doing or are acting on expert advice.

Money is a means of gaining emotional and material security, and you like to buy items that you know will stand the test of time. You aren't interested in buying the latest fashions – even though you like to look good, you much prefer to buy items that are classic and won't date.

MONEY

HEALTH

One of your biggest health problems is your ability to worry. What's more, you find it very difficult to confide in others so you tend to bottle up your fears, which only makes them seem worse than ever. It can also be very hard for you to switch off from your work at the end of each day. You may work longer hours than strictly necessary, and even when you aren't working you may be thinking about it. It is important for you to explore ways of relaxing and dividing your life into compartments, or your loved ones may think you are chained to your desk!

The most vulnerable areas of your body are your knees and teeth. As you get older you may suffer from bone complaints, such as arthritis or rheumatism. It will do you good to take gentle exercise and also to find constructive ways of expressing any bottled-up anger that you may be feeling. You may also suffer from skin complaints, such as eczema, whenever life gets on top of you.

Hobbies that are completely unconnected with your work will help you to unwind, especially if they get you out into the fresh air. Gardening suits you very well and you will probably enjoy growing your own fruit and vegetables.

If you are a typical Capricorn, the problem may not lie in starting a job but in knowing when to stop. Your deep-rooted sense of responsibility means you don't like to leave tasks unfinished and you would rather burn the midnight oil on a project than lie awake worrying about it. However, this can easily become such a habit that you lose sight of what is important and what is trivial. As a result, you can develop workaholic tendencies, to the eventual detriment of your health and family life.

It is essential for you to learn to delegate. Even though you are absolutely convinced that if a job is worth doing well you have to do it yourself, you need to hand over the reins every now and then and let someone else have a go. If you don't, you will soon burn yourself out and be incapable of doing your best.

Any job that involves taking responsibility and being practical will suit you down to the ground. Financial services such as banking and investments are ideal for you, as is anything connected with property. Big business, politics and government work can also appeal, especially if linked with tradition or preserving the status quo. You could be interested in architecture or working on historic buildings, and you might also enjoy something connected with history.

CAREER

AQUARIUS

21 JANUARY – 18 FEBRUARY

If you are a typical Aquarian you probably spend most of your life feeling like a square peg in a round hole. It is difficult to fit in with other people because you don't always have a lot in common with them. You seem to approach life from a completely different angle and it can be hard to find any common ground. Not that you usually mind, of course! You may even take pleasure in knowing that you are different from everyone else.

You are the third of the Air signs, so you live chiefly in your mind. You much prefer taking an intellectual approach to life to getting caught up in dramatic emotional scenes. In fact, you simply can't cope when the atmosphere becomes too intense – it makes you want to run in the opposite direction. You are clever and intellectual, and may even be streets ahead of everyone else around you. Aquarius is the sign of the future

QUALITY: *Fixed*

ELEMENT: *Air*

RULING PLANET: *Uranus*

and Aquarians are often way ahead of the game in many ways.

You have such a strong ability to think that you can sometimes believe you are the only one with all the answers. You enjoy getting involved in heated debates – but only if you can win them! Yet you are also very honest so you will be happy to own up if you don't know something or you aren't sure of your ground. Unfortunately, this honesty can lead to some very blunt statements that have other people wincing, and there may be times when it would be better to temper your views or even keep them to yourself. You have a very cut-and-dried, highly logical way of looking at the world and you firmly believe that life would be so much easier if everyone else behaved in the same way!

RELATIONSHIPS

Being an Air sign means that you enjoy communicating with other people. You love exchanging ideas and understanding what makes people tick. You are happiest when dealing with the realm of thought, but you are not so confident when it comes to showing your feelings. You may attempt to intellectualize your emotions rather than deal with the reality of them, and you may take refuge in books and theories rather than get swept up in powerful emotional encounters.

You have a strong need for independence and you loathe the idea of being tied to your partner's apron strings. Even though you may love your family and adore your home, you like to tell yourself you are a free spirit who can come and go as you please – you can't cope with anyone who wants you to account for every moment you are away from them. Aquarius is a sign of tremendous loyalty so it's unlikely you'll be unfaithful unless there are very good reasons for it.

As far as you are concerned, sex is not the most important facet of a long-term emotional relationship. After the first fine careless rapture has evaporated between you and your partner, you are much more interested in what goes on in their mind. If they aren't a match for you intellectually, you may eventually look for someone who is.

Money is a useful commodity to you but no more than that. You are unlikely to hoard your spare cash and gloat over it every evening – the very idea revolts you. You are happy when you have some savings in the bank because you know you can draw on them in an emergency, although you are much more likely to spend them on a fabulous holiday or your latest interest.

However, this lack of concern for money and what it can buy means you may never be in the market for expensive holidays and flashy cars. You believe that other things are more important than mere status symbols and you secretly pity anyone who thinks otherwise. If you have lots of money, then that's wonderful.

If you don't, then so what? Even so, your traditional ruler Saturn means you are likely to be diligent about keeping track of your finances. You will also be quick to question any mistakes or discrepancies in your bank balance or credit card account. You may not be very materialistic but you are certainly no fool, either!

When you do have money to spare, you enjoy spending it on travel, books and other activities that stimulate your brain. You may also enjoy giving money away to humanitarian causes, although you would never advertise the fact.

MONEY

HEALTH

The sign of Aquarius rules eyesight, and many Aquarians have to wear spectacles or contact lenses. Your sign also rules the circulation of the blood and this can be a problem for you, especially if you have a sedentary life; you can easily become chilled and find it hard to get warm again. Your ankles can also be vulnerable to accidents and mishaps, and if you play sports or go jogging you should always wear shoes that give your ankles proper support.

Taking exercise for its own sake is an idea that leaves you cold. You can't see the point of rush-ing up and down a field chasing a ball. Even so, you may be a fast runner and might also enjoy playing tennis. Exercise regimes that keep you fit while also allowing you to relax are an excellent choice, and you could be very interested in yoga or tai chi. Meditation will also help you unwind.

You enjoy good food but you are more likely to be a vegetarian than to gorge yourself on lots of meat. You have a keen interest in animal welfare and it may go against the grain to eat them. Many Aquarians become vegetarians, or even vegans, in their teens and never see any reason to change. However, this doesn't mean that you eat a model diet because chocolate may be a major weakness for you!

Making it big in a career doesn't mean a lot to you. You have no need for the status of having made your way in the material world. Instead, you need to do something significant with your life so you know you have done your bit to help the world. As a result, you may not hanker for a job that gives you the key to the executive washroom or your own fleet of private jets. Instead, you will prefer to do something worthwhile and, ideally, with a humanitarian slant.

The most important aspect of your job or career is its intellectual opportunities. You will quickly become bored with any job that doesn't allow you to use your brain, and you may also balk at the idea of taking orders from people who aren't nearly as clever as you. In the end, you may get fed up and walk out. Jobs that involve writing, communication and selling ideas are more in your line, although you have to believe in what you are doing. For instance, you will not be able to bring yourself to sell expensive products that you think are shoddy or poor value.

Being self-employed suits you very well because you have the motivation to get on with your work and you will also enjoy the independence that comes from being your own boss.

CAREER

PISCES

19 FEBRUARY – 20 MARCH

You belong to one of the kindest and most sensitive signs in the zodiac. It is second nature to you to help other people and you may have a strong attraction to charitable and voluntary work. You are highly attuned to other people's feelings, which can make you act like a psychic sponge, soaking up the atmosphere around you. This is thanks to your Water element, which reduces the boundaries between you and other people and makes you highly susceptible to atmosphere. As a result, there are times when you need to protect yourself against unpleasantness and un-wanted energies. Some Pisceans are so highly attuned to what is going on around them that they are very intuitive and may even be psychic. If this is true of you, you need to find ways to con-trol and regulate these gifts – other-wise you may be bombarded with im-pressions, emotions

QUALITY: *Mutable*
ELEMENT: *Water*
RULING PLANET: *Neptune*

and impulses that you pick up from the people and places around you.

Reality is a very difficult area of life for you. You like to escape ugly facts and disagreeable knowledge whenever possible, and this can make you bury your head in the sand. In extreme cases, it can lead to trouble when you go out of your way to avoid harsh reality because you simply can't deal with it. You may ignore warning signs from others, you may fail to spot situations that are about to turn into disasters and you may also pretend that things aren't nearly as bad as they obviously are. Ideally, you should find strategies and techniques that help you to deal with life as it is, warts and all. You may then find that it runs much more smoothly because you are able to anticipate problems before they arrive, rather than convince yourself that bad things will never happen.

RELATIONSHIPS

You need to know that you are loved and cared for, and you enjoy showing affection to others. Your desire for everything to be just the way you want it, with no unpleasantness, anger or bitterness, means that you may turn a blind eye to the more unpalatable areas of any relationship. You simply pretend that they don't exist. You may allow problems to reach crisis point before you are prepared to do anything about them, and even then you can be bewildered about what went wrong. All you wanted was to be happy!

Your huge heart and innate need for romance make you a very rewarding and loving partner. You readily put yourself out for your loved ones and will do almost anything for them.

Unfortunately you can sometimes choose partners and lovers who don't deserve you and who take you for a ride. They can exploit your innocence and slight gullibility, so they may tell you lies in a calculated attempt to appeal to your soft heart and make you do what they want.

Sex is important for you because it allows you to show your feelings for your partner. You may even find that you enter an otherworldly state through sex. Some Pisceans enjoy intrigue and fantasy, and so can become involved in a double life in which they get up to all sorts of games and subterfuge.

This is not a topic that sets your heart leaping with excitement! Although you want enough money to live on, with a little left over for treats, you are not interested in money for its own sake. You may fantasize about what it would be like to be a millionaire but you are not interested in playing the stock market or working round the clock in order to turn this dream into reality. No one could accuse you of being penny-pinching or miserly because you will willingly share your money and possessions when you have them.

Your reluctance to face up to unpleasant facts may make it a struggle for you to keep abreast of your finances. Your instinctive reaction may be to ignore those nasty envelopes that drop through the letterbox – especially when things are tricky in the rest of your life. You hope that your finances will take care of themselves, so it may be a good idea to set up banking arrangements where bills are paid on time directly from your account.

When spending money, you love buying luxurious and beautiful objects. You might have a big collection of perfumes, expensive toiletries and other items with which to pamper yourself. You have such good taste that your wardrobe is probably the envy of many, and you may spend a lot of money on clothes and shoes.

MONEY

HEALTH

Your traditional ruler, Jupiter, gives you a liking for the good things in life. You enjoy fine wines and delicious foods, and if you aren't careful these can lead to weight gain over the years. You might also find that you can feel liverish if you eat and drink too well.

Your modern ruler is Neptune, which can make you sensitive to allergies and possibly even intolerant to certain foods. You should certainly try to keep away from any foods that don't suit you because your very sensitive metabolism will struggle to cope with them. Some Pisceans find that they respond much better to complementary medicine, such as homeopathy and healing, than to more traditional forms of treatment. If you often feel het up, nervy or so anxious that it makes you ill, you could benefit from practising a relaxation technique such as yoga or meditation. This will also help you to keep your emotions in check, because if left to flow unimpeded they can have a powerful influence on your health.

The area of the body ruled by Pisces is the feet, and many Pisceans find it difficult to buy shoes that fit them. Having a regular pedicure or seeing a chiropodist can make all the difference to your well-being, and you may also benefit from reflexology.

Pisces is a dual sign and you are certainly capable of showing two sides of your character in your career. You may work in one of the most sophisticated professions or you might dedicate your life to serving humanity.

Many Pisceans are drawn to highly glamorous fields, such as the cinema, beauty business, fashion industry and the world of dance. Actors, dancers, artists, poets, singers and writers abound in this sign. Yet you may reject all that and become involved in the other Piscean extreme: working with people down on their luck, or rejected by society. You could be attracted to working in an institution, whether a hospital, prison or religious community. This will bring out your marvellous compassion and ability to help everyone, no matter what they have done or who they are. You may even see this as a vocation, because many Pisceans live their lives according to their spiritual or religious beliefs.

However, wherever you work you need amenable colleagues and pleasant surroundings. You will soon become unhappy if you have nothing in common with your workmates or you aren't appreciated. Certainly, it's easy for you to downplay your talents as you are naturally modest and dislike pushing yourself forward. Whatever your job, ideally it should bring out your creativity.

CAREER

PART TWO

THE PLANETS

Now that you are familiar with the main characteristics of your Sun sign, you can begin to add to your knowledge and understanding of your personality. Although the Sun is a very important factor in your planetary picture, by no means does it tell the whole story. The sign positions of the other planets at the time of your birth provide further information about your character. Some of this information may complement the main characteristics of your Sun sign, but some of it might be contradictory. It is these conflicts within our planetary pictures that make us fully rounded, complex human beings rather than two-dimensional characters lacking internal inconsistencies or contradictions.

Six planets are described on the following pages: the Moon, Mercury, Venus, Mars, Jupiter and Saturn. The Moon rules our instinctive emotions, Mercury rules our ability to communicate, Venus rules our ability to show love, Mars rules our drive and energy, Jupiter rules our expansion on physical and intellectual levels and Saturn rules our stability and authority. Look up the interpretation relating to the zodiac sign occupied by each planet at the time of birth (which you can find out by using the planetary charts in Part Three), and discover how the planets have shaped and influenced your life.

THE MOON

THE MOON IN ARIES   QUALITY: *Cardinal*   ELEMENT: *Fire*

You have a strong need to push yourself. You are instinctively competitive, with a strong urge to win, though you may not be consciously aware of this as it is second nature. You prefer to be a leader, not a follower, and sooner or later you will break out from being under the yoke. Assert your independence! You are capable of great achievements, thanks to your energy, drive and ambition.

You find any form of tedious routine hard to stomach, and if life becomes too predictable you will react by doing something exciting or daredevil. This impetuous streak can land you in trouble, especially if you were born with the Sun in a Fire or Air sign; if in a Water or Earth sign, you may find it hard to resolve your need for security with your urge for freedom.

Your emotions flare up easily and you can be hot-headed. Although you are capable of great warmth, the emotion that comes easiest is anger. You can be impatient, and get annoyed if others drag their feet. But your anger soon subsides and you rarely bear a grudge.

You have an instinctive need for emotional and physical security, and you feel very unsettled when these are threatened. Your Taurus Moon will stabilize and ground you if you have the Sun in an Air or Fire sign, but will increase your need for security if in a Water or Earth sign.

You have strong emotional needs, making you loving and affectionate. You delight in caring for those you love, and they know they can count on your loyalty, but your need for emotional security can make you possessive and jealous. This trait may be so ingrained that it operates unconsciously, which is when problems can start. Partners may not like being treated as your private property!

Your need for stability means that you don't like change. You hanker for a quiet life, free from disruptions, and you quickly feel unsettled when your routine is disturbed. You believe it is better to stay with the devil you know, and you can become stuck in a rut as a result. You have a natural aptitude for finance and you enjoy making investments, including property; one of your primary concerns in life is to live somewhere comfortable.

THE MOON IN TAURUS   QUALITY: *Fixed*   ELEMENT: *Earth*

The Moon's position at the time of your birth shows how you instinctively react to situations. It also reveals what is familiar to you and what can nurture you through life.

THE MOON IN GEMINI

QUALITY: *Mutable*   ELEMENT: *Air*

You are a real live wire! Witty, bright, articulate and lively, you are terrific company, and there's nothing you like better than a good gossip. You are especially voluble on the subject of your family and close friends. Yet you also enjoy talking about more serious subjects as you are intelligent and have an inquisitive mind. You love keeping informed, and have a high respect for education. These traits are emphasized if your Sun is in Gemini, and highlighted if your Sun occupies another Air sign or a Fire sign. The Moon in Gemini will liven up the Sun if it is in a Water or Earth sign.

This aptitude for words can make you a gifted writer, teacher, journalist or salesperson, and you instinctively tune into other people. But you become impatient when life is boring or predictable – it can even make you feel sluggish or physically ill. You find it hard to deal with complex or messy emotions; you prefer operating on an intellectual level, so will try to distract yourself by keeping busy or thinking about other things.

The Moon is at home in Cancer, because this is its ruling sign. You enjoy taking care of others and are very protective of loved ones. You are, however, extremely sensitive emotionally and easily hurt. Sometimes you can feel rather defensive and may imagine that people are attacking you when they aren't. As a result, you can be quite moody at times. It is second nature for you to express your emotions – indeed, they can flood out without any conscious effort on your part! If your Sun is in an Air or Fire sign you may find it hard to cope with your strong emotions, while if your Sun is in a Water or Earth sign you are extremely loving.

Family ties are very important to you. You may also be the family historian, with stories of the past and a precious collection of keepsakes. It is difficult for you to sever your ties with the past, as you cannot bear to say goodbye. Any form of parting is a potential emotional disruption and it can take you a long time to recover. Emotional security is paramount and you need to live in a comfortable home; you tend to stay in the same place for years as you hate having to uproot.

THE MOON IN CANCER

QUALITY: *Cardinal*   ELEMENT: *Water*

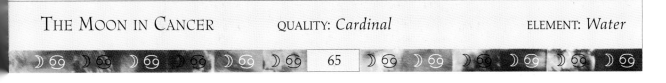

THE MOON IN LEO

QUALITY: *Fixed*   ELEMENT: *Fire*

All the world's a stage to you and you feel happiest when you are basking in the spotlight. You have a deep need to be noticed and appreciated, and you feel very uncomfortable if you are relegated to the sidelines. If this happens regularly, or you feel that people are ignoring you too often, you may use dramatic ploys to capture their attention once more. You also like to be treated as someone special, because this reassures you that you are valued. When things go badly, you instinctively put on a good front. You may feel crushed inside but you will wear a brave smile in public. You need to protect your pride, because this gives you a sense of emotional security. The show must go on! This is especially true if your Sun is in a Water or Earth sign. You may be more carefree if it is in an Air or Fire sign.

One of your most endearing qualities is your ability to show love and affection. The people you care about are left in no doubt about your feelings for them, thanks to your loyalty and generosity. You are also an enthusiastic participator in life and enjoy getting involved in new projects, especially if they are creative. Issues connected with family matters and children are important to you, and you may even defend the interests of children in some way.

Worrying is second nature to you. You have an almost overpowering need to live in an orderly, secure and predictable universe, so you fret whenever life throws a spanner in the works. And, since life has a habit of doing this with annoying frequency, you spend a lot of your time feeling anxious, het up and nervy. You are especially prone to this if your Sun is in a Water or Earth sign. As far as you are concerned, the best way to cope with the random nature of life is to be as practical, reliable and methodical as possible. Work is a great antidote for you when life gets you down, and offers a good escape route when you are trying to avoid confronting painful emotional situations.

You have an instinctive need to be of service to others, whether voluntarily or as an employee. And because you are a perfectionist you will work tirelessly to do the best possible job. You are secretly convinced that you are second-rate and that it's only a matter of time before the rest of the world cottons on. This makes you a perfectionist. It can also make you critical of others' shortcomings. What they don't realize is that you are even more critical of your own. And what you don't realize is that you are probably much more capable than most of the people around you.

THE MOON IN VIRGO

QUALITY: *Mutable*   ELEMENT: *Earth*

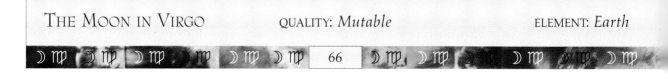

THE MOON IN LIBRA

QUALITY: *Cardinal* ELEMENT: *Air*

Peace at any price? You certainly have a horror of conflict and disagreements, and you may put up with a lot of ill-treatment because of your desire to keep things on an even keel. This is especially likely if you also have the Sun or Venus in Libra. It may feel unsafe to lose your temper, so you have a tendency to swallow your anger or even deny that it exists. Of course, this has many benefits as well as disadvantages. It makes you a born diplomat and someone who can mediate in many difficult situations. You also have an innate charm and sensitivity that makes you deservedly popular. People love you for your gentle and considerate nature.

Love and affection come very high on your list of priorities, and you are a very loving and romantic partner. You may even be emotionally dependent on your partner. You are also idealistic, making you reluctant to view situations as they really are, so you may put a gloss on a troubled relationship, refusing to admit to yourself how you really feel about it. This is partly because you do not like being on your own. You are much happier in a partnership than out of one, even when the relationship makes you unhappy or is on the rocks.

Your emotions run very deep. So deep, in fact, that you may spend your life peeling back layers of feelings, like peeling an onion. You are extremely reluctant to discuss your emotions with anyone else because you are immensely private. You lock them away from public gaze yet you may endlessly go over them in your mind. In extreme cases, this can lead to obsessions and buried grudges. It is rare for someone with this placing to have sailed through life unscathed. Usually, you carry huge emotional scars and you have probably weathered storms that would have destroyed lesser mortals. When the going gets tough you tend to withdraw from the fray, either mentally or physically. You are also something of an enigma to the people in your life. They love you but they may not understand you.

You have tremendous powers of concentration and a love of detective work, making you a born researcher. You instinctively analyse situations, working out exactly what happened and why. This allows you to feel in control of what is going on, and that in turn helps to boost your emotional security. This is particularly true if your Sun is in a Water or Earth sign. If you suspect your partner is not being honest with you, you may start to feel jealous or possessive.

THE MOON IN SCORPIO

QUALITY: *Fixed* ELEMENT: *Water*

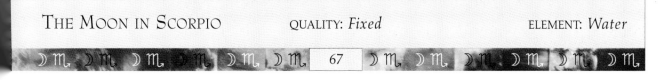

THE MOON IN SAGITTARIUS QUALITY: *Mutable* ELEMENT: *Fire*

The grass is always greener for you! You are an instinctive wanderer and your innate need for personal freedom means you hate to be tied down. You adore all forms of travel, whether mental or physical, and have a deep need to amass knowledge. It makes you feel safe. No matter how many books you own, you always want more because a new interest is usually awakening in you – especially if your Sun is in an Air or Fire sign. You talk about your enthusiasms with missionary zeal, and may even try to convert others to your latest interest. Religion, politics, spiritual quests and environmental issues may be particularly dear to your heart. You are always looking for ways to make the world a better place.

You are an eternal optimist, convinced that everything will work out for the best. You always manage to see the silver lining, even when things have gone badly wrong. This is partly because you feel uncomfortable when looking at the darker side of life and you may deal with emotional problems by adopting a decidedly philosophical approach to them. You may also laugh at them; you are blessed with a lively sense of humour and an ability to see the funny side of life. This, combined with your gregarious nature and your instinctive generosity, makes you very popular.

Life is a serious business for you. Your strong sense of duty gives you a tendency to step into the breach when things go wrong or when you feel that no one else is taking proper responsibility. As a child, you may have had an old head on young shoulders. People count on you in a crisis because you keep a cool head and have an air of being a rock that they can depend on. You also have a highly developed set of morals, and may be rather disapproving when people misbehave. If your Sun is in a Water or Earth sign you will have a real drive to assume responsibility for others.

All this comes at a price, of course. You are prone to bouts of worry and depression, made all the worse by your knowledge that life can be very unfair. You are often left holding the baby because everyone knows your conscience won't allow you to do anything less. Ambitions drive you and you have a great need to be a success. You are cautious in your relationships and may find it a struggle to show your feelings. This, coupled with your natural shyness, gives you an emotional reserve. When you feel threatened emotionally, you may try to preserve your safety by controlling the other person or even policing their actions. Your greatest saving grace is your dry sense of humour.

THE MOON IN CAPRICORN QUALITY: *Cardinal* ELEMENT: *Earth*

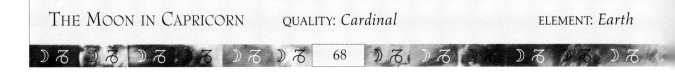

THE MOON IN AQUARIUS   QUALITY: *Fixed*   ELEMENT: *Air*

You have a great gift for friendship. Partners may come and go but your friends will not desert you. This may upset some partners, but as far as you are concerned that is too bad. You feel uncomfortable when showing your feelings and prefer to maintain an emotional distance. Loved ones may experience this as cool detachment on your part. When up against it emotionally, you have a tendency to intellectualize your feelings. This helps you to feel in control of them. If your Sun is in an Air or Earth sign, you will feel especially wary of intense emotional encounters.

You also have a horror of being tied down emotionally – you need to feel you still have your freedom, even when in a committed relationship.

No matter what sign your Sun occupies, you can be unconventional and rebellious at times. You may even delight in being shocking and stirring people up to make them think. You cannot abide intellectual complacency – nor do you believe in clinging on to doctrines or ideologies simply because they are part of the status quo. Nevertheless, you can be very reluctant to change your mind when you think you are in the right. Humanitarian causes appeal to you and you are prepared to champion issues that are too controversial for popular taste.

At times you feel as though you have one foot in this world and one foot in a wonderland of your own making. You may be present in body but your spirit might well have decamped to other realms. You are highly sensitive to atmospheres, and can soak them up like a sponge. You may even have psychic abilities that increase this tendency to absorb the emotions and energies around you. When life becomes too tough you tend to escape into a world of your own, or you may become addicted to whatever makes things bearable for you.

You might feel as though you have a layer of skin missing because you are so sensitive to the undercurrents around you. It doesn't take much to hurt your feelings or rob you of your confidence. Being aware of how life can cut you down to size makes you supremely compassionate towards others. You may even be drawn to a career or spiritual path that enables you to take care of people, or work to reduce the world's suffering. Nevertheless, you need to erect emotional boundaries that prevent you taking on everyone's troubles as though they were your own – especially if your Sun is in a Water sign. You also need to find ways of preventing people taking advantage of your good nature and kind heart.

THE MOON IN PISCES   QUALITY: *Mutable*   ELEMENT: *Water*

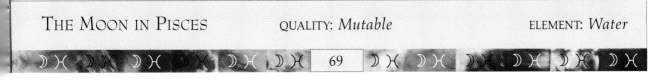

MERCURY

MERCURY IN ARIES   QUALITY: *Cardinal*   ELEMENT: *Fire*

You have great enthusiasm for life and throw yourself into it wholeheartedly. You soon become restless if you have to spend too long in one place or doing something you find boring or tedious. When working on new ideas, you are full of energy at first, but once the excitement passes you will look for someone else to do all the donkey work and tidy up loose ends. You will be busy searching for the next project!

When talking to people, you are direct and confident. You tend to speak first and only later wonder whether you said the right thing. Not that it usually matters because you have a natural enthusiasm that wins people over. You enjoy learning but may have no qualms about disagreeing with your teacher when you think they have got something wrong. Your opinions are highly subjective and are coloured by your own experiences. It is very hard for you to divorce your ego from your ideas. Whenever you are distracted, you may be slightly accident-prone, especially to your head or hands. Concentrate on what you are doing, particularly when in a hurry.

You are blessed with a good brain, though sometimes you may not think so, as it takes a while for new ideas and concepts to sink in. It is hard for you to grasp abstract thoughts and you feel on much safer ground when dealing with concrete facts. Nevertheless, even though your mind may work at a slower pace than others', you are able to remember those hard-learned facts. You may also have a much more solid grasp of ideas because you have spent such a long time grappling with them and trying to make sense of them.

You think and communicate in a very practical and careful way. You like to deal with the facts and are often able to discuss difficult subjects in an unemotional way. You can appear matter-of-fact and in control. There are times when you hold very fixed opinions, making you reluctant to accept any viewpoint if it differs from your own. You may also shy away from ideas or suggestions that seem to threaten your material or emotional security, and you can be very dogmatic in rejecting them. However, once the idea has sunk in you are usually prepared to reconsider your views.

MERCURY IN TAURUS   QUALITY: *Fixed*   ELEMENT: *Earth*

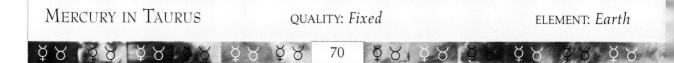

Mercury rules the way we communicate. It governs our thoughts, speech, actions and opinions. It can also indicate the areas of life that we enjoy thinking about.

MERCURY IN GEMINI   QUALITY: *Mutable*   ELEMENT: *Air*

You love to keep on the move, both physically and mentally, and are always ready to embrace new ideas. You loathe the thought of becoming mentally stagnant or set in your ways, and in extreme cases this can send you in the opposite direction, making you unnecessarily restless and flighty. You may get involved in new interests just for the sake of it, or find it hard to settle to anything for long. Try to stick at projects even after boredom sets in – or you may never finish anything!

Communication is extremely important to you and you love keeping in touch with friends and family. The growth of the internet is a godsend because it allows you to send flurries of messages at the click of a mouse, and you also enjoy surfing the web. You love chatting on the phone, writing notes, sending letters and gossiping with friends. You are sociable, lively and excellent company, and you are also very bright. You enjoy reading books, magazines and newspapers. They help satisfy your curiosity about life, even though a new interest is always waiting around the corner. It is part of what helps to keep you alive and alert.

You are family-minded, liking to talk and think about your nearest and dearest. Memories often fill your thoughts and you may take delight in being the family archivist. You may also be very interested in history because you like the continuity of ideas. Your emotions have a powerful influence on your thoughts and it can be hard for you to separate your feelings from your ideas. This means you can be subjective and may feel emotionally threatened by ideas that run counter to your beliefs.

Fears and worries may nag away at you, especially if problems affect your home life in some way.

You are blessed with a retentive memory, particularly over things you feel strongly about. Bald facts may leave you cold yet you are much more likely to remember them if they spark off an emotional reaction. People enjoy your company as you are sympathetic and understanding. You make an effort to tune into them, both mentally and emotionally. You can prefer to communicate through feelings rather than words, so you may judge someone's mood by the way you feel when you are with them rather than by what they say.

MERCURY IN CANCER   QUALITY: *Cardinal*   ELEMENT: *Water*

MERCURY IN LEO QUALITY: *Fixed* ELEMENT: *Fire*

Creative ideas come easily to you. You take pride in making the best use of your mind, especially if you know that your efforts will be appreciated by others. You may even work extra-hard if the results will be greeted by an enthusiastic audience. When learning new subjects, you will fare best if you can have some sort of creative involvement, or you may quickly lose interest. You enjoy coming up with new ideas and will steadfastly defend them in the face of criticism. However, sometimes you may be so wrapped up in them that you feel threatened if they are challenged. This can make you reluctant to reconsider your views, and you may be dogmatic, strong-willed and utterly convinced that you are in the right.

You have a very energetic, warm and affectionate way of communicating with others. You may sprinkle your conversation with heartfelt endearments, or you may send loved ones little notes containing carefully worded messages. When taking part in a conversation you may have to fight against a natural tendency to take centre stage or at least to direct everyone's ideas. Even though you may make some very valuable contributions, you need to surrender the conversational limelight every now and then.

Nervous energy has a tendency to sweep through you, leaving you jittery and restless. You need plenty of positive outlets for all this energy, otherwise you can find it difficult to settle to anything for long. You may also have difficulty sleeping because your mind mulls over whichever problems are currently besetting you. You have a very quick and agile mind, and are able to grasp important points and ideas. You approach problems in a very logical way, thinking through every aspect and analysing them in great detail. This can pay dividends as it allows you to see what others have missed. Unfortunately, it can also mean that sometimes you get bogged down with detail and are unable to see the wood for the trees.

People depend on you because you are reliable, practical and organized. You like to do things properly and will take care to present written information as neatly and precisely as possible. When particularly worried about something, you can become a perfectionist, continually making adjustments and corrections to whatever you are working on. You have a tendency to be hard on yourself because you have very high standards and will not hesitate to be self-critical when you fail to meet them. You can also be critical of others when they fail to come up to scratch.

MERCURY IN VIRGO QUALITY: *Mutable* ELEMENT: *Earth*

MERCURY IN LIBRA QUALITY: *Cardinal* ELEMENT: *Air*

Charming and diplomatic, you communicate in a very pleasing, harmonious way. You instinctively have the knack of saying the right thing at the right time, choosing your words carefully in order to bring out the best in other people and avoid any hint of trouble or discord. You may also be unable to say when you don't like something because you have such a strong need to maintain harmony. This can lead to an inner sense of resentment, followed by angry outbursts when you finally feel compelled to say what you really think and redress the balance. Even so, you like to maintain objective viewpoints because you pride yourself on being able to see more than one side to the story. Sometimes, you may be able to appreciate so many differing points of view that you are completely unable to decide where you stand. You also have a dislike of falling out with people, so may prefer to sit on the fence rather than commit yourself one way or the other.

You are intelligent and you enjoy discussing ideas. However, you may be reluctant to spend too long thinking about things that you find repellent or unsettling. This may mean that you sometimes bury your head in the sand rather than confront someone about their objectionable behaviour or stand up for yourself.

Your thoughts run very deep but you may be reluctant to reveal them to many people. This may be because you need to trust someone before you will talk to them in depth. It may also be because some of your ideas are so profound or troubling that you keep them to yourself. For instance, you may enjoy thinking about life and death topics that are too complex for everyday conversation. You are, nevertheless, capable of having penetrating ideas and taking part in deep conversations. Your natural ability to look beyond the surface of a situation makes you a born researcher or detective.

There are times when you like to keep your thoughts to yourself, and on occasion you may come across as being secretive, furtive or elusive. If you have had bad experiences in the past you may be suspicious of people's motives, wondering if they are going to let you down again in the future. You have a good memory and may store up past resentments and slights if you are unable to discuss them or find other ways of releasing them. When you make up your mind about something, it will take a lot to make you change it. You may dig in your heels and refuse to alter your opinion, even to the point of wilfulness.

MERCURY IN SCORPIO QUALITY: *Fixed* ELEMENT: *Water*

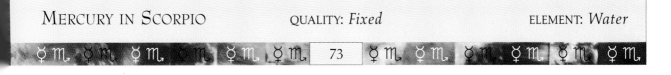

MERCURY IN SAGITTARIUS

QUALITY: *Mutable*   ELEMENT: *Fire*

You are no stranger to big ideas! Your natural enthusiasm means you embrace new ideas with great fervour, and you can get carried away when deciding how to make something happen. You may take a slapdash approach to the practicalities because you believe you did all the hard work when you had the idea in the first place. Now you hope that a willing helper will step in and take the boring tasks away from you. You have wide-ranging interests and you pride yourself on keeping an open mind, so you are receptive to all sorts of ideas, concepts and beliefs. Religions, philosophies and moral codes all fascinate you, and in the course of your life you may follow several religions or spiritual beliefs.

You enjoy travel and keeping on the move, and may feel suffocated if you have to spend too long in one place. If you can't travel in person you will do it from the comfort of your armchair, losing yourself in books and watching informative television programmes. You may be an eternal student, always fascinated by ideas and curious to learn more about the world. Your shelves may groan with books, reflecting all your past interests. Teaching comes naturally to you, whether you do it for a living or you simply enjoy passing on your knowledge in informal ways.

You approach life with a down-to-earth attitude. You like to keep your feet on the ground so that you know what is going on. This may mean mulling things over in great detail before you feel satisfied that you have understood what is happening. You take pride in being businesslike and responsible, so you will go into things very seriously. Responsibilities will be met with diligence and care, because you loathe the idea of being slipshod and not doing things properly. If you feel that you have let yourself down you will worry about it. This serious attitude can spill over into depression when things are not going well. You can be pessimistic, and when you feel insecure or shy you come across as reserved and formal.

Your ideas can be conservative because you have a traditionalist's outlook on life. You like to do things by the book and may feel unsettled when someone wants to break the rules or stray from accepted methods. It is hard for you to switch off from work and you may bring it home with you. This can mean you find it difficult to relax and unwind, as you have such a strong sense of responsibility and duty that you feel you should be doing something rather than sitting doing nothing. You value education and credentials, and may acquire more qualifications as you get older.

MERCURY IN CAPRICORN

QUALITY: *Cardinal*   ELEMENT: *Earth*

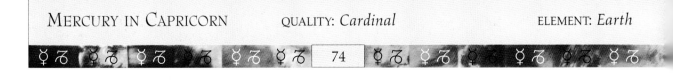

MERCURY IN AQUARIUS   QUALITY: *Fixed*   ELEMENT: *Air*

Independent thinking is essential to you. You loathe the idea of slavishly following other people's beliefs or swallowing their thoughts without question. On the contrary, you enjoy evaluating accepted ideas and concepts and, if necessary, pulling them to pieces or pointing out their faults. You have no qualms about highlighting the flaws in someone's arguments or destroying their sacred cows if you disagree with them. This can make people treat you with trepidation, but it also means you are no slave to accepted ideas and can ask pertinent questions when necessary. You may see it as your job to be the catalyst, the rebel who roots out other people's complacent ideas and points out sloppy thinking. However, you can be just as reluctant to change your mind when someone argues with you, and you may doggedly hold on to your opinions come what may, convinced that you are in the right.

Friends are very important to you, and you probably have a wide-ranging social life drawn from various cultures and classes. You are much more interested in someone's brain than their background, and will quickly withdraw from anyone who is unable to think for themselves. Some of your ideas may be sheer brilliance and years ahead of their time, while others may be bizarre.

You may find it a struggle to keep your feet on the ground as your mind is always floating off to other realms. This is especially likely when you are confronted by unpleasant ideas or unpalatable facts – fantasy can then offer an attractive escape route. You may vanish into a world of make-believe and daydreams. This can be very inspirational, especially if you are able to make use of your creative and artistic talents. However, it can sometimes lead you astray, making you reluctant to face up to reality. It will help if you can find positive outlets for your fertile imagination, and have a sympathetic confidant that you can talk to whenever you are worried about something. Poetry, music and romantic art all appeal to you greatly and you may have a special affinity for them.

You are highly intuitive and may absorb the atmosphere around you without being aware of it. This means you can be strongly affected by people who are angry, depressed or disturbed, and you may need to limit the amount of time you spend with them. You may even have psychic abilities or extrasensory perception. People find you sympathetic and compassionate, and at times you may tune into them so completely that you lose all sense of boundaries. Again, you may need to protect yourself from this tendency.

MERCURY IN PISCES   QUALITY: *Mutable*   ELEMENT: *Water*

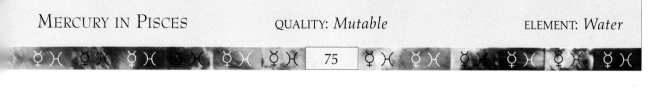

VENUS

VENUS IN ARIES   QUALITY: *Cardinal*   ELEMENT: *Fire*

You have an impulsive attitude to loving relationships. You leap into them, sometimes head first, without holding back. For you, it's the experience and sense of adventure that count. When you meet someone that you like, you don't stop to ask yourself whether they are a good bet. If you are unlucky, this can lead to a broken heart as you tend to expect the best from people until they disappoint you. You can have a childlike, innocent belief that no one will hurt you. But do you learn from your mistakes? Probably not!

Although you enjoy having others around you, you also want to maintain your independence. You don't like having to account for your every move – you need to do your own thing. Equally, you don't want your partner to be clingy or possessive. You enjoy showing affection and have a hearty enjoyment of sex, but feel trapped and uncomfortable when involved in intensely passionate or melodramatic scenes. Though you are loyal to those you love, a relationship is always at its best when still new; when familiarity sets in, you can struggle to keep things going.

This is a very tactile, sensuous placing. You have a great appreciation of the good things in life – fine wines, delicious food, luxurious silks, delectable scents. You enjoy pampering yourself and your loved ones. You love the natural world and derive much pleasure from beautiful surroundings. You may also enjoy growing fruit and vegetables, even if you only have a windowbox.

Love is very important to you, and you can be a very warm, affectionate and passionate lover. Your relationships are central to your well-being and you will do your utmost to protect them. This can lead to possessiveness – reluctance to let your loved one out of your sight. You may also try to hold on to a relationship long after it should have ended, through fear of emotional upheaval and starting again. You are immensely loyal, taking your emotional commitments very seriously. You feel bewildered when people betray your trust, as love is such an important business for you. How can it not be for everyone else? When looking for a partner, their appearance means a lot to you. As far as you are concerned, love is definitely not blind!

VENUS IN TAURUS   QUALITY: *Fixed*   ELEMENT: *Earth*

Venus rules love and affection, and its placing in our charts shows how we react emotionally to others. The sign it occupies can also reveal our idealized image of women.

Venus in Gemini

QUALITY: *Mutable*   ELEMENT: *Air*

Brains are more important than beauty when looking for a partner – you will quickly lose interest if you suspect that they only have grey fluff between their ears. It is essential for you to be with people who are intelligent, witty and clever. You love ideas and enjoy discussing them with people who are suitable foils for you. You also like keeping in touch with everyone, whether by phone, e-mail, letter or in person. You are very sociable and enjoy meeting new people.

When it comes to love, you prefer to keep things on a bright and breezy level. You break out in a cold sweat if your partner is jealous, possessive or controlling, and your instinct may be to rush off in the opposite direction as quickly as possible. Rather than allow yourself to experience deep and possibly unsettling emotions, you prefer to control them by talking or writing about them. You need to have an intellectual grasp of the way you are feeling, but this may be a way of avoiding difficult situations. As a result, loved ones may sometimes feel that you are emotionally detached from them.

If you love someone, they always know it. You will try to take care of them at all times. You are also openly affectionate and probably believe in the healing power of hugs. If you are skilled in the kitchen you will take great pleasure in cooking for your loved ones. This is fine if your loved ones appreciate your brand of maternal loving, but you may have to temper it for people with a strong urge for freedom and independence. You can tread a fine line between offering a safe haven from the world and being suffocating. If you don't have family nearby, you may create a second family out of your friends. They always know they can count on you for support, sympathy and affection.

It is essential for you to live in a peaceful environment. Ideally, you should own your home, as this will add to your emotional security. Your need to feel safe in relationships may mean you tend to cling on to them long after they should have ended, and you may be quite tenacious about keeping hold of people who should have left your life.

Venus in Cancer

QUALITY: *Cardinal*   ELEMENT: *Water*

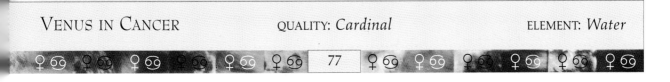

VENUS IN LEO

QUALITY: *Fixed*   ELEMENT: *Fire*

You are very demonstrative, generous and affectionate towards the people you love. You don't want to leave them in any doubt about the way you feel and you are thrilled when they return the compliment. You take tremendous pleasure in spoiling your loved ones, and giving presents is a very important part of that process. You will spend a long time choosing the perfect gift or arranging treats for them. Romance plays a big role in your love life, because it is a way of keeping the relationship alive and proving that you appreciate one another. You will be very miserable with a partner who takes you for granted. Little dramas that arise from time to time also help to keep things alive for you. However, you should beware of trying to dominate your partner by being too bossy or controlling.

When looking for a partner, you need someone that you can feel proud of. You may find someone with stunning looks or you might choose a partner who is very successful. You are very loyal to the people you love and expect no less in return. Your natural dramatic flair may give you acting talent or it may mean that you enjoy being the centre of attention within your own social circle. Creative activities are second nature to you.

You take great pleasure and emotional satisfaction in being of service to other people. This may even have a devotional quality to it, and you may see it as part of your life's work to meet other people's needs. You also take pleasure in being practical, logical and organized. You enjoy thinking things through and turning your sharp wits to knotty problems. You may do this in such a modest, unassuming way that people don't realize how valuable you are – until they need you in a crisis and you aren't around! In loving relationships, you instinctively take a back seat. You are reluctant to push yourself forward, in case you are rejected, and you also don't want to draw too much attention to yourself. Potential lovers may have to pursue you quite diligently before you are ready to succumb. This is not helped by your tendency to criticize yourself, and also other people.

You may take your pleasures in a modest way as well. Perhaps you limit your intake of high-calorie foods, or alcohol, or you enjoy eating as healthily as possible. Vegetarianism and other special diets may appeal to you because you have a natural empathy with them. You enjoy taking care of your body and your idea of bliss may be staying at a health farm.

VENUS IN VIRGO

QUALITY: *Mutable*   ELEMENT: *Earth*

VENUS IN LIBRA

QUALITY: *Cardinal*   ELEMENT: *Air*

Love makes your world go round. You may feel at a loss when you are not involved in a loving relationship and it can be very hard for you to be alone. You need to be one half of a couple, and even if your relationship has long since passed its best you will be reluctant to leave until something better comes along. Even then, your natural dislike of hurting people will make it difficult for you to cut your losses. Even if you are generally happy in your relationship, your motto is 'Anything for a quiet life'. You need a balanced, harmonious atmosphere and this may make you too conciliatory sometimes. You would rather endure problems in a relationship than cause a fuss by mentioning them. Besides, you may instinctively shy away from unpleasant scenes and rows.

You are a born romantic, making you an ideal partner. However, you can also be idealistic and will turn a blind eye to any failings in your loved ones. Because you have such a need for harmony and you want everyone to get on well together, you can feel very uncomfortable when in the company of someone you don't like. You may feel guilty and will try to overcompensate. This can lead to misunderstandings because you send out confusing signals.

For you, loving relationships have an all-or-nothing quality. You like to do things wholeheartedly or not at all, and this applies to your love life as well, so you may throw yourself into a new relationship, extracting every ounce of emotional drama from it and having a wonderful time in the process! You may even enjoy tempestuous scenes, compulsive obsessions, stormy break-ups and passionate reconciliations. This can be an exhausting combination for anyone who wants an uneventful relationship, but you thrive on it. You find it almost impossible to divorce love from sex, and you may even have sexual fantasies about friends because there is always some form of sensual link between you and the important people in your life.

Because you invest so much emotion in your relationships, jealousy and control often cause problems. You like to keep a firm hand on the relationship and when things are going badly you may suspect that your partner is up to no good. If your suspicions are confirmed, this can make you reluctant to trust partners in the future. Your friendships are also coloured by emotional intensity, yet you have the gift of being able to love people very deeply. They know they can count on your loyalty and support.

VENUS IN SCORPIO

QUALITY: *Fixed*   ELEMENT: *Water*

VENUS IN SAGITTARIUS QUALITY: *Mutable* ELEMENT: *Fire*

One of the qualities that you look for in friends and lovers is honesty. You need to be able to trust people. However, your own desire for·honesty may mean that you unconsciously hurt people by telling them the plain, unvarnished truth. You may then be bewildered when they object to your comments. After all, you were only telling them the facts! When looking for a partner, you are attracted to people who are broad-minded, independent and who won't cling to you. Although you are demonstrative and affectionate, you loathe the thought of someone hanging on to your coat-tails or restricting your freedom through their emotional demands. You like to think of yourself as a free spirit. You have an idealistic vision of what a relationship should be, and will strive to turn it into reality even if it does not fit your partner's idea of heaven.

You are drawn to beliefs and philosophies, and these may affect the way you behave to your loved ones. As your beliefs change, so will the tenor of your close relationships. Ideally, your partner should share your beliefs or your general view of life. You have a tremendous love of travel and you enjoy rising to challenges. You may even have important relationships with people from other countries or cultures.

You have a strong need for material security and you will not be truly happy unless you have a roof over your head and money in the bank. You may also require a happy family gathered around you in order to feel fully secure. You take love very seriously because you are so wary of being rejected and hurt. Even though you may not be very demonstrative, you need deep and lasting loving relationships, and anything less simply will not do. So, when looking for a partner you will be drawn to people who appear to be good bets, who won't let you down and, probably, who have a good income or earning ability. You have a healthy respect for money and what it can buy, and you need a partner who thinks the same way. It will cause problems between you if your partner does not share this respect.

It is difficult for you to show your feelings openly, and this may make you appear aloof, distant or uncaring. You may exercise a tight control over your feelings, fighting back any emotional outbursts and also ensuring that your partner does the same. You are certainly reluctant to be demonstrative in public because you like to maintain your dignity in front of others. Your reputation means a lot to you.

VENUS IN CAPRICORN QUALITY: *Cardinal* ELEMENT: *Earth*

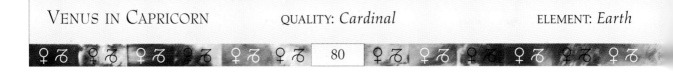

VENUS IN AQUARIUS

QUALITY: *Fixed*   ELEMENT: *Air*

You have a strong need for emotional independence and you hate feeling tied down to someone or something. Even when you are in a close and long-lasting relationship, a part of you remains unattached and free. This may make you seem slightly detached and distant, even with close friends and family. You feel uncomfortable when someone expresses intense feelings or shows their emotions, and you may try to rationalize your responses as a way of controlling them. Although you are capable of great love, you may find it very hard to translate your feelings into words. Instead, you will discuss your emotions in the abstract or as part of an intellectual theory.

Friends and groups are very important to you, and you will be an active member of them. You may also have strong humanitarian impulses, and these could help to influence your spare-time activities. In your search for a partner, you will instinctively avoid anyone who you feel is stupid or unable to think for themselves. You will also avoid potential partners who might be possessive or want to restrict your freedom in other ways. You may take pleasure in being controversial, rebellious or extremist, especially if you want to shock someone who is being stuffy or prim. You will enjoy getting a rise out of them.

Love and affection mean the world to you. You are a born romantic, who tends to idealize your relationships. It is very easy for you to drift into a fantasy world whenever real life fails to meet your expectations, especially if you are in danger of having your feelings hurt. You are immensely sensitive and you may feel as though you have a layer of emotional 'skin' missing. Situations that would not bother other people may affect you deeply. You may even be psychic, enabling you to tune into others on a very deep level. This means you can establish very powerful and enriching relationships with people, but you may also be highly susceptible to negative energies that you easily absorb. You need to develop some form of defence mechanism to cope with this.

You are blessed with tremendous compassion, so you may always be the one who offers a shoulder to cry on. Again, you need to avoid soaking up other people's problems like a sponge. Even so, you are capable of selfless love and may be instinctively drawn to lame ducks and lost causes. This may also be part of the spiritual path that you feel drawn to. Unfortunately, a lack of discrimination and a strong empathy for people in trouble means you can sometimes be gullible and your good nature can be exploited.

VENUS IN PISCES

QUALITY: *Mutable*   ELEMENT: *Water*

MARS

MARS IN ARIES QUALITY: *Cardinal* ELEMENT: *Fire*

You are energetic, dynamic and raring to go. You view life as a series of adventures and competitions, and you are determined to get as much out of the experiences as possible. You jump at the chance to do something new because you view it as a challenge. There may be obstacles involved but you won't let these put you off your stroke – you can even feel excited at the chance to prove your worth in the face of adversity. This is a very positive quality but sometimes you can get carried away and become quite impetuous, reckless and even foolhardy. You are impatient for quick results so can soon become bored with whatever goal you are pursuing and want to move on to the next adventure, rather than follow through the current one.

Your natural assertiveness makes you no stranger to the idea of getting what you want from life. You see no reason not to ask for it and you can be very direct in this. As far as you are concerned, it is a waste of time to beat about the bush. You have tremendous sexual drive and energy, and enjoy the thrill of the chase.

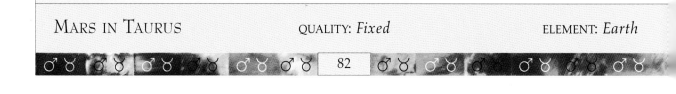

You have very strong ideas about life on which you are not prepared to budge. This can make you steadfast and resolute at best, but it can also turn into obstinacy and pig-headedness on occasion. You have a strong urge to maintain the status quo and you are wary of introducing change for the sake of it. At heart, you are a traditionalist and you are prepared to fight for what you believe in. This may mean that you view innovation with suspicion and would rather stick with the devil you know than branch out in new and untried directions. Part of this may be caused by a slightly lazy streak and also a need for emotional and physical security.

When it comes to asking for what you want, you are very straightforward and you can be quite unmoving!

Sex is extremely important to you, and you can be very earthy and sensual. You may also be prone to sexual jealousy, making you want to treat your partner like a possession. However, this can be self-defeating. Fidelity is an essential element of close relationships and you may reveal quite a temper if you think you have been betrayed.

MARS IN TAURUS QUALITY: *Fixed* ELEMENT: *Earth*

Mars rules our drive, energy and impetus. It indicates the directions in which we are motivated. The sign it occupies can also reveal our idealized image of men.

MARS IN GEMINI

QUALITY: *Mutable*　　　ELEMENT: *Air*

Words can be your weapon in life. You use them to assert yourself, to make an impact on people and to get what you want. You are a fast talker and you enjoy taking part in debates and light-hearted verbal sparring matches because you know you will probably win them. It is also good fun for you to hone your already sharp brain through some intellectual combat. You have a lot of nervous energy and may struggle to channel it in one direction for long. You can frequently be distracted by new interests, fresh excitements or enticing opportunities, so that you leave a trail of unfinished projects behind you. This is partly because you are not sure what you want from life – there are so many options open to you that you are reluctant to commit yourself to anything. It is far more exciting to see what life will bring.

When looking for a partner you are very attracted to people with minds of their own. What starts as a sexual relationship may eventually turn into a solid friendship. When the right opportunity comes along you can be very flirtatious and even unfaithful.

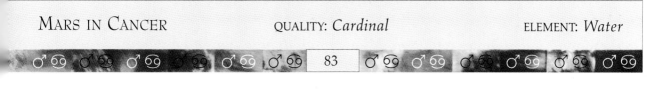

You may look back on your life so far and wonder how on earth you have achieved so much. You might not know how you have reached your current position – it seems to have happened of its own accord. This is because you can take an indirect approach to life, and you may even be unconscious of most of your goals and ambitions. Even if other people see you as ambitious, you do not recognize this trait in yourself because you are so unaware of it. Nevertheless, when you do assert yourself it is in a sympathetic and sensitive way, and you will try to tune into the feelings of the other people involved. You have no desire to hurt them or to make yourself unpopular.

You have a strong urge to stay connected with your roots as this boosts your emotional security. If a member of the family or a close friend is under threat, you are prepared to fight tooth and nail on their behalf and you can be fiercely protective of them. Your sexual desires are closely linked with your emotions, and although you are capable of great passion you can also withdraw emotionally when the atmosphere is wrong.

MARS IN CANCER

QUALITY: *Cardinal*　　　ELEMENT: *Water*

MARS IN LEO   QUALITY: *Fixed*   ELEMENT: *Fire*

One of the great blessings of this placing is tremendous confidence and self-assurance. You assert yourself with dignity and warmth, although you can sometimes become rather regal if you think the situation warrants it. After all, Leo is the sign of royalty and you may want to remind other people to take you seriously! Your innate love of drama means that life is often exciting when you are around, and you enjoy knowing that you are the centre of attention. You certainly need a lot of recognition from others and can feel quite irritated if you have to spend too long out of the limelight.

You have plenty of energy and an abundant vitality, which means you are always eagerly awaiting the next adventure. If other people fail to share your enthusiasm, you may become quite impatient with them and might even fall into the trap of bossing them around so they will do what you want. Sometimes this placing can create a rather arrogant belief in your own importance, and also the determination that everyone else should follow your lead and do what you want. When looking for a partner you may be drawn to someone who is larger than life, and you will certainly want a lover who is as demonstrative and sexually motivated as you.

Hard work is second nature to you. You believe in channelling all your energy into tasks and chores, and you are especially diligent when it comes to being of service to others and carrying out your duties. There is no danger of you shirking your responsibilities or expecting someone else to do your dirty work for you. You are very discriminating and have high standards, and can become quite irritated when other people fail to live up to them. They may be left in no doubt about their faults! However, even though you are critical of others you are probably much tougher on yourself. Although you have the drive to make a lot of progress in your work, you may get bogged down in too much attention to detail and will worry about what might happen if things go wrong. You need to develop strategies that will help you to control your perfectionist streak.

Although Virgo is an Earth sign, sex may not come very high up on your list of relationship priorities. It may be more important that your partner is clean, tidy and shares your understanding of the importance of hygiene. Your natural sense of modesty may prevent you being as sexually open as you would sometimes like. There might also be a tendency to let your sex life become somewhat routine.

MARS IN VIRGO   QUALITY: *Mutable*   ELEMENT: *Earth*

MARS IN LIBRA

QUALITY: *Cardinal* ELEMENT: *Air*

There is an inbuilt contradiction with this placing. The natural drive of Mars is to assert oneself, yet Libra is more concerned with the happiness of others – so you may find it hard to strike a balance between voicing your own desires and fitting in with those of the people in your life. You might also be so aware that there are at least two sides to every story that you feel reluctant to stick your neck out or insist that things are done in the way you want. Nevertheless, when you are assertive you behave in a charming and diplomatic way, and you will do your best to create an air of harmony and conciliation. You will also want things to be as fair as possible.

Your natural indecisiveness means that you are sometimes reluctant to make up your mind. You may be faced with too many options to feel confident about choosing the right one. A strong need to please your partner can interfere with your ability to ask for what you want, and you need to find a balance between these two instincts. Romance is important to you but sex may be rather off-putting, especially if it involves too much passion or mess. You may also give much of the power and control in your relationship to your partner.

As far as you are concerned, you are only interested in doing things that have meaning for you. You are simply not prepared to invest a lot of energy in any activities that are a waste of time or insignificant. This intensity of purpose and belief in the importance of what you do can make you uncompromising and stubborn. It may be impossible to get you to change your mind, but if you do concede defeat you can bear a grudge about it for a long time afterwards. Control issues are likely to cause problems for you in relationships because you have a very strong need to be the one who calls the shots. It can be hard for you to learn to compromise, and to trust other people enough to leave the decision-making to them.

Nevertheless, this is a placing with enormous emotional power and endurance. You may have to cope with situations and problems that would be too much for most people, yet somehow you get through them and emerge stronger as a result. You can also learn to transform yourself through your experiences, and this is one of your greatest strengths. Partners find you passionate, intense and loyal, and your most intimate relationships have an all-or-nothing quality. At its best, sex has a transformative quality for you.

MARS IN SCORPIO

QUALITY: *Fixed* ELEMENT: *Water*

Mars in Sagittarius

QUALITY: *Mutable* ELEMENT: *Fire*

An innate sense of optimism gives you tremendous resilience and energy. No matter what life throws at you, you bounce back like a rubber ball sooner or later, convinced that things will be different next time. Whether or not they are is another matter. Your beliefs and personal philosophy guide your actions, and your wonderful honesty prevents you doing things that go against the grain or run counter to your moral code. Even if you thought you could get away with such behaviour in the eyes of the world, you would find it hard to live with yourself. When other people behave in ways you don't like, you can be blunt to the point of tactlessness when telling them what you think of them.

Ideally, you like life to have an exciting quality. If things become too boring you will probably dream up a scheme or project that will give you something to look forward to. Your adventurous spirit makes you a natural traveller and you enjoy visiting far-flung places or going on voyages of expedition. In your sex life you need to maintain some sexual and emotional freedom. You can't bear the thought of being tied down, even if you have been married for more years than you care to remember. You may also enjoy the thrill of the chase more than the conquest.

One of your greatest strengths is your self-discipline. You have high standards and you are determined not to let yourself down. It is important for you to make a success of your life and also to win respect from the people around you. Although you may not make a song and dance about it, you are quietly ambitious and always keep one eye on your long-term goals and objectives. You may even map out your strategy in a calculated way, plotting what each move should be and when you should make it. Material success is very important to you and you will work hard to attain it. This is not because you want to flaunt status symbols or show off, but rather it is simply because money will buy you a secure home and a comfortable life.

Convention and tradition are important to you and you can worry about what other people think about you. You like to do things by the book. When looking for a partner, you want someone who will share your earthy sexiness. You also need someone who will work hard to create a safe environment for the two of you. You can be self-controlled and rather reserved, especially if you are secretly frightened of being rejected by loved ones.

Mars in Capricorn

QUALITY: *Cardinal* ELEMENT: *Earth*

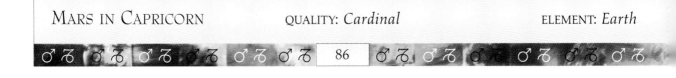

MARS IN AQUARIUS

QUALITY: *Fixed*　　　　ELEMENT: *Air*

Naturally quirky and unconventional, you can assert yourself in ways that people don't expect. Your energy levels are erratic, veering between dynamism and lethargy. Above all, you are determined to be an individual and someone who is true to yourself. Other people's expectations have little or no bearing on the way you behave because you have to do what feels right for you. It is essential for you to live your life with a sense of independence and freedom. You hate being restricted by society's rules and strictures, and there may be times when you are deliberately unconventional or contradictory in order to make this point. Sometimes this rebellious streak holds you back from achieving what you want because you can be your own worst enemy or set people against you. You are quite prepared to stand up for the things that you believe in, even if these shock society as a whole, and humanitarian causes and animal welfare may be dear to your heart.

In sexual relationships you have a strong need to feel that you are essentially a free spirit, so you may have a slight air of detachment. You can't bear being with someone who is possessive or jealous. You also need a partner who is intelligent and, most important of all, a good friend.

There are times when it is difficult for you to assert yourself because you are so tuned into the feelings of the people around you that you don't want to hurt or upset them. You may worry about losing the affection of others if you say things they don't want to hear, and you can also be reluctant to face up to unpleasant facts. As a result, you may go along with situations that you aren't happy about until you finally lose your temper and put your foot down. It would be better to train yourself to speak up earlier and avoid such scenes. Even when you do assert yourself, you may not be entirely sure how you do it, because you can do it unconsciously.

Your energy levels are strongly influenced by your emotions, so you may quickly become listless when you feel unhappy and be full of energy when things are going well. Romance and fantasies play important roles in your sex life. At its best you see sex as the chance to attain a spiritual union with your partner, yet you can also be intrigued by sexual games and the idea of playing the field. Some people with this placing can be very promiscuous, taking pleasure in carving numerous notches on their bedposts.

MARS IN PISCES

QUALITY: *Mutable*　　　　ELEMENT: *Water*

JUPITER

JUPITER IN ARIES QUALITY: *Cardinal* ELEMENT: *Fire*

You are full of enthusiasm and vibrant energy. Life is an adventure and you want to enjoy as much of it as possible. You have an innate confidence that propels you through life even when things are difficult. Other people can see this as a charming, naive quality – you never lose faith that things will get better in time. But if taken to extremes, it can lead to foolish risk-taking or a refusal to see the writing on the wall. This is when you can be reckless, and miss opportunities.

You are a natural athlete, and you certainly have a competitive nature. You may enjoy taking part in sports and athletics, and might carry several scars as trophies from some of your more daredevil exploits. You are a born leader because you have a strong sense of where you are going in life and what you want to achieve. But sometimes these leadership qualities can turn into a slight tendency to bully others or to insist that you are right. You may also be happy to blow your own trumpet, and sometimes you can do it rather loudly.

You like to make slow and steady progress through life. You want to enjoy yourself along the way and ensure that everyone has as good a time as possible. Something else that you want to achieve is a healthy bank balance and a comfortable standard of living. You aren't interested in roughing it and will work hard to be able to afford the good life. You thoroughly enjoy your creature comforts, although sometimes you can over-indulge. As a result, you may have to find a compromise between endless dieting and eating whatever you fancy. There is also a slight tendency for you to place so much importance on money and possessions that you become rather materialistic. This would be a great shame because your innate generosity is one of your most endearing qualities.

Something else that ensures your popularity is your tremendous sense of humour. You are gregarious, sociable and affectionate, and also faithful – loved ones know where they stand with you. You may take great pleasure from being surrounded by beauty and also from being in the open air. Nature can be a tremendous solace and inspiration for you.

JUPITER IN TAURUS QUALITY: *Fixed* ELEMENT: *Earth*

Jupiter describes the ways in which we expand in life. It shows our ability to grow and the way we accumulate experience. It also reveals our faith and beliefs.

JUPITER IN GEMINI

QUALITY: *Mutable*   ELEMENT: *Air*

Communicating is of prime importance to you. It gives you a lot of satisfaction to talk to other people, and especially to get involved in spirited discussions and lively conversations. You enjoy showing off your mental and verbal skills, and you may also love hearing the sound of your own voice! You like to chat about whatever happens to interest you at that moment. You have wide-ranging interests and an intellectual curiosity about the world.

However, there is a danger that you can become so broad-minded and open to ideas that you never settle to anything for long. You can be one of those people who knows a little about a lot but has never studied anything in great depth. It will help to concentrate on one or two subjects and to acquire more than just superficial knowledge.

You are blessed with a sense of optimism and an ability to talk yourself out of any tight spots! Versatility and flexibility are two of your greatest strengths, but you can be so restless that you seek change for its own sake and find it hard to relax.

Family contacts are very important to you. If you don't have a family of your own, or you don't get on well with them, you will create your own network of people that you consider to be family. You like the sense that you are giving one another emotional support and that you are linked by enduring bonds of affection. It is easy for you to show loved ones that you care for them, and they will benefit from your generous, protective and loving nature. Children mean a lot to you, and you will be at pains to encourage their intellectual growth from an early age, teaching them to

read or discussing wide-ranging topics with them. You can also take pleasure from cooking, and it may be a way of restoring your faith in life when things are going badly.

Worry can be a problem for you. It may be difficult to trust that everything will work itself out and you might spend a lot of time fretting about things that may never happen. You excel at business because you are shrewd and have the great incentive of wanting to earn enough money to create a safe and comfortable home environment.

JUPITER IN CANCER

QUALITY: *Cardinal*   ELEMENT: *Water*

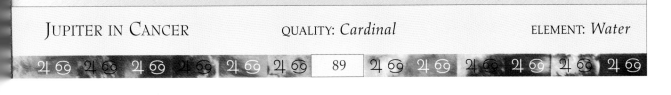

JUPITER IN LEO

QUALITY: *Fixed* ELEMENT: *Fire*

You certainly know how to stand out in a crowd! For a start, you may enjoy dressing in a flamboyant and dramatic way, and you may take particular care over your hair. It is important for you to look your best and you might spend more than your budget allows on fashionable clothes and expensive accessories. You might also judge others by their appearance, quickly learning to add up the cost of their outfits and assess their social status accordingly. Unfortunately, this can make you arrogant and snobbish, and this is something that you need to guard against.

Even so, you are terrific company and deservedly popular. Friends and loved ones revel in your expansive, generous and exuberant company. You are an optimist, although this may be partly due to a self-centred conviction that life couldn't possibly let you down – it wouldn't dare! You enjoy taking centre stage and may feel irritated or put out when other people rob you of the limelight for too long. As a result, you can flourish in the world of show-business although you will need to keep your feet on the ground and not believe too much of your own publicity. You have marvellous organizational skills, but you must take care not to let these turn into bossiness.

This placing is a curious combination of warring energies. Jupiter encourages expansion but Virgo likes to concentrate on details. As a result, you can sometimes veer between taking the long view and a broad-minded approach to life, and seeking refuge in tiny details and precise facts. Nevertheless, if you can find a compromise between such opposing viewpoints, you will be capable of tremendous intellectual work and will gain a well-developed analytical viewpoint. Such gifts mean you can make enormous progress through life. People trust you because they know you will do your best while keeping a sense of humour that will prevent you taking yourself too seriously.

You gain a lot of emotional satisfaction from being of service to others and doing your work to the best of your abilities. At times, such activities may even have a devotional quality to them and you may seek refuge in them when other areas of your life are difficult. You enjoy working with words and take pleasure in study and research. Meticulous and practical, you are quick to criticize yourself when you fail to meet your own high standards. Others have a much higher opinion of you than you do of yourself, and encourage you to relax more and worry less over details.

JUPITER IN VIRGO

QUALITY: *Mutable* ELEMENT: *Earth*

JUPITER IN LIBRA   QUALITY: *Cardinal*   ELEMENT: *Air*

Relationships are extremely important to you. You can feel as if you are only half alive if you have to spend too long by yourself, and you have an abiding need for a permanent partner in your life. Being part of a relationship helps you to blossom and develop. However, such a strong emphasis on relationships means you may be reluctant to end a partnership when it is over because you have such a powerful dislike of being on your own. In addition, it might also mean that you put up with relationship problems that other people simply would not tolerate.

Business partnerships work very well for you and you may find it much easier to make money when working as part of a team than when you are left to your own devices. Money is certainly important to you because it allows you to enjoy all the good things in life. You will happily buy gifts for loved ones and they will appreciate your open-hearted generosity. Taking exercise may not come particularly high on your list of priorities and this can eventually lead to weight gain and a sluggish metabolism, especially if you are busy living the high life in the meantime. You enjoy taking a broad-minded approach to life and you are always at pains to play fair by others.

Have you ever wondered why life is so full of ups and downs for you? It is because you have a tendency to live life to the full and you need a strong emotional involvement with whatever you are doing. Sometimes this means you can take things to extremes. This is true of your relationships, your career and other aspects of your life. You may have a powerful yearning to find a belief or philosophy that gives meaning to your life, and you are likely to choose something that is intense and has a transformative quality. It may also act like a form of psychoanalysis on you,

and you will respond to this very well. It will give you increased confidence in your abilities.

Sometimes it can be difficult for you to be open about your emotions. Your instincts may tell you to keep your innermost thoughts and feelings to yourself, in case they are betrayed or trivialized. Nevertheless, if you can bring yourself to confide in treasured companions you will gain a tremendous amount from the experience, and so will they. You are an excellent judge of character and should be able to trust your intuition, knowing who to confide in and who to keep at arm's length. It is easy for you to make money but just as easy to spend it, thanks to your impulsive generosity.

JUPITER IN SCORPIO   QUALITY: *Fixed*   ELEMENT: *Water*

JUPITER IN SAGITTARIUS   QUALITY: *Mutable*   ELEMENT: *Fire*

Optimistic, positive and enthusiastic, you like to throw yourself into life because you are confident that everything will work out well. And strangely enough it does, perhaps because you are not prepared for anything less to happen. Your positive attitude also attracts positive situations and people. You have a great love of life and are always eager to know what is around the next corner. Even when things go badly for you, you quickly recover your equilibrium and are all set for the next adventure. A philosophical approach to life helps you to take problems on the chin, learn from them and then put them behind you. However, you need to guard against a tendency towards blind optimism, in which you have a Pollyanna-ish attitude and refuse to acknowledge problems and difficulties.

It is very important for you to have something to believe in. This may not be a conventional religion or belief, provided it gives you faith and conviction. You also set great store by knowledge, and you may be the eternal student, always studying or being fascinated by new subjects. Travel can appeal to you too, and you enjoy visiting far-flung corners of the globe. The grass may sometimes be greener on the other side of the fence, making you restless and unsettled.

You are no stranger to hard work and you will willingly roll up your sleeves if that is what is required. You have a strong sense of diligence and a very practical streak, making you someone who can be relied upon to do what is expected of them. People put their trust in you because they are encouraged by your quiet confidence and self-assurance. You are responsible, capable and efficient. However, you need to guard against a tendency to take on too much work or to work around the clock to the detriment of your private life.

You believe that it is necessary to work your way steadily to the top and you would rather do this than attain a sudden success that you are unable to sustain.

You are able to combine optimism with reality and common sense, giving you the best of both worlds. However, occasionally you may be overtaken by depression or a miserable conviction that things are going wrong. You can also be guilty of the belief that you are right and everyone else is deluding themselves. Luckily, your wonderful, dry sense of humour is your saving grace and you have a marvellous ability to laugh at yourself and send yourself up.

JUPITER IN CAPRICORN   QUALITY: *Cardinal*   ELEMENT: *Earth*

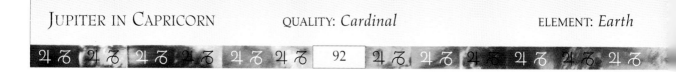

JUPITER IN AQUARIUS

QUALITY: *Fixed*   ELEMENT: *Air*

You have a strong sense of individuality and your many friends will vouch for the fact that you are your own person. You have no desire to be anything less and you have a quirky originality that is very engaging and interesting. People enjoy being with you because you are intelligent, tolerant and lively. You have a strong sense of justice and you are always quick to stand up for what you think is right. This can sometimes lead you into battles with authority figures, especially if you believe that they are blindly following rules and not thinking things through properly.

Humanitarian causes are especially important to you. However, you may sometimes be intolerant of people who do not share your views, and you can take a moral stance that insists you are the only person who is in the right.

Science can interest you and you may also have good technological abilities. You need to find a faith that you can believe in wholeheartedly. It may be something of your own invention or it could be a mixture of several different philosophies – this does not bother you in the slightest. What matters is to find something that is true for you and not coloured by other people's beliefs and opinions. You are warm and gregarious, making you a popular person to have around.

Faith is a very important part of your life. You may not be able to give your faith or philosophy a name, as it may not fit in with accepted ideas or creeds. Occasionally it can offer an escape route from the problems you encounter in life. Nevertheless, you are very receptive to other people's beliefs and you will happily take part in discussions about them. You have tremendous compassion, empathy, sensitivity and kindness, making you a natural confidant. Many people may unburden themselves to you and you might even choose a job that involves listening to other people's problems. You might be drawn to a vocation or follow a spiritual path through life.

It is easy for you to express your emotions, and you enjoy showing affection to loved ones. You have such a powerful ability to tune into the people around you that you may be very intuitive and possibly even psychic. If so, you need to develop techniques that will help you to protect yourself from negative energies and people who rely on you too heavily. Sometimes you can be prone to worry, in which case practices such as yoga and meditation can help you to relax. You are ideally suited to any form of deep contemplation and it can give your life a powerful focus and meaning.

JUPITER IN PISCES

QUALITY: *Mutable*   ELEMENT: *Water*

SATURN

SATURN IN ARIES

QUALITY: *Cardinal*   ELEMENT: *Fire*

This is a strange mixture of energies because Saturn urges caution and a measured approach, while Aries sees life as one long adventure and is sometimes careless about taking risks. As a result you will have to work hard to find a balance between these differing energies within you. You may find that you alternate between bouts of derring-do and occasions when you feel hidebound and hesitant about pushing yourself forward. With time and self-knowledge you will be able to marry your enterprising nature with a healthy dash of common sense. You will be single-minded about achieving goals and proving yourself in the world, and will feel much more confident about your abilities and resources.

You may have a strong aptitude for sports, and will work hard to do your best. Even so, you should guard against being foolhardy because this could result in possible injury. Whenever the pace of life slows down too much, you can become bored, stale and even depressed. It can be difficult for to you to accept a lot of respon-sibility and you may develop childish ploys in order to escape it.

You have a great respect for tradition and conven-tion because you believe they are the frameworks on which society is built. It therefore goes against the grain for you to be unconventional or to buck trends. As a result, you may sometimes feel scared of breaking out of your personal ruts. You may develop a strict routine that gives you emo-tional security yet acts rather like a straitjacket, and it can be hard for you to alter this. You can certainly be very tough on yourself and you have high standards, especially when it comes to hard work and being reliable. You are probably renowned for your patience, diligence, reliability and persistence. It is important for you to gain the approval of others.

Fear of losing control can make you behave in very rigid, buttoned-up ways. You may frown on too much levity, even if you secretly long to join in. You can also be very strict with yourself over food and drink, and you may monitor your intake very carefully. Too much financial extravagance worries you, so you might count the pennies and budget carefully, even when you can afford to indulge yourself.

SATURN IN TAURUS

QUALITY: *Fixed*   ELEMENT: *Earth*

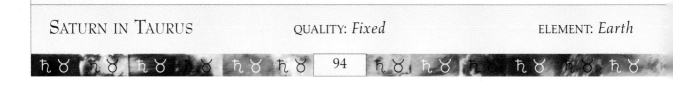

Saturn is the planet of rules and limitations. It helps us to set boundaries and is the small voice inside us telling us what we should and should not do.

SATURN IN GEMINI

QUALITY: *Mutable* ELEMENT: *Air*

You have a very good brain! You enjoy using your mind and thinking problems through, and probably have a strong intellectual bent. You may also have some scientific ability and are able to understand complicated theories and concepts. However, thinking about such things and discussing them are entirely different matters for you. There may be times when you feel tongue-tied or lost for words, and you are always reluctant to speak just for the sake of it. Sometimes people may find you rather too taciturn or silent, which can make them uncomfortable. They may also misunderstand your silences for sulking or disapproval, so it might be helpful to explain how you are feeling at these times.

Your attitude towards duties and responsibilities is coloured by how interesting they are! You are far more likely to work hard at jobs that engage your mind than at tasks that require almost no mental input. If you are confronted by many of these you will find it a struggle to finish them, and you will be strongly critical of yourself for this, which may make the problem worse.

You are far more sensitive than you like to admit, and you may worry about revealing too much of what you probably regard as your Achilles heel. You are at pains to protect yourself from slights and hurts, and this can give you an air of reserve and defensiveness. Rather than reveal your strong feelings you prefer to keep them to yourself, which can leave loved ones wondering how you really feel about them. They may withdraw from you in a reflection of your own behaviour, which can create a vicious circle. Ideally, you need to muster the courage to reveal your affectionate nature.

Emotional security is very important to you and you will work hard to create a stable home environment. You believe in investing in property as soon as you can afford it, and you take your family responsibilities very seriously. As a result, you may be the one who regularly visits old or difficult members of the family, simply because you believe it is your duty. You like saving money and can be a shrewd investor. You may also have good business sense, with the ability to persist in your chosen profession even when times are hard.

SATURN IN CANCER

QUALITY: *Cardinal* ELEMENT: *Water*

SATURN IN LEO QUALITY: *Fixed* ELEMENT: *Fire*

You have a strong sense of where you are going in life and you take pride in this. It gives you a feeling of security to know that you are doing a good job in whichever walk of life you have chosen and that other people respect you for it. You may even take this area of your life rather seriously, placing a lot of emphasis on it and working towards your ambitions with great single-mindedness. Relationships, your social life and your family may have to take a back seat to your ambitions, because you channel so much effort and energy into them.

Even so, you are capable of tremendous love and affection, although sometimes you may have difficulty in showing your feelings. You are certainly extremely loyal and you will move heaven and earth in order to protect your loved ones. They know they can rely on your affection. It will do you good to bring out your creative talents, and these will help you to lighten up and not take things quite so seriously. When you talk to yourself, you tend to be very strict and uncompromising. You may also persuade yourself to do what you think is expected of you, rather than what you would secretly like to do. This can have quite a restrictive effect on you. Perhaps you need to play more!

The virtues of hard work, discipline and patience are very important to you. You do your best to be of service to others whenever possible, often putting yourself out in order to help people. If you do anything less you feel you are letting yourself – and them – down. Sometimes this can mean that you act in very selfless ways because you dare not do otherwise. Besides, your inner voice is so strict that you will criticize yourself repeatedly if you do not carry out what you believe to be your duty.

You excel at work because you are so reliable, methodical and painstaking. Your organizational skills are excellent, so other people tend to rely on you to make things happen. However, you can sometimes get bogged down in petty details that you will worry endlessly about. You may need to reach a compromise between being what you consider to be slapdash and what others think of as perfectionist. It may also be necessary for you to tone down your criticism of the people in your life: you can be quite cutting sometimes and you may also have standards that no one could ever hope to attain – not even you! Yet your innate modesty prevents you from recognizing how capable and hard-working you really are.

SATURN IN VIRGO QUALITY: *Mutable* ELEMENT: *Earth*

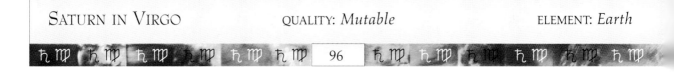

SATURN IN LIBRA
QUALITY: *Cardinal* ELEMENT: *Air*

You put a lot of hard work and effort into your relationships. You take them seriously and you want them to be a success. Tact, diplomacy and a quiet charm make you popular and ensure that you get on well with others. In addition to these qualities, you place much value on your responsibilities and pride yourself on not letting people down. If you make promises you will do your utmost to keep them, and you are always at pains to be fair when sorting out problems with people. However, deep down you may have a fear of relationships that prevents you getting as close to loved ones as you would like – something can hold you back from true intimacy. You may find practical reasons for this, such as the pressure of work or outside commitments, but privately you will know that these are simply excuses for something that goes much deeper and which you will probably never want to explore in great detail.

Your inner voice will always take you to task when you think you have let someone down or you are not being as kind or favourable to them as you should. You may also be so keen to foster a sense of balance and harmony in your relationships that you end up putting your own needs second.

Feelings run very deep for you. In fact, they may be so deep that you are reluctant to explore them in too much detail and you feel it would be better to leave well alone. Nevertheless, your emotions are powerful and profound, and they may have a transforming effect on your life if you let them. You can certainly learn a lot from experiencing your deepest feelings so it is in your interests to acknowledge these as much as possible. It will also help your relationships if you can be more open about the way you feel – otherwise partners may suspect that you are always holding something back and they will never be able to establish a true intimacy with you.

One area in which you are happy to channel your emotions and energy is your career. You are a shrewd operator and you are probably very successful in your job. Even if you haven't got there yet, you want to reach a position of authority and power and you won't rest until you attain this. It is vital for you to have an emotional investment in your career and you will feel depressed and cheated if this is not possible. You can excel at work that involves helping people who are at rock bottom or who want to transform their lives.

SATURN IN SCORPIO
QUALITY: *Fixed* ELEMENT: *Water*

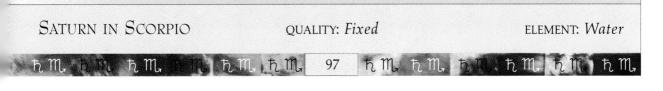

SATURN IN SAGITTARIUS   QUALITY: *Mutable*   ELEMENT: *Fire*

You have a tremendous respect for the power of knowledge and will work hard throughout your life to increase your education and add to your experience. You have the concentration needed to focus on subjects in a lot of depth, and you also have the staying power and determination to continue with them through thick and thin. This is helped by the fact that you can remember important facts, sometimes for years at a time. Philosophy, religion and spiritual beliefs are all important ingredients of a happy and fulfilling life for you, and you are not afraid to examine these beliefs in detail to make sure they are right for you. When life is tough, you can gain tremendous emotional reassurance from your beliefs.

You are honest and straightforward, sometimes to the point of tactlessness. You loathe the idea of pussyfooting around or not being true to yourself. You don't mind the thought of being at variance with commonly held beliefs and opinions, and may even see it as an interesting challenge to defend your ideas in the teeth of opposition. However, other challenges can make you feel inadequate and you may tell yourself that you will never be able to meet them. This may be partly true if you have a habit of taking on more responsibility than you can comfortably manage.

Responsibilities and duties come easily to you because you have an innate understanding of their importance in life. You want to do your best and you hate the thought of being incompetent or letting someone down. You are a tireless, assiduous and highly disciplined worker who will not be satisfied unless you know you have performed to your best abilities. You are not the sort of person who works with one eye on the clock. Instead, you may still be at your desk when everyone else has gone home, and if this trend is allowed to continue you can become a workaholic who never has a break. You will do this from the best of motives, but your relationships, home life and health can all eventually suffer.

It is important for you to take plenty of exercise to avoid stiffness in your joints – it will also help you to work off any worry that you have incurred through your job.

You have great organizational abilities but sometimes you need to avoid being too controlling. It may also help you to delegate to others. One of your greatest strengths is your marvellous sense of humour, and this can act as a much-needed safety valve. It will help to counter what can sometimes be a very strict and harsh opinion of yourself.

SATURN IN CAPRICORN   QUALITY: *Cardinal*   ELEMENT: *Earth*

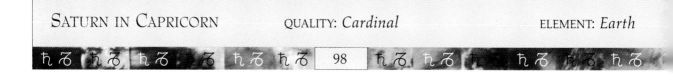

SATURN IN AQUARIUS

QUALITY: *Fixed* ELEMENT: *Air*

This placing means you have to combine the traditionalism of Saturn with the iconoclasm of Aquarius. This is not easy and you may swing between being bogged down by convention and worry about what people think of you, and a deep-seated need to do your own thing regardless of anyone else's opinions. Ideally, you should find a middle way in which you are able to have the best of both worlds, but this can take you a long time to achieve. One way to resolve this dilemma is to work hard at all the things you are good at, so you can take pride in your achievements and gain a better sense of your own worth. Otherwise, you may feel too timid to stick your neck out or express your considerable individuality and originality.

Friends are a very important ingredient in your life, and you may be particularly drawn to people who are much older than you. You certainly see nothing strange in having friends of all ages and social groups because you are more interested in who they are than what they are. Humanitarian goals mean a lot to you and you may work hard to help others. You can become heavily involved in group activities, especially if these work to improve the world in some way. You might also have some scientific ability.

You are naturally modest and have a charming tendency towards self-effacement. However, there are times, such as when you are feeling insecure, when you take this to extremes and put yourself down. This will not do you any favours since it invites others to follow suit and also further reduces your self-esteem. One way to counter this is to have a strong faith or philosophy that acts like a compass, giving you something to work towards and believe in. It will give you a much-needed sense of security to feel that you can immerse yourself in something that is bigger than yourself.

Harsh realities can take their toll on you. You may struggle to face up to them, preferring to retreat into a world of your own or to ignore them as much as possible. As a result, you may shy away from taking on responsibilities or duties because your inner voice tells you that you cannot cope, even when you can. Ideally, you need someone who can bolster your confidence, and accepting challenges and meeting them will also help to increase your faith in yourself. You are very sensitive and compassionate, and you may work to help others in practical or resourceful ways. Your imagination is very powerful and you need to find positive outlets for it – otherwise it can lead to worry.

SATURN IN PISCES

QUALITY: *Mutable* ELEMENT: *Water*

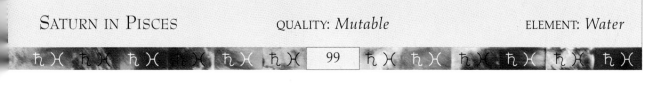

PART THREE

THE CHARTS

This section contains all the information you need in order to calculate your unique planetary picture. Remember that to calculate this accurately you must first convert your birth time to GMT, as explained in the step-by-step instructions on pages 8–9. This may take your birthday one day forward or back from the day on which you celebrate your birthday. Once you have calculated your birth time and date for Greenwich, you can consult the relevant pages in this section to discover the positions of the planets on that day.

The planetary information is arranged year by year, from 1930 to 2010 (the chart begins on page 104). Systematically work your way through the positions of each planet on the day you were born, starting with the Sun and ending with Saturn. Photocopy the blank chart on page 128 to record all your planetary details. Take care when looking up the position of a planet on a day when it moved signs. Make sure you find the right sign for the time you were born. Except for the Sun and Moon, all the planets listed here occasionally appear to move backwards through the skies, and may move back into their previous sign before moving on again. The Sun has the most regular orbit of all the planets, but does not always change signs on the same day each year, due to the differences between sidereal time (star time) and geocentric time (Earth time).

WORLD TIME ZONES

The map below shows the time zones across the world. Find the country in which you were born and check how many hours ahead or behind GMT it is. You can then deduct or add the corresponding number of hours to your birth time *(see also pages 8–9 for instructions)*. Don't forget to check whether Daylight Saving Time (summer time) was in operation when you were born. British Summer Time is shown on the page opposite; for other countries you should either contact an appropriate local authority or consult the ACS American Atlas or the ACS International Atlas (Thomas S. Shanks; ACS publications, San Diego) to find out. Once you have calculated your birth time, then refer to your year of birth in the planetary-position chart *(pages 104–127)* to discover your planetary picture, recording the information in your blank chart as you go.

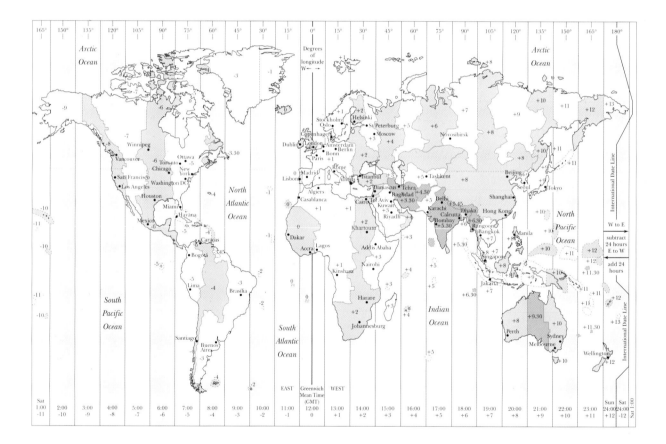

BRITISH SUMMER TIME

This chart lists the dates for British Summer Time (BST) between 1930 and 2010. If you were born in the UK during any of these periods, you must deduct one hour from your birth time to convert it to GMT. Until and including 1980, BST began each spring at 02:00 GMT on the day listed and reverted to GMT each autumn at 03:00 BST. Since 1981, BST has begun at 01:00 GMT and ended at 02:00 BST. For some years you will need to deduct two hours (*see Double Summer Time below*).

Year	Dates		Year	Dates		Year	Dates
1930	13 April to 5 October		1959	19 April to 4 October		1994	27 March to 23 October
1931	19 April to 4 October		1960	10 April to 2 October		1995	26 March to 22 October
1932	17 April to 2 October		1961	26 March to 29 October		1996	31 March to 27 October
1933	9 April to 8 October		1962	25 March to 28 October		1997	30 March to 26 October
1934	22 April to 7 October		1963	31 March to 27 October		1998	29 March to 25 October
1935	14 April to 6 October		1964	22 March to 25 October		1999	28 March to 31 October
1936	19 April to 4 October		1965	21 March to 24 October		2000	26 March to 29 October
1937	18 April to 3 October		1966	20 March to 23 October		2001	25 March to 28 October
1938	10 April to 2 October		1967	19 March to 29 October		2002	31 March to 27 October
1939	16 April to 19 November		1968	18 February to 31 December		2003	30 March to 26 October
1940	25 February to 31 December		1969	1 January to 31 December		2004	28 March to 31 October
1941	1 January to 4 May		1970	1 January to 31 December		2005	27 March to 30 October
1941	10 August to 31 December		1971	1 January to 31 October		2006	26 March to 29 October
1942	1 January to 5 April		1972	19 March to 29 October		2007	25 March to 28 October
1942	9 August to 31 December		1973	18 March to 28 October		2008	30 March to 26 October
1943	1 January to 4 April		1974	17 March to 27 October		2009	29 March to 25 October
1943	15 August to 31 December		1975	16 March to 26 October		2010	28 March to 31 October
1944	1 January to 2 April		1976	21 March to 24 October			
1944	17 September to 31 December		1977	20 March to 23 October			
1945	1 January to 2 April		1978	19 March to 29 October			
1945	15 July to 7 October		1979	18 March to 28 October			
1946	14 April to 6 October		1980	16 March to 26 October			
1947	16 March to 13 April		1981	29 March to 25 October			
1947	10 August to 2 November		1982	28 March to 24 October			
1948	14 March to 31 October		1983	27 March to 23 October			
1949	3 April to 30 October		1984	25 March to 28 October			
1950	16 April to 22 October		1985	31 March to 27 October			
1951	15 April to 21 October		1986	30 March to 26 October			
1952	20 April to 26 October		1987	29 March to 25 October			
1953	19 April to 4 October		1988	27 March to 23 October			
1954	11 April to 3 October		1989	26 March to 29 October			
1955	17 April to 2 October		1990	25 March to 28 October			
1956	22 April to 7 October		1991	31 March to 27 October			
1957	14 April to 6 October		1992	29 March to 25 October			
1958	20 April to 5 October		1993	28 March to 24 October			

Double Summer Time

In the United Kingdom, Double Summer Time operated from 1941 to 1945 and also in 1947. During the dates listed below, the local time was two hours ahead of GMT, so you should deduct two hours to convert births during these dates to GMT.

1941	4 May to 10 August
1942	5 April to 9 August
1943	4 April to 15 August
1944	2 April to 17 September
1945	2 April to 15 July
1947	13 April to 10 August

1930

SUN

♑	1 Jan	00:00
♒	20 Jan	18:33
♓	19 Feb	09:00
♈	21 Mar	08:30
♉	20 Apr	20:06
♊	21 May	19:42
♋	22 Jun	03:53
♌	23 Jul	14:42
♍	23 Aug	21:27
♎	23 Sep	18:36
♏	24 Oct	03:26
♐	23 Nov	00:35
♑	22 Dec	13:40

MOON

♑	1 Jan	00:00
♒	1 Jan	18:30
♓	4 Jan	07:05
♈	6 Jan	18:28
♉	9 Jan	02:59
♊	11 Jan	07:35
♋	13 Jan	08:35
♌	15 Jan	07:38
♍	17 Jan	06:57
♎	19 Jan	08:45
♏	21 Jan	14:25
♐	23 Jan	23:56
♑	26 Jan	11:53
♒	29 Jan	00:35
♓	31 Jan	12:59
♈	3 Feb	00:23
♉	5 Feb	09:49
♊	7 Feb	16:08
♋	9 Feb	18:56
♌	11 Feb	19:01
♍	13 Feb	18:14
♎	15 Feb	18:51
♏	17 Feb	22:45
♐	20 Feb	06:49
♑	22 Feb	18:13
♒	25 Feb	06:57
♓	27 Feb	19:13
♈	2 Mar	06:09
♉	4 Mar	15:19
♊	6 Mar	22:16
♋	9 Mar	02:35
♌	11 Mar	04:26
♍	13 Mar	04:54
♎	15 Mar	05:44
♏	17 Mar	08:46
♐	19 Mar	15:24
♑	22 Mar	01:40
♒	24 Mar	14:05
♓	27 Mar	02:24
♈	29 Mar	13:00
♉	31 Mar	21:24
♊	3 Apr	03:43
♋	5 Apr	08:11
♌	7 Apr	11:09
♍	9 Apr	13:11
♎	11 Apr	15:17
♏	13 Apr	18:45
♐	16 Apr	00:50
♑	18 Apr	10:08
♒	20 Apr	21:59
♓	23 Apr	10:24
♈	25 Apr	21:10
♉	28 Apr	05:09
♊	30 Apr	10:26
♋	2 May	13:54
♌	4 May	16:32
♍	6 May	19:11
♎	8 May	22:30
♏	11 May	03:07
♐	13 May	09:39
♑	15 May	18:40
♒	18 May	06:04
♓	20 May	18:34
♈	23 May	05:56
♉	25 May	14:16
♊	27 May	19:07
♋	29 May	21:26
♌	31 May	22:45
♍	3 Jun	00:37
♎	5 Jun	04:04
♏	7 Jun	09:30
♐	9 Jun	16:56
♑	12 Jun	02:21
♒	14 Jun	13:39
♓	17 Jun	02:12
♈	19 Jun	14:15
♉	21 Jun	23:36
♊	24 Jun	05:01
♋	26 Jun	06:58
♌	28 Jun	07:07
♍	30 Jun	07:29
♎	2 Jul	09:47
♏	4 Jul	14:56
♐	6 Jul	22:50
♑	9 Jul	08:50
♒	11 Jul	20:23
♓	14 Jul	08:58
♈	16 Jul	21:26
♉	19 Jul	07:55
♊	21 Jul	14:40
♋	23 Jul	17:23
♌	25 Jul	17:19
♍	27 Jul	16:35
♎	29 Jul	17:18
♏	31 Jul	21:05
♐	3 Aug	04:25
♑	5 Aug	14:35
♒	8 Aug	02:27
♓	10 Aug	15:03
♈	13 Aug	03:33
♉	15 Aug	14:38
♊	17 Aug	22:46
♋	20 Aug	03:02
♌	22 Aug	03:58
♍	24 Aug	03:14
♎	26 Aug	02:58
♏	28 Aug	05:11
♐	30 Aug	11:05
♑	1 Sep	20:36
♒	4 Sep	08:28
♓	6 Sep	21:07
♈	9 Sep	09:22
♉	11 Sep	20:18
♊	14 Sep	05:01
♋	16 Sep	10:43
♌	18 Sep	13:19
♍	20 Sep	13:46
♎	22 Sep	13:44
♏	24 Sep	15:08
♐	26 Sep	19:35
♑	29 Sep	03:49
♒	1 Oct	15:10
♓	4 Oct	03:48
♈	6 Oct	15:52
♉	9 Oct	02:15
♊	11 Oct	10:30
♋	13 Oct	16:30
♌	15 Oct	20:20
♍	17 Oct	22:26
♎	19 Oct	23:44
♏	22 Oct	01:33
♐	24 Oct	05:24
♑	26 Oct	12:27
♒	28 Oct	22:54
♓	31 Oct	11:23
♈	2 Nov	23:35
♉	5 Nov	09:38
♊	7 Nov	16:59
♋	9 Nov	22:05
♌	12 Nov	01:46
♍	14 Nov	04:42
♎	16 Nov	07:27
♏	18 Nov	10:37
♐	20 Nov	15:01
♑	22 Nov	21:42
♒	25 Nov	07:23
♓	27 Nov	19:33
♈	30 Nov	08:07
♉	2 Dec	18:32
♊	5 Dec	01:32
♋	7 Dec	05:32
♌	9 Dec	07:53
♍	11 Dec	10:04
♎	13 Dec	13:05
♏	15 Dec	17:20
♐	17 Dec	22:55
♑	20 Dec	06:12
♒	22 Dec	15:44
♓	25 Dec	03:36
♈	27 Dec	16:30
♉	30 Dec	03:52

MERCURY

♑	1 Jan	00:00
♒	2 Jan	10:26
♑	23 Jan	00:30
♒	15 Feb	15:09
♓	9 Mar	22:39
♈	26 Mar	23:37
♉	10 Apr	17:06
♊	1 May	05:31
♉	17 May	11:06
♊	14 Jun	20:10
♋	4 Jul	22:11
♌	19 Jul	02:44
♍	4 Aug	02:39
♎	26 Aug	18:05
♍	20 Sep	02:16
♎	11 Oct	04:45
♏	29 Oct	14:35
♐	17 Nov	05:31
♑	6 Dec	20:58

VENUS

♑	1 Jan	00:00
♒	24 Jan	00:22
♓	16 Feb	22:12
♈	12 Mar	22:34
♉	6 Apr	02:58
♊	30 Apr	12:37
♋	25 May	04:37
♌	19 Jun	04:39
♍	14 Jul	16:35
♎	10 Aug	00:54
♏	7 Sep	04:06
♐	12 Oct	02:45
♏	22 Nov	07:44

MARS

♑	1 Jan	00:00
♒	6 Feb	18:21
♓	17 Mar	05:55
♈	24 Apr	17:27
♉	3 Jun	03:16
♊	14 Jul	12:55
♋	28 Aug	11:28
♌	20 Oct	14:44

JUPITER

♊	1 Jan	00:00
♋	26 Jun	22:42

SATURN

♑	1 Jan	00:00

1931

SUN

♑	1 Jan	00:00
♒	21 Jan	00:18
♓	19 Feb	14:41
♈	21 Mar	14:07
♉	21 Apr	01:40
♊	22 May	01:16
♋	22 Jun	09:28
♌	23 Jul	20:22
♍	24 Aug	03:11
♎	24 Sep	00:24
♏	24 Oct	09:16
♐	23 Nov	06:25
♑	22 Dec	19:30

MOON

♉	1 Jan	00:00
♊	1 Jan	11:35
♋	3 Jan	15:21
♌	5 Jan	16:32
♍	7 Jan	17:06
♎	9 Jan	18:49
♏	11 Jan	22:41
♐	14 Jan	04:51
♑	16 Jan	13:02
♒	18 Jan	23:04
♓	21 Jan	10:55
♈	23 Jan	23:55
♉	26 Jan	12:10
♊	28 Jan	21:19
♋	31 Jan	02:10
♌	2 Feb	03:25
♍	4 Feb	02:57
♎	6 Feb	02:55
♏	8 Feb	05:05
♐	10 Feb	10:22
♑	12 Feb	18:39
♒	15 Feb	05:15
♓	17 Feb	17:24
♈	20 Feb	06:21
♉	22 Feb	18:54
♊	25 Feb	05:13
♋	27 Feb	11:47
♌	1 Mar	14:25
♍	3 Mar	14:21
♎	5 Mar	13:33
♏	7 Mar	14:03
♐	9 Mar	17:30
♑	12 Mar	00:39
♒	14 Mar	11:04
♓	16 Mar	23:27
♈	19 Mar	12:24
♉	22 Mar	00:45
♊	24 Mar	11:19
♋	26 Mar	19:05
♌	28 Mar	23:29
♍	31 Mar	00:58
♎	2 Apr	00:50
♏	4 Apr	00:51
♐	6 Apr	02:52
♑	8 Apr	08:21
♒	10 Apr	17:40
♓	13 Apr	05:49
♈	15 Apr	18:48
♉	18 Apr	06:51
♊	20 Apr	16:56
♋	23 Apr	00:43
♌	25 Apr	06:04
♍	27 Apr	09:10
♎	29 Apr	10:35
♏	1 May	11:26
♐	3 May	13:14
♑	5 May	17:36
♒	8 May	01:37
♓	10 May	13:02
♈	13 May	01:57
♉	15 May	13:54
♊	17 May	23:27
♋	20 May	06:26
♌	22 May	11:28
♍	24 May	15:07
♎	26 May	17:51
♏	28 May	20:08
♐	30 May	22:48
♑	2 Jun	03:08
♒	4 Jun	10:24
♓	6 Jun	21:01
♈	9 Jun	09:44
♉	11 Jun	21:55
♊	14 Jun	07:22
♋	16 Jun	13:38
♌	18 Jun	17:37
♍	20 Jun	20:33
♎	22 Jun	23:23
♏	25 Jun	02:35
♐	27 Jun	06:27
♑	29 Jun	11:35
♒	1 Jul	18:57
♓	4 Jul	05:10
♈	6 Jul	17:40
♉	9 Jul	06:14
♊	11 Jul	16:14
♋	13 Jul	22:31
♌	16 Jul	01:42
♍	18 Jul	03:22
♎	20 Jul	05:06
♏	22 Jul	07:57
♐	24 Jul	12:19
♑	26 Jul	18:23
♒	29 Jul	02:25
♓	31 Jul	12:46
♈	3 Aug	01:10
♉	5 Aug	14:05
♊	8 Aug	01:02
♋	10 Aug	08:11
♌	12 Aug	11:31
♍	14 Aug	12:26
♎	16 Aug	12:45
♏	18 Aug	14:11
♐	20 Aug	17:47
♑	22 Aug	23:59
♒	25 Aug	08:38
♓	27 Aug	19:28
♈	30 Aug	07:57
♉	1 Sep	20:59
♊	4 Sep	08:44
♋	6 Sep	17:15
♌	8 Sep	21:48
♍	10 Sep	23:04
♎	12 Sep	22:43
♏	14 Sep	22:41
♐	17 Sep	00:40
♑	19 Sep	05:48
♒	21 Sep	14:18
♓	24 Sep	01:29
♈	26 Sep	14:10
♉	29 Sep	03:07
♊	1 Oct	15:04
♋	4 Oct	00:38
♌	6 Oct	06:50
♍	8 Oct	09:34
♎	10 Oct	09:50
♏	12 Oct	09:17
♐	14 Oct	09:51
♑	16 Oct	13:19
♒	18 Oct	20:39
♓	21 Oct	07:33
♈	23 Oct	20:21
♉	26 Oct	09:21
♊	28 Oct	20:48
♋	31 Oct	06:27
♌	2 Nov	13:40
♍	4 Nov	18:08
♎	6 Nov	20:03
♏	8 Nov	20:21
♐	10 Nov	20:39
♑	12 Nov	22:52
♒	15 Nov	04:41
♓	17 Nov	14:33
♈	20 Nov	03:09
♉	22 Nov	16:00
♊	25 Nov	03:12
♋	27 Nov	12:10
♌	29 Nov	19:06
♍	2 Dec	00:17
♎	4 Dec	03:45
♏	6 Dec	05:43
♐	8 Dec	07:04
♑	10 Dec	09:18
♒	12 Dec	14:10
♓	14 Dec	22:51
♈	17 Dec	10:50
♉	19 Dec	23:46
♊	22 Dec	11:00
♋	24 Dec	19:22
♌	27 Dec	01:17
♍	29 Dec	05:41
♎	31 Dec	09:18

MERCURY

♑	1 Jan	00:00
♒	11 Feb	12:28
♓	2 Mar	17:28
♈	18 Mar	22:09
♉	3 Apr	13:38
♊	11 Jun	07:27
♋	26 Jun	13:49
♌	10 Jul	19:56
♍	28 Jul	23:25
♎	4 Oct	18:27
♏	22 Oct	02:09
♐	10 Nov	04:27
♑	2 Dec	00:00
♐	20 Dec	08:00

VENUS

♏	1 Jan	00:00
♐	3 Jan	20:03
♑	6 Feb	12:25
♒	5 Mar	21:46
♓	31 Mar	19:04
♈	26 Apr	02:10
♉	21 May	02:39
♊	14 Jun	23:05
♋	9 Jul	15:35
♌	3 Aug	03:30
♍	27 Aug	10:43
♎	20 Sep	14:15
♏	14 Oct	15:45
♐	7 Nov	16:32
♑	1 Dec	17:29
♒	25 Dec	19:44

MARS

♌	1 Jan	00:00
♋	16 Feb	14:27
♌	30 Mar	04:38
♍	10 Jun	14:58
♎	1 Aug	16:38
♏	17 Sep	08:44
♐	30 Oct	12:47
♑	10 Dec	03:11

JUPITER

♋	1 Jan	00:00
♌	17 Jul	07:52

SATURN

♑	1 Jan	00:00

1932

SUN

♑	1 Jan	00:00
♒	21 Jan	06:07
♓	19 Feb	20:29
♈	20 Mar	19:54
♉	20 Apr	07:28
♊	21 May	07:07
♋	21 Jun	15:23
♌	23 Jul	02:18
♍	23 Aug	09:07
♎	23 Sep	06:16
♏	23 Oct	15:04
♐	22 Nov	12:11
♑	22 Dec	01:15

MOON

♎	1 Jan	00:00
♏	2 Jan	12:24
♐	4 Jan	15:16
♑	6 Jan	18:37
♒	8 Jan	23:44
♓	11 Jan	07:50
♈	13 Jan	19:08
♉	16 Jan	08:03
♊	18 Jan	19:48
♋	21 Jan	04:23
♌	23 Jan	09:40
♍	25 Jan	12:47
♎	27 Jan	15:08
♏	29 Jan	17:43
♐	31 Jan	21:07
♑	3 Feb	01:39
♒	5 Feb	07:49
♓	7 Feb	16:15
♈	10 Feb	03:18
♉	12 Feb	16:05
♊	15 Feb	04:28
♋	17 Feb	14:03
♌	19 Feb	19:49
♍	21 Feb	22:25
♎	23 Feb	23:22
♏	26 Feb	00:20
♐	28 Feb	02:39
♑	1 Mar	07:07
♒	3 Mar	14:01
♓	5 Mar	23:16
♈	8 Mar	10:36
♉	10 Mar	23:20
♊	13 Mar	12:03
♋	15 Mar	22:46
♌	18 Mar	05:56
♍	20 Mar	09:19
♎	22 Mar	09:57
♏	24 Mar	09:35
♐	26 Mar	10:07
♑	28 Mar	13:08
♒	30 Mar	19:31
♓	2 Apr	05:05
♈	4 Apr	16:53
♉	7 Apr	05:44
♊	9 Apr	18:27
♋	12 Apr	05:47
♌	14 Apr	14:22
♍	16 Apr	19:22
♎	18 Apr	21:00
♏	20 Apr	20:34
♐	22 Apr	19:58
♑	24 Apr	21:15
♒	27 Apr	02:05
♓	29 Apr	10:56
♈	1 May	22:47
♉	4 May	11:46
♊	7 May	00:20
♋	9 May	11:35
♌	11 May	20:47
♍	14 May	03:14
♎	16 May	06:33
♏	18 May	07:15
♐	20 May	06:48
♑	22 May	07:13
♒	24 May	10:31
♓	26 May	17:58
♈	29 May	05:09
♉	31 May	18:05
♊	3 Jun	06:33
♋	5 Jun	17:21
♌	8 Jun	02:15
♍	10 Jun	09:07
♎	12 Jun	13:42
♏	14 Jun	16:00
♐	16 Jun	16:46
♑	18 Jun	17:31
♒	20 Jun	20:12
♓	23 Jun	02:26
♈	25 Jun	12:34
♉	28 Jun	01:08
♊	30 Jun	13:35
♋	3 Jul	00:07
♌	5 Jul	08:19
♍	7 Jul	14:33
♎	9 Jul	19:13
♏	11 Jul	22:28
♐	14 Jul	00:38
♑	16 Jul	02:36
♒	18 Jul	05:45
♓	20 Jul	11:35
♈	22 Jul	20:52
♉	25 Jul	08:55
♊	27 Jul	21:27
♋	30 Jul	08:08
♌	1 Aug	15:57
♍	3 Aug	21:15
♎	6 Aug	00:56
♏	8 Aug	03:50
♐	10 Aug	06:32
♑	12 Aug	09:39
♒	14 Aug	13:54
♓	16 Aug	20:14
♈	19 Aug	05:18
♉	21 Aug	16:56
♊	24 Aug	05:34
♋	26 Aug	16:50
♌	29 Aug	01:03
♍	31 Aug	05:59
♎	2 Sep	08:32
♏	4 Sep	10:06
♐	6 Sep	12:00
♑	8 Sep	15:12
♒	10 Sep	20:16
♓	13 Sep	03:31
♈	15 Sep	13:01
♉	18 Sep	00:34
♊	20 Sep	13:14
♋	23 Sep	01:14
♌	25 Sep	10:32
♍	27 Sep	16:07
♎	29 Sep	18:22
♏	1 Oct	18:44
♐	3 Oct	19:03
♑	5 Oct	21:00
♒	8 Oct	01:44
♓	10 Oct	09:27
♈	12 Oct	19:36
♉	15 Oct	07:24
♊	17 Oct	20:03
♋	20 Oct	08:27
♌	22 Oct	18:57
♍	25 Oct	02:03
♎	27 Oct	05:16
♏	29 Oct	05:31
♐	31 Oct	04:40
♑	2 Nov	04:55
♒	4 Nov	08:06
♓	6 Nov	15:07
♈	9 Nov	01:25
♉	11 Nov	13:34
♊	14 Nov	02:14
♋	16 Nov	14:32
♌	19 Nov	01:36
♍	21 Nov	10:09
♎	23 Nov	15:08
♏	25 Nov	16:38
♐	27 Nov	15:59
♑	29 Nov	15:17
♒	1 Dec	16:47
♓	3 Dec	22:08
♈	6 Dec	07:35
♉	8 Dec	19:42
♊	11 Dec	08:26
♋	13 Dec	20:28
♌	16 Dec	07:13
♍	18 Dec	16:09
♎	20 Dec	22:32
♏	23 Dec	01:53
♐	25 Dec	02:43
♑	27 Dec	02:31
♒	29 Dec	03:23
♓	31 Dec	07:17

MERCURY

♐	1 Jan	00:00
♑	14 Jan	12:47
♒	5 Feb	02:37
♓	23 Feb	00:50
♈	9 Mar	20:21
♉	15 May	22:50
♊	2 Jun	23:05
♋	16 Jun	22:30
♌	2 Jul	08:17
♍	27 Jul	20:38
♌	10 Aug	07:32
♍	9 Sep	07:21
♎	26 Sep	01:15
♏	13 Oct	15:42
♐	2 Nov	20:28

VENUS

♒	1 Jan	00:00
♓	19 Jan	01:52
♈	12 Feb	16:59
♉	9 Mar	02:07
♊	5 Apr	00:19
♋	6 May	09:04
♊	13 Jul	10:34
♋	28 Jul	12:36
♌	8 Sep	19:45
♍	7 Oct	05:46
♎	2 Nov	04:02
♏	27 Nov	00:07
♐	21 Dec	07:43

MARS

♑	1 Jan	00:00
♒	18 Jan	00:35
♓	25 Feb	02:37
♈	3 Apr	07:02
♉	12 May	10:54
♊	22 Jun	09:20
♋	4 Aug	19:53
♌	20 Sep	19:44
♍	13 Nov	21:26

JUPITER

♌	1 Jan	00:00
♍	11 Aug	07:16

SATURN

♑	1 Jan	00:00
♒	24 Feb	02:47
♑	13 Aug	11:15
♒	20 Nov	02:10

1933

SUN

♑	1 Jan	00:00
♒	20 Jan	11:53
♓	19 Feb	02:17
♈	21 Mar	01:44
♉	20 Apr	13:19
♊	21 May	12:57
♋	21 Jun	21:12
♌	23 Jul	08:06
♍	23 Aug	14:53
♎	23 Sep	12:02
♏	23 Oct	20:49
♐	22 Nov	17:54
♑	22 Dec	06:58

MOON

♓	1 Jan	00:00
♈	2 Jan	15:14
♉	5 Jan	02:37
♊	7 Jan	15:20
♋	10 Jan	03:17
♌	12 Jan	13:27
♍	14 Jan	21:42
♎	17 Jan	04:03
♏	19 Jan	08:25
♐	21 Jan	10:55
♑	23 Jan	12:18
♒	25 Jan	13:57
♓	27 Jan	17:31
♈	30 Jan	00:21
♉	1 Feb	10:40
♊	3 Feb	23:05
♋	6 Feb	11:14
♌	8 Feb	21:17
♍	11 Feb	04:43
♎	13 Feb	09:59
♏	15 Feb	13:47
♐	17 Feb	16:43
♑	19 Feb	19:23
♒	21 Feb	22:29
♓	24 Feb	02:56
♈	26 Feb	09:43
♉	28 Feb	19:20
♊	3 Mar	07:18
♋	5 Mar	19:43
♌	8 Mar	06:18
♍	10 Mar	13:42
♎	12 Mar	18:03
♏	14 Mar	20:28
♐	16 Mar	22:19
♑	19 Mar	00:47
♒	21 Mar	04:39
♓	23 Mar	10:16
♈	25 Mar	17:50
♉	28 Mar	03:32
♊	30 Mar	15:14
♋	2 Apr	03:50
♌	4 Apr	15:17
♍	6 Apr	23:33
♎	9 Apr	04:01
♏	11 Apr	05:32
♐	13 Apr	05:52
♑	15 Apr	06:54
♒	17 Apr	10:03
♓	19 Apr	15:54
♈	22 Apr	00:14
♉	24 Apr	10:31
♊	26 Apr	22:18
♋	29 Apr	10:59
♌	1 May	23:07
♍	4 May	08:41
♎	6 May	14:17
♏	8 May	16:07
♐	10 May	15:43
♑	12 May	15:15
♒	14 May	16:46
♓	16 May	21:34
♈	19 May	05:46
♉	21 May	16:27
♊	24 May	04:32
♋	26 May	17:12
♌	29 May	05:34
♍	31 May	16:06
♎	2 Jun	23:15
♏	5 Jun	02:25
♐	7 Jun	02:32

MOON (1933, continued)

♑ 9 Jun 01:33
♒ 11 Jun 01:41
♓ 13 Jun 04:50
♈ 15 Jun 11:51
♉ 17 Jun 22:12
♊ 20 Jun 10:26
♋ 22 Jun 23:07
♌ 25 Jun 11:17
♍ 27 Jun 22:01
♎ 30 Jun 06:11
♏ 2 Jul 10:57
♐ 4 Jul 12:32
♑ 6 Jul 12:16
♒ 8 Jul 12:05
♓ 10 Jul 14:02
♈ 12 Jul 19:31
♉ 15 Jul 04:49
♊ 17 Jul 16:45
♋ 20 Jul 05:25
♌ 22 Jul 17:19
♍ 25 Jul 03:36
♎ 27 Jul 11:45
♏ 29 Jul 17:22
♐ 31 Jul 20:27
♑ 2 Aug 21:41
♒ 4 Aug 22:22
♓ 7 Aug 00:11
♈ 9 Aug 04:41
♉ 11 Aug 12:45
♊ 13 Aug 23:58
♋ 16 Aug 12:33
♌ 19 Aug 00:23
♍ 21 Aug 10:08
♎ 23 Aug 17:30
♏ 25 Aug 22:45
♐ 28 Aug 02:22
♑ 30 Aug 04:52
♒ 1 Sep 07:00
♓ 3 Sep 09:44
♈ 5 Sep 14:15
♉ 7 Sep 21:35
♊ 10 Sep 08:01
♋ 12 Sep 20:25
♌ 15 Sep 08:31
♍ 17 Sep 18:14
♎ 20 Sep 00:52
♏ 22 Sep 05:00
♐ 24 Sep 07:49
♑ 26 Sep 10:23
♒ 28 Sep 13:27
♓ 30 Sep 17:27
♈ 2 Oct 22:51
♉ 5 Oct 06:18
♊ 7 Oct 16:18
♋ 10 Oct 04:30
♌ 12 Oct 17:02
♍ 15 Oct 03:25
♎ 17 Oct 10:08
♏ 19 Oct 13:28
♐ 21 Oct 14:54
♑ 23 Oct 16:14
♒ 25 Oct 18:49
♓ 27 Oct 23:18
♈ 30 Oct 05:41
♉ 1 Nov 13:53
♊ 4 Nov 00:02
♋ 6 Nov 12:05
♌ 9 Nov 00:58
♍ 11 Nov 12:24
♎ 13 Nov 20:13
♏ 15 Nov 23:52
♐ 18 Nov 00:35
♑ 20 Nov 00:24
♒ 22 Nov 01:21
♓ 24 Nov 04:50
♈ 26 Nov 11:13
♉ 28 Nov 20:03
♊ 1 Dec 06:45
♋ 3 Dec 18:53
♌ 6 Dec 07:49
♍ 8 Dec 20:00
♎ 11 Dec 05:19
♏ 13 Dec 10:27
♐ 15 Dec 11:49
♑ 17 Dec 11:08
♒ 19 Dec 10:38
♓ 21 Dec 12:15
♈ 23 Dec 17:16
♉ 26 Dec 01:43
♊ 28 Dec 12:43
♋ 31 Dec 01:07

MERCURY

♐ 1 Jan 00:00
♑ 8 Jan 10:25
♒ 27 Jan 22:39
♓ 14 Feb 05:07
♈ 3 Mar 10:49
♓ 25 Mar 21:49
♈ 17 Apr 15:27
♉ 10 May 07:43
♊ 25 May 14:27
♋ 8 Jun 14:12
♌ 27 Jun 01:12
♍ 2 Sep 05:45
♎ 18 Sep 03:48
♏ 6 Oct 15:05
♐ 30 Oct 04:27
♏ 16 Nov 02:07
♐ 12 Dec 03:44

VENUS

♐ 1 Jan 00:00
♑ 14 Jan 09:57
♒ 7 Feb 10:30
♓ 3 Mar 11:25
♈ 27 Mar 13:58
♉ 20 Apr 19:01
♊ 15 May 02:47
♋ 8 Jun 13:01
♌ 3 Jul 01:30
♍ 27 Jul 16:45
♎ 21 Aug 12:24
♏ 15 Sep 14:55
♐ 11 Oct 04:32
♑ 6 Nov 16:02
♒ 5 Dec 18:01

MARS

♍ 1 Jan 00:00
♎ 6 Jul 22:03
♏ 26 Aug 06:34
♐ 9 Oct 11:35
♑ 19 Nov 07:19
♒ 28 Dec 03:43

JUPITER

♎ 1 Jan 00:00
♏ 10 Sep 05:11

SATURN

♒ 1 Jan 00:00

1934

SUN

♑ 1 Jan 00:00
♒ 20 Jan 17:37
♓ 19 Feb 08:02
♈ 21 Mar 07:28
♉ 20 Apr 19:01
♊ 21 May 18:35
♋ 22 Jun 02:48
♌ 23 Jul 13:43
♍ 23 Aug 20:32
♎ 23 Sep 17:46
♏ 24 Oct 02:37
♐ 22 Nov 23:45
♑ 22 Dec 12:50

MOON

♋ 1 Jan 00:00
♌ 2 Jan 13:56
♍ 5 Jan 02:09
♎ 7 Jan 12:21
♏ 9 Jan 19:11
♐ 11 Jan 22:18
♑ 13 Jan 22:37
♒ 15 Jan 21:56
♓ 17 Jan 22:18
♈ 20 Jan 01:28
♉ 22 Jan 08:27
♊ 24 Jan 18:54
♋ 27 Jan 07:24
♌ 29 Jan 20:12
♍ 1 Feb 08:01
♎ 3 Feb 18:00
♏ 6 Feb 01:32
♐ 8 Feb 06:15
♑ 10 Feb 08:24
♒ 12 Feb 08:57
♓ 14 Feb 09:28
♈ 16 Feb 11:40
♉ 18 Feb 17:04
♊ 21 Feb 02:17
♋ 23 Feb 14:23
♌ 26 Feb 03:14
♍ 28 Feb 14:46
♎ 3 Mar 00:02
♏ 5 Mar 06:59
♐ 7 Mar 11:59
♑ 9 Mar 15:22
♒ 11 Mar 17:36
♓ 13 Mar 19:26
♈ 15 Mar 22:00
♉ 18 Mar 02:46
♊ 20 Mar 10:52
♋ 22 Mar 22:13
♌ 25 Mar 11:03
♍ 27 Mar 22:45
♎ 30 Mar 07:37
♏ 1 Apr 13:36
♐ 3 Apr 17:37
♑ 5 Apr 20:46
♒ 7 Apr 23:43
♓ 10 Apr 02:52
♈ 12 Apr 06:40
♉ 14 Apr 11:56
♊ 16 Apr 19:42
♋ 19 Apr 06:27
♌ 21 Apr 19:10
♍ 24 Apr 07:20
♎ 26 Apr 16:33
♏ 28 Apr 22:07
♐ 1 May 01:02
♑ 3 May 02:54
♒ 5 May 05:06
♓ 7 May 08:26
♈ 9 May 13:09
♉ 11 May 19:24
♊ 14 May 03:38
♋ 16 May 14:18
♌ 19 May 02:55
♍ 21 May 15:36
♎ 24 May 03:11
♏ 26 May 07:52
♐ 28 May 10:29
♑ 30 May 11:12
♒ 1 Jun 11:55
♓ 3 Jun 14:07
♈ 5 Jun 18:32
♉ 8 Jun 01:17
♊ 10 Jun 10:14
♋ 12 Jun 21:14
♌ 15 Jun 09:53
♍ 17 Jun 22:52
♎ 20 Jun 09:59
♏ 22 Jun 17:25
♐ 24 Jun 20:50
♑ 26 Jun 21:25
♒ 28 Jun 21:03
♓ 30 Jun 21:38
♈ 3 Jul 00:31
♉ 5 Jul 06:48
♊ 7 Jul 15:56
♋ 10 Jul 03:21
♌ 12 Jul 16:08
♍ 15 Jul 05:07
♎ 17 Jul 16:48
♏ 20 Jul 01:31
♐ 22 Jul 06:28
♑ 24 Jul 08:04
♒ 26 Jul 07:44
♓ 28 Jul 07:21
♈ 30 Jul 08:46
♉ 1 Aug 13:25
♊ 3 Aug 21:49
♋ 6 Aug 09:13
♌ 8 Aug 22:08
♍ 11 Aug 10:59
♎ 13 Aug 22:33
♏ 16 Aug 07:51
♐ 18 Aug 14:12
♑ 20 Aug 17:27
♒ 22 Aug 18:19
♓ 24 Aug 18:08
♈ 26 Aug 18:44
♉ 28 Aug 21:55
♊ 31 Aug 04:56
♋ 2 Sep 15:41
♌ 5 Sep 04:32
♍ 7 Sep 17:17
♎ 10 Sep 04:23
♏ 12 Sep 13:20
♐ 14 Sep 20:04
♑ 17 Sep 00:36
♒ 19 Sep 03:07
♓ 21 Sep 04:14
♈ 23 Sep 05:13
♉ 25 Sep 07:47
♊ 27 Sep 13:34
♋ 29 Sep 23:15
♌ 2 Oct 11:45
♍ 5 Oct 00:31
♎ 7 Oct 11:21
♏ 9 Oct 19:32
♐ 12 Oct 01:32
♑ 14 Oct 06:04
♒ 16 Oct 09:32
♓ 18 Oct 12:10
♈ 20 Oct 14:29
♉ 22 Oct 17:35
♊ 24 Oct 22:58
♋ 27 Oct 07:46
♌ 29 Oct 19:43
♍ 1 Nov 08:36
♎ 3 Nov 19:41
♏ 6 Nov 03:33
♐ 8 Nov 08:33
♑ 10 Nov 11:57
♒ 12 Nov 14:52
♓ 14 Nov 17:57
♈ 16 Nov 21:26
♉ 19 Nov 01:47
♊ 21 Nov 07:48
♋ 23 Nov 16:26
♌ 26 Nov 03:54
♍ 28 Nov 16:52
♎ 1 Dec 04:39
♏ 3 Dec 13:06
♐ 5 Dec 17:53
♑ 7 Dec 20:09
♒ 9 Dec 21:34
♓ 11 Dec 23:31
♈ 14 Dec 02:51
♉ 16 Dec 07:57
♊ 18 Dec 14:58
♋ 21 Dec 00:11
♌ 23 Dec 11:38
♍ 26 Dec 00:32
♎ 28 Dec 13:00
♏ 30 Dec 22:42

MERCURY

♐ 1 Jan 00:00
♑ 11 Jan 18:40
♒ 20 Jan 11:45
♓ 6 Feb 17:24
♈ 15 Apr 04:14
♉ 2 May 18:45
♊ 16 May 23:44
♋ 1 Jun 08:22
♌ 9 Jun 13:50
♍ 25 Jun 02:18
♎ 10 Sep 11:30
♏ 30 Sep 14:46
♐ 6 Dec 06:42
♑ 25 Dec 14:59

VENUS

♒ 1 Jan 00:00
♓ 6 Apr 09:23
♈ 6 May 08:54
♉ 2 Jun 10:11
♊ 28 Jun 09:38
♋ 23 Jul 18:22
♌ 17 Aug 15:45
♍ 11 Sep 03:32
♎ 5 Oct 07:56
♏ 29 Oct 07:37
♐ 22 Nov 05:00
♑ 16 Dec 01:39

MARS

♒ 1 Jan 00:00
♓ 4 Feb 04:14
♈ 14 Mar 09:09
♉ 22 Apr 15:40
♊ 2 Jun 16:21
♋ 15 Jul 21:33
♌ 30 Aug 13:44
♍ 18 Oct 04:59
♎ 11 Dec 09:32

JUPITER

♎ 1 Jan 00:00
♏ 11 Oct 04:55

SATURN

♒ 1 Jan 00:00

1935

SUN

♑ 1 Jan 00:00
♒ 20 Jan 23:29
♓ 19 Feb 13:52
♈ 21 Mar 13:18
♉ 21 Apr 00:51
♊ 22 May 00:25
♋ 22 Jun 08:38
♌ 23 Jul 19:33
♍ 24 Aug 02:24
♎ 23 Sep 23:39
♏ 24 Oct 08:30
♐ 23 Nov 05:36
♑ 22 Dec 18:38

MOON

♏ 1 Jan 00:00
♐ 2 Jan 04:27
♑ 4 Jan 06:44
♒ 6 Jan 07:04
♓ 8 Jan 07:18
♈ 10 Jan 09:03
♉ 12 Jan 13:25
♊ 14 Jan 20:43
♋ 17 Jan 06:38
♌ 19 Jan 18:27
♍ 22 Jan 07:20
♎ 24 Jan 20:00
♏ 27 Jan 06:46
♐ 29 Jan 14:11
♑ 31 Jan 17:48
♒ 2 Feb 18:26
♓ 4 Feb 17:47
♈ 6 Feb 17:49
♉ 8 Feb 20:23
♊ 11 Feb 02:36
♋ 13 Feb 12:24
♌ 16 Feb 00:35
♍ 18 Feb 13:33
♎ 21 Feb 02:03
♏ 23 Feb 13:05
♐ 25 Feb 21:41
♑ 28 Feb 03:05
♒ 2 Mar 05:16
♓ 4 Mar 05:13
♈ 6 Mar 04:41
♉ 8 Mar 05:43
♊ 10 Mar 10:12
♋ 12 Mar 18:52
♌ 15 Mar 06:48
♍ 17 Mar 19:52
♎ 20 Mar 08:08
♏ 22 Mar 18:45
♐ 25 Mar 03:24
♑ 27 Mar 09:49
♒ 29 Mar 13:42
♓ 31 Mar 15:15
♈ 2 Apr 15:32
♉ 4 Apr 16:18
♊ 6 Apr 19:36
♋ 9 Apr 02:49
♌ 11 Apr 13:52
♍ 14 Apr 02:47
♎ 16 Apr 15:01
♏ 19 Apr 01:10
♐ 21 Apr 09:06
♑ 23 Apr 15:14
♒ 25 Apr 19:44
♓ 27 Apr 22:40
♈ 30 Apr 00:27
♉ 2 May 02:10
♊ 4 May 05:26
♋ 6 May 11:51
♌ 8 May 21:55
♍ 11 May 10:26
♎ 13 May 22:48
♏ 16 May 08:56
♐ 18 May 16:13
♑ 20 May 21:21
♒ 23 May 01:09
♓ 25 May 04:14
♈ 27 May 06:59
♉ 29 May 09:59
♊ 31 May 14:11
♋ 2 Jun 20:44
♌ 5 Jun 06:20
♍ 7 Jun 18:26
♎ 10 Jun 07:00
♏ 12 Jun 17:36
♐ 15 Jun 00:57
♑ 17 Jun 05:21
♒ 19 Jun 07:56
♓ 21 Jun 09:56
♈ 23 Jun 12:21
♉ 25 Jun 15:54
♊ 27 Jun 21:07
♋ 30 Jun 04:08
♌ 2 Jul 14:13
♍ 5 Jul 02:09
♎ 7 Jul 14:53
♏ 10 Jul 02:15
♐ 12 Jul 10:28
♑ 14 Jul 15:03
♒ 16 Jul 16:54
♓ 18 Jul 17:31
♈ 20 Jul 18:33
♉ 22 Jul 21:21
♊ 25 Jul 02:42
♋ 27 Jul 10:44
♌ 29 Jul 21:04
♍ 1 Aug 09:21
♎ 3 Aug 21:55
♏ 6 Aug 09:57
♐ 8 Aug 19:25
♑ 11 Aug 01:10
♒ 13 Aug 03:22
♓ 15 Aug 03:19
♈ 17 Aug 02:55
♉ 19 Aug 04:08
♊ 21 Aug 08:26
♋ 23 Aug 16:17
♌ 26 Aug 03:01
♍ 28 Aug 15:21
♎ 31 Aug 04:08
♏ 2 Sep 16:22
♐ 5 Sep 02:49
♑ 7 Sep 10:08
♒ 9 Sep 13:44
♓ 11 Sep 14:15
♈ 13 Sep 13:21
♉ 15 Sep 13:11
♊ 17 Sep 15:48
♋ 19 Sep 22:27
♌ 22 Sep 08:50
♍ 24 Sep 21:19
♎ 27 Sep 10:06
♏ 29 Sep 22:06
♐ 2 Oct 08:41
♑ 4 Oct 17:03
♒ 6 Oct 22:21
♓ 9 Oct 00:27
♈ 11 Oct 00:21
♉ 12 Oct 23:54
♊ 15 Oct 01:18
♋ 17 Oct 06:21
♌ 19 Oct 15:36
♍ 22 Oct 03:45
♎ 24 Oct 16:32
♏ 27 Oct 04:15
♐ 29 Oct 14:18
♑ 31 Oct 22:31
♒ 3 Nov 04:39
♓ 5 Nov 08:21
♈ 7 Nov 09:54
♉ 9 Nov 10:29
♊ 11 Nov 11:53
♋ 13 Nov 15:57
♌ 15 Nov 23:51
♍ 18 Nov 11:11
♎ 20 Nov 23:53
♏ 23 Nov 11:36
♐ 25 Nov 21:09
♑ 28 Nov 04:29
♒ 30 Nov 10:00
♓ 2 Dec 14:03
♈ 4 Dec 16:53
♉ 6 Dec 19:04
♊ 8 Dec 21:37
♋ 11 Dec 01:54
♌ 13 Dec 09:07
♍ 15 Dec 19:33
♎ 18 Dec 07:59
♏ 20 Dec 20:03
♐ 23 Dec 05:45
♑ 25 Dec 12:28
♒ 27 Dec 16:46
♓ 29 Dec 19:42
♈ 31 Dec 22:16

MERCURY

♑ 1 Jan 00:00
♒ 13 Jan 01:20
♓ 16 Feb 11:16
♈ 18 Mar 21:54
♉ 8 Apr 18:40
♈ 24 Apr 12:29
♉ 8 May 17:20
♊ 29 May 19:27
♋ 20 Jun 17:59
♌ 13 Jul 22:22
♍ 16 Aug 20:39
♎ 3 Sep 09:33
♍ 28 Sep 15:52
♎ 12 Oct 18:03
♏ 10 Nov 01:24
♐ 29 Nov 07:06
♑ 18 Dec 08:29

VENUS

♒ 1 Jan 00:00
♓ 8 Jan 22:44
♈ 1 Feb 21:37
♉ 26 Feb 00:30
♊ 22 Mar 10:30
♋ 16 Apr 07:37
♌ 11 May 22:02
♍ 7 Jun 19:12
♎ 7 Jul 20:33
♏ 9 Nov 16:35
♐ 8 Dec 14:36

MARS

♎ 1 Jan 00:00
♏ 29 Jul 17:33
♐ 16 Sep 12:59
♑ 28 Oct 18:22
♒ 7 Dec 04:34

JUPITER

♏ 1 Jan 00:00
♐ 9 Nov 02:56

SATURN

♒ 1 Jan 00:00
♓ 14 Feb 14:09

1936

SUN

♑ 1 Jan 00:00
♒ 21 Jan 05:12
♓ 19 Feb 19:33
♈ 20 Mar 18:58
♉ 20 Apr 06:32
♊ 21 May 06:08
♋ 21 Jun 14:22
♌ 23 Jul 01:18
♍ 23 Aug 08:11
♎ 23 Sep 05:26
♏ 23 Oct 14:19
♐ 22 Nov 11:25
♑ 22 Dec 00:27

MOON

♈ 1 Jan 00:00
♉ 3 Jan 01:11
♊ 5 Jan 05:04
♋ 7 Jan 10:29
♌ 9 Jan 18:02
♍ 12 Jan 04:05
♎ 14 Jan 16:11
♏ 17 Jan 04:39
♐ 19 Jan 15:12
♑ 21 Jan 22:19
♒ 24 Jan 02:03
♓ 26 Jan 03:35
♈ 28 Jan 04:36
♉ 30 Jan 06:38
♊ 1 Feb 10:39
♋ 3 Feb 16:58
♌ 6 Feb 01:48
♍ 8 Feb 12:55
♎ 10 Feb 23:46
♏ 13 Feb 12:25
♐ 15 Feb 23:57
♑ 18 Feb 08:21
♒ 20 Feb 12:47
♓ 22 Feb 13:56
♈ 24 Feb 13:35
♉ 26 Feb 13:30
♊ 28 Feb 16:30
♋ 1 Mar 22:26
♌ 4 Mar 07:21
♍ 6 Mar 18:18
♎ 9 Mar 06:26
♏ 11 Mar 19:04
♐ 14 Mar 07:06
♑ 16 Mar 16:52
♒ 18 Mar 22:52
♓ 21 Mar 00:59
♈ 23 Mar 00:32
♉ 25 Mar 00:32
♊ 27 Mar 00:32
♋ 31 Mar 13:04
♌ 3 Apr 00:08
♍ 5 Apr 12:31
♎ 8 Apr 01:05
♏ 10 Apr 13:03
♐ 12 Apr 23:23
♑ 15 Apr 06:49
♒ 17 Apr 10:38
♓ 19 Apr 11:21
♈ 21 Apr 10:37
♉ 23 Apr 10:38
♊ 25 Apr 13:23
♋ 27 Apr 20:04
♌ 30 Apr 06:22
♍ 2 May 18:43
♎ 5 May 07:17
♏ 7 May 18:54
♐ 10 May 04:57
♑ 12 May 12:48
♒ 14 May 17:53
♓ 16 May 20:14
♈ 18 May 20:48
♉ 20 May 21:12
♊ 22 May 23:20
♋ 25 May 04:42
♌ 27 May 13:48
♍ 30 May 01:39
♎ 1 Jun ...
♈ 13 Jun 02:47
♉ 15 Jun 04:49
♊ 17 Jun 06:30
♋ 19 Jun 09:09
♌ 21 Jun 14:06
♍ 23 Jun 22:16
♎ 26 Jun 09:24
♏ 28 Jun 21:53
♐ 1 Jul 09:27
♑ 3 Jul 18:34
♒ 6 Jul 00:57
♓ 8 Jul 05:11
♈ 10 Jul 08:10
♉ 12 Jul 10:46
♊ 14 Jul 13:39
♋ 16 Jul 17:28
♌ 18 Jul 22:58
♍ 21 Jul 06:54
♎ 23 Jul 17:31
♏ 26 Jul 05:54
♐ 28 Jul 17:56
♑ 31 Jul 03:24
♒ 2 Aug 09:26
♓ 4 Aug 12:36
♈ 6 Aug 14:22
♉ 8 Aug 16:12
♊ 10 Aug 19:12
♋ 12 Aug 23:52
♌ 15 Aug 06:20
♍ 17 Aug 14:45
♎ 20 Aug 01:17
♏ 22 Aug 13:36
♐ 25 Aug 02:10
♑ 27 Aug 12:35
♒ 29 Aug 19:13
♓ 31 Aug 22:06
♈ 2 Sep 22:43
♉ 4 Sep 23:04
♊ 7 Sep 00:55
♋ 9 Sep 05:16
♌ 11 Sep 12:13
♍ 13 Sep 21:20
♎ 16 Sep 08:13
♏ 18 Sep 20:33
♐ 21 Sep 09:25
♑ 23 Sep 20:53
♒ 26 Sep 04:53
♓ 28 Sep 08:39
♈ 30 Sep 09:10
♉ 2 Oct 08:25
♊ 4 Oct 08:37
♋ 6 Oct 11:29
♌ 8 Oct 17:45
♍ 11 Oct 03:02
♎ 13 Oct 14:19
♏ 16 Oct 02:47
♐ 18 Oct 15:38
♑ 21 Oct 03:38
♒ 23 Oct 13:00
♓ 25 Oct 18:28
♈ 27 Oct 20:10
♉ 29 Oct 19:34
♊ 31 Oct 18:50
♋ 2 Nov 20:01
♌ 5 Nov 00:37
♍ 7 Nov 09:00
♎ 9 Nov 20:15
♏ 12 Nov 08:52
♐ 14 Nov 21:34
♑ 17 Nov 09:21
♒ 19 Nov 19:11
♓ 22 Nov 02:04
♈ 24 Nov 05:37
♉ 26 Nov 06:29
♊ 28 Nov 06:12
♋ 30 Nov 06:40
♌ 2 Dec 09:44
♍ 4 Dec 16:31
♎ 7 Dec 02:56
♏ 9 Dec 15:28
♐ 12 Dec 04:07
♑ 14 Dec 15:26
♒ 17 Dec 00:43
♓ 19 Dec 07:44
♈ 21 Dec 12:27
♉ 23 Dec 15:06
♊ 25 Dec 16:25
♋ 27 Dec 17:37
♌ 29 Dec 20:14

MERCURY

♑ 1 Jan 00:00
♒ 3 Jan 03:52
♓ 13 Mar 06:40
♈ 31 Mar 05:09
♉ 15 Apr 01:46
♊ 1 May 01:30
♋ 8 Jul 20:48
♌ 23 Jul 15:40

(continued)

♍ 7 Aug 23:00
♍ 27 Aug 17:43
♏ 2 Nov 11:00
♐ 21 Nov 00:39
♑ 10 Dec 06:40

VENUS
♏ 1 Jan 00:00
♐ 3 Jan 14:17
♑ 28 Jan 14:00
♒ 22 Feb 04:15
♓ 17 Mar 14:54
♈ 11 Apr 00:41
♉ 5 May 10:53
♊ 29 May 21:40
♋ 23 Jun 08:17
♌ 17 Jul 17:51
♍ 11 Aug 02:11
♎ 4 Sep 10:02
♏ 28 Sep 18:36
♐ 23 Oct 05:01
♑ 16 Nov 18:36
♒ 11 Dec 14:52

MARS
♒ 1 Jan 00:00
♓ 14 Jan 14:00
♈ 22 Feb 04:09
♉ 1 Apr 21:30
♊ 13 May 09:17
♋ 25 Jun 21:54
♌ 10 Aug 09:43
♍ 26 Sep 14:52
♎ 14 Nov 14:53

JUPITER
♐ 1 Jan 00:00
♑ 2 Dec 08:39

SATURN
♓ 1 Jan 00:00

1937

SUN
♑ 1 Jan 00:00
♒ 20 Jan 11:01
♓ 19 Feb 01:21
♈ 21 Mar 00:45
♉ 20 Apr 12:20
♊ 21 May 11:58
♋ 21 Jun 20:12
♌ 23 Jul 07:07
♍ 23 Aug 13:58
♎ 23 Sep 11:13
♏ 23 Oct 20:07
♐ 22 Nov 17:17
♑ 22 Dec 06:22

MOON
♌ 1 Jan 00:00
♍ 1 Jan 01:46
♎ 3 Jan 10:55
♏ 5 Jan 22:58
♐ 8 Jan 11:43
♑ 10 Jan 22:54
♒ 13 Jan 07:25
♓ 15 Jan 13:29
♈ 17 Jan 17:49
♉ 19 Jan 21:07
♊ 21 Jan 23:54
♋ 24 Jan 02:38
♌ 26 Jan 06:08
♍ 28 Jan 11:31
♎ 30 Jan 19:50
♏ 2 Feb 07:11
♐ 4 Feb 19:59
♑ 7 Feb 07:34
♒ 9 Feb 16:00
♓ 11 Feb 21:10
♈ 14 Feb 00:12
♉ 16 Feb 02:35
♊ 18 Feb 05:23
♋ 20 Feb 09:04
♌ 22 Feb 13:51
♍ 24 Feb 20:05
♎ 27 Feb 04:27
♏ 1 Mar 15:23
♐ 4 Mar 04:08
♑ 6 Mar 16:23
♒ 9 Mar 01:36
♓ 11 Mar 06:50
♈ 13 Mar 09:00
♉ 15 Mar 09:54
♊ 17 Mar 11:19
♋ 19 Mar 14:25
♌ 21 Mar 19:36
♍ 24 Mar 02:44
♎ 26 Mar 11:47
♏ 28 Mar 22:51
♐ 31 Mar 11:33
♑ 3 Apr 00:17
♒ 5 Apr 10:39
♓ 7 Apr 17:00
♈ 9 Apr 19:29
♉ 11 Apr 19:40
♊ 13 Apr 19:35
♋ 15 Apr 21:03
♌ 18 Apr 01:12
♍ 20 Apr 08:16
♎ 22 Apr 17:51
♏ 25 Apr 05:21
♐ 27 Apr 18:05
♑ 30 Apr 06:57
♒ 2 May 18:09
♓ 5 May 01:57
♈ 7 May 05:48
♉ 9 May 06:32
♊ 11 May 05:57
♋ 13 May 06:00
♌ 15 May 08:28
♍ 17 May 14:19
♎ 19 May 23:35
♏ 22 May 11:18
♐ 25 May 00:10
♑ 27 May 12:54
♒ 30 May 00:13
♓ 1 Jun 08:58
♈ 3 Jun 14:22
♉ 5 Jun 16:36
♊ 7 Jun 16:46
♋ 9 Jun 16:32
♌ 11 Jun 17:45
♍ 13 Jun 22:01
♎ 16 Jun 06:08
♏ 18 Jun 17:31
♐ 21 Jun 06:26
♑ 23 Jun 18:58
♒ 26 Jun 05:54
♓ 28 Jun 14:37
♈ 30 Jun 20:51
♉ 3 Jul 00:35
♊ 5 Jul 02:16
♋ 7 Jul 02:54
♌ 9 Jul 03:59
♍ 11 Jul 07:16
♎ 13 Jul 14:04
♏ 16 Jul 00:36
♐ 18 Jul 13:20
♑ 21 Jul 01:51
♒ 23 Jul 12:20
♓ 25 Jul 20:21
♈ 28 Jul 02:16
♉ 30 Jul 06:32
♊ 1 Aug 09:29
♋ 3 Aug 11:34
♌ 5 Aug 13:36
♍ 7 Aug 16:54
♎ 9 Aug 22:59
♏ 12 Aug 08:37
♐ 14 Aug 20:59
♑ 17 Aug 09:38
♒ 19 Aug 20:05
♓ 22 Aug 03:29
♈ 24 Aug 08:24
♉ 26 Aug 11:57
♊ 28 Aug 15:02
♋ 30 Aug 18:04
♌ 1 Sep 21:21
♍ 4 Sep 01:35
♎ 6 Sep 07:48
♏ 8 Sep 17:00
♐ 11 Sep 04:59
♑ 13 Sep 17:52
♒ 16 Sep 04:51
♓ 18 Sep 12:19
♈ 20 Sep 16:31
♉ 22 Sep 18:50
♊ 24 Sep 20:46
♋ 26 Sep 23:25
♌ 29 Sep 03:14
♍ 1 Oct 08:29
♎ 3 Oct 15:32
♏ 6 Oct 00:55
♐ 8 Oct 12:44
♑ 11 Oct 01:47
♒ 13 Oct 13:38
♓ 15 Oct 22:04
♈ 18 Oct 02:33
♉ 20 Oct 04:10
♊ 22 Oct 04:40
♋ 24 Oct 05:47
♌ 26 Oct 08:43
♍ 28 Oct 14:02
♎ 30 Oct 21:47
♏ 2 Nov 07:49
♐ 4 Nov 19:46
♑ 7 Nov 08:50
♒ 9 Nov 21:19
♓ 12 Nov 07:08
♈ 14 Nov 13:00
♉ 16 Nov 15:12
♊ 18 Nov 15:10
♋ 20 Nov 14:48
♌ 22 Nov 15:55
♍ 24 Nov 19:56
♎ 27 Nov 03:22
♏ 29 Nov 13:46
♐ 2 Dec 02:06
♑ 4 Dec 15:08
♒ 7 Dec 03:41
♓ 9 Dec 14:22
♈ 11 Dec 21:55
♉ 14 Dec 01:50
♊ 16 Dec 02:43
♋ 18 Dec 02:03
♌ 20 Dec 01:49
♍ 22 Dec 03:57
♎ 24 Dec 09:53
♏ 26 Dec 19:45
♐ 29 Dec 08:12
♑ 31 Dec 21:17

MERCURY
♑ 1 Jan 00:00
♑ 1 Jan 16:41
♒ 9 Jan 21:29
♓ 14 Feb 00:26
♈ 6 Mar 14:06
♈ 23 Mar 03:42
♉ 7 Apr 01:10
♊ 13 Jun 02:22
♋ 1 Jul 02:22
♌ 15 Jul 04:12
♍ 31 Jul 21:07
♎ 8 Oct 01:14
♏ 26 Oct 01:14
♐ 13 Nov 19:26
♑ 3 Dec 23:51

VENUS
♒ 1 Jan 00:00
♓ 6 Jan 03:18
♈ 2 Feb 10:40
♉ 9 Mar 13:20
♊ 14 Apr 04:20
♋ 4 Jun 06:41
♊ 7 Jul 21:13
♋ 4 Aug 20:14
♌ 31 Aug 00:08
♍ 25 Sep 04:03
♎ 19 Oct 16:34
♏ 12 Nov 19:43
♐ 6 Dec 18:06
♑ 30 Dec 14:43

MARS
♏ 1 Jan 00:00
♏ 5 Jan 20:40
♐ 13 Mar 03:17
♑ 14 May 22:52
♒ 8 Aug 22:14
♓ 30 Sep 09:08
♈ 11 Nov 18:31
♓ 21 Dec 17:46

JUPITER
♑ 1 Jan 00:00
♒ 20 Dec 04:06

SATURN
♓ 1 Jan 00:00
♈ 25 Apr 06:30
♓ 18 Oct 03:41

1938

SUN
♑ 1 Jan 00:00
♒ 20 Jan 16:59
♓ 19 Feb 07:20
♈ 21 Mar 06:43
♉ 20 Apr 18:15
♊ 21 May 17:51
♋ 22 Jun 02:04
♌ 23 Jul 12:58
♍ 23 Aug 19:46
♎ 23 Sep 17:00
♏ 24 Oct 00:55
♐ 22 Nov 23:07
♑ 22 Dec 12:14

MOON
♑ 1 Jan 00:00
♒ 3 Jan 09:32
♓ 5 Jan 20:07
♈ 8 Jan 04:29
♉ 10 Jan 10:06
♊ 12 Jan 12:50
♋ 14 Jan 13:22
♌ 16 Jan 13:10
♍ 18 Jan 14:13
♎ 20 Jan 18:28
♏ 23 Jan 02:55
♐ 25 Jan 14:52
♑ 28 Jan 03:58
♒ 30 Jan 16:00
♓ 2 Feb 01:59
♈ 4 Feb 09:55
♉ 6 Feb 15:59
♊ 8 Feb 20:08
♋ 10 Feb 22:26
♌ 12 Feb 23:34
♍ 15 Feb 00:57
♎ 17 Feb 04:28
♏ 19 Feb 11:37
♐ 21 Feb 22:34
♑ 24 Feb 11:28
♒ 26 Feb 23:36
♓ 1 Mar 09:14
♈ 3 Mar 16:17
♉ 5 Mar 21:30
♊ 8 Mar 01:34
♋ 10 Mar 04:46
♌ 12 Mar 07:32
♍ 14 Mar 10:06
♎ 16 Mar 14:08
♏ 18 Mar 20:54
♐ 21 Mar 07:01
♑ 23 Mar 19:32
♒ 26 Mar 07:56
♓ 28 Mar 17:52
♈ 31 Mar 00:34
♉ 2 Apr 04:43
♊ 4 Apr 07:34
♋ 6 Apr 10:08
♌ 8 Apr 13:05
♍ 10 Apr 16:51
♎ 12 Apr 22:02
♏ 15 Apr 05:21
♐ 17 Apr 15:20
♑ 20 Apr 03:32
♒ 22 Apr 16:11
♓ 25 Apr 02:54
♈ 27 Apr 10:09
♉ 29 Apr 14:02
♊ 1 May 15:45
♋ 3 May 16:51
♌ 5 May 18:42
♍ 7 May 22:17
♎ 10 May 04:06
♏ 12 May 12:16
♐ 14 May 22:41
♑ 17 May 10:51
♒ 19 May 23:38
♓ 22 May 11:09
♈ 24 May 19:36
♉ 27 May 00:17
♊ 29 May 01:52
♋ 31 May 01:53
♌ 2 Jun 02:09
♍ 4 Jun 04:22
♎ 6 Jun 09:36
♏ 8 Jun 18:01
♐ 11 Jun 04:58
♑ 13 Jun 17:21
♒ 16 Jun 06:08
♓ 18 Jun 18:03
♈ 21 Jun 03:40
♉ 23 Jun 09:50
♊ 25 Jun 12:25
♋ 27 Jun 12:27
♌ 29 Jun 11:46
♍ 1 Jul 12:24
♎ 3 Jul 16:09
♏ 5 Jul 23:49
♐ 8 Jul 10:46
♑ 10 Jul 23:22
♒ 13 Jul 12:06
♓ 15 Jul 23:56
♈ 18 Jul 10:03
♉ 20 Jul 17:31
♊ 22 Jul 21:43
♋ 24 Jul 22:55
♌ 26 Jul 22:26
♍ 28 Jul 22:17
♎ 31 Jul 00:35
♏ 2 Aug 06:50
♐ 4 Aug 17:02
♑ 7 Aug 05:34
♒ 9 Aug 18:15
♓ 12 Aug 05:45
♈ 14 Aug 15:35
♉ 16 Aug 23:26
♊ 19 Aug 04:51
♋ 21 Aug 07:40
♌ 23 Aug 08:27
♍ 25 Aug 08:43
♎ 27 Aug 10:26
♏ 29 Aug 15:26
♐ 1 Sep 00:30
♑ 3 Sep 12:30
♒ 6 Sep 01:11
♓ 8 Sep 12:29
♈ 10 Sep 21:41
♉ 13 Sep 04:54
♊ 15 Sep 10:23
♋ 17 Sep 14:10
♌ 19 Sep 16:26
♍ 21 Sep 18:01
♎ 23 Sep 20:19
♏ 26 Sep 00:57
♐ 28 Sep 09:02
♑ 30 Sep 20:21
♒ 3 Oct 08:58
♓ 5 Oct 20:27
♈ 8 Oct 05:23
♉ 10 Oct 11:43
♊ 12 Oct 16:11
♋ 14 Oct 19:31
♌ 16 Oct 22:20
♍ 19 Oct 01:09
♎ 21 Oct 04:43
♏ 23 Oct 10:00
♐ 25 Oct 17:54
♑ 28 Oct 04:39
♒ 30 Oct 17:09
♓ 2 Nov 05:09
♈ 4 Nov 14:35
♉ 6 Nov 20:41
♊ 9 Nov 00:04
♋ 11 Nov 02:00
♌ 13 Nov 03:50
♍ 15 Nov 06:38
♎ 17 Nov 11:04
♏ 19 Nov 17:26
♐ 22 Nov 01:57
♑ 24 Nov 12:38
♒ 27 Nov 00:59
♓ 29 Nov 13:30
♈ 2 Dec 00:03
♉ 4 Dec 07:01
♊ 6 Dec 10:19
♋ 8 Dec 11:08
♌ 10 Dec 11:18
♍ 12 Dec 12:38
♎ 14 Dec 16:28
♏ 16 Dec 23:13
♐ 19 Dec 08:31
♑ 21 Dec 19:39
♒ 24 Dec 07:59
♓ 26 Dec 20:41
♈ 29 Dec 08:15
♉ 31 Dec 16:48

MERCURY
♐ 1 Jan 00:00
♑ 6 Jan 21:38
♒ 12 Jan 22:31
♓ 8 Feb 13:17
♈ 27 Feb 03:01
♉ 15 Mar 00:03
♊ 1 Apr 13:24
♋ 23 Apr 13:56
♌ 16 May 17:46
♊ 11 Jun 00:32
♋ 22 Jun 13:09
♌ 26 Jul 22:55
♍ 3 Sep 02:59
♎ 1 Oct 04:19
♏ 18 Oct 12:44
♐ 6 Nov 23:33

VENUS
♐ 1 Jan 00:00
♑ 23 Jan 11:16
♒ 16 Feb 09:01
♓ 12 Mar 09:21
♈ 5 Apr 13:47
♉ 29 Apr 23:36
♊ 24 May 15:56
♋ 18 Jun 16:38
♌ 14 Jul 05:45
♍ 9 Aug 16:27
♎ 7 Sep 01:37
♏ 13 Oct 18:50
♏ 15 Nov 16:07

MARS
♓ 1 Jan 00:00
♈ 30 Jan 12:44
♉ 19 May 09:07
♉ 12 Mar 07:48
♌ 23 Apr 18:40

JUPITER
♑ 1 Jan 00:00
♒ 14 Jan 07:47
♓ 31 Jul 00:00
♈ 29 Dec 18:35

SATURN
♈ 1 Jan 00:00
♈ 14 Jan 10:31

1939

SUN
♑ 1 Jan 00:00
♒ 20 Jan 22:51
♓ 19 Feb 13:10
♈ 21 Mar 12:29
♉ 20 Apr 23:56
♊ 21 May 23:27
♋ 22 Jun 07:40
♌ 23 Jul 18:37
♍ 24 Aug 01:32
♎ 23 Sep 22:50
♏ 24 Oct 07:46
♐ 23 Nov 04:59
♑ 22 Dec 18:06

MOON
♋ 1 Jan 00:00
♌ 2 Jan 21:20
♍ 4 Jan 22:20
♎ 6 Jan 21:32
♏ 8 Jan 21:08
♐ 10 Jan 23:11
♑ 13 Jan 04:54
♒ 15 Jan 14:10
♓ 18 Jan 01:44
♈ 20 Jan 14:15
♉ 23 Jan 02:51
♊ 25 Jan 14:42
♋ 28 Jan 00:29
♌ 30 Jan 06:50
♍ 1 Feb 09:22
♎ 3 Feb 09:06
♏ 5 Feb 08:03
♐ 7 Feb 08:30
♑ 9 Feb 12:22
♒ 11 Feb 20:24
♓ 14 Feb 07:42
♈ 16 Feb 20:22
♉ 19 Feb 08:52
♊ 21 Feb 20:24
♋ 24 Feb 06:19
♌ 26 Feb 13:48
♍ 28 Feb 18:07
♎ 2 Mar 19:30
♏ 4 Mar 19:17
♐ 6 Mar 19:26
♑ 8 Mar 22:00
♒ 11 Mar 04:23
♓ 13 Mar 14:36
♈ 16 Mar 03:02
♉ 18 Mar 15:32
♊ 21 Mar 02:41
♋ 23 Mar 11:59
♌ 25 Mar 19:15
♍ 28 Mar 00:20
♎ 30 Mar 03:15
♏ 1 Apr 04:39
♐ 3 Apr 05:49
♑ 5 Apr 08:22
♒ 7 Apr 13:48
♓ 9 Apr 22:47
♈ 12 Apr 10:34
♉ 14 Apr 23:05
♊ 17 Apr 10:14
♋ 19 Apr 18:57
♌ 22 Apr 01:17
♍ 24 Apr 05:44
♎ 26 Apr 08:55
♏ 28 Apr 11:27
♐ 30 Apr 14:02
♑ 2 May 17:36
♒ 4 May 23:11
♓ 7 May 07:34
♈ 9 May 18:41
♉ 12 May 07:10
♊ 14 May 18:41
♋ 17 May 03:28
♌ 19 May 09:07
♋ 21 May 12:23
♌ 23 May 14:34
♍ 25 May 16:51
♎ 27 May 20:06
♏ 30 May 00:48
♐ 1 Jun 07:15
♑ 3 Jun 15:50
♒ 6 Jun 02:41
♓ 8 Jun 15:05
♈ 11 Jun 03:11
♉ 13 Jun 12:43
♊ 15 Jun 18:33
♋ 17 Jun 21:07
♌ 19 Jul 07:08
♍ 21 Jul 08:11
♎ 23 Jul 12:04
♏ 25 Jul 19:10
♐ 28 Jul 04:51
♑ 30 Jul 16:15
♒ 2 Aug 04:42
♓ 4 Aug 17:23
♈ 7 Aug 04:48
♉ 9 Aug 13:06
♊ 13 Aug 18:10
♌ 15 Aug 17:19
♍ 17 Aug 17:04
♎ 19 Aug 19:20
♏ 22 Aug 01:14
♐ 24 Aug 10:34
♑ 26 Aug 22:09
♒ 29 Aug 10:43
♓ 3 Sep 10:48
♉ 5 Sep 20:02
♊ 10 Sep 04:12
♌ 14 Sep 03:39
♎ 18 Sep 09:02
♐ 23 Sep 04:24
♒ 25 Sep 17:00
♓ 30 Sep 18:29
♉ 5 Oct 08:17
♋ 7 Oct 12:10
♌ 9 Oct 13:46
♍ 11 Oct 14:16
♎ 13 Oct 15:19
♏ 15 Oct 18:36
♐ 20 Oct 11:40
♑ 25 Oct 12:28
♒ 27 Oct 23:09
♓ 30 Oct 07:31
♈ 1 Nov 13:42
♉ 3 Nov 18:02
♊ 5 Nov 20:57
♋ 7 Nov 23:03
♌ 10 Nov 01:14
♍ 12 Nov 04:42
♎ 14 Nov 10:42
♏ 16 Nov 20:01
♐ 19 Nov 08:00
♑ 21 Nov 20:36
♒ 24 Nov 07:23
♓ 26 Nov 15:09
♈ 28 Nov 20:12
♉ 30 Nov 23:34
♊ 3 Dec 02:23
♋ 5 Dec 05:23
♌ 7 Dec 08:57
♍ 9 Dec 13:33
♎ 11 Dec 19:51
♏ 14 Dec 04:43
♐ 16 Dec 16:14
♑ 19 Dec 05:03
♒ 21 Dec 16:32
♓ 24 Dec 00:37
♈ 26 Dec 05:03
♉ 28 Dec 07:05
♊ 30 Dec 08:29

MERCURY
♐ 1 Jan 00:00
♑ 12 Jan 07:58
♒ 1 Feb 17:57
♓ 19 Feb 08:10
♈ 7 Mar 09:14
♉ 13 May 13:43
♊ 31 May 02:46
♋ 13 Jun 23:02
♌ 30 Jun 06:41
♍ 7 Sep 04:59
♎ 23 Sep 07:48
♏ 11 Oct 05:20
♐ 1 Nov 07:04
♑ 3 Dec 07:22
♐ 13 Dec 19:17

VENUS
♏ 1 Jan 00:00
♐ 4 Jan 21:48
♑ 6 Feb 09:20
♒ 5 Mar 13:29
♓ 31 Mar 08:35
♈ 25 Apr 14:29
♉ 20 May 14:13
♊ 14 Jun 10:11
♋ 9 Jul 02:25
♌ 2 Aug 14:12
♍ 26 Aug 21:24
♎ 20 Sep 01:03
♏ 14 Oct 02:42
♐ 7 Nov 03:41
♑ 1 Dec 04:52
♒ 25 Dec 07:26

MARS
♏ 1 Jan 00:00
♐ 29 Jan 09:49
♑ 21 Mar 07:26
♒ 25 May 00:20
♓ 21 Jul 19:31
♈ 24 Sep 01:14
♓ 19 Nov 15:57

JUPITER
♓ 1 Jan 00:00
♈ 11 May 14:09
♓ 30 Oct 00:45
♈ 20 Dec 17:03

SATURN
♈ 1 Jan 00:00
♉ 6 Jul 05:46
♉ 22 Sep 05:18

1940

SUN
♑ 1 Jan 00:00
♒ 21 Jan 04:45
♓ 19 Feb 19:04
♈ 20 Mar 18:24
♉ 20 Apr 05:51
♊ 21 May 05:23
♋ 21 Jun 13:37
♌ 23 Jul 00:35
♍ 23 Aug 07:29
♎ 23 Sep 04:46
♏ 23 Oct 13:40
♐ 22 Nov 10:49
♑ 22 Dec 23:55

MOON
♒ 1 Jan 00:00
♓ 1 Jan 10:44
♈ 3 Jan 14:36
♉ 5 Jan 20:13
♊ 8 Jan 03:30
♋ 10 Jan 12:42
♌ 13 Jan 00:03
♍ 15 Jan 12:56
♎ 18 Jan 01:16
♏ 20 Jan 10:32
♐ 22 Jan 15:35
♑ 24 Jan 17:11
♒ 26 Jan 17:12
♓ 28 Jan 17:43
♈ 30 Jan 20:18
♉ 2 Feb 01:36
♊ 4 Feb 09:27
♋ 6 Feb 19:22
♌ 9 Feb 06:59
♍ 11 Feb 19:50
♎ 14 Feb 08:36
♏ 16 Feb 19:10
♐ 19 Feb 01:47
♑ 21 Feb 04:19
♒ 23 Feb 04:12

♎ 25 Feb 03:29
♏ 27 Feb 04:14
♐ 29 Feb 07:55
♑ 2 Mar 15:03
♒ 5 Mar 01:08
♓ 7 Mar 13:08
♈ 10 Mar 02:01
♉ 12 Mar 14:45
♊ 15 Mar 01:53
♋ 17 Mar 09:57
♌ 19 Mar 14:15
♍ 21 Mar 15:21
♎ 23 Mar 14:48
♏ 25 Mar 14:34
♐ 27 Mar 16:31
♑ 29 Mar 22:00
♒ 1 Apr 07:14
♓ 3 Apr 19:11
♈ 6 Apr 08:10
♉ 8 Apr 20:39
♊ 11 Apr 07:33
♋ 13 Apr 16:04
♌ 15 Apr 21:44
♍ 18 Apr 00:35
♎ 20 Apr 01:23
♏ 22 Apr 01:33
♐ 24 Apr 02:49
♑ 26 Apr 06:50
♒ 28 Apr 14:39
♓ 1 May 01:56
♈ 3 May 14:52
♉ 6 May 03:13
♊ 8 May 13:34
♋ 10 May 21:34
♌ 13 May 03:23
♍ 15 May 07:18
♎ 17 May 09:41
♏ 19 May 11:21
♐ 21 May 13:00
♑ 23 May 16:35
♒ 25 May 23:19
♓ 28 May 09:39
♈ 30 May 22:19
♉ 2 Jun 10:44
♊ 4 Jun 20:50
♋ 7 Jun 04:02
♌ 9 Jun 09:01
♍ 11 Jun 12:41
♎ 13 Jun 15:44
♏ 15 Jun 18:32
♐ 17 Jun 21:34
♑ 20 Jun 01:45
♒ 22 Jun 08:15
♓ 24 Jun 17:56
♈ 27 Jun 06:13
♉ 29 Jun 18:53
♊ 2 Jul 05:16
♋ 4 Jul 12:11
♌ 6 Jul 16:12
♍ 8 Jul 18:45
♎ 10 Jul 21:07
♏ 13 Jul 00:07
♐ 15 Jul 04:05
♑ 17 Jul 09:18
♒ 19 Jul 16:22
♓ 22 Jul 01:59
♈ 24 Jul 14:02
♉ 27 Jul 02:57
♊ 29 Jul 14:04
♋ 31 Jul 21:32
♌ 3 Aug 01:20
♍ 5 Aug 02:51
♎ 7 Aug 03:50
♏ 9 Aug 05:46
♐ 11 Aug 09:29
♑ 13 Aug 15:15
♒ 15 Aug 23:08
♓ 18 Aug 09:10
♈ 20 Aug 21:14
♉ 23 Aug 10:17
♊ 25 Aug 22:13
♋ 28 Aug 06:54
♌ 30 Aug 11:32
♍ 1 Sep 12:57
♎ 3 Sep 12:54
♏ 5 Sep 13:17
♐ 7 Sep 15:36
♑ 9 Sep 20:46
♒ 12 Sep 04:52
♓ 14 Sep 15:26
♈ 17 Sep 03:43
♉ 19 Sep 16:46
♊ 22 Sep 05:06
♋ 24 Sep 14:58
♌ 26 Sep 21:09
♍ 28 Sep 23:42
♎ 30 Sep 23:47
♏ 2 Oct 23:12
♐ 4 Oct 23:54
♑ 7 Oct 03:29
♒ 9 Oct 10:44
♓ 11 Oct 21:18
♈ 14 Oct 09:50
♉ 16 Oct 22:50
♊ 19 Oct 11:00
♋ 21 Oct 21:18
♌ 24 Oct 04:51
♍ 26 Oct 09:10
♎ 28 Oct 10:37
♏ 30 Oct 10:25
♐ 1 Nov 10:21
♑ 3 Nov 12:23
♒ 5 Nov 18:04
♓ 8 Nov 03:46
♈ 10 Nov 16:13
♉ 13 Nov 05:13
♊ 15 Nov 17:01
♋ 18 Nov 02:53
♌ 20 Nov 10:39
♍ 22 Nov 16:11
♎ 24 Nov 19:25
♏ 26 Nov 20:45
♐ 28 Nov 21:19
♑ 30 Nov 22:51
♒ 3 Dec 03:13
♓ 5 Dec 11:36
♈ 7 Dec 23:27
♉ 10 Dec 12:28
♊ 13 Dec 00:08
♋ 15 Dec 09:20
♌ 17 Dec 16:17
♍ 19 Dec 21:35
♎ 22 Dec 01:37
♏ 24 Dec 04:30
♐ 26 Dec 06:37
♑ 28 Dec 08:59
♒ 30 Dec 13:09

MERCURY

♐ 1 Jan 00:00
♑ 6 Jan 07:56
♒ 25 Jan 10:15
♓ 11 Feb 14:01
♈ 4 Mar 10:10
♓ 8 Mar 01:26
♈ 17 Apr 04:57
♉ 6 May 21:14
♊ 21 May 13:59
♋ 4 Jun 22:29
♌ 26 Jun 14:33
♋ 21 Jul 01:39
♌ 11 Aug 17:06
♍ 29 Aug 11:11
♎ 14 Sep 11:34
♏ 3 Oct 12:14
♐ 9 Dec 12:45

VENUS

♒ 1 Jan 00:00
♓ 18 Jan 14:00
♈ 12 Feb 05:51
♉ 8 Mar 16:26
♊ 4 Apr 18:10
♋ 6 May 18:47
♊ 5 Jul 16:17
♋ 1 Aug 02:21
♌ 8 Sep 16:59
♍ 6 Oct 21:10
♎ 1 Nov 17:24
♏ 26 Nov 12:32
♐ 20 Dec 19:37

MARS

♓ 1 Jan 00:00
♈ 4 Jan 00:06
♉ 17 Feb 01:54
♊ 1 Apr 18:41
♋ 17 May 14:46
♌ 3 Jul 10:32
♍ 19 Aug 15:58
♎ 5 Oct 14:22
♏ 20 Nov 17:16

JUPITER

♈ 1 Jan 00:00
♉ 16 May 07:55

SATURN

♈ 1 Jan 00:00
♉ 20 Mar 09:41

1941

SUN

♑ 1 Jan 00:00
♒ 20 Jan 10:34
♓ 19 Feb 00:57
♈ 21 Mar 00:21
♉ 20 Apr 11:51
♊ 21 May 11:23
♋ 21 Jun 19:34
♌ 23 Jul 06:27
♍ 23 Aug 13:17
♎ 23 Sep 10:33
♏ 23 Oct 19:28
♐ 22 Nov 16:38
♑ 22 Dec 05:45

MOON

♒ 1 Jan 00:00
♓ 1 Jan 20:35
♈ 4 Jan 07:35
♉ 6 Jan 20:29
♊ 9 Jan 08:27
♋ 11 Jan 17:34
♌ 13 Jan 23:40
♍ 16 Jan 03:46
♎ 18 Jan 07:00
♏ 20 Jan 10:04
♐ 22 Jan 13:17
♑ 24 Jan 17:01
♒ 26 Jan 22:06
♓ 29 Jan 05:35
♈ 31 Jan 16:02
♉ 3 Feb 04:41
♊ 5 Feb 17:10
♋ 8 Feb 02:58
♌ 10 Feb 09:08
♍ 12 Feb 12:21
♎ 14 Feb 14:08
♏ 16 Feb 15:53
♐ 18 Feb 18:37
♑ 20 Feb 22:54
♒ 23 Feb 05:02
♓ 25 Feb 13:19
♈ 27 Feb 23:55
♉ 2 Mar 12:24
♊ 5 Mar 01:12
♋ 7 Mar 12:04
♌ 9 Mar 19:19
♍ 11 Mar 22:52
♎ 13 Mar 23:52
♏ 16 Mar 00:03
♐ 18 Mar 01:08
♑ 20 Mar 04:25
♒ 22 Mar 10:34
♓ 24 Mar 19:30
♈ 27 Mar 06:40
♉ 29 Mar 19:14
♊ 1 Apr 08:07
♋ 3 Apr 19:44
♌ 6 Apr 04:26
♍ 8 Apr 09:21
♎ 10 Apr 10:55
♏ 12 Apr 10:32
♐ 14 Apr 10:08
♑ 16 Apr 11:39
♒ 18 Apr 16:31
♓ 21 Apr 01:07
♈ 23 Apr 12:35
♉ 26 Apr 01:23
♊ 28 Apr 14:11
♋ 1 May 01:56
♌ 3 May 11:34
♍ 5 May 18:06
♎ 7 May 21:12
♏ 9 May 21:34
♐ 11 May 20:50
♑ 13 May 21:04
♒ 16 May 00:15
♓ 18 May 07:34
♈ 20 May 18:34
♉ 23 May 07:27
♊ 25 May 20:10
♋ 28 May 07:37
♌ 30 May 17:16
♍ 2 Jun 00:39
♎ 4 Jun 05:17
♏ 6 Jun 07:14
♐ 8 Jun 07:24
♑ 10 Jun 07:32
♒ 12 Jun 09:42
♓ 14 Jun 15:34
♈ 17 Jun 01:31
♉ 19 Jun 14:03
♊ 22 Jun 02:45
♋ 24 Jun 13:51
♌ 26 Jun 22:55
♍ 29 Jun 06:03
♎ 1 Jul 11:17
♏ 3 Jul 14:34
♐ 5 Jul 16:14
♑ 7 Jul 17:21
♒ 9 Jul 19:36
♓ 12 Jul 00:42
♈ 14 Jul 09:35
♉ 16 Jul 21:30
♊ 19 Jul 10:10
♋ 21 Jul 21:15
♌ 24 Jul 05:48
♍ 26 Jul 12:04
♎ 28 Jul 16:41
♏ 30 Jul 20:09
♐ 1 Aug 22:50
♑ 4 Aug 01:17
♒ 6 Aug 04:32
♓ 8 Aug 09:51
♈ 10 Aug 18:13
♉ 13 Aug 05:32
♊ 15 Aug 18:10
♋ 18 Aug 05:38
♌ 20 Aug 14:16
♍ 22 Aug 19:53
♎ 24 Aug 23:22
♏ 27 Aug 01:49
♐ 29 Aug 04:13
♑ 31 Aug 07:18
♒ 2 Sep 11:39
♓ 4 Sep 17:52
♈ 7 Sep 02:29
♉ 9 Sep 13:32
♊ 12 Sep 02:06
♋ 14 Sep 14:09
♌ 16 Sep 23:36
♍ 19 Sep 05:29
♎ 21 Sep 08:18
♏ 23 Sep 09:24
♐ 25 Sep 10:25
♑ 27 Sep 12:45
♒ 29 Sep 17:17
♓ 2 Oct 00:18
♈ 4 Oct 09:38
♉ 6 Oct 20:52
♊ 9 Oct 09:23
♋ 11 Oct 21:53
♌ 14 Oct 08:29
♍ 16 Oct 15:36
♎ 18 Oct 18:54
♏ 20 Oct 19:26
♐ 22 Oct 19:01
♑ 24 Oct 19:40
♒ 26 Oct 23:03
♓ 29 Oct 05:51
♈ 31 Oct 15:38
♉ 3 Nov 03:19
♊ 5 Nov 15:53
♋ 8 Nov 04:26
♌ 10 Nov 15:49
♍ 13 Nov 00:29
♎ 15 Nov 05:22
♏ 17 Nov 06:40
♐ 19 Nov 05:54
♑ 21 Nov 05:12
♒ 23 Nov 06:47
♓ 25 Nov 12:09
♈ 27 Nov 21:27
♉ 30 Nov 09:19
♊ 2 Dec 22:00
♋ 5 Dec 10:22
♌ 7 Dec 21:43
♍ 10 Dec 07:13
♎ 12 Dec 13:46
♏ 14 Dec 16:52
♐ 16 Dec 17:10
♑ 18 Dec 16:27
♒ 20 Dec 16:54
♓ 22 Dec 20:33
♈ 25 Dec 04:24
♉ 27 Dec 15:43
♊ 30 Dec 04:27

MERCURY

♑ 1 Jan 00:00
♒ 16 Jan 22:37
♓ 3 Feb 13:09
♒ 8 Mar 00:00
♓ 16 Mar 12:27
♈ 12 Apr 07:19
♉ 28 Apr 23:10
♊ 13 May 00:51
♋ 29 May 17:33
♌ 6 Aug 05:58
♍ 21 Aug 05:18
♎ 6 Sep 23:58
♏ 28 Sep 09:22
♐ 29 Oct 20:35
♏ 11 Nov 20:11
♐ 3 Dec 00:11
♑ 22 Dec 03:54

VENUS

♐ 1 Jan 00:00
♑ 13 Jan 21:30
♒ 6 Feb 21:49
♓ 2 Mar 22:33
♈ 27 Mar 00:58
♉ 20 Apr 05:54
♊ 14 May 13:37
♋ 7 Jun 23:53
♌ 2 Jul 12:33
♍ 27 Jul 04:13
♎ 21 Aug 00:30
♏ 15 Sep 04:02
♐ 10 Oct 19:22
♑ 6 Nov 10:17
♒ 5 Dec 23:05

MARS

♏ 1 Jan 00:00
♐ 4 Jan 19:43
♑ 17 Feb 23:33
♒ 2 Apr 11:46
♓ 16 May 05:05
♈ 2 Jul 05:17

JUPITER

♉ 1 Jan 00:00
♊ 26 May 12:48

SATURN

♉ 1 Jan 00:00

1942

SUN

♑ 1 Jan 00:00
♒ 20 Jan 16:24
♓ 19 Feb 06:47
♈ 21 Mar 06:11
♉ 20 Apr 17:40
♊ 21 May 17:09
♋ 22 Jun 01:17
♌ 23 Jul 12:08
♍ 23 Aug 18:59
♎ 23 Sep 16:17
♏ 24 Oct 01:16
♐ 22 Nov 22:31
♑ 22 Dec 11:40

MOON

♊ 1 Jan 00:00
♋ 1 Jan 16:42
♌ 4 Jan 03:33
♍ 6 Jan 12:43
♎ 8 Jan 19:49
♏ 11 Jan 00:25
♐ 13 Jan 02:32
♑ 15 Jan 03:07
♒ 17 Jan 03:53
♓ 19 Jan 06:43
♈ 21 Jan 13:08
♉ 23 Jan 23:19
♊ 26 Jan 11:44
♋ 29 Jan 00:04
♌ 31 Jan 10:37
♍ 2 Feb 18:58
♎ 5 Feb 01:18
♏ 7 Feb 05:56
♐ 9 Feb 09:07
♑ 11 Feb 11:19
♒ 13 Feb 13:28
♓ 15 Feb 16:51
♈ 17 Feb 22:47
♉ 20 Feb 07:58
♊ 22 Feb 19:48
♋ 25 Feb 08:16
♌ 27 Feb 19:06
♍ 2 Mar 03:06
♎ 4 Mar 08:23
♏ 6 Mar 11:50
♐ 8 Mar 14:28
♑ 10 Mar 17:09
♒ 12 Mar 20:31
♓ 15 Mar 01:09
♈ 17 Mar 07:41
♉ 19 Mar 16:39
♊ 22 Mar 04:01
♋ 24 Mar 16:33
♌ 27 Mar 04:05
♍ 29 Mar 12:37
♎ 31 Mar 17:37
♏ 2 Apr 19:55
♐ 4 Apr 21:05
♑ 6 Apr 22:42
♒ 9 Apr 01:57
♓ 11 Apr 07:20
♈ 13 Apr 14:49
♉ 16 Apr 00:18
♊ 18 Apr 11:37
♋ 21 Apr 00:10
♌ 23 Apr 12:22
♍ 25 Apr 22:03
♎ 28 Apr 03:50
♏ 30 Apr 05:59
♐ 2 May 06:03
♑ 4 May 06:05
♒ 6 May 07:56
♓ 8 May 12:44
♈ 10 May 20:32
♉ 13 May 06:37
♊ 15 May 18:15
♋ 18 May 06:49
♌ 20 May 19:22
♍ 23 May 06:08
♎ 25 May 13:22
♏ 27 May 16:32
♐ 29 May 16:39
♑ 31 May 15:44
♒ 2 Jun 16:00
♓ 4 Jun 19:14
♈ 7 Jun 02:11
♉ 9 Jun 12:16
♊ 12 Jun 00:12
♋ 14 Jun 12:50
♌ 17 Jun 01:20
♍ 19 Jun 12:34
♎ 21 Jun 21:05
♏ 24 Jun 01:51
♐ 26 Jun 03:09
♑ 28 Jun 02:30
♒ 30 Jun 02:01
♓ 2 Jul 03:46
♈ 4 Jul 09:11
♉ 6 Jul 18:23
♊ 9 Jul 06:10
♋ 11 Jul 18:52
♌ 14 Jul 07:08
♍ 16 Jul 18:09
♎ 19 Jul 03:02
♏ 21 Jul 09:02
♐ 23 Jul 11:58
♑ 25 Jul 12:38
♒ 27 Jul 12:37
♓ 29 Jul 13:49
♈ 31 Jul 17:56
♉ 3 Aug 01:48
♊ 5 Aug 12:55
♋ 8 Aug 01:31
♌ 10 Aug 13:40
♍ 13 Aug 00:09
♎ 15 Aug 08:31
♏ 17 Aug 14:38
♐ 19 Aug 18:35
♑ 21 Aug 20:47
♒ 23 Aug 22:07
♓ 25 Aug 23:56
♈ 28 Aug 03:39
♉ 30 Aug 10:29
♊ 1 Sep 20:41
♋ 4 Sep 09:01
♌ 6 Sep 21:16
♍ 9 Sep 07:31
♎ 11 Sep 15:05
♏ 13 Sep 20:19
♐ 15 Sep 23:58
♑ 18 Sep 02:48
♒ 20 Sep 05:27
♓ 22 Sep 08:34
♈ 24 Sep 12:57
♉ 26 Sep 19:35
♊ 29 Sep 05:05
♋ 1 Oct 17:03
♌ 4 Oct 05:36
♍ 6 Oct 16:14
♎ 8 Oct 23:33
♏ 11 Oct 03:47
♐ 13 Oct 06:11
♑ 15 Oct 08:14
♒ 17 Oct 11:01
♓ 19 Oct 15:05
♈ 21 Oct 20:37
♉ 24 Oct 03:52
♊ 26 Oct 13:19
♋ 29 Oct 01:00
♌ 31 Oct 13:49
♍ 3 Nov 01:19
♎ 5 Nov 09:22
♏ 7 Nov 13:27
♐ 9 Nov 14:47
♑ 11 Nov 15:18
♒ 13 Nov 16:49
♓ 15 Nov 20:28
♈ 18 Nov 02:31
♉ 20 Nov 10:38
♊ 22 Nov 20:35
♋ 25 Nov 08:17
♌ 27 Nov 21:10
♍ 30 Nov 09:30
♎ 2 Dec 18:56
♏ 5 Dec 00:07
♐ 7 Dec 01:34
♑ 9 Dec 01:07
♒ 11 Dec 00:57
♓ 13 Dec 02:56
♈ 15 Dec 08:05
♉ 17 Dec 16:17
♊ 20 Dec 02:46
♋ 22 Dec 14:46
♌ 25 Dec 03:36
♍ 27 Dec 16:11
♎ 30 Dec 02:45

MERCURY

♑ 1 Jan 00:00
♒ 9 Jan 15:24
♓ 17 Mar 00:11
♈ 5 Apr 07:07
♉ 20 Apr 13:43
♊ 5 May 04:38
♋ 12 Jul 20:24
♌ 29 Jul 04:24
♍ 13 Aug 01:48
♎ 31 Aug 08:28
♏ 7 Nov 01:45
♐ 25 Nov 20:26
♑ 14 Dec 22:22

VENUS

♒ 1 Jan 00:00
♓ 6 Apr 13:15
♈ 6 May 02:26
♉ 2 Jun 00:26
♊ 27 Jun 22:19
♋ 23 Jul 06:10
♌ 17 Aug 03:05
♍ 10 Sep 14:38
♎ 4 Oct 18:58
♏ 28 Oct 18:41
♐ 21 Nov 16:08
♑ 15 Dec 12:53

MARS

♈ 1 Jan 00:00
♉ 11 Jan 22:21
♊ 7 Mar 08:05
♋ 26 Apr 06:18
♌ 14 Jun 03:56
♍ 1 Aug 08:27
♎ 17 Sep 10:11
♏ 1 Nov 22:37
♐ 15 Dec 16:51

JUPITER

♊ 1 Jan 00:00
♋ 10 Jun 10:36

SATURN

♉ 1 Jan 00:00
♊ 8 May 19:40

1943

SUN

♑ 1 Jan 00:00
♒ 20 Jan 22:19
♓ 19 Feb 12:41
♈ 21 Mar 12:03
♉ 20 Apr 23:32
♊ 21 May 23:03
♋ 22 Jun 07:13
♌ 23 Jul 18:05
♍ 24 Aug 00:55
♎ 23 Sep 22:12
♏ 24 Oct 07:09
♐ 23 Nov 04:22
♑ 22 Dec 17:30

MOON

♎ 1 Jan 00:00
♏ 1 Jan 09:40
♐ 3 Jan 12:34
♑ 5 Jan 12:35
♒ 7 Jan 11:42
♓ 9 Jan 12:03
♈ 11 Jan 15:21
♉ 13 Jan 22:22
♊ 16 Jan 08:39
♋ 18 Jan 20:54
♌ 21 Jan 09:44
♍ 23 Jan 22:03
♎ 26 Jan 08:47
♏ 28 Jan 16:51
♐ 30 Jan 21:34
♑ 1 Feb 23:16
♒ 3 Feb 23:11
♓ 5 Feb 23:08
♈ 8 Feb 01:01
♉ 10 Feb 06:18
♊ 12 Feb 15:25
♋ 15 Feb 03:25
♌ 17 Feb 16:19
♍ 20 Feb 04:20
♎ 22 Feb 14:30
♏ 24 Feb 22:25
♐ 27 Feb 03:59
♑ 1 Mar 07:19
♒ 3 Mar 08:57
♓ 5 Mar 09:55
♈ 7 Mar 11:42
♉ 9 Mar 15:54
♊ 11 Mar 23:39
♋ 14 Mar 10:51
♌ 16 Mar 23:41
♍ 19 Mar 11:43
♎ 21 Mar 21:21
♏ 24 Mar 04:23
♐ 26 Mar 09:24
♑ 28 Mar 13:05
♒ 30 Mar 15:57
♓ 1 Apr 18:27
♈ 3 Apr 21:18
♉ 6 Apr 01:38
♊ 8 Apr 08:42
♋ 10 Apr 19:03
♌ 13 Apr 07:40
♍ 15 Apr 19:59
♎ 18 Apr 05:41
♏ 20 Apr 12:04
♐ 22 Apr 15:57
♑ 24 Apr 18:40
♒ 26 Apr 21:21
♓ 29 Apr 00:36
♈ 1 May 04:40
♉ 3 May 09:57
♊ 5 May 17:16
♋ 8 May 03:17
♌ 10 May 15:39
♍ 13 May 04:22
♎ 15 May 14:45
♏ 17 May 21:20
♐ 20 May 00:33
♑ 22 May 02:00
♒ 24 May 03:23
♓ 26 May 05:58
♈ 28 May 10:17
♉ 30 May 16:25
♊ 2 Jun 00:30
♋ 4 Jun 10:46
♌ 6 Jun 23:03
♍ 9 Jun 12:04
♎ 11 Jun 23:22
♏ 14 Jun 06:59
♐ 16 Jun 10:36
♑ 18 Jun 11:30
♒ 20 Jun 11:34
♓ 22 Jun 12:37
♈ 24 Jun 15:53
♉ 26 Jun 21:52
♊ 29 Jun 06:27
♋ 1 Jul 17:14
♌ 4 Jul 05:40
♍ 6 Jul 18:45
♎ 9 Jul 06:45
♏ 11 Jul 15:41
♐ 13 Jul 20:37
♑ 15 Jul 22:07
♒ 17 Jul 21:46
♓ 19 Jul 21:31
♈ 21 Jul 23:09
♉ 24 Jul 03:53
♊ 26 Jul 12:04
♋ 28 Jul 23:04
♌ 31 Jul 11:43
♍ 3 Aug 00:46
♎ 5 Aug 12:52
♏ 7 Aug 22:40
♐ 10 Aug 05:09
♑ 12 Aug 08:10
♒ 14 Aug 08:37
♓ 16 Aug 08:07
♈ 18 Aug 08:33
♉ 20 Aug 11:40
♊ 22 Aug 18:35
♋ 25 Aug 05:07
♌ 27 Aug 17:50
♍ 30 Aug 06:47
♎ 1 Sep 18:34
♏ 4 Sep 04:21
♐ 6 Sep 11:39
♑ 8 Sep 16:14
♒ 10 Sep 18:18
♓ 12 Sep 18:47
♈ 14 Sep 19:09
♉ 16 Sep 21:15
♊ 19 Sep 02:43
♋ 21 Sep 12:11
♌ 24 Sep 00:34
♍ 26 Sep 13:31
♎ 29 Sep 00:57

- ♏ 1 Oct 10:05
- ♐ 3 Oct 17:03
- ♑ 5 Oct 22:11
- ♒ 8 Oct 01:40
- ♓ 10 Oct 03:45
- ♈ 12 Oct 05:12
- ♉ 14 Oct 07:26
- ♊ 16 Oct 12:07
- ♋ 18 Oct 20:28
- ♌ 21 Oct 08:13
- ♍ 23 Oct 21:10
- ♎ 26 Oct 08:38
- ♏ 28 Oct 17:15
- ♐ 30 Oct 23:15
- ♑ 2 Nov 03:37
- ♒ 4 Nov 07:10
- ♓ 6 Nov 10:16
- ♈ 8 Nov 13:11
- ♉ 10 Nov 16:33
- ♊ 12 Nov 21:32
- ♋ 15 Nov 05:23
- ♌ 17 Nov 16:28
- ♍ 20 Nov 05:22
- ♎ 22 Nov 17:19
- ♏ 25 Nov 02:09
- ♐ 27 Nov 07:35
- ♑ 29 Nov 10:43
- ♒ 1 Dec 13:02
- ♓ 3 Dec 15:36
- ♈ 5 Dec 19:00
- ♉ 7 Dec 23:30
- ♊ 10 Dec 05:33
- ♋ 12 Dec 13:47
- ♌ 15 Dec 00:37
- ♍ 17 Dec 13:23
- ♎ 20 Dec 01:56
- ♏ 22 Dec 11:46
- ♐ 24 Dec 17:44
- ♑ 26 Dec 20:24
- ♒ 28 Dec 21:21
- ♓ 30 Dec 22:17

MERCURY

- ♑ 1 Jan 00:00
- ♒ 3 Jan 08:27
- ♑ 27 Jan 23:43
- ♒ 15 Feb 19:00
- ♓ 11 Mar 05:00
- ♈ 28 Mar 11:20
- ♉ 12 Apr 04:57
- ♊ 30 Apr 15:56
- ♉ 26 May 10:05
- ♊ 14 Jun 00:47
- ♋ 6 Jul 09:05
- ♌ 20 Jul 16:08
- ♍ 5 Aug 10:34
- ♎ 27 Aug 00:37
- ♍ 25 Sep 09:56
- ♎ 11 Oct 23:28
- ♏ 30 Oct 23:38
- ♐ 18 Nov 13:39
- ♑ 8 Dec 01:48

VENUS

- ♑ 1 Jan 00:00
- ♒ 8 Jan 10:03
- ♓ 1 Feb 09:02
- ♈ 25 Feb 12:05
- ♉ 21 Mar 22:25
- ♊ 15 Apr 20:12
- ♋ 11 May 11:57
- ♌ 7 Jun 12:09
- ♍ 7 Jul 23:56
- ♎ 9 Nov 18:26
- ♏ 8 Dec 07:45

MARS

- ♐ 1 Jan 00:00
- ♑ 26 Jan 19:10
- ♒ 8 Mar 12:42
- ♓ 17 Apr 10:26
- ♈ 27 May 09:26
- ♉ 7 Jul 23:05
- ♊ 23 Aug 23:58

JUPITER

- ♋ 1 Jan 00:00
- ♌ 30 Jun 21:46

SATURN

- ♊ 1 Jan 00:00

1944

SUN

- ♑ 1 Jan 00:00
- ♒ 21 Jan 04:08
- ♓ 19 Feb 18:28
- ♈ 20 Mar 17:49
- ♉ 20 Apr 05:18
- ♊ 21 May 04:51
- ♋ 21 Jun 13:03
- ♌ 22 Jul 23:56
- ♍ 23 Aug 06:47
- ♎ 23 Sep 04:02
- ♏ 23 Oct 12:56
- ♐ 22 Nov 10:08
- ♑ 21 Dec 23:15

MOON

- ♓ 1 Jan 00:00
- ♈ 2 Jan 00:34
- ♉ 4 Jan 04:59
- ♊ 6 Jan 11:45
- ♋ 8 Jan 20:48
- ♌ 11 Jan 07:58
- ♍ 13 Jan 20:39
- ♎ 16 Jan 09:29
- ♏ 18 Jan 20:28
- ♐ 21 Jan 03:54
- ♑ 23 Jan 07:27
- ♒ 25 Jan 08:10
- ♓ 27 Jan 07:48
- ♈ 29 Jan 08:15
- ♉ 31 Jan 11:07
- ♊ 2 Feb 17:18
- ♋ 5 Feb 02:40
- ♌ 7 Feb 14:20
- ♍ 10 Feb 03:08
- ♎ 12 Feb 15:55
- ♏ 15 Feb 03:24
- ♐ 17 Feb 12:15
- ♑ 19 Feb 17:33
- ♒ 21 Feb 19:27
- ♓ 23 Feb 19:09
- ♈ 25 Feb 18:31
- ♉ 27 Feb 19:36
- ♊ 1 Mar 00:06
- ♋ 3 Mar 08:38
- ♌ 5 Mar 20:20
- ♍ 8 Mar 09:19
- ♎ 10 Mar 21:55
- ♏ 13 Mar 09:12
- ♐ 15 Mar 18:31
- ♑ 18 Mar 01:14
- ♒ 20 Mar 04:55
- ♓ 22 Mar 05:59
- ♈ 24 Mar 05:42
- ♉ 26 Mar 06:01
- ♊ 28 Mar 08:59
- ♋ 30 Mar 16:00
- ♌ 2 Apr 02:54
- ♍ 4 Apr 15:49
- ♎ 7 Apr 04:22
- ♏ 9 Apr 15:12
- ♐ 12 Apr 00:03
- ♑ 14 Apr 06:56
- ♒ 16 Apr 11:46
- ♓ 18 Apr 14:28
- ♈ 20 Apr 15:36
- ♉ 22 Apr 16:29
- ♊ 24 Apr 18:59
- ♋ 27 Apr 00:49
- ♌ 29 Apr 10:36
- ♍ 1 May 23:05
- ♎ 4 May 11:40
- ♏ 6 May 22:18
- ♐ 9 May 06:27
- ♑ 11 May 12:33
- ♒ 13 May 17:10
- ♓ 15 May 20:35
- ♈ 17 May 23:04
- ♉ 20 May 01:16
- ♊ 22 May 04:27
- ♋ 24 May 10:04
- ♌ 26 May 19:05
- ♍ 29 May 06:59
- ♎ 31 May 19:38
- ♏ 3 Jun 06:32
- ♐ 5 Jun 14:28
- ♑ 7 Jun 19:41
- ♒ 9 Jun 23:13
- ♓ 12 Jun 01:59
- ♈ 14 Jun 04:41
- ♉ 16 Jun 07:52
- ♊ 18 Jun 12:11
- ♋ 20 Jun 18:29
- ♌ 23 Jun 03:26
- ♍ 25 Jun 14:58
- ♎ 28 Jun 03:40
- ♏ 30 Jun 15:11
- ♐ 2 Jul 23:39
- ♑ 5 Jul 04:42
- ♒ 7 Jul 07:14
- ♓ 9 Jul 08:39
- ♈ 11 Jul 10:19
- ♉ 13 Jul 13:17
- ♊ 15 Jul 18:12
- ♋ 18 Jul 01:22
- ♌ 20 Jul 10:51
- ♍ 22 Jul 22:25
- ♎ 25 Jul 11:08
- ♏ 27 Jul 23:17
- ♐ 30 Jul 08:50
- ♑ 1 Aug 14:43
- ♒ 3 Aug 17:11
- ♓ 5 Aug 17:35
- ♈ 7 Aug 17:44
- ♉ 9 Aug 19:20
- ♊ 11 Aug 23:39
- ♋ 14 Aug 07:04
- ♌ 16 Aug 17:08
- ♍ 19 Aug 05:01
- ♎ 21 Aug 17:48
- ♏ 24 Aug 06:13
- ♐ 26 Aug 16:52
- ♑ 29 Aug 00:13
- ♒ 31 Aug 03:45
- ♓ 2 Sep 04:15
- ♈ 4 Sep 03:27
- ♉ 6 Sep 03:29
- ♊ 8 Sep 06:14
- ♋ 10 Sep 12:47
- ♌ 12 Sep 22:51
- ♍ 15 Sep 11:01
- ♎ 17 Sep 23:48
- ♏ 20 Sep 12:11
- ♐ 22 Sep 23:17
- ♑ 25 Sep 07:56
- ♒ 27 Sep 13:10
- ♓ 29 Sep 14:58
- ♈ 1 Oct 14:30
- ♉ 3 Oct 13:46
- ♊ 5 Oct 15:00
- ♋ 7 Oct 19:57
- ♌ 10 Oct 05:04
- ♍ 12 Oct 17:05
- ♎ 15 Oct 15:56
- ♏ 17 Oct 18:04
- ♐ 20 Oct 04:50
- ♑ 22 Oct 13:49
- ♒ 24 Oct 20:19
- ♓ 26 Oct 23:54
- ♈ 29 Oct 00:54
- ♉ 31 Oct 00:45
- ♊ 2 Nov 01:29
- ♋ 4 Nov 05:05
- ♌ 6 Nov 12:55
- ♍ 8 Nov 23:59
- ♎ 11 Nov 12:45
- ♏ 14 Nov 00:48
- ♐ 16 Nov 11:02
- ♑ 18 Nov 19:20
- ♒ 21 Nov 01:47
- ♓ 23 Nov 06:19
- ♈ 25 Nov 08:57
- ♉ 27 Nov 10:23
- ♊ 29 Nov 11:55
- ♋ 1 Dec 15:17
- ♌ 3 Dec 21:53
- ♍ 6 Dec 08:04
- ♎ 8 Dec 20:29
- ♏ 11 Dec 08:42
- ♐ 13 Dec 18:51
- ♑ 16 Dec 02:22
- ♒ 18 Dec 07:44
- ♓ 20 Dec 11:40
- ♈ 22 Dec 14:43
- ♉ 24 Dec 17:25
- ♊ 26 Dec 20:26
- ♋ 29 Dec 00:44
- ♌ 31 Dec 07:20

MERCURY

- ♑ 1 Jan 00:00
- ♒ 12 Feb 14:18
- ♓ 3 Mar 02:45
- ♈ 19 Mar 07:43
- ♉ 3 Apr 17:29
- ♊ 11 Jun 11:47
- ♋ 27 Jun 03:40
- ♌ 11 Jul 07:42
- ♍ 28 Jul 23:44
- ♎ 5 Oct 03:18
- ♏ 22 Oct 11:33
- ♐ 10 Nov 11:10
- ♑ 1 Dec 15:31
- ♐ 23 Dec 23:22

VENUS

- ♏ 1 Jan 00:00
- ♐ 3 Jan 04:44
- ♑ 28 Jan 03:11
- ♒ 21 Feb 16:40
- ♓ 17 Mar 02:47
- ♈ 10 Apr 12:10
- ♉ 4 May 22:04
- ♊ 29 May 08:40
- ♋ 22 Jun 19:12
- ♌ 17 Jul 04:47
- ♍ 10 Aug 13:13
- ♎ 3 Sep 21:17
- ♏ 28 Sep 06:12
- ♐ 22 Oct 17:08
- ♑ 16 Nov 07:26
- ♒ 11 Dec 04:48

MARS

- ♊ 1 Jan 00:00
- ♋ 28 Mar 09:55
- ♌ 22 May 14:17
- ♍ 12 Jul 02:55
- ♎ 29 Aug 00:24
- ♏ 13 Oct 12:10
- ♐ 25 Nov 16:12

JUPITER

- ♌ 1 Jan 00:00
- ♍ 26 Jul 01:04

SATURN

- ♊ 1 Jan 00:00
- ♋ 20 Jun 07:48

1945

SUN

- ♑ 1 Jan 00:00
- ♒ 20 Jan 09:54
- ♓ 19 Feb 00:15
- ♈ 20 Mar 23:38
- ♉ 20 Apr 11:07
- ♊ 21 May 10:41
- ♋ 21 Jun 18:53
- ♌ 23 Jul 05:46
- ♍ 23 Aug 12:36
- ♎ 23 Sep 09:50
- ♏ 23 Oct 18:44
- ♐ 22 Nov 15:56
- ♑ 22 Dec 05:04

MOON

- ♌ 1 Jan 00:00
- ♍ 2 Jan 16:49
- ♎ 5 Jan 04:44
- ♏ 7 Jan 17:13
- ♐ 10 Jan 03:56
- ♑ 12 Jan 11:28
- ♒ 14 Jan 15:57
- ♓ 16 Jan 18:28
- ♈ 18 Jan 20:21
- ♉ 20 Jan 22:48
- ♊ 23 Jan 02:35
- ♋ 25 Jan 08:05
- ♌ 27 Jan 15:33
- ♍ 30 Jan 01:09
- ♎ 1 Feb 12:46
- ♏ 4 Feb 01:23
- ♐ 6 Feb 12:58
- ♑ 8 Feb 21:30
- ♒ 11 Feb 02:12
- ♓ 13 Feb 03:53
- ♈ 15 Feb 04:13
- ♉ 17 Feb 05:05
- ♊ 19 Feb 08:01
- ♋ 21 Feb 13:43
- ♌ 23 Feb 21:59
- ♍ 26 Feb 08:14
- ♎ 28 Feb 19:57
- ♏ 3 Mar 08:33
- ♐ 5 Mar 20:45
- ♑ 8 Mar 06:38
- ♒ 10 Mar 12:40
- ♓ 12 Mar 14:50
- ♈ 14 Mar 14:33
- ♉ 16 Mar 13:55
- ♊ 18 Mar 15:05
- ♋ 20 Mar 19:32
- ♌ 23 Mar 03:32
- ♍ 25 Mar 14:11
- ♎ 28 Mar 02:15
- ♏ 30 Mar 14:50
- ♐ 2 Apr 03:08
- ♑ 4 Apr 13:52
- ♒ 6 Apr 21:29
- ♓ 9 Apr 01:11
- ♈ 11 Apr 01:38
- ♉ 13 Apr 00:40
- ♊ 15 Apr 00:31
- ♋ 17 Apr 03:14
- ♌ 19 Apr 09:52
- ♍ 21 Apr 20:04
- ♎ 24 Apr 08:15
- ♏ 26 Apr 20:53
- ♐ 29 Apr 08:56
- ♑ 1 May 19:40
- ♒ 4 May 04:06
- ♓ 6 May 09:21
- ♈ 8 May 11:25
- ♉ 10 May 11:25
- ♊ 12 May 11:12
- ♋ 14 May 12:51
- ♌ 16 May 17:57
- ♍ 19 May 02:56
- ♎ 21 May 14:43
- ♏ 24 May 03:21
- ♐ 26 May 15:12
- ♑ 29 May 01:25
- ♒ 31 May 09:35
- ♓ 2 Jun 15:26
- ♈ 4 Jun 18:51
- ♉ 6 Jun 20:24
- ♊ 8 Jun 21:15
- ♋ 10 Jun 23:02
- ♌ 13 Jun 03:20
- ♍ 15 Jun 11:08
- ♎ 17 Jun 22:07
- ♏ 20 Jun 10:36
- ♐ 22 Jun 22:28
- ♑ 25 Jun 08:15
- ♒ 27 Jun 15:37
- ♓ 29 Jun 20:52
- ♈ 2 Jul 00:30
- ♉ 4 Jul 03:05
- ♊ 6 Jul 05:20
- ♋ 8 Jul 08:11
- ♌ 10 Jul 12:44
- ♍ 12 Jul 19:58
- ♎ 15 Jul 06:13
- ♏ 17 Jul 18:29
- ♐ 20 Jul 06:36
- ♑ 22 Jul 16:29
- ♒ 24 Jul 23:17
- ♓ 27 Jul 03:27
- ♈ 29 Jul 06:08
- ♉ 31 Jul 08:29
- ♊ 2 Aug 11:24
- ♋ 4 Aug 15:23
- ♌ 6 Aug 21:06
- ♍ 9 Aug 04:24
- ♎ 11 Aug 14:21
- ♏ 14 Aug 02:25
- ♐ 16 Aug 14:56
- ♑ 19 Aug 01:31
- ♒ 21 Aug 08:33
- ♓ 23 Aug 12:05
- ♈ 25 Aug 13:30
- ♉ 27 Aug 13:54
- ♊ 29 Aug 16:47
- ♋ 31 Aug 21:00
- ♌ 3 Sep 03:20
- ♍ 5 Sep 11:37
- ♎ 7 Sep 21:49
- ♏ 10 Sep 09:48
- ♐ 12 Sep 22:38
- ♑ 15 Sep 10:12
- ♒ 17 Sep 18:20
- ♓ 19 Sep 22:19
- ♈ 21 Sep 23:11
- ♉ 23 Sep 22:54
- ♊ 25 Sep 23:32
- ♋ 28 Sep 02:39
- ♌ 30 Sep 08:47
- ♍ 2 Oct 17:34
- ♎ 5 Oct 04:17
- ♏ 7 Oct 16:24
- ♐ 10 Oct 05:18
- ♑ 12 Oct 17:33
- ♒ 15 Oct 03:07
- ♓ 17 Oct 08:34
- ♈ 19 Oct 10:09
- ♉ 21 Oct 09:31
- ♊ 23 Oct 08:50
- ♋ 25 Oct 10:11
- ♌ 27 Oct 14:56
- ♍ 29 Oct 23:12
- ♎ 1 Nov 10:08
- ♏ 3 Nov 22:30
- ♐ 6 Nov 11:13
- ♑ 8 Nov 23:36
- ♒ 11 Nov 09:59
- ♓ 13 Nov 17:05
- ♈ 15 Nov 20:25
- ♉ 17 Nov 20:48
- ♊ 19 Nov 20:03
- ♋ 21 Nov 20:14
- ♌ 23 Nov 23:12
- ♍ 26 Nov 06:00
- ♎ 28 Nov 16:19
- ♏ 1 Dec 04:43
- ♐ 3 Dec 17:30
- ♑ 6 Dec 05:24
- ♒ 8 Dec 15:35
- ♓ 10 Dec 23:21
- ♈ 13 Dec 04:16
- ♉ 15 Dec 06:30
- ♊ 17 Dec 07:03
- ♋ 19 Dec 07:28
- ♌ 21 Dec 09:31
- ♍ 23 Dec 14:44
- ♎ 25 Dec 23:45
- ♏ 28 Dec 11:43
- ♐ 31 Dec 00:33

MERCURY

- ♐ 1 Jan 00:00
- ♑ 14 Jan 03:05
- ♒ 5 Feb 09:21
- ♓ 23 Feb 11:26
- ♈ 11 Mar 06:45
- ♉ 16 May 15:22
- ♊ 4 Jun 10:30
- ♋ 18 Jun 12:28
- ♌ 3 Jul 15:39
- ♍ 26 Jul 14:48
- ♌ 17 Aug 08:50
- ♍ 10 Sep 07:21
- ♎ 27 Sep 12:09
- ♏ 15 Oct 00:14
- ♐ 3 Nov 23:07

VENUS

- ♒ 1 Jan 00:00
- ♓ 5 Jan 19:19
- ♈ 2 Feb 08:07
- ♉ 11 Mar 11:18
- ♈ 7 Apr 19:16
- ♉ 4 Jun 22:58
- ♊ 7 Jul 16:21
- ♋ 4 Aug 11:00
- ♌ 30 Aug 13:05
- ♍ 24 Sep 16:07
- ♎ 19 Oct 04:10
- ♏ 12 Nov 07:05
- ♐ 6 Dec 05:23

MARS

- ♐ 1 Jan 00:00
- ♑ 5 Jan 19:31
- ♒ 14 Feb 09:58
- ♓ 25 Mar 03:44
- ♈ 2 May 20:29
- ♉ 11 Jun 11:53
- ♊ 23 Jul 08:59
- ♋ 7 Sep 20:56
- ♌ 11 Nov 21:05
- ♋ 26 Dec 15:05

JUPITER

- ♍ 1 Jan 00:00
- ♎ 25 Aug 06:06

SATURN

- ♋ 1 Jan 00:00

1946

SUN

- ♑ 1 Jan 00:00
- ♒ 20 Jan 15:45
- ♓ 19 Feb 06:09
- ♈ 21 Mar 05:33
- ♉ 20 Apr 17:03
- ♊ 21 May 16:34
- ♋ 22 Jun 00:45
- ♌ 23 Jul 11:38
- ♍ 23 Aug 18:27
- ♎ 23 Sep 15:41
- ♏ 24 Oct 00:35
- ♐ 22 Nov 21:47
- ♑ 22 Dec 10:54

MOON

- ♐ 1 Jan 00:00
- ♑ 2 Jan 12:11
- ♒ 4 Jan 21:38
- ♓ 7 Jan 04:47
- ♈ 9 Jan 09:56
- ♉ 11 Jan 13:26
- ♊ 13 Jan 15:43
- ♋ 15 Jan 17:33
- ♌ 17 Jan 20:04
- ♍ 20 Jan 00:41
- ♎ 22 Jan 08:32
- ♏ 24 Jan 19:40
- ♐ 27 Jan 08:28
- ♑ 29 Jan 20:18
- ♒ 1 Feb 05:24
- ♓ 3 Feb 11:33
- ♈ 5 Feb 15:38
- ♉ 7 Feb 18:47
- ♊ 9 Feb 21:46
- ♋ 12 Feb 00:59
- ♌ 14 Feb 04:51
- ♍ 16 Feb 10:03
- ♎ 18 Feb 17:36
- ♏ 21 Feb 04:05
- ♐ 23 Feb 16:41
- ♑ 26 Feb 05:02
- ♒ 28 Feb 14:35
- ♓ 2 Mar 20:25
- ♈ 4 Mar 23:24
- ♉ 7 Mar 01:09
- ♊ 9 Mar 03:12
- ♋ 11 Mar 06:29
- ♌ 13 Mar 11:15
- ♍ 15 Mar 17:33
- ♎ 18 Mar 01:41
- ♏ 20 Mar 12:05
- ♐ 23 Mar 00:31
- ♑ 25 Mar 13:18
- ♒ 27 Mar 23:51
- ♓ 30 Mar 06:26
- ♈ 1 Apr 09:17
- ♉ 3 Apr 09:57
- ♊ 5 Apr 10:25
- ♋ 7 Apr 12:21
- ♌ 9 Apr 16:38
- ♍ 11 Apr 23:21
- ♎ 14 Apr 08:14
- ♏ 16 Apr 19:04
- ♐ 19 Apr 07:30
- ♑ 21 Apr 20:29
- ♒ 24 Apr 07:57
- ♓ 26 Apr 15:55
- ♈ 28 Apr 19:46
- ♉ 30 Apr 20:31
- ♊ 2 May 20:04
- ♋ 4 May 20:23
- ♌ 6 May 23:05
- ♍ 9 May 04:58
- ♎ 11 May 13:54
- ♏ 14 May 01:09
- ♐ 16 May 13:46
- ♑ 19 May 02:42
- ♒ 21 May 14:32
- ♓ 23 May 23:39
- ♈ 26 May 05:05
- ♉ 28 May 07:04
- ♊ 30 May 06:55
- ♋ 1 Jun 06:29
- ♌ 3 Jun 07:40
- ♍ 5 Jun 11:57
- ♎ 7 Jun 19:57
- ♏ 10 Jun 07:05
- ♐ 12 Jun 19:51
- ♑ 15 Jun 08:40
- ♒ 17 Jun 20:16
- ♓ 20 Jun 05:43
- ♈ 22 Jun 12:20
- ♉ 24 Jun 15:56
- ♊ 26 Jun 17:08
- ♋ 28 Jun 17:11
- ♌ 30 Jun 17:48
- ♍ 2 Jul 20:45
- ♎ 5 Jul 03:21
- ♏ 7 Jul 13:42
- ♐ 10 Jul 02:21
- ♑ 12 Jul 15:06
- ♒ 15 Jul 02:17
- ♓ 17 Jul 11:16
- ♈ 19 Jul 17:59
- ♉ 21 Jul 22:36
- ♊ 24 Jul 01:19
- ♋ 26 Jul 02:44
- ♌ 28 Jul 03:58
- ♍ 30 Jul 06:33
- ♎ 1 Aug 12:05
- ♏ 3 Aug 21:23
- ♐ 6 Aug 09:37
- ♑ 8 Aug 22:24
- ♒ 11 Aug 09:24
- ♓ 13 Aug 17:41
- ♈ 15 Aug 23:37
- ♉ 18 Aug 04:00
- ♊ 20 Aug 07:23
- ♋ 22 Aug 10:07
- ♌ 24 Aug 12:38
- ♍ 26 Aug 15:54
- ♎ 28 Aug 21:15
- ♏ 31 Aug 05:50
- ♐ 2 Sep 17:32
- ♑ 5 Sep 06:24
- ♒ 7 Sep 17:42
- ♓ 10 Sep 01:46
- ♈ 12 Sep 06:49
- ♉ 14 Sep 10:04
- ♊ 16 Sep 12:46
- ♋ 18 Sep 15:42
- ♌ 20 Sep 19:13
- ♍ 22 Sep 23:38
- ♎ 25 Sep 05:40
- ♏ 27 Sep 14:13
- ♐ 30 Sep 01:33
- ♑ 2 Oct 14:30
- ♒ 5 Oct 02:28
- ♓ 7 Oct 11:09
- ♈ 9 Oct 16:05
- ♉ 11 Oct 18:21
- ♊ 13 Oct 19:37
- ♋ 15 Oct 21:23
- ♌ 18 Oct 00:35
- ♍ 20 Oct 05:36
- ♎ 22 Oct 12:34
- ♏ 24 Oct 21:41
- ♐ 27 Oct 09:04
- ♑ 29 Oct 22:00
- ♒ 1 Nov 10:37
- ♓ 3 Nov 20:32
- ♈ 6 Nov 02:28
- ♉ 8 Nov 04:49
- ♊ 10 Nov 05:08
- ♋ 12 Nov 05:16
- ♌ 14 Nov 06:53
- ♍ 16 Nov 11:05
- ♎ 18 Nov 18:13
- ♏ 21 Nov 03:58
- ♐ 23 Nov 15:44
- ♑ 26 Nov 04:40
- ♒ 28 Nov 17:30
- ♓ 1 Dec 04:30
- ♈ 3 Dec 12:06
- ♉ 5 Dec 15:49
- ♊ 7 Dec 16:30
- ♋ 9 Dec 15:50
- ♌ 11 Dec 15:47
- ♍ 13 Dec 18:09
- ♎ 16 Dec 00:08
- ♏ 18 Dec 09:43
- ♐ 20 Dec 21:49
- ♑ 23 Dec 10:51
- ♒ 25 Dec 23:30
- ♓ 28 Dec 10:44
- ♈ 30 Dec 19:31

MERCURY

- ♐ 1 Jan 00:00
- ♑ 9 Jan 14:10
- ♒ 29 Jan 07:23
- ♓ 15 Feb 15:43
- ♈ 4 Mar 09:26
- ♓ 1 Apr 18:17
- ♈ 16 Apr 14:55
- ♉ 11 May 14:29
- ♊ 27 May 04:14
- ♋ 10 Jun 02:01
- ♌ 27 Jun 19:08
- ♍ 3 Sep 16:30
- ♎ 19 Sep 14:34
- ♏ 7 Oct 21:21
- ♐ 30 Oct 11:23
- ♏ 20 Nov 20:16
- ♐ 13 Dec 00:03

VENUS

- ♑ 1 Jan 00:00
- ♒ 22 Jan 22:28
- ♓ 15 Feb 20:12
- ♈ 11 Mar 20:32
- ♉ 5 Apr 01:01
- ♊ 29 Apr 11:00
- ♋ 24 May 03:40
- ♌ 18 Jun 05:01
- ♍ 13 Jul 19:23
- ♎ 9 Aug 08:35
- ♏ 7 Sep 00:16
- ♐ 16 Oct 10:45
- ♏ 8 Nov 08:56

MARS

- ♋ 1 Jan 00:00
- ♌ 22 Apr 19:32
- ♍ 20 Jun 08:32
- ♎ 9 Aug 13:17
- ♏ 24 Sep 16:35
- ♐ 6 Nov 18:23
- ♑ 17 Dec 10:56

JUPITER

- ♎ 1 Jan 00:00
- ♏ 25 Sep 10:19

SATURN

- ♋ 1 Jan 00:00
- ♌ 2 Aug 14:42

1947

SUN

♑	1 Jan	00:00
♒	20 Jan	21:32
♓	19 Feb	11:52
♈	21 Mar	11:13
♉	20 Apr	22:40
♊	21 May	22:10
♋	22 Jun	06:19
♌	23 Jul	17:15
♍	24 Aug	00:09
♎	23 Sep	21:29
♏	24 Oct	06:26
♐	23 Nov	03:38
♑	22 Dec	16:43

MOON

♈	1 Jan	00:00
♉	2 Jan	01:06
♊	4 Jan	03:26
♋	6 Jan	03:28
♌	8 Jan	02:54
♍	10 Jan	03:45
♎	12 Jan	07:54
♏	14 Jan	16:16
♐	17 Jan	04:03
♑	19 Jan	17:11
♒	22 Jan	05:37
♓	24 Jan	16:23
♈	27 Jan	01:11
♉	29 Jan	07:46
♊	31 Jan	11:52
♋	2 Feb	13:39
♌	4 Feb	14:02
♍	6 Feb	14:42
♎	8 Feb	17:40
♏	11 Feb	00:29
♐	13 Feb	11:16
♑	16 Feb	00:12
♒	18 Feb	12:39
♓	20 Feb	22:58
♈	23 Feb	06:58
♉	25 Feb	13:08
♊	27 Feb	17:47
♋	1 Mar	20:59
♌	3 Mar	23:00
♍	6 Mar	00:47
♎	8 Mar	03:51
♏	10 Mar	09:51
♐	12 Mar	19:34
♑	15 Mar	08:01
♒	17 Mar	20:36
♓	20 Mar	06:58
♈	22 Mar	14:23
♉	24 Mar	19:29
♊	26 Mar	23:16
♋	29 Mar	02:26
♌	31 Mar	05:22
♍	2 Apr	08:31
♎	4 Apr	12:40
♏	6 Apr	18:57
♐	9 Apr	04:13
♑	11 Apr	16:09
♒	14 Apr	04:52
♓	16 Apr	15:48
♈	18 Apr	23:26
♉	21 Apr	03:56
♊	23 Apr	06:28
♋	25 Apr	08:23
♌	27 Apr	10:44
♍	29 Apr	14:15
♎	1 May	19:24
♏	4 May	02:36
♐	6 May	12:10
♑	8 May	23:55
♒	11 May	12:41
♓	14 May	00:21
♈	16 May	08:57
♉	18 May	13:52
♊	20 May	15:52
♋	22 May	16:27
♌	24 May	17:18
♍	26 May	19:50
♎	29 May	00:54
♏	31 May	08:43
♐	2 Jun	18:54
♑	5 Jun	06:52
♒	7 Jun	19:38
♓	10 Jun	07:47
♈	12 Jun	17:34
♉	14 Jun	23:46
♊	17 Jun	02:22
♋	19 Jun	02:33
♌	21 Jun	02:07
♍	23 Jun	03:02
♎	25 Jun	06:52
♏	27 Jun	14:17
♐	30 Jun	00:46
♑	2 Jul	13:03
♒	5 Jul	01:50
♓	7 Jul	14:03
♈	10 Jul	00:35
♉	12 Jul	08:12
♊	14 Jul	12:17
♋	16 Jul	13:15
♌	18 Jul	12:35
♍	20 Jul	12:19
♎	22 Jul	14:34
♏	24 Jul	20:41
♐	27 Jul	06:41
♑	29 Jul	19:02
♒	1 Aug	07:50
♓	3 Aug	19:49
♈	6 Aug	06:20
♉	8 Aug	14:44
♊	10 Aug	20:18
♋	12 Aug	22:50
♌	14 Aug	23:07
♍	16 Aug	22:49
♎	19 Aug	00:04
♏	21 Aug	04:45
♐	23 Aug	13:35
♑	26 Aug	01:31
♒	28 Aug	14:18
♓	31 Aug	02:04
♈	2 Sep	12:03
♉	4 Sep	20:11
♊	7 Sep	02:19
♋	9 Sep	06:12
♌	11 Sep	08:03
♍	13 Sep	08:51
♎	15 Sep	10:17
♏	17 Sep	14:11
♐	19 Sep	21:50
♑	22 Sep	08:58
♒	24 Sep	21:38
♓	27 Sep	09:25
♈	29 Sep	18:59
♉	2 Oct	02:16
♊	4 Oct	07:44
♋	6 Oct	11:47
♌	8 Oct	14:42
♍	10 Oct	16:57
♎	12 Oct	19:32
♏	14 Oct	23:46
♐	17 Oct	06:53
♑	19 Oct	17:14
♒	22 Oct	05:39
♓	24 Oct	17:46
♈	27 Oct	03:31
♉	29 Oct	10:16
♊	31 Oct	14:36
♋	2 Nov	17:32
♌	4 Nov	20:04
♍	6 Nov	22:55
♎	9 Nov	02:43
♏	11 Nov	08:03
♐	13 Nov	15:34
♑	16 Nov	01:37
♒	18 Nov	13:45
♓	21 Nov	02:17
♈	23 Nov	12:54
♉	25 Nov	20:06
♊	27 Nov	23:56
♋	30 Nov	01:31
♌	2 Dec	02:30
♍	4 Dec	04:24
♎	6 Dec	08:14
♏	8 Dec	14:25
♐	10 Dec	22:50
♑	13 Dec	09:14
♒	15 Dec	21:16
♓	18 Dec	09:59
♈	20 Dec	21:37
♉	23 Dec	06:12
♊	25 Dec	10:47
♋	27 Dec	12:03
♌	29 Dec	11:42
♍	31 Dec	11:47

MERCURY

♐	1 Jan	00:00
♑	3 Jan	01:47
♒	21 Jan	21:06
♓	8 Feb	01:32
♈	16 Apr	04:31
♉	4 May	06:03
♊	18 May	13:34
♋	2 Jun	13:41
♌	10 Aug	17:41
♍	26 Aug	14:50
♎	11 Sep	20:55
♏	1 Oct	15:26
♐	7 Dec	12:32
♑	26 Dec	23:18

VENUS

♏	1 Jan	00:00
♐	5 Jan	16:46
♑	6 Feb	05:42
♒	5 Mar	05:09
♓	30 Mar	22:15
♈	25 Apr	03:03
♉	20 May	02:06
♊	13 Jun	21:36
♋	8 Jul	13:30
♌	2 Aug	01:07
♍	26 Aug	08:18
♎	19 Sep	12:01
♏	13 Oct	13:49
♐	6 Nov	14:59
♑	30 Nov	16:23
♒	24 Dec	19:13

MARS

♑	1 Jan	00:00
♒	25 Jan	11:45
♓	4 Mar	16:47
♈	11 Apr	23:03
♉	21 May	03:40
♊	1 Jul	03:35
♋	13 Aug	21:26
♌	1 Oct	02:31
♍	1 Dec	11:44

JUPITER

♏	1 Jan	00:00
♐	24 Oct	03:00

SATURN

♌	1 Jan	00:00

1948

SUN

♑	1 Jan	00:00
♒	21 Jan	03:19
♓	19 Feb	17:37
♈	20 Mar	16:57
♉	20 Apr	04:25
♊	21 May	03:58
♋	21 Jun	12:11
♌	22 Jul	23:08
♍	23 Aug	06:03
♎	23 Sep	03:22
♏	23 Oct	12:18
♐	22 Nov	09:29
♑	21 Dec	22:34

MOON

♍	1 Jan	00:00
♎	2 Jan	14:10
♏	4 Jan	19:51
♐	7 Jan	04:41
♑	9 Jan	15:41
♒	12 Jan	03:54
♓	14 Jan	16:36
♈	17 Jan	04:44
♉	19 Jan	14:43
♊	21 Jan	21:02
♋	23 Jan	23:24
♌	25 Jan	23:00
♍	27 Jan	21:56
♎	29 Jan	22:30
♏	1 Feb	02:28
♐	3 Feb	10:26
♑	5 Feb	21:30
♒	8 Feb	09:59
♓	10 Feb	22:37
♈	13 Feb	10:38
♉	15 Feb	21:09
♊	18 Feb	04:56
♋	20 Feb	09:09
♌	22 Feb	10:07
♍	24 Feb	09:23
♎	26 Feb	09:06
♏	28 Feb	11:24
♐	1 Mar	17:42
♑	4 Mar	03:51
♒	6 Mar	16:15
♓	9 Mar	04:54
♈	11 Mar	16:33
♉	14 Mar	02:41
♊	16 Mar	10:46
♋	18 Mar	16:14
♌	20 Mar	18:58
♍	22 Mar	19:43
♎	24 Mar	20:02
♏	26 Mar	21:50
♐	29 Mar	02:47
♑	31 Mar	11:34
♒	2 Apr	23:19
♓	5 Apr	11:56
♈	7 Apr	23:29
♉	10 Apr	08:59
♊	12 Apr	16:20
♋	14 Apr	21:42
♌	17 Apr	01:16
♍	19 Apr	03:31
♎	21 Apr	05:17
♏	23 Apr	07:50
♐	25 Apr	12:32
♑	27 Apr	20:22
♒	30 Apr	07:16
♓	2 May	19:44
♈	5 May	07:29
♉	7 May	16:48
♊	9 May	23:20
♋	12 May	03:39
♌	14 May	06:39
♍	16 May	09:15
♎	18 May	12:07
♏	20 May	15:56
♐	22 May	21:22
♑	25 May	05:08
♒	27 May	15:31
♓	30 May	03:46
♈	1 Jun	15:55
♉	4 Jun	01:44
♊	6 Jun	08:07
♋	8 Jun	11:29
♌	10 Jun	13:12
♍	12 Jun	14:49
♎	14 Jun	17:34
♏	16 Jun	22:04
♐	19 Jun	04:29
♑	21 Jun	12:51
♒	23 Jun	23:16
♓	26 Jun	11:24
♈	28 Jun	23:56
♉	1 Jul	10:40
♊	3 Jul	17:48
♋	5 Jul	21:07
♌	7 Jul	21:53
♍	9 Jul	22:04
♎	11 Jul	23:31
♏	14 Jul	03:28
♐	16 Jul	10:11
♑	18 Jul	19:14
♒	21 Jul	06:03
♓	23 Jul	18:13
♈	26 Jul	06:58
♉	28 Jul	18:34
♊	31 Jul	03:02
♋	2 Aug	07:21
♌	4 Aug	08:14
♍	6 Aug	07:33
♎	8 Aug	07:30
♏	10 Aug	09:57
♐	12 Aug	15:50
♑	15 Aug	00:52
♒	17 Aug	12:03
♓	20 Aug	00:23
♈	22 Aug	13:06
♉	25 Aug	01:04
♊	27 Aug	10:40
♋	29 Aug	16:34
♌	31 Aug	18:42
♍	2 Sep	18:21
♎	4 Sep	17:36
♏	6 Sep	18:35
♐	8 Sep	22:52
♑	11 Sep	06:57
♒	13 Sep	17:59
♓	16 Sep	06:27
♈	18 Sep	19:02
♉	21 Sep	06:46
♊	23 Sep	16:40
♋	25 Sep	23:46
♌	28 Sep	03:35
♍	30 Sep	04:41
♎	2 Oct	04:30
♏	4 Oct	04:59
♐	6 Oct	07:55
♑	8 Oct	14:31
♒	11 Oct	00:43
♓	13 Oct	13:04
♈	16 Oct	01:37
♉	18 Oct	12:54
♊	20 Oct	22:15
♋	23 Oct	05:22
♌	25 Oct	10:10
♍	27 Oct	12:54
♎	29 Oct	14:16
♏	31 Oct	15:32
♐	2 Nov	18:11
♑	4 Nov	23:40
♒	7 Nov	08:42
♓	9 Nov	20:34
♈	12 Nov	09:13
♉	14 Nov	20:24
♊	17 Nov	05:02
♋	19 Nov	11:12
♌	21 Nov	15:33
♍	23 Nov	18:49
♎	25 Nov	21:33
♏	28 Nov	00:19
♐	30 Nov	03:52
♑	2 Dec	09:17
♒	4 Dec	17:32
♓	7 Dec	04:46
♈	9 Dec	17:30
♉	12 Dec	05:09
♊	14 Dec	13:44
♋	16 Dec	19:01
♌	18 Dec	22:03
♍	21 Dec	00:19
♎	23 Dec	03:00
♏	25 Dec	06:39
♐	27 Dec	11:29
♑	29 Dec	17:47

MERCURY

♑	1 Jan	00:00
♒	14 Jan	10:07
♓	2 Feb	00:46
♒	21 Feb	00:00
♓	18 Mar	08:14
♈	9 Apr	02:26
♉	25 Apr	01:39
♊	9 May	04:39
♋	28 May	10:51
♌	28 Jun	17:58
♍	11 Jul	20:56
♌	2 Aug	13:55
♍	17 Aug	08:44
♎	3 Sep	15:47
♏	27 Sep	07:19
♎	17 Oct	03:34
♏	10 Nov	02:19
♐	29 Nov	15:09
♑	18 Dec	16:47

VENUS

♒	1 Jan	00:00
♓	18 Jan	02:14
♈	11 Feb	18:51
♉	8 Mar	07:00
♊	4 Apr	12:40
♋	7 May	08:28
♊	29 Jun	07:59
♋	3 Aug	02:16
♌	8 Sep	13:41
♍	6 Oct	12:26
♎	1 Nov	06:42
♏	26 Nov	00:55
♐	20 Dec	07:29

MARS

♍	1 Jan	00:00
♌	12 Feb	10:28
♍	18 May	20:54
♎	17 Jul	05:26
♏	3 Sep	13:58
♐	17 Oct	05:44
♑	26 Nov	21:59

JUPITER

♐	1 Jan	00:00
♑	15 Nov	10:38

SATURN

♌	1 Jan	00:00
♍	19 Sep	04:36

1949

SUN

♑	1 Jan	00:00
♒	20 Jan	09:09
♓	18 Feb	23:28
♈	20 Mar	22:49
♉	20 Apr	10:18
♊	21 May	09:51
♋	21 Jun	18:03
♌	23 Jul	04:57
♍	23 Aug	11:49
♎	23 Sep	09:06
♏	23 Oct	18:03
♐	22 Nov	15:17
♑	22 Dec	04:23

MOON

♑	1 Jan	00:00
♒	1 Jan	02:08
♓	3 Jan	12:59
♈	6 Jan	01:41
♉	8 Jan	14:03
♊	10 Jan	23:31
♋	13 Jan	04:57
♌	15 Jan	07:08
♍	17 Jan	07:52
♎	19 Jan	09:03
♏	21 Jan	12:00
♐	23 Jan	17:09
♑	26 Jan	00:22
♒	28 Jan	09:27
♓	30 Jan	20:27
♈	2 Feb	09:05
♉	4 Feb	21:57
♊	7 Feb	08:41
♋	9 Feb	15:23
♌	11 Feb	18:01
♍	13 Feb	18:06
♎	15 Feb	17:44
♏	17 Feb	18:53
♐	19 Feb	22:50
♑	22 Feb	05:51
♒	24 Feb	15:26
♓	27 Feb	02:54
♈	1 Mar	15:36
♉	4 Mar	04:33
♊	6 Mar	16:06
♋	9 Mar	00:22
♌	11 Mar	04:34
♍	13 Mar	05:24
♎	15 Mar	04:40
♏	17 Mar	04:26
♐	19 Mar	06:31
♑	21 Mar	12:05
♒	23 Mar	21:11
♓	26 Mar	08:50
♈	28 Mar	21:42
♉	31 Mar	10:30
♊	2 Apr	22:03
♋	5 Apr	07:10
♌	7 Apr	13:00
♍	9 Apr	15:32
♎	11 Apr	15:48
♏	13 Apr	15:28
♐	15 Apr	16:24
♑	17 Apr	20:16
♒	20 Apr	04:00
♓	22 Apr	15:08
♈	25 Apr	04:01
♉	27 Apr	16:41
♊	30 Apr	03:48
♋	2 May	12:44
♌	4 May	19:12
♍	6 May	23:12
♎	9 May	01:07
♏	11 May	01:54
♐	13 May	02:57
♑	15 May	05:57
♒	17 May	12:19
♓	19 May	22:26
♈	22 May	11:02
♉	24 May	23:42
♊	27 May	10:27
♋	29 May	18:39
♌	1 Jun	00:36
♍	3 Jun	04:54
♎	5 Jun	07:58
♏	7 Jun	10:14
♐	9 Jun	12:24
♑	11 Jun	15:40
♒	13 Jun	21:27
♓	16 Jun	06:39
♈	18 Jun	18:45
♉	21 Jun	07:31
♊	23 Jun	18:20
♋	26 Jun	02:02
♌	28 Jun	07:01
♍	30 Jun	10:27
♎	2 Jul	13:22
♏	4 Jul	16:22
♐	6 Jul	19:45
♑	9 Jul	00:03
♒	11 Jul	06:09
♓	13 Jul	15:02
♈	16 Jul	02:43
♉	18 Jul	15:36
♊	21 Jul	02:58
♋	23 Jul	10:52
♌	25 Jul	15:19
♍	27 Jul	17:36
♎	29 Jul	19:20
♏	31 Jul	21:44
♐	3 Aug	01:25
♑	5 Aug	06:36
♒	7 Aug	13:34
♓	9 Aug	22:46
♈	12 Aug	10:20
♉	14 Aug	23:18
♊	17 Aug	11:23
♋	19 Aug	20:15
♌	22 Aug	01:08
♍	24 Aug	02:56
♎	26 Aug	03:25
♏	28 Aug	04:20
♐	30 Aug	07:01
♑	1 Sep	12:05
♒	3 Sep	19:37
♓	6 Sep	05:27
♈	8 Sep	17:14
♉	11 Sep	06:13
♊	13 Sep	18:47
♋	16 Sep	04:52
♌	18 Sep	11:05
♍	20 Sep	13:34
♎	22 Sep	13:42
♏	24 Sep	13:21
♐	26 Sep	14:22
♑	28 Sep	18:07
♒	1 Oct	01:14
♓	3 Oct	11:20
♈	5 Oct	23:28
♉	8 Oct	12:27
♊	11 Oct	01:03
♋	13 Oct	11:51
♌	15 Oct	19:35
♍	17 Oct	23:43
♎	20 Oct	00:48
♏	22 Oct	00:19
♐	24 Oct	00:08
♑	26 Oct	02:11
♒	28 Oct	07:51
♓	30 Oct	17:22
♈	2 Nov	05:35
♉	4 Nov	18:37
♊	7 Nov	06:55
♋	9 Nov	17:35
♌	12 Nov	02:01
♍	14 Nov	07:43
♎	16 Nov	10:36
♏	18 Nov	11:19
♐	20 Nov	11:16
♑	22 Nov	12:20
♒	24 Nov	16:25
♓	27 Nov	00:36
♈	29 Nov	12:18
♉	2 Dec	01:22
♊	4 Dec	13:29
♋	6 Dec	23:32
♌	9 Dec	07:28
♍	11 Dec	13:32
♎	13 Dec	17:45
♏	15 Dec	20:14
♐	17 Dec	21:32
♑	19 Dec	23:00
♒	22 Dec	02:25
♓	24 Dec	09:20
♈	26 Dec	20:05
♉	29 Dec	08:58
♊	31 Dec	21:13

MERCURY

♑	1 Jan	00:00
♒	6 Jan	08:53
♓	14 Mar	09:52
♈	1 Apr	16:02
♉	16 Apr	14:56
♊	2 May	02:20
♋	10 Jul	03:20
♌	25 Jul	05:20
♍	9 Aug	09:05
♎	28 Aug	15:48
♏	3 Nov	18:58
♐	22 Nov	09:07
♑	11 Dec	13:38

VENUS

♐	1 Jan	00:00
♑	13 Jan	09:01
♒	6 Feb	09:06
♓	2 Mar	09:39
♈	26 Mar	11:54
♉	19 Apr	16:44
♊	14 May	00:26
♋	7 Jun	10:48
♌	1 Jul	23:41
♍	26 Jul	15:44
♎	20 Aug	12:39
♏	14 Sep	17:13
♐	10 Oct	10:19
♑	6 Nov	04:54
♒	6 Dec	06:06

MARS

♑	1 Jan	00:00
♒	4 Jan	17:50
♓	11 Feb	18:06
♈	21 Mar	22:03
♉	30 Apr	02:33
♊	10 Jun	00:57
♋	23 Jul	05:55
♌	7 Sep	04:52
♍	27 Oct	00:59
♎	26 Dec	05:24

JUPITER

♑	1 Jan	00:00
♒	12 Apr	19:18
♑	27 Jun	18:30
♒	30 Nov	20:08

SATURN

♍	1 Jan	00:00
♌	3 Apr	03:40
♍	29 May	12:58

1950

SUN

♑	1 Jan	00:00
♒	20 Jan	15:00
♓	19 Feb	05:18
♈	21 Mar	04:36
♉	20 Apr	16:00
♊	21 May	15:28
♋	21 Jun	23:37
♌	23 Jul	10:30
♍	23 Aug	17:24
♎	23 Sep	14:44
♏	23 Oct	23:45
♐	22 Nov	21:03
♑	22 Dec	10:14

MOON

♊	1 Jan	00:00
♋	3 Jan	06:57
♌	5 Jan	13:58
♍	7 Jan	19:06
♎	9 Jan	23:09
♏	12 Jan	02:28
♐	14 Jan	05:16
♑	16 Jan	08:07
♒	18 Jan	12:07
♓	20 Jan	18:42
♈	23 Jan	04:38
♉	25 Jan	17:08
♊	28 Jan	05:43
♋	30 Jan	15:50
♌	1 Feb	22:34
♍	4 Feb	02:37
♎	6 Feb	05:19
♏	8 Feb	07:51
♐	10 Feb	10:52
♑	12 Feb	14:45
♒	14 Feb	19:58
♓	17 Feb	03:11
♈	19 Feb	13:01
♉	22 Feb	01:12
♊	24 Feb	14:03
♋	27 Feb	01:03
♌	1 Mar	08:31
♍	3 Mar	12:25
♎	5 Mar	14:01
♏	7 Mar	14:56
♐	9 Mar	16:38
♑	11 Mar	20:07
♒	14 Mar	01:53
♓	16 Mar	10:00
♈	18 Mar	20:21
♉	21 Mar	08:33
♊	23 Mar	21:28
♋	26 Mar	09:17
♌	28 Mar	18:05
♍	30 Mar	23:01
♎	2 Apr	00:41
♏	4 Apr	00:36
♐	6 Apr	00:37
♑	8 Apr	02:30
♒	10 Apr	07:25
♓	12 Apr	15:38
♈	15 Apr	02:32
♉	17 Apr	15:00
♊	20 Apr	03:55
♋	22 Apr	16:02
♌	25 Apr	01:58
♍	27 Apr	08:30
♎	29 Apr	11:25
♏	1 May	11:38
♐	3 May	10:51
♑	5 May	11:08
♒	7 May	14:22
♓	9 May	21:34
♈	12 May	08:18
♉	14 May	20:59
♊	17 May	09:53
♋	19 May	21:51
♌	22 May	08:07
♍	24 May	15:51
♎	26 May	20:26
♏	28 May	22:01
♐	30 May	21:44
♑	1 Jun	21:27
♒	3 Jun	23:18

♓ 6 Jun 04:58
♈ 8 Jun 14:44
♉ 11 Jun 03:13
♊ 13 Jun 16:05
♋ 16 Jun 03:45
♌ 18 Jun 13:38
♍ 20 Jun 21:32
♎ 23 Jun 03:10
♏ 25 Jun 06:19
♐ 27 Jun 07:26
♑ 29 Jun 07:49
♒ 1 Jul 09:20
♓ 3 Jul 13:52
♈ 5 Jul 22:25
♉ 8 Jul 10:14
♊ 10 Jul 23:02
♋ 13 Jul 10:34
♌ 15 Jul 19:53
♍ 18 Jul 03:06
♎ 20 Jul 08:34
♏ 22 Jul 12:27
♐ 24 Jul 14:56
♑ 26 Jul 16:40
♒ 28 Jul 18:56
♓ 30 Jul 23:19
♈ 2 Aug 07:03
♉ 4 Aug 18:06
♊ 7 Aug 06:44
♋ 9 Aug 18:27
♌ 12 Aug 03:37
♍ 14 Aug 10:04
♎ 16 Aug 14:31
♏ 18 Aug 17:49
♐ 20 Aug 20:36
♑ 22 Aug 23:23
♒ 25 Aug 02:53
♓ 27 Aug 08:02
♈ 29 Aug 15:45
♉ 1 Sep 02:19
♊ 3 Sep 14:46
♋ 6 Sep 02:54
♌ 8 Sep 12:34
♍ 10 Sep 18:55
♎ 12 Sep 22:28
♏ 15 Sep 00:27
♐ 17 Sep 02:13
♑ 19 Sep 04:49
♒ 21 Sep 09:00
♓ 23 Sep 15:10
♈ 25 Sep 23:32
♉ 28 Sep 10:09
♊ 30 Sep 22:27
♋ 3 Oct 11:00
♌ 5 Oct 21:40
♍ 8 Oct 04:54
♎ 10 Oct 08:29
♏ 12 Oct 09:31
♐ 14 Oct 09:44
♑ 16 Oct 10:56
♒ 18 Oct 14:27
♓ 20 Oct 20:53
♈ 23 Oct 05:59
♉ 25 Oct 17:03
♊ 28 Oct 05:23
♋ 30 Oct 18:04
♌ 2 Nov 05:38
♍ 4 Nov 14:21
♎ 6 Nov 19:11
♏ 8 Nov 20:29
♐ 10 Nov 19:52
♑ 12 Nov 19:26
♒ 14 Nov 21:15
♓ 17 Nov 02:39
♈ 19 Nov 11:40
♉ 21 Nov 23:08
♊ 24 Nov 11:39
♋ 27 Nov 00:14
♌ 29 Nov 12:02
♍ 1 Dec 21:54
♎ 4 Dec 04:29
♏ 6 Dec 07:20
♐ 8 Dec 07:17
♑ 10 Dec 06:17
♒ 12 Dec 06:35
♓ 14 Dec 10:11
♈ 16 Dec 17:59
♉ 18 Dec 05:10
♊ 21 Dec 17:50
♋ 24 Dec 06:18
♌ 26 Dec 17:46
♍ 29 Dec 03:42
♎ 31 Dec 11:20

MERCURY
♑ 1 Jan 00:00
♒ 1 Jan 12:40
♑ 15 Jan 07:36
♒ 14 Feb 19:13
♓ 7 Mar 22:05
♈ 24 Mar 15:52
♉ 8 Apr 11:13
♊ 14 Jun 14:33
♋ 2 Jul 14:58
♌ 16 Jul 17:09
♍ 2 Aug 02:44
♎ 27 Aug 14:17
♍ 10 Sep 19:16
♎ 9 Oct 14:41
♏ 27 Oct 10:37
♐ 15 Nov 03:11
♑ 5 Dec 01:58

VENUS
♒ 1 Jan 00:00
♓ 6 Apr 15:14
♈ 5 May 19:20
♉ 1 Jun 14:19
♊ 27 Jun 10:45
♋ 22 Jul 17:50
♌ 16 Aug 14:18
♍ 10 Sep 01:38
♎ 4 Oct 05:51
♏ 28 Oct 05:33
♐ 21 Nov 03:03
♑ 14 Dec 23:54

MARS
♎ 1 Jan 00:00
♍ 28 Mar 11:05
♎ 11 Jun 20:27
♏ 10 Aug 16:48
♐ 25 Sep 19:49
♑ 6 Nov 06:41
♒ 15 Dec 08:59

JUPITER
♒ 1 Jan 00:00
♓ 15 Apr 08:59
♒ 16 Sep 00:00
♓ 1 Dec 19:57

SATURN
♍ 1 Jan 00:00
♎ 20 Nov 15:50

1951

SUN
♑ 1 Jan 00:00
♒ 20 Jan 20:53
♓ 19 Feb 11:10
♈ 21 Mar 10:26
♉ 20 Apr 21:49
♊ 21 May 21:16
♋ 22 Jun 05:25
♌ 23 Jul 16:21
♍ 23 Aug 23:17
♎ 23 Sep 20:37
♏ 24 Oct 05:37
♐ 23 Nov 02:52
♑ 22 Dec 16:01

MOON
♎ 1 Jan 00:00
♏ 2 Jan 15:58
♐ 4 Jan 17:39
♑ 6 Jan 17:32
♒ 8 Jan 17:36
♓ 10 Jan 19:56
♈ 13 Jan 02:06
♉ 15 Jan 12:11
♊ 18 Jan 00:36
♋ 20 Jan 13:06
♌ 23 Jan 00:12
♍ 25 Jan 09:26
♎ 27 Jan 16:46
♏ 29 Jan 22:04
♐ 1 Feb 01:17
♑ 3 Feb 02:53
♒ 5 Feb 04:04
♓ 7 Feb 06:29
♈ 9 Feb 11:43
♉ 11 Feb 20:34
♊ 14 Feb 08:19
♋ 16 Feb 20:52
♌ 19 Feb 08:01
♍ 21 Feb 16:43
♎ 23 Feb 23:01
♏ 26 Feb 03:31
♐ 28 Feb 06:50
♑ 2 Mar 09:30
♒ 4 Mar 12:11
♓ 6 Mar 15:46
♈ 8 Mar 21:16
♉ 11 Mar 05:33
♊ 13 Mar 16:36
♋ 16 Mar 05:06
♌ 18 Mar 16:45
♍ 21 Mar 01:39
♎ 23 Mar 07:21
♏ 25 Mar 10:36
♐ 27 Mar 12:41
♑ 29 Mar 14:51
♒ 31 Mar 18:03
♓ 2 Apr 22:45
♈ 5 Apr 05:16
♉ 7 Apr 13:53
♊ 10 Apr 00:41
♋ 12 Apr 13:05
♌ 15 Apr 01:18
♍ 17 Apr 11:07
♎ 19 Apr 17:14
♏ 21 Apr 19:55
♐ 23 Apr 20:40
♑ 25 Apr 21:20
♒ 27 Apr 23:33
♓ 30 Apr 04:14
♈ 2 May 11:27
♉ 4 May 20:47
♊ 7 May 07:51
♋ 9 May 20:13
♌ 12 May 08:50
♍ 14 May 19:44
♎ 17 May 03:06
♏ 19 May 06:24
♐ 21 May 06:44
♑ 23 May 06:08
♒ 25 May 06:42
♓ 27 May 10:06
♈ 29 May 16:54
♉ 1 Jun 02:34
♊ 3 Jun 14:03
♋ 6 Jun 02:32
♌ 8 Jun 15:12
♍ 11 Jun 02:47
♎ 13 Jun 11:31
♏ 15 Jun 16:17
♐ 17 Jun 17:27
♑ 19 Jun 16:38
♒ 21 Jun 16:04
♓ 23 Jun 17:50
♈ 25 Jun 23:14
♉ 28 Jun 08:18
♊ 30 Jun 19:52
♋ 3 Jul 08:28
♌ 5 Jul 21:01
♍ 8 Jul 08:36
♎ 10 Jul 18:05
♏ 13 Jul 00:19
♐ 15 Jul 03:03
♑ 17 Jul 03:15
♒ 19 Jul 02:42
♓ 21 Jul 03:29
♈ 23 Jul 07:22
♉ 25 Jul 15:07
♊ 28 Jul 02:08
♋ 30 Jul 14:43
♌ 2 Aug 03:08
♍ 4 Aug 14:19
♎ 6 Aug 23:35
♏ 9 Aug 06:24
♐ 11 Aug 10:31
♑ 13 Aug 12:19
♒ 15 Aug 12:53
♓ 17 Aug 13:53
♈ 19 Aug 16:59
♉ 21 Aug 23:27
♊ 24 Aug 09:28
♋ 26 Aug 21:45
♌ 29 Aug 10:10
♍ 31 Aug 21:00
♎ 3 Sep 05:32
♏ 5 Sep 11:49
♐ 7 Sep 16:12
♑ 9 Sep 19:07
♒ 11 Sep 21:12
♓ 13 Sep 23:22
♈ 16 Sep 02:48
♉ 18 Sep 08:42
♊ 20 Sep 17:47
♋ 23 Sep 05:35
♌ 25 Sep 18:08
♍ 28 Sep 05:06
♎ 30 Sep 13:09
♏ 2 Oct 18:24
♐ 4 Oct 21:48
♑ 7 Oct 00:30
♒ 9 Oct 03:19
♓ 11 Oct 06:47
♈ 13 Oct 11:20
♉ 15 Oct 17:37
♊ 18 Oct 02:22
♋ 20 Oct 13:43
♌ 23 Oct 02:25
♍ 25 Oct 14:02
♎ 27 Oct 22:26
♏ 30 Oct 03:10
♐ 1 Nov 05:20
♑ 3 Nov 06:40
♒ 5 Nov 08:43
♓ 7 Nov 12:23
♈ 9 Nov 17:53
♉ 12 Nov 01:08
♊ 14 Nov 10:16
♋ 16 Nov 21:28
♌ 19 Nov 10:12
♍ 21 Nov 22:36
♎ 24 Nov 08:09
♏ 26 Nov 13:32
♐ 28 Nov 15:20
♑ 30 Nov 15:23
♒ 2 Dec 15:45
♓ 4 Dec 18:08
♈ 6 Dec 23:18
♉ 9 Dec 07:05
♊ 11 Dec 16:54
♋ 14 Dec 04:23
♌ 16 Dec 17:05
♍ 19 Dec 05:53
♎ 21 Dec 16:41
♏ 23 Dec 23:39
♐ 26 Dec 02:27
♑ 28 Dec 02:24
♒ 30 Dec 01:36

MERCURY
♑ 1 Jan 00:00
♒ 9 Feb 17:51
♓ 28 Feb 13:05
♈ 16 Mar 11:54
♉ 2 Apr 03:28
♈ 1 May 21:25
♉ 15 May 01:41
♊ 9 Jun 08:44
♋ 24 Jun 03:14
♌ 9 Jul 13:39
♍ 27 Jul 15:24
♎ 2 Oct 14:26
♏ 19 Oct 21:53
♐ 8 Nov 04:59
♑ 1 Dec 20:41
♐ 12 Dec 12:40

VENUS
♑ 1 Jan 00:00
♒ 7 Jan 21:11
♓ 31 Jan 20:15
♈ 24 Feb 23:27
♉ 21 Mar 10:06
♊ 15 Apr 08:34
♋ 11 May 01:42
♌ 7 Jun 05:10
♍ 8 Jul 04:54
♎ 9 Nov 18:48
♏ 8 Dec 00:19

MARS
♒ 1 Jan 00:00
♓ 22 Jan 13:06
♈ 1 Mar 22:04
♉ 10 Apr 09:37
♊ 21 May 15:32
♋ 3 Jul 23:42
♌ 18 Aug 10:56
♍ 5 Oct 00:20
♎ 24 Nov 06:12

JUPITER
♓ 1 Jan 00:00
♈ 21 Apr 14:57

SATURN
♎ 1 Jan 00:00
♍ 7 Mar 12:14
♎ 13 Aug 16:44

1952

SUN
♑ 1 Jan 00:00
♒ 21 Jan 02:39
♓ 19 Feb 16:57
♈ 20 Mar 16:14
♉ 20 Apr 03:37
♊ 21 May 03:04
♋ 21 Jun 11:13
♌ 22 Jul 22:08
♍ 23 Aug 05:03
♎ 23 Sep 02:24
♏ 23 Oct 11:23
♐ 22 Nov 08:36
♑ 21 Dec 21:44

MOON
♒ 1 Jan 00:00
♓ 1 Jan 02:11
♈ 3 Jan 05:42
♉ 5 Jan 12:44
♊ 7 Jan 22:43
♋ 10 Jan 10:35
♌ 12 Jan 23:20
♍ 15 Jan 12:01
♎ 17 Jan 23:20
♏ 20 Jan 07:44
♐ 22 Jan 12:41
♑ 24 Jan 13:39
♒ 26 Jan 13:07
♓ 28 Jan 12:46
♈ 30 Jan 14:33
♉ 1 Feb 19:51
♊ 4 Feb 04:55
♋ 6 Feb 16:44
♌ 9 Feb 05:36
♍ 11 Feb 18:02
♎ 14 Feb 05:01
♏ 16 Feb 13:45
♐ 18 Feb 19:43
♑ 20 Feb 22:50
♒ 22 Feb 23:49
♓ 25 Feb 00:01
♈ 27 Feb 01:12
♉ 29 Feb 05:02
♊ 2 Mar 12:37
♋ 4 Mar 23:41
♌ 7 Mar 12:31
♍ 10 Mar 00:52
♎ 12 Mar 11:17
♏ 14 Mar 19:21
♐ 17 Mar 01:16
♑ 19 Mar 05:20
♒ 21 Mar 07:55
♓ 23 Mar 09:39
♈ 25 Mar 11:34
♉ 27 Mar 15:06
♊ 29 Mar 21:36
♋ 1 Apr 07:39
♌ 3 Apr 20:10
♍ 6 Apr 08:41
♎ 8 Apr 18:56
♏ 11 Apr 02:14
♐ 13 Apr 07:08
♑ 15 Apr 10:42
♒ 17 Apr 13:44
♓ 19 Apr 16:41
♈ 21 Apr 19:57
♉ 24 Apr 00:15
♊ 26 Apr 06:41
♋ 28 Apr 16:06
♌ 1 May 04:13
♍ 3 May 16:58
♎ 6 May 03:39
♏ 8 May 10:49
♐ 10 May 14:51
♑ 12 May 17:09
♒ 14 May 19:15
♓ 16 May 22:06
♈ 19 May 02:07
♉ 21 May 07:30
♊ 23 May 14:38
♋ 26 May 00:06
♌ 28 May 12:00
♍ 31 May 00:57
♎ 2 Jun 12:26
♏ 4 Jun 20:20
♐ 7 Jun 00:21
♑ 9 Jun 01:47
♒ 11 Jun 02:27
♓ 13 Jun 04:01
♈ 15 Jun 07:29
♉ 17 Jun 13:11
♊ 19 Jun 21:04
♋ 22 Jun 07:04
♌ 24 Jun 19:03
♍ 27 Jun 08:07
♎ 29 Jun 20:19
♏ 2 Jul 05:26
♐ 4 Jul 10:27
♑ 6 Jul 12:03
♒ 8 Jul 11:55
♓ 10 Jul 12:00
♈ 12 Jul 13:56
♉ 14 Jul 18:46
♊ 17 Jul 02:38
♋ 19 Jul 13:05
♌ 22 Jul 01:21
♍ 24 Jul 14:25
♎ 27 Jul 02:54
♏ 29 Jul 13:05
♐ 31 Jul 19:38
♑ 2 Aug 22:28
♒ 4 Aug 22:41
♓ 6 Aug 22:05
♈ 8 Aug 22:34
♉ 11 Aug 01:46
♊ 13 Aug 08:37
♋ 15 Aug 18:53
♌ 18 Aug 07:19
♍ 20 Aug 20:23
♎ 23 Aug 08:42
♏ 25 Aug 19:11
♐ 28 Aug 02:54
♑ 30 Aug 07:24
♒ 1 Sep 09:03
♓ 3 Sep 09:00
♈ 5 Sep 08:58
♉ 7 Sep 10:48
♊ 9 Sep 16:06
♋ 12 Sep 01:24
♌ 14 Sep 13:39
♍ 17 Sep 02:42
♎ 19 Sep 14:42
♏ 22 Sep 00:44
♐ 24 Sep 08:33
♑ 26 Sep 14:06
♒ 28 Sep 17:25
♓ 30 Sep 18:53
♈ 2 Oct 19:34
♉ 4 Oct 21:06
♊ 7 Oct 01:15
♋ 9 Oct 09:16
♌ 11 Oct 20:51
♍ 14 Oct 09:51
♎ 16 Oct 21:45
♏ 19 Oct 07:10
♐ 21 Oct 14:12
♑ 23 Oct 19:29
♒ 25 Oct 23:28
♓ 28 Oct 02:23
♈ 30 Oct 04:35
♉ 1 Nov 06:59
♊ 3 Nov 11:02
♋ 5 Nov 18:13
♌ 8 Nov 04:57
♍ 10 Nov 17:47
♎ 13 Nov 05:58
♏ 15 Nov 15:19
♐ 17 Nov 21:34
♑ 20 Nov 01:41
♒ 22 Nov 04:52
♓ 24 Nov 07:55
♈ 26 Nov 11:10
♉ 28 Nov 14:55
♊ 30 Nov 19:53
♋ 3 Dec 03:09
♌ 5 Dec 13:23
♍ 8 Dec 01:58
♎ 10 Dec 14:36
♏ 13 Dec 00:39
♐ 15 Dec 07:00
♑ 17 Dec 10:18
♒ 19 Dec 12:03
♓ 21 Dec 13:46
♈ 23 Dec 16:30
♉ 25 Dec 20:46
♊ 28 Dec 02:48
♋ 30 Dec 10:54

MERCURY
♐ 1 Jan 00:00
♑ 13 Jan 06:45
♒ 3 Feb 01:38
♓ 20 Feb 18:55
♈ 7 Mar 17:10
♉ 14 May 14:44
♊ 31 May 15:26
♋ 14 Jun 12:22
♌ 30 Jun 10:27
♍ 7 Sep 12:03
♎ 23 Sep 18:46
♏ 11 Oct 13:06
♐ 1 Nov 05:34

VENUS
♏ 1 Jan 00:00
♐ 2 Jan 18:45
♑ 27 Jan 15:58
♒ 21 Feb 04:43
♓ 16 Mar 14:18
♈ 9 Apr 23:18
♉ 4 May 08:55
♊ 28 May 19:19
♋ 22 Jun 05:47
♌ 16 Jul 15:23
♍ 9 Aug 23:58
♎ 3 Sep 08:18
♏ 27 Sep 17:36
♐ 22 Oct 05:02
♑ 15 Nov 20:03
♒ 10 Dec 18:31

MARS
♎ 1 Jan 00:00
♏ 20 Jan 01:33
♐ 27 Aug 18:54
♑ 12 Oct 04:45
♒ 21 Nov 19:40
♓ 30 Dec 21:36

JUPITER
♈ 1 Jan 00:00
♉ 28 Apr 20:51

SATURN
♎ 1 Jan 00:00

1953

SUN
♑ 1 Jan 00:00
♒ 20 Jan 08:22
♓ 18 Feb 22:42
♈ 20 Mar 22:01
♉ 20 Apr 09:26
♊ 21 May 08:53
♋ 21 Jun 17:00
♌ 23 Jul 03:53
♍ 23 Aug 10:46
♎ 23 Sep 08:06
♏ 23 Oct 17:07
♐ 22 Nov 14:23
♑ 22 Dec 03:32

MOON
♋ 1 Jan 00:00
♌ 1 Jan 21:18
♍ 4 Jan 09:41
♎ 6 Jan 22:37
♏ 9 Jan 09:44
♐ 11 Jan 17:15
♑ 13 Jan 20:55
♒ 15 Jan 21:58
♓ 17 Jan 22:07
♈ 19 Jan 23:09
♉ 22 Jan 02:21
♊ 24 Jan 08:21
♋ 26 Jan 17:07
♌ 29 Jan 04:06
♍ 31 Jan 16:36
♎ 3 Feb 05:32
♏ 5 Feb 17:21
♐ 8 Feb 02:21
♑ 10 Feb 07:32
♒ 12 Feb 09:17
♓ 14 Feb 08:58
♈ 16 Feb 08:31
♉ 18 Feb 09:51
♊ 20 Feb 14:27
♋ 22 Feb 22:48
♌ 25 Feb 10:06
♍ 27 Feb 22:51
♎ 2 Mar 11:41
♏ 4 Mar 23:31
♐ 7 Mar 09:20
♑ 9 Mar 16:10
♒ 11 Mar 19:38
♓ 13 Mar 20:17
♈ 15 Mar 19:39
♉ 17 Mar 19:45
♊ 19 Mar 22:35
♋ 22 Mar 05:30
♌ 24 Mar 16:15
♍ 27 Mar 05:04
♎ 29 Mar 17:52
♏ 1 Apr 05:20
♐ 3 Apr 14:59
♑ 5 Apr 22:29
♒ 8 Apr 03:28
♓ 10 Apr 05:50
♈ 12 Apr 06:19
♉ 14 Apr 06:32
♊ 16 Apr 08:27
♋ 18 Apr 13:53
♌ 20 Apr 23:27
♍ 23 Apr 11:53
♎ 26 Apr 00:41
♏ 28 Apr 11:52
♐ 30 Apr 20:53
♑ 3 May 03:55
♒ 5 May 09:13
♓ 7 May 12:47
♈ 9 May 14:49
♉ 11 May 16:12
♊ 13 May 18:27
♋ 15 May 23:17
♌ 18 May 07:47
♍ 20 May 19:31
♎ 23 May 08:16
♏ 25 May 19:33
♐ 28 May 04:09
♑ 30 May 10:17
♒ 1 Jun 14:46
♓ 3 Jun 18:12
♈ 5 Jun 21:02
♉ 7 Jun 23:42
♊ 10 Jun 03:03
♋ 12 Jun 08:18
♌ 14 Jun 16:28
♍ 17 Jun 03:37
♎ 19 Jun 16:17
♏ 22 Jun 03:58
♐ 24 Jun 12:48
♑ 26 Jun 18:29
♒ 28 Jun 21:52
♓ 1 Jul 00:09
♈ 3 Jul 02:24
♉ 5 Jul 05:54
♊ 7 Jul 09:43
♋ 9 Jul 15:55
♌ 12 Jul 00:28
♍ 14 Jul 11:29
♎ 17 Jul 00:04
♏ 19 Jul 12:17
♐ 21 Jul 21:59
♑ 24 Jul 04:07
♒ 26 Jul 07:03
♓ 28 Jul 08:07
♈ 30 Jul 08:56
♉ 1 Aug 10:57
♊ 3 Aug 15:11
♋ 5 Aug 22:00
♌ 8 Aug 07:16
♍ 10 Aug 18:34
♎ 13 Aug 07:09
♏ 15 Aug 19:44
♐ 18 Aug 06:30
♑ 20 Aug 13:53
♒ 22 Aug 17:29
♓ 24 Aug 18:12
♈ 26 Aug 17:46
♉ 28 Aug 18:11
♊ 30 Aug 21:07
♋ 2 Sep 03:30
♌ 4 Sep 13:05
♍ 7 Sep 00:48
♎ 9 Sep 13:28
♏ 12 Sep 02:06
♐ 14 Sep 13:32
♑ 16 Sep 22:21
♒ 19 Sep 03:30
♓ 21 Sep 05:07
♈ 23 Sep 04:31
♉ 25 Sep 03:45
♊ 27 Sep 05:01
♋ 29 Sep 09:57
♌ 1 Oct 18:54
♍ 4 Oct 06:41
♎ 6 Oct 19:28
♏ 9 Oct 07:57
♐ 11 Oct 19:20
♑ 14 Oct 04:52
♒ 16 Oct 11:35
♓ 18 Oct 14:56
♈ 20 Oct 15:27
♉ 22 Oct 14:47
♊ 24 Oct 15:05
♋ 26 Oct 18:24
♌ 29 Oct 01:55
♍ 31 Oct 13:05
♎ 3 Nov 01:51
♏ 5 Nov 14:12
♐ 8 Nov 01:07
♑ 10 Nov 10:19
♒ 12 Nov 17:31
♓ 14 Nov 22:18
♈ 17 Nov 00:36
♉ 19 Nov 01:15
♊ 21 Nov 01:55
♋ 23 Nov 04:32
♌ 25 Nov 10:41
♍ 27 Nov 20:41
♎ 30 Nov 09:06
♏ 2 Dec 21:31
♐ 5 Dec 08:09
♑ 7 Dec 16:33
♒ 9 Dec 23:00
♓ 12 Dec 03:47
♈ 14 Dec 07:07
♉ 16 Dec 09:23
♊ 18 Dec 11:28
♋ 20 Dec 14:40
♌ 22 Dec 20:23
♍ 25 Dec 05:24
♎ 27 Dec 17:11
♏ 30 Dec 05:43

MERCURY
♐ 1 Jan 00:00
♑ 6 Jan 13:24
♒ 25 Jan 19:11
♓ 11 Feb 23:57
♈ 2 Mar 19:21
♓ 15 Mar 21:17
♈ 17 Apr 16:48
♉ 8 May 06:24
♊ 23 May 03:59
♋ 6 Jun 08:24
♌ 26 Jun 11:01
♋ 28 Jul 13:41
♌ 11 Aug 14:05
♍ 30 Aug 22:59
♎ 15 Sep 21:45
♏ 4 Oct 16:41
♐ 31 Oct 15:50
♏ 6 Nov 22:19
♐ 10 Dec 14:49
♑ 30 Dec 17:14

VENUS
♒ 1 Jan 00:00
♓ 5 Jan 11:11
♈ 2 Feb 05:55
♉ 14 Mar 18:58
♈ 31 Mar 05:18
♉ 5 Jun 10:34
♊ 7 Jul 10:30
♋ 4 Aug 01:09
♌ 30 Aug 01:35
♍ 24 Sep 03:48
♎ 18 Oct 15:27
♏ 11 Nov 18:12
♐ 5 Dec 16:24
♑ 29 Dec 12:54

MARS
♓ 1 Jan 00:00
♈ 8 Feb 01:07
♉ 20 Mar 06:54
♊ 1 May 06:08
♋ 14 Jun 03:49
♌ 29 Jul 19:26
♍ 14 Sep 17:59
♎ 1 Nov 14:19
♏ 20 Dec 11:23

JUPITER
♉ 1 Jan 00:00
♊ 9 May 15:34

SATURN
♎ 1 Jan 00:00
♏ 22 Oct 15:36

1954

SUN
♑ 1 Jan 00:00
♒ 20 Jan 14:12
♓ 19 Feb 04:33
♈ 21 Mar 03:54
♉ 20 Apr 15:20
♊ 21 May 14:48
♋ 21 Jun 22:55
♌ 23 Jul 09:45
♍ 23 Aug 16:36
♎ 23 Sep 13:56
♏ 23 Oct 22:57
♐ 22 Nov 20:15
♑ 22 Dec 09:25

MOON
♏ 1 Jan 00:00
♐ 1 Jan 16:40
♑ 4 Jan 00:46
♒ 6 Jan 06:10
♓ 8 Jan 09:43
♈ 10 Jan 12:27
♉ 12 Jan 15:10
♊ 14 Jan 18:30
♋ 16 Jan 23:01
♌ 19 Jan 05:25
♍ 21 Jan 14:14
♎ 24 Jan 01:30
♏ 26 Jan 14:04
♐ 29 Jan 01:43
♑ 31 Jan 10:27
♒ 2 Feb 15:38
♓ 4 Feb 18:04
♈ 6 Feb 19:15
♉ 9 Feb 20:47
♊ 10 Feb 23:55
♋ 13 Feb 05:10
♌ 15 Feb 12:36
♍ 17 Feb 22:01
♎ 20 Feb 09:15
♏ 22 Feb 21:44
♐ 25 Feb 10:01
♑ 27 Feb 19:58
♒ 2 Mar 02:07
♓ 4 Mar 04:33
♈ 6 Mar 04:41
♉ 8 Mar 04:33
♊ 10 Mar 06:07
♋ 12 Mar 10:38
♌ 14 Mar 18:17
♍ 17 Mar 04:22
♎ 19 Mar 15:58
♏ 22 Mar 04:27
♐ 24 Mar 16:57
♑ 27 Mar 03:56
♒ 29 Mar 11:38
♓ 31 Mar 15:17
♈ 2 Apr 15:40
♉ 4 Apr 14:43
♊ 6 Apr 14:40
♋ 8 Apr 17:29
♌ 11 Apr 00:06
♍ 13 Apr 10:03
♎ 15 Apr 21:58
♏ 18 Apr 10:33
♐ 20 Apr 22:55
♑ 23 Apr 10:12
♒ 25 Apr 19:03
♓ 28 Apr 00:22
♈ 30 Apr 02:09
♉ 2 May 01:43
♊ 4 May 01:07
♋ 6 May 02:30
♌ 8 May 07:29
♍ 10 May 16:23
♎ 13 May 04:04
♏ 15 May 16:42
♐ 18 May 04:54
♑ 20 May 15:49
♒ 23 May 00:49
♓ 25 May 07:09
♈ 27 May 10:32
♉ 29 May 11:34
♊ 31 May 11:41
♋ 2 Jun 12:46
♌ 4 Jun 16:35
♍ 7 Jun 00:07
♎ 9 Jun 10:59
♏ 11 Jun 23:50
♐ 14 Jun 11:38
♑ 16 Jun 22:06
♒ 19 Jun 06:26
♓ 21 Jun 12:37
♈ 23 Jun 16:44
♉ 25 Jun 19:09
♊ 27 Jun 20:42
♋ 29 Jun 22:36
♌ 2 Jul 02:17
♍ 4 Jul 08:56
♎ 6 Jul 18:54
♏ 9 Jul 07:04
♐ 11 Jul 19:19
♑ 14 Jul 05:40
♒ 16 Jul 13:20
♓ 18 Jul 18:33
♈ 20 Jul 22:08
♉ 23 Jul 00:53
♊ 25 Jul 03:31
♋ 27 Jul 06:42
♌ 29 Jul 11:11
♍ 31 Jul 17:50
♎ 3 Aug 03:14
♏ 5 Aug 15:03
♐ 8 Aug 03:33
♑ 10 Aug 14:21
♒ 12 Aug 21:55
♓ 15 Aug 02:17
♈ 17 Aug 04:38
♉ 19 Aug 06:26
♊ 21 Aug 08:57
♋ 23 Aug 12:50
♌ 25 Aug 18:23
♍ 28 Aug 01:44
♎ 30 Aug 11:12
♏ 1 Sep 22:49
♐ 4 Sep 11:33
♑ 6 Sep 23:10
♒ 9 Sep 07:31
♓ 11 Sep 11:55
♈ 13 Sep 13:23
♉ 15 Sep 13:45
♊ 17 Sep 14:55
♋ 19 Sep 18:13
♌ 22 Sep 00:04
♍ 24 Sep 08:11
♎ 26 Sep 18:11
♏ 29 Sep 05:52
♐ 1 Oct 18:42
♑ 4 Oct 07:05
♒ 6 Oct 16:46
♓ 8 Oct 22:17
♈ 10 Oct 23:59
♉ 12 Oct 23:32
♊ 14 Oct 23:10
♋ 17 Oct 00:50
♌ 19 Oct 05:41
♍ 21 Oct 13:45
♎ 24 Oct 00:12
♏ 26 Oct 12:11
♐ 29 Oct 00:59
♑ 31 Oct 13:37
♒ 3 Nov 00:23
♓ 5 Nov 07:35
♈ 7 Nov 10:43
♉ 9 Nov 10:49
♊ 11 Nov 09:51
♋ 13 Nov 10:00
♌ 15 Nov 13:03
♍ 17 Nov 19:53
♎ 20 Nov 06:03
♏ 22 Nov 18:13
♐ 25 Nov 07:02
♑ 27 Nov 19:24
♒ 30 Nov 06:20
♓ 2 Dec 14:39
♈ 4 Dec 19:35
♉ 6 Dec 21:23
♊ 8 Dec 21:17
♋ 10 Dec 21:07
♌ 12 Dec 22:49
♍ 15 Dec 03:54
♎ 17 Dec 12:52
♏ 20 Dec 00:44
♐ 22 Dec 13:35
♑ 25 Dec 01:41
♒ 27 Dec 12:01
♓ 29 Dec 20:10

MERCURY
♑ 1 Jan 00:00
♒ 18 Jan 07:44
♓ 4 Feb 18:03
♈ 13 Apr 11:35
♉ 30 Apr 11:26
♊ 14 May 13:58
♋ 30 May 16:13
♌ 7 Aug 14:44
♍ 22 Aug 17:42
♎ 8 Sep 08:06
♏ 29 Sep 04:07
♎ 4 Nov 12:37
♏ 11 Nov 10:25
♐ 4 Dec 07:03
♑ 23 Dec 12:10

VENUS
♑ 1 Jan 00:00
♒ 22 Jan 09:21
♓ 15 Feb 10:28
♈ 11 Mar 07:22
♉ 4 Apr 11:56
♊ 28 Apr 22:04
♋ 23 May 15:04
♌ 17 Jun 17:05
♍ 13 Jul 08:43
♎ 9 Aug 00:34
♏ 6 Sep 23:29
♐ 23 Oct 22:08
♏ 27 Oct 10:43

MARS
♏ 1 Jan 00:00
♐ 9 Feb 19:18
♑ 12 Apr 16:28
♐ 3 Jul 07:23
♑ 24 Aug 13:23
♒ 21 Oct 12:03
♓ 4 Dec 07:42

JUPITER
♊ 1 Jan 00:00
♋ 24 May 04:44

SATURN
♏ 1 Jan 00:00

1955

SUN
♑ 1 Jan 00:00
♒ 20 Jan 20:02
♓ 19 Feb 10:19
♈ 21 Mar 09:36
♉ 20 Apr 20:58
♊ 21 May 20:25
♋ 22 Jun 04:32
♌ 23 Jul 15:25
♍ 23 Aug 22:19
♎ 23 Sep 19:41
♏ 24 Oct 04:44
♐ 23 Nov 02:01
♑ 22 Dec 15:11

MOON
♓ 1 Jan 00:00
♈ 1 Jan 01:57
♉ 3 Jan 05:25
♊ 5 Jan 07:05
♋ 7 Jan 08:01
♌ 9 Jan 09:42
♍ 11 Jan 13:43
♎ 13 Jan 21:15
♏ 16 Jan 08:15
♐ 18 Jan 21:02
♑ 21 Jan 09:10
♒ 23 Jan 18:59
♓ 26 Jan 02:11
♈ 28 Jan 07:20
♉ 30 Jan 11:06
♊ 1 Feb 14:03
♋ 3 Feb 16:37
♌ 5 Feb 19:29
♍ 7 Feb 23:43
♎ 10 Feb 06:34
♏ 12 Feb 16:39
♐ 15 Feb 05:08
♑ 17 Feb 17:35
♒ 20 Feb 03:33
♓ 22 Feb 10:10
♈ 24 Feb 14:06
♉ 26 Feb 16:47
♊ 28 Feb 19:24
♋ 2 Mar 22:40
♌ 5 Mar 02:49
♍ 7 Mar 08:09
♎ 9 Mar 15:20
♏ 12 Mar 01:05
♐ 14 Mar 13:14
♑ 17 Mar 02:02
♒ 19 Mar 12:47
♓ 21 Mar 19:45
♈ 23 Mar 23:10
♉ 26 Mar 00:32
♊ 28 Mar 01:42
♋ 30 Mar 04:06
♌ 1 Apr 08:21
♍ 3 Apr 14:31
♎ 5 Apr 22:34
♏ 8 Apr 08:38
♐ 10 Apr 20:42
♑ 13 Apr 09:41
♒ 15 Apr 21:20
♓ 18 Apr 05:29
♈ 20 Apr 09:30
♉ 22 Apr 10:30
♊ 24 Apr 10:24
♋ 26 Apr 11:09
♌ 28 Apr 14:09
♍ 30 Apr 19:58
♎ 3 May 04:26
♏ 5 May 15:04
♐ 8 May 03:19
♑ 10 May 16:19
♒ 13 May 04:30
♓ 15 May 13:54
♈ 17 May 19:21
♉ 19 May 21:12
♊ 21 May 20:57
♋ 23 May 20:33
♌ 25 May 21:53
♍ 28 May 02:16
♎ 30 May 10:08
♏ 1 Jun 20:54
♐ 4 Jun 09:24
♑ 6 Jun 22:21
♒ 9 Jun 10:30
♓ 11 Jun 20:32
♈ 14 Jun 03:24
♉ 16 Jun 06:50
♊ 18 Jun 07:37
♋ 20 Jun 07:16
♌ 22 Jun 07:37
♍ 24 Jun 10:27
♎ 26 Jun 16:56
♏ 29 Jun 03:05
♐ 1 Jul 15:34
♑ 4 Jul 04:30
♒ 6 Jul 16:19
♓ 9 Jul 02:09
♈ 11 Jul 09:33
♉ 13 Jul 14:21
♊ 15 Jul 16:43
♋ 17 Jul 17:30
♌ 19 Jul 18:04
♍ 21 Jul 20:07
♎ 24 Jul 01:16
♏ 26 Jul 10:19
♐ 28 Jul 22:24
♑ 31 Jul 11:19
♒ 2 Aug 22:52
♓ 5 Aug 08:04
♈ 7 Aug 15:00
♉ 9 Aug 20:03
♊ 11 Aug 23:34
♋ 14 Aug 01:51
♌ 16 Aug 03:34
♍ 18 Aug 05:58
♎ 20 Aug 10:34
♏ 22 Aug 18:38
♐ 25 Aug 06:04
♑ 27 Aug 18:57
♒ 30 Aug 06:36
♓ 1 Sep 15:23
♈ 3 Sep 21:24
♉ 6 Sep 01:37
♊ 8 Sep 04:59
♋ 10 Sep 08:01
♌ 12 Sep 11:02
♍ 14 Sep 14:34
♎ 16 Sep 19:36
♏ 19 Sep 03:19
♐ 21 Sep 14:12
♑ 24 Sep 03:01
♒ 26 Sep 15:08
♓ 29 Sep 00:13
♈ 1 Oct 05:47
♉ 3 Oct 08:52
♊ 5 Oct 11:00
♋ 7 Oct 13:23
♌ 9 Oct 16:42
♍ 11 Oct 21:12
♎ 14 Oct 03:14
♏ 16 Oct 11:24
♐ 18 Oct 22:08
♑ 21 Oct 10:52
♒ 23 Oct 23:33
♓ 26 Oct 09:38
♈ 28 Oct 15:46
♉ 30 Oct 18:30
♊ 1 Nov 19:23
♋ 3 Nov 20:12
♌ 5 Nov 22:20
♍ 8 Nov 02:37
♎ 10 Nov 09:16
♏ 12 Nov 18:13
♐ 15 Nov 05:17
♑ 17 Nov 17:59
♒ 20 Nov 06:59
♓ 22 Nov 18:11
♈ 25 Nov 01:48
♉ 27 Nov 05:27
♊ 29 Nov 06:11
♋ 1 Dec 05:47
♌ 3 Dec 06:08
♍ 5 Dec 08:50
♎ 7 Dec 14:49
♏ 10 Dec 00:00
♐ 12 Dec 11:34
♑ 15 Dec 00:24
♒ 17 Dec 13:20
♓ 20 Dec 01:02
♈ 22 Dec 10:06
♉ 24 Dec 15:33
♊ 26 Dec 17:33
♋ 28 Dec 17:18
♌ 30 Dec 16:37

MERCURY
♑ 1 Jan 00:00
♒ 10 Jan 23:05
♓ 17 Mar 20:50
♈ 6 Apr 16:15
♉ 22 Apr 02:58
♊ 6 May 13:05
♋ 13 Jul 14:45
♌ 30 Jul 17:23
♍ 14 Aug 13:08
♎ 1 Sep 12:06
♏ 8 Nov 06:57
♐ 27 Nov 04:35
♑ 16 Dec 06:07

VENUS
♏ 1 Jan 00:00
♐ 6 Jan 06:49
♑ 6 Feb 01:16
♒ 4 Mar 20:22
♓ 30 Mar 11:31
♈ 24 Apr 15:13
♉ 19 May 13:36
♊ 13 Jun 08:38
♋ 8 Jul 00:16
♌ 1 Aug 11:43
♍ 25 Aug 18:53
♎ 18 Sep 22:41
♏ 13 Oct 00:39
♐ 6 Nov 02:03
♑ 30 Nov 03:43
♒ 24 Dec 06:53

MARS
♓ 1 Jan 00:00
♈ 15 Jan 04:34
♉ 26 Feb 10:23
♊ 10 Apr 23:09
♋ 26 May 00:50
♌ 11 Jul 09:23
♍ 27 Aug 10:14
♎ 13 Oct 11:20
♏ 29 Nov 01:34

JUPITER
♋ 1 Jan 00:00
♌ 13 Jun 00:07
♍ 17 Nov 03:59

SATURN
♏ 1 Jan 00:00

1956

SUN
♑ 1 Jan 00:00
♒ 21 Jan 01:49
♓ 19 Feb 16:05
♈ 20 Mar 15:21
♉ 20 Apr 02:44
♊ 21 May 02:13
♋ 21 Jun 10:24
♌ 22 Jul 21:20
♍ 23 Aug 04:15
♎ 23 Sep 01:36
♏ 23 Oct 10:35
♐ 22 Nov 07:50
♑ 21 Dec 21:00

MOON
♌ 1 Jan 00:00
♍ 1 Jan 17:31
♎ 3 Jan 21:44
♏ 6 Jan 06:00
♐ 8 Jan 17:33
♑ 11 Jan 06:34
♒ 13 Jan 19:20
♓ 16 Jan 06:48
♈ 18 Jan 16:18
♉ 20 Jan 23:12
♊ 23 Jan 03:06
♋ 25 Jan 04:20
♌ 27 Jan 04:07
♍ 29 Jan 04:18
♎ 31 Jan 06:56
♏ 2 Feb 13:34
♐ 5 Feb 00:13
♑ 7 Feb 13:09
♒ 10 Feb 01:52
♓ 12 Feb 12:52
♈ 14 Feb 21:49
♉ 17 Feb 04:49
♊ 19 Feb 09:51
♋ 21 Feb 12:50
♌ 23 Feb 14:11
♍ 25 Feb 15:05
♎ 27 Feb 17:21
♏ 29 Feb 22:45
♐ 3 Mar 08:10
♑ 5 Mar 20:33
♒ 8 Mar 09:20
♓ 10 Mar 20:12
♈ 13 Mar 04:27
♉ 15 Mar 10:32
♊ 17 Mar 15:12
♋ 19 Mar 18:48
♌ 21 Mar 21:31
♍ 23 Mar 23:53
♎ 26 Mar 03:00
♏ 28 Mar 08:19
♐ 30 Mar 16:56
♑ 2 Apr 04:38
♒ 4 Apr 17:25
♓ 7 Apr 04:38
♈ 9 Apr 12:47
♉ 11 Apr 18:04
♊ 13 Apr 21:31
♋ 16 Apr 00:15
♌ 18 Apr 03:01
♍ 20 Apr 06:17
♎ 22 Apr 10:37
♏ 24 Apr 16:45
♐ 27 Apr 01:26
♑ 29 Apr 12:45
♒ 2 May 01:28
♓ 4 May 13:16
♈ 6 May 22:06
♉ 9 May 03:24
♊ 11 May 06:01
♋ 13 May 07:21
♌ 15 May 08:52
♍ 17 May 11:40
♎ 19 May 16:26
♏ 21 May 23:27
♐ 24 May 08:47
♑ 26 May 20:12
♒ 29 May 08:52
♓ 31 May 21:10
♈ 3 Jun 07:05
♉ 5 Jun 13:22
♊ 7 Jun 16:10
♋ 9 Jun 16:42
♌ 11 Jun 16:45
♍ 13 Jun 18:04
♎ 15 Jun 21:59
♏ 18 Jun 05:03
♐ 20 Jun 14:56
♑ 23 Jun 02:43
♒ 25 Jun 15:26
♓ 28 Jun 03:55
♈ 30 Jun 14:43
♉ 2 Jul 22:26
♊ 5 Jul 02:26
♋ 7 Jul 03:20
♌ 9 Jul 02:42
♍ 11 Jul 02:35
♎ 13 Jul 04:55
♏ 15 Jul 10:57
♐ 17 Jul 20:38
♑ 20 Jul 08:41
♒ 22 Jul 21:29
♓ 25 Jul 09:51
♈ 27 Jul 20:54
♉ 30 Jul 05:41
♊ 1 Aug 11:16
♋ 3 Aug 13:33
♌ 5 Aug 13:27
♍ 7 Aug 12:50
♎ 9 Aug 13:51
♏ 11 Aug 18:21
♐ 14 Aug 03:00
♑ 16 Aug 14:48
♒ 19 Aug 03:38
♓ 21 Aug 15:48
♈ 24 Aug 02:30
♉ 26 Aug 11:24
♊ 28 Aug 18:00
♋ 30 Aug 21:52
♌ 1 Sep 23:14
♍ 3 Sep 23:21
♎ 6 Sep 00:05
♏ 8 Sep 03:27
♐ 10 Sep 10:46
♑ 12 Sep 21:46
♒ 15 Sep 10:28
♓ 17 Sep 22:34
♈ 20 Sep 08:48
♉ 22 Sep 17:01
♊ 24 Sep 23:25
♋ 27 Sep 04:00
♌ 29 Sep 06:49
♍ 1 Oct 08:25
♎ 3 Oct 10:02
♏ 5 Oct 13:19
♐ 7 Oct 19:46
♑ 10 Oct 05:48
♒ 12 Oct 18:10
♓ 15 Oct 06:25
♈ 17 Oct 16:36
♉ 20 Oct 00:08
♊ 22 Oct 05:29
♋ 24 Oct 09:24
♌ 26 Oct 12:27
♍ 28 Oct 15:10
♎ 30 Oct 18:10
♏ 1 Nov 22:25
♐ 4 Nov 04:57
♑ 6 Nov 14:24
♒ 9 Nov 02:20
♓ 11 Nov 14:51
♈ 14 Nov 01:37
♉ 16 Nov 09:13
♊ 18 Nov 13:45
♋ 20 Nov 16:18
♌ 22 Nov 18:10
♍ 24 Nov 20:32
♎ 27 Nov 00:11
♏ 29 Nov 05:35
♐ 1 Dec 12:59
♑ 3 Dec 22:36
♒ 6 Dec 10:17
♓ 8 Dec 22:57
♈ 11 Dec 10:37
♉ 13 Dec 19:16
♊ 16 Dec 00:07
♋ 18 Dec 01:52
♌ 20 Dec 02:12
♍ 22 Dec 02:56
♎ 24 Dec 05:39
♏ 26 Dec 11:09
♐ 28 Dec 19:20
♑ 31 Dec 05:37

MERCURY
♑ 1 Jan 00:00
♒ 4 Jan 09:17
♑ 2 Feb 12:18
♒ 15 Feb 06:35
♓ 11 Mar 10:28
♈ 28 Mar 22:42
♉ 12 Apr 17:10
♊ 29 Apr 22:42
♋ 6 Jul 19:03
♌ 21 Jul 05:35
♍ 5 Aug 19:07
♎ 26 Aug 13:30
♍ 29 Sep 21:26
♎ 11 Oct 07:31
♏ 31 Oct 08:20
♐ 18 Nov 21:43
♑ 8 Dec 07:11

VENUS
♒ 1 Jan 00:00
♓ 17 Jan 14:22
♈ 11 Feb 07:47
♉ 7 Mar 21:32
♊ 4 Apr 07:23
♋ 8 May 02:17
♊ 23 Jun 12:10
♋ 4 Aug 09:49
♌ 8 Sep 09:24
♍ 6 Oct 03:13
♎ 31 Oct 19:40
♏ 25 Nov 13:02
♐ 19 Dec 19:07

MARS
♏ 1 Jan 00:00
♐ 14 Jan 02:28
♑ 28 Feb 20:05
♒ 14 Apr 23:40
♓ 3 Jun 07:52
♈ 6 Dec 11:24

JUPITER
♍ 1 Jan 00:00
♌ 18 Jan 02:05
♍ 7 Jul 19:02
♎ 13 Dec 02:17

SATURN
♏ 1 Jan 00:00
♐ 12 Jan 18:45
♏ 14 May 03:47
♐ 10 Oct 15:11

1957

SUN
♑ 1 Jan 00:00
♒ 20 Jan 07:39
♓ 18 Feb 21:59
♈ 20 Mar 21:17
♉ 20 Apr 08:42
♊ 21 May 08:11
♋ 21 Jun 16:21
♌ 23 Jul 03:15
♍ 23 Aug 10:08
♎ 23 Sep 07:27
♏ 23 Oct 16:25
♐ 22 Nov 13:40
♑ 22 Dec 02:49

MOON
♑ 1 Jan 00:00
♒ 2 Jan 17:25
♓ 5 Jan 06:05
♈ 7 Jan 18:23
♉ 10 Jan 04:27
♊ 12 Jan 10:44
♋ 14 Jan 13:06
♌ 16 Jan 12:51
♍ 18 Jan 12:04
♎ 20 Jan 12:55
♏ 22 Jan 17:03
♐ 25 Jan 00:52
♑ 27 Jan 11:33
♒ 29 Jan 23:42
♓ 1 Feb 12:21
♈ 4 Feb 00:42
♉ 6 Feb 11:38

♊	8 Feb	19:35
♋	10 Feb	23:29
♌	13 Feb	00:19
♍	14 Feb	23:17
♎	16 Feb	22:50
♏	19 Feb	01:06
♐	21 Feb	07:23
♑	23 Feb	17:27
♒	26 Feb	05:43
♓	28 Feb	18:25
♈	3 Mar	06:31
♉	5 Mar	17:21
♊	8 Mar	02:04
♋	10 Mar	07:45
♌	12 Mar	10:12
♍	14 Mar	10:20
♎	16 Mar	09:59
♏	18 Mar	11:15
♐	20 Mar	15:54
♑	23 Mar	00:35
♒	25 Mar	12:18
♓	28 Mar	01:00
♈	30 Mar	12:55
♉	1 Apr	23:11
♊	4 Apr	07:31
♋	6 Apr	13:38
♌	8 Apr	17:25
♍	10 Apr	19:13
♎	12 Apr	20:09
♏	14 Apr	21:46
♐	17 Apr	01:43
♑	19 Apr	09:09
♒	21 Apr	19:54
♓	24 Apr	08:23
♈	26 Apr	20:22
♉	29 Apr	06:18
♊	1 May	13:47
♋	3 May	19:09
♌	5 May	22:54
♍	8 May	01:37
♎	10 May	03:58
♏	12 May	06:49
♐	14 May	11:14
♑	16 May	18:14
♒	19 May	04:13
♓	21 May	16:21
♈	24 May	04:34
♉	26 May	14:43
♊	28 May	21:47
♋	31 May	02:06
♌	2 Jun	01:16
♍	4 Jun	07:00
♎	6 Jun	09:46
♏	8 Jun	13:41
♐	10 Jun	19:10
♑	13 Jun	02:37
♒	15 Jun	12:24
♓	18 Jun	00:15
♈	20 Jun	12:46
♉	22 Jun	23:39
♊	25 Jun	07:07
♋	27 Jun	11:01
♌	29 Jun	12:31
♍	1 Jul	13:24
♎	3 Jul	15:17
♏	5 Jul	19:10
♐	8 Jul	01:21
♑	10 Jul	09:35
♒	12 Jul	19:43
♓	15 Jul	07:33
♈	17 Jul	20:15
♉	20 Jul	07:58
♊	22 Jul	16:34
♋	24 Jul	21:05
♌	26 Jul	22:17
♍	28 Jul	22:00
♎	30 Jul	22:20
♏	2 Aug	01:01
♐	4 Aug	06:48
♑	6 Aug	15:24
♒	9 Aug	02:02
♓	11 Aug	14:02
♈	14 Aug	02:46
♉	16 Aug	15:01
♊	19 Aug	00:52
♋	21 Aug	06:49
♌	23 Aug	08:51
♍	25 Aug	08:26
♎	27 Aug	07:42
♏	29 Aug	08:46
♐	31 Aug	13:08
♑	2 Sep	21:06
♒	5 Sep	07:50
♓	7 Sep	20:04
♈	10 Sep	08:45
♉	12 Sep	20:58
♊	15 Sep	07:27
♋	17 Sep	14:50
♌	19 Sep	18:31
♍	21 Sep	19:12
♎	23 Sep	18:33
♏	25 Sep	18:41
♐	27 Sep	21:28
♑	30 Sep	04:00
♒	2 Oct	14:04
♓	5 Oct	02:18
♈	7 Oct	14:57
♉	10 Oct	02:48
♊	12 Oct	13:01
♋	14 Oct	20:55
♌	17 Oct	02:00
♍	19 Oct	04:24
♎	21 Oct	05:04
♏	23 Oct	05:31
♐	25 Oct	07:34
♑	27 Oct	12:41
♒	29 Oct	21:33
♓	1 Nov	09:19
♈	3 Nov	22:00
♉	6 Nov	09:38
♊	8 Nov	19:09
♋	11 Nov	02:24
♌	13 Nov	07:37
♍	15 Nov	11:07
♎	17 Nov	13:26
♏	19 Nov	15:18
♐	21 Nov	17:52
♑	23 Nov	22:30
♒	26 Nov	06:17
♓	28 Nov	17:16
♈	1 Dec	05:57
♉	3 Dec	17:48
♊	6 Dec	03:01
♋	8 Dec	09:16
♌	10 Dec	13:24
♍	12 Dec	16:29
♎	14 Dec	19:23
♏	16 Dec	22:26
♐	19 Dec	02:31
♑	21 Dec	07:47
♒	23 Dec	15:19
♓	26 Dec	01:41
♈	28 Dec	14:13
♉	31 Dec	02:38

MERCURY

♑	1 Jan	00:00
♒	12 Feb	14:30
♓	4 Mar	11:34
♈	20 Mar	19:48
♉	4 Apr	23:38
♊	12 Jun	13:40
♋	28 Jun	17:08
♌	12 Jul	19:42
♍	30 Jul	01:44
♎	6 Oct	11:09
♏	23 Oct	20:51
♐	11 Nov	18:01
♑	2 Dec	11:19
♐	28 Dec	17:31

VENUS

♐	1 Jan	00:00
♑	12 Jan	20:23
♒	5 Feb	20:17
♓	1 Mar	20:40
♈	25 Mar	22:46
♉	19 Apr	03:29
♊	13 May	11:08
♋	6 Jun	21:35
♌	1 Jul	10:43
♍	26 Jul	03:10
♎	20 Aug	00:44
♏	14 Sep	06:20
♐	10 Oct	01:16
♑	5 Nov	23:46
♒	6 Dec	15:26

MARS

♈	1 Jan	00:00
♉	28 Jan	14:19
♊	17 Mar	21:34
♋	4 May	15:22
♌	21 Jun	12:18
♍	8 Aug	05:28
♎	24 Sep	04:32
♏	8 Nov	21:04
♐	23 Dec	01:30

JUPITER

♎	1 Jan	00:00
♍	19 Feb	15:38
♎	7 Aug	02:11

SATURN

♐	1 Jan	00:00

1958

SUN

♑	1 Jan	00:00
♒	20 Jan	13:29
♓	19 Feb	03:49
♈	21 Mar	03:06
♉	20 Apr	14:28
♊	21 May	13:52
♋	21 Jun	21:57
♌	23 Jul	08:51
♍	23 Aug	15:46
♎	23 Sep	13:09
♏	23 Oct	22:12
♐	22 Nov	19:30
♑	22 Dec	08:40

MOON

♉	1 Jan	00:00
♊	2 Jan	12:22
♋	4 Jan	18:22
♌	6 Jan	21:22
♍	8 Jan	22:59
♎	11 Jan	00:52
♏	13 Jan	04:03
♐	15 Jan	08:50
♑	17 Jan	15:13
♒	19 Jan	23:23
♓	22 Jan	09:42
♈	24 Jan	22:03
♉	27 Jan	10:57
♊	29 Jan	21:48
♋	1 Feb	04:41
♌	3 Feb	07:38
♍	5 Feb	08:11
♎	7 Feb	08:24
♏	9 Feb	10:04
♐	11 Feb	14:12
♑	13 Feb	20:56
♒	16 Feb	05:52
♓	18 Feb	16:40
♈	21 Feb	05:02
♉	23 Feb	18:05
♊	26 Feb	05:53
♋	28 Feb	14:17
♌	2 Mar	18:27
♍	4 Mar	19:15
♎	6 Mar	18:36
♏	8 Mar	18:35
♐	10 Mar	20:57
♑	13 Mar	02:37
♒	15 Mar	11:28
♓	17 Mar	22:42
♈	20 Mar	11:17
♉	23 Mar	00:16
♊	25 Mar	12:20
♋	27 Mar	21:53
♌	30 Mar	03:46
♍	1 Apr	06:01
♎	3 Apr	05:54
♏	5 Apr	05:17
♐	7 Apr	06:07
♑	9 Apr	10:01
♒	11 Apr	17:42
♓	14 Apr	04:39
♈	16 Apr	17:23
♉	19 Apr	06:17
♊	21 Apr	18:03
♋	24 Apr	03:47
♌	26 Apr	10:44
♍	28 Apr	14:41
♎	30 Apr	16:07
♏	2 May	16:15
♐	4 May	16:44
♑	6 May	19:21
♒	9 May	01:30
♓	11 May	11:27
♈	13 May	23:58
♉	16 May	12:50
♊	19 May	00:14
♋	21 May	09:23
♌	23 May	16:15
♍	25 May	21:00
♎	27 May	23:56
♏	30 May	01:34
♐	1 Jun	02:54
♑	3 Jun	05:23
♒	5 Jun	10:34
♓	7 Jun	19:24
♈	10 Jun	07:21
♉	12 Jun	20:13
♊	15 Jun	07:31
♋	17 Jun	16:04
♌	19 Jun	22:04
♍	22 Jun	02:23
♎	24 Jun	05:43
♏	26 Jun	08:31
♐	28 Jun	11:12
♑	30 Jun	14:33
♒	2 Jul	19:45
♓	5 Jul	03:57
♈	7 Jul	15:18
♉	10 Jul	04:10
♊	12 Jul	15:47
♋	15 Jul	00:16
♌	17 Jul	05:31
♍	19 Jul	08:42
♎	21 Jul	11:12
♏	23 Jul	13:58
♐	25 Jul	17:26
♑	27 Jul	21:53
♒	30 Jul	03:53
♓	1 Aug	12:12
♈	3 Aug	23:15
♉	6 Aug	12:05
♊	9 Aug	00:17
♋	11 Aug	09:26
♌	13 Aug	14:44
♍	15 Aug	17:07
♎	17 Aug	18:17
♏	19 Aug	19:50
♐	21 Aug	22:48
♑	24 Aug	03:39
♒	26 Aug	10:28
♓	28 Aug	19:25
♈	31 Aug	06:36
♉	2 Sep	19:24
♊	5 Sep	08:07
♋	7 Sep	18:23
♌	10 Sep	00:42
♍	12 Sep	03:20
♎	14 Sep	03:45
♏	16 Sep	03:50
♐	18 Sep	15:17
♑	20 Sep	09:13
♒	22 Sep	16:04
♓	25 Sep	01:34
♈	27 Sep	13:08
♉	30 Sep	01:58
♊	2 Oct	14:51
♋	5 Oct	02:01
♌	7 Oct	09:51
♍	9 Oct	13:50
♎	11 Oct	14:44
♏	13 Oct	14:12
♐	15 Oct	14:09
♑	17 Oct	16:23
♒	19 Oct	22:04
♓	22 Oct	07:20
♈	24 Oct	19:11
♉	27 Oct	08:08
♊	29 Oct	20:50
♋	1 Nov	08:09
♌	3 Nov	17:03
♍	5 Nov	22:46
♎	8 Nov	01:17
♏	10 Nov	01:30
♐	12 Nov	01:03
♑	14 Nov	01:55
♒	16 Nov	05:53
♓	18 Nov	13:57
♈	21 Nov	01:29
♉	23 Nov	14:31
♊	26 Nov	03:01
♋	28 Nov	13:52
♌	30 Nov	22:41
♍	3 Dec	05:18
♎	5 Dec	09:31
♏	7 Dec	11:29
♐	9 Dec	12:02
♑	11 Dec	12:47
♒	13 Dec	15:38
♓	15 Dec	22:12
♈	18 Dec	08:46
♉	20 Dec	21:38
♊	23 Dec	10:09
♋	25 Dec	20:33
♌	28 Dec	04:34
♍	30 Dec	10:41

MERCURY

♐	1 Jan	00:00
♑	14 Jan	10:03
♒	6 Feb	15:21
♓	24 Feb	21:44
♈	12 Mar	17:32
♉	2 Apr	19:18
♈	10 Apr	13:52
♉	17 May	01:53
♊	5 Jun	20:59
♋	20 Jun	02:21
♌	4 Jul	23:46
♍	26 Jul	10:08
♌	23 Aug	14:32
♍	11 Sep	01:10
♎	28 Sep	22:46
♏	16 Oct	08:52
♐	5 Nov	02:36

VENUS

♒	1 Jan	00:00
♓	6 Apr	16:00
♈	5 May	12:00
♉	1 Jun	04:08
♊	26 Jun	23:09
♋	22 Jul	05:26
♌	16 Aug	01:29
♍	9 Sep	12:36
♎	3 Oct	16:44
♏	27 Oct	16:27
♐	20 Nov	14:00
♑	14 Dec	10:55

MARS

♐	1 Jan	00:00
♑	3 Feb	18:57
♒	17 Mar	07:11
♓	27 Apr	02:31
♈	7 Jun	06:21
♉	21 Jul	07:04
♊	21 Sep	05:26
♉	29 Oct	00:01

JUPITER

♎	1 Jan	00:00
♏	13 Jan	12:52
♎	20 Mar	19:14
♏	7 Sep	08:52

SATURN

♐	1 Jan	00:00

1959

SUN

♑	1 Jan	00:00
♒	20 Jan	19:19
♓	19 Feb	09:38
♈	21 Mar	08:55
♉	20 Apr	20:17
♊	21 May	19:43
♋	22 Jun	03:50
♌	23 Jul	14:46
♍	23 Aug	21:44
♎	23 Sep	19:09
♏	24 Oct	04:12
♐	23 Nov	01:28
♑	22 Dec	14:35

MOON

♍	1 Jan	00:00
♎	1 Jan	15:22
♏	3 Jan	18:42
♐	5 Jan	20:56
♑	7 Jan	22:50
♒	10 Jan	01:52
♓	12 Jan	07:40
♈	14 Jan	17:10
♉	17 Jan	05:33
♊	19 Jan	18:16
♋	22 Jan	04:47
♌	24 Jan	12:14
♍	26 Jan	17:14
♎	28 Jan	20:55
♏	31 Jan	00:06
♐	2 Feb	03:11
♑	4 Feb	06:29
♒	6 Feb	10:41
♓	8 Feb	16:51
♈	11 Feb	01:55
♉	13 Feb	13:48
♊	16 Feb	02:40
♋	18 Feb	13:51
♌	20 Feb	21:38
♍	23 Feb	02:06
♎	25 Feb	04:29
♏	27 Feb	06:15
♐	1 Mar	08:33
♑	3 Mar	12:06
♒	5 Mar	17:17
♓	8 Mar	00:26
♈	10 Mar	09:54
♉	12 Mar	21:37
♊	15 Mar	10:31
♋	17 Mar	22:28
♌	20 Mar	07:23
♍	22 Mar	12:28
♎	24 Mar	14:27
♏	26 Mar	14:54
♐	28 Mar	15:32
♑	30 Mar	17:49
♒	1 Apr	22:42
♓	4 Apr	06:23
♈	6 Apr	16:33
♉	9 Apr	04:32
♊	11 Apr	17:25
♋	14 Apr	05:48
♌	16 Apr	15:55
♍	18 Apr	22:28
♎	21 Apr	01:19
♏	23 Apr	01:34
♐	25 Apr	00:59
♑	27 Apr	01:33
♒	29 Apr	04:56
♓	1 May	11:59
♈	3 May	22:19
♉	6 May	10:39
♊	8 May	23:35
♋	11 May	11:57
♌	13 May	22:41
♍	16 May	06:38
♎	18 May	11:07
♏	20 May	12:25
♐	22 May	11:51
♑	24 May	11:24
♒	26 May	13:10
♓	28 May	18:43
♈	31 May	04:19
♉	2 Jun	16:37
♊	5 Jun	05:36
♋	7 Jun	17:44
♌	10 Jun	04:19
♍	12 Jun	12:51
♎	14 Jun	18:42
♏	16 Jun	21:39
♐	18 Jun	22:15
♑	20 Jun	22:02
♒	22 Jun	23:01
♓	25 Jun	03:10
♈	27 Jun	11:28
♉	29 Jun	23:11
♊	2 Jul	12:06
♋	5 Jul	00:04
♌	7 Jul	10:08
♍	9 Jul	18:16
♎	12 Jul	00:27
♏	14 Jul	04:34
♐	16 Jul	06:42
♑	18 Jul	07:42
♒	20 Jul	09:05
♓	22 Jul	12:41
♈	24 Jul	19:54
♉	27 Jul	06:44
♊	29 Jul	19:24
♋	1 Aug	07:24
♌	3 Aug	17:10
♍	6 Aug	00:30
♎	8 Aug	05:57
♏	10 Aug	10:00
♐	12 Aug	12:59
♑	14 Aug	15:19
♒	16 Aug	17:54
♓	18 Aug	22:00
♈	21 Aug	04:52
♉	23 Aug	14:59
♊	26 Aug	03:19
♋	28 Aug	15:34
♌	31 Aug	01:34
♍	2 Sep	08:31
♎	4 Sep	12:57
♏	6 Sep	15:53
♐	8 Sep	18:21
♑	10 Sep	21:05
♒	13 Sep	00:44
♓	15 Sep	05:54
♈	17 Sep	13:17
♉	19 Sep	23:13
♊	22 Sep	11:16
♋	24 Sep	23:50
♌	27 Sep	10:37
♍	29 Sep	18:04
♎	1 Oct	22:09
♏	3 Oct	23:54
♐	6 Oct	00:55
♑	8 Oct	02:29
♒	10 Oct	06:13
♓	12 Oct	12:06
♈	14 Oct	20:20
♉	17 Oct	06:40
♊	19 Oct	18:40
♋	22 Oct	07:23
♌	24 Oct	19:04
♍	27 Oct	03:49
♎	29 Oct	08:42
♏	31 Oct	10:14
♐	2 Nov	10:02
♑	4 Nov	10:05
♒	6 Nov	12:14
♓	8 Nov	17:36
♈	11 Nov	02:10
♉	13 Nov	13:05
♊	16 Nov	01:17
♋	18 Nov	13:57
♌	21 Nov	02:04
♍	23 Nov	12:08
♎	25 Nov	18:42
♏	27 Nov	21:22
♐	29 Nov	21:12
♑	1 Dec	20:11
♒	3 Dec	20:35
♓	6 Dec	00:17
♈	8 Dec	08:00
♉	10 Dec	18:56
♊	13 Dec	07:25
♋	15 Dec	20:01
♌	18 Dec	07:58
♍	20 Dec	18:30
♎	23 Dec	02:29
♏	25 Dec	07:01
♐	27 Dec	08:16
♑	29 Dec	07:38
♒	31 Dec	07:15

MERCURY

♐	1 Jan	00:00
♑	10 Jan	16:48
♒	30 Jan	15:42
♓	17 Feb	02:15
♈	5 Mar	11:53
♉	12 May	19:48
♊	28 May	17:36
♋	11 Jun	14:11
♌	28 Jun	16:32
♍	5 Sep	02:28
♎	21 Sep	01:20
♏	9 Oct	04:02
♐	31 Oct	01:17
♏	25 Nov	11:53
♐	13 Dec	15:42

VENUS

♑	1 Jan	00:00
♒	7 Jan	08:17
♓	31 Jan	07:29
♈	24 Feb	10:53
♉	20 Mar	21:56
♊	14 Apr	21:08
♋	10 May	15:45
♌	6 Jun	22:43
♍	8 Jul	12:08
♌	20 Sep	03:02
♍	25 Sep	08:15
♎	9 Nov	18:11
♏	7 Dec	16:42

MARS

♉	1 Jan	00:00
♊	10 Feb	13:58
♋	10 Apr	09:47
♌	1 Jun	02:26
♍	20 Jul	11:04
♎	5 Sep	22:47
♏	21 Oct	09:41
♐	3 Dec	18:09

JUPITER

♏	1 Jan	00:00
♐	10 Feb	13:46
♏	24 Apr	14:11
♐	5 Oct	14:40

SATURN

♐	1 Jan	00:00
♑	5 Jan	13:33

1960

SUN

♑	1 Jan	00:00
♒	21 Jan	01:11
♓	19 Feb	15:27
♈	20 Mar	14:43
♉	20 Apr	02:06
♊	21 May	01:34
♋	21 Jun	09:43
♌	22 Jul	20:38
♍	23 Aug	03:35
♎	23 Sep	00:59
♏	23 Oct	10:02
♐	22 Nov	07:19
♑	21 Dec	20:27

MOON

♒	1 Jan	00:00
♓	2 Jan	09:19
♈	4 Jan	15:22
♉	7 Jan	01:23
♊	9 Jan	13:46
♋	12 Jan	02:24
♌	14 Jan	14:00
♍	17 Jan	00:04
♎	19 Jan	08:15
♏	21 Jan	14:00
♐	23 Jan	17:03
♑	25 Jan	18:00
♒	27 Jan	18:19
♓	29 Jan	19:57
♈	1 Feb	00:40
♉	3 Feb	09:17
♊	5 Feb	20:59
♋	8 Feb	09:38
♌	10 Feb	21:09
♍	13 Feb	06:35
♎	15 Feb	13:56
♏	17 Feb	19:24
♐	19 Feb	23:12
♑	22 Feb	01:40
♒	24 Feb	03:33
♓	26 Feb	06:04
♈	28 Feb	10:38
♉	1 Mar	18:19
♊	4 Mar	05:08
♋	6 Mar	17:37
♌	9 Mar	05:25
♍	11 Mar	14:48
♎	13 Mar	21:20
♏	16 Mar	01:38
♐	18 Mar	04:38
♑	20 Mar	07:15
♒	22 Mar	10:10
♓	24 Mar	14:02
♈	26 Mar	19:30
♉	29 Mar	03:14
♊	31 Mar	13:32
♋	3 Apr	01:46
♌	5 Apr	14:01
♍	8 Apr	00:02
♎	10 Apr	06:36
♏	12 Apr	10:02
♐	14 Apr	11:38
♑	16 Apr	13:01
♒	18 Apr	15:32
♓	20 Apr	19:56
♈	23 Apr	02:23
♉	25 Apr	10:51
♊	27 Apr	21:17
♋	30 Apr	09:23
♌	2 May	21:59
♍	5 May	08:59
♎	7 May	16:31
♏	9 May	20:07
♐	11 May	20:56
♑	13 May	20:51
♒	15 May	21:52
♓	18 May	01:24
♈	20 May	07:56
♉	22 May	17:00
♊	25 May	03:55
♋	27 May	16:07
♌	30 May	04:51
♍	1 Jun	16:38
♎	4 Jun	01:32
♏	6 Jun	06:20
♐	8 Jun	07:31
♑	10 Jun	06:48
♒	12 Jun	06:23
♓	14 Jun	08:18
♈	16 Jun	13:43
♉	18 Jun	22:34
♊	21 Jun	09:46
♋	23 Jun	22:10
♌	26 Jun	10:52
♍	28 Jun	22:53
♎	1 Jul	08:47
♏	3 Jul	15:09
♐	5 Jul	17:43
♑	7 Jul	17:35
♒	9 Jul	16:43
♓	11 Jul	17:19
♈	13 Jul	21:07
♉	16 Jul	04:49
♊	18 Jul	15:41
♋	21 Jul	04:09
♌	23 Jul	16:46
♍	26 Jul	04:32
♎	28 Jul	14:34
♏	30 Jul	21:55
♐	2 Aug	02:05
♑	4 Aug	03:26
♒	6 Aug	03:21
♓	8 Aug	03:43
♈	10 Aug	06:22
♉	12 Aug	12:36
♊	14 Aug	22:30
♋	17 Aug	10:43
♌	19 Aug	23:18
♍	22 Aug	10:42
♎	24 Aug	20:10
♏	27 Aug	03:24
♐	29 Aug	08:20
♑	31 Aug	11:09
♒	2 Sep	12:36
♓	4 Sep	13:51

♈ 6 Sep 16:26
♉ 8 Sep 21:45
♊ 11 Sep 06:32
♋ 13 Sep 18:11
♌ 16 Sep 06:47
♍ 18 Sep 18:07
♎ 21 Sep 02:59
♏ 23 Sep 09:18
♐ 25 Sep 13:42
♑ 27 Sep 16:54
♒ 29 Sep 19:33
♓ 1 Oct 22:15
♈ 4 Oct 01:47
♉ 6 Oct 07:09
♊ 8 Oct 15:17
♋ 11 Oct 02:19
♌ 13 Oct 14:55
♍ 16 Oct 02:41
♎ 18 Oct 11:33
♏ 20 Oct 17:06
♐ 22 Oct 20:16
♑ 24 Oct 22:29
♒ 27 Oct 00:58
♓ 29 Oct 04:27
♈ 31 Oct 09:12
♉ 2 Nov 15:28
♊ 4 Nov 23:45
♋ 7 Nov 10:26
♌ 9 Nov 23:00
♍ 12 Nov 11:24
♎ 14 Nov 21:08
♏ 17 Nov 02:54
♐ 19 Nov 05:17
♑ 21 Nov 06:03
♒ 23 Nov 07:05
♓ 25 Nov 09:50
♈ 27 Nov 14:51
♉ 29 Nov 22:00
♊ 2 Dec 07:01
♋ 4 Dec 17:53
♌ 7 Dec 06:22
♍ 9 Dec 19:14
♎ 12 Dec 06:11
♏ 14 Dec 13:14
♐ 16 Dec 16:07
♑ 18 Dec 16:17
♒ 20 Dec 15:49
♓ 22 Dec 16:48
♈ 24 Dec 20:35
♉ 27 Dec 03:31
♊ 29 Dec 13:02

MERCURY
♐ 1 Jan 00:00
♑ 4 Jan 08:25
♒ 23 Jan 06:17
♓ 9 Feb 10:13
♈ 16 Apr 02:22
♉ 4 May 16:46
♊ 19 May 03:27
♋ 2 Jun 20:31
♌ 1 Jul 01:14
♋ 6 Jul 01:23
♌ 10 Aug 17:50
♍ 27 Aug 03:12
♎ 12 Sep 06:30
♏ 1 Oct 17:17
♐ 7 Dec 17:30
♑ 27 Dec 07:21

VENUS
♏ 1 Jan 00:00
♐ 2 Jan 08:43
♑ 27 Jan 04:46
♒ 20 Feb 16:48
♓ 16 Mar 01:54
♈ 9 Apr 10:33
♉ 3 May 19:56
♊ 28 May 06:12
♋ 21 Jun 16:34
♌ 16 Jul 02:12
♍ 9 Aug 10:54
♎ 2 Sep 19:30
♏ 27 Sep 05:13
♐ 21 Oct 17:13
♑ 15 Nov 08:58
♒ 10 Dec 08:35

MARS
♐ 1 Jan 00:00
♑ 14 Jan 05:00
♒ 23 Feb 04:12
♓ 2 Apr 06:25
♈ 11 May 07:20
♉ 20 Jun 09:05
♊ 2 Aug 04:32
♋ 21 Sep 04:07

JUPITER
♐ 1 Jan 00:00
♑ 1 Mar 13:10
♐ 10 Jun 01:53
♑ 26 Oct 03:01

SATURN
♑ 1 Jan 00:00

1961

SUN
♑ 1 Jan 00:00
♒ 20 Jan 07:02
♓ 18 Feb 21:17
♈ 20 Mar 20:33
♉ 20 Apr 07:56
♊ 21 May 07:23
♋ 21 Jun 15:31
♌ 23 Jul 02:24
♍ 23 Aug 09:19
♎ 23 Sep 06:43
♏ 23 Oct 15:48
♐ 22 Nov 13:08
♑ 22 Dec 02:20

MOON
♊ 1 Jan 00:00
♋ 1 Jan 00:22
♌ 3 Jan 12:54
♍ 6 Jan 01:49
♎ 8 Jan 13:32
♏ 10 Jan 22:09
♐ 13 Jan 02:41
♑ 15 Jan 03:42
♒ 17 Jan 02:56
♓ 19 Jan 02:32
♈ 21 Jan 04:27
♉ 23 Jan 09:52
♊ 25 Jan 18:50
♋ 28 Jan 06:22
♌ 30 Jan 19:06
♍ 2 Feb 07:49
♎ 4 Feb 19:28
♏ 7 Feb 04:51
♐ 9 Feb 11:02
♑ 11 Feb 13:51
♒ 13 Feb 14:15
♓ 15 Feb 13:53
♈ 17 Feb 14:41
♉ 19 Feb 18:22
♊ 22 Feb 01:52
♋ 24 Feb 12:49
♌ 27 Feb 01:35
♍ 1 Mar 14:12
♎ 4 Mar 01:22
♏ 6 Mar 10:24
♐ 8 Mar 17:04
♑ 10 Mar 21:19
♒ 12 Mar 23:29
♓ 15 Mar 00:27
♈ 17 Mar 01:33
♉ 19 Mar 04:26
♊ 21 Mar 10:33
♋ 23 Mar 20:23
♌ 26 Mar 08:49
♍ 28 Mar 21:30
♎ 31 Mar 08:22
♏ 2 Apr 16:37
♐ 4 Apr 22:34
♑ 7 Apr 02:52
♒ 9 Apr 06:03
♓ 11 Apr 08:32
♈ 13 Apr 10:56
♉ 15 Apr 14:17
♊ 17 Apr 19:55
♋ 20 Apr 04:50
♌ 22 Apr 16:43
♍ 25 Apr 05:31
♎ 27 Apr 16:35
♏ 30 Apr 00:27
♐ 2 May 05:25
♑ 4 May 08:40
♒ 6 May 11:24
♓ 8 May 14:23
♈ 10 May 17:56
♉ 12 May 22:26
♊ 15 May 04:35
♋ 17 May 13:17
♌ 20 May 00:45
♍ 22 May 13:39
♎ 25 May 01:18
♏ 27 May 09:35
♐ 29 May 14:11
♑ 31 May 16:21
♒ 2 Jun 17:45
♓ 4 Jun 19:51
♈ 6 Jun 23:24
♉ 9 Jun 04:38
♊ 11 Jun 11:41
♋ 13 Jun 20:50
♌ 16 Jun 08:16
♍ 18 Jun 21:12
♎ 21 Jun 09:32
♏ 23 Jun 18:51
♐ 26 Jun 00:06
♑ 28 Jun 02:00
♒ 30 Jun 02:18
♓ 2 Jul 02:53
♈ 4 Jul 05:12
♉ 6 Jul 10:02
♊ 8 Jul 17:28
♋ 11 Jul 03:13
♌ 13 Jul 14:57
♍ 16 Jul 03:55
♎ 18 Jul 16:39
♏ 21 Jul 03:05
♐ 23 Jul 09:42
♑ 25 Jul 12:29
♒ 27 Jul 12:42
♓ 29 Jul 12:13
♈ 31 Jul 12:56
♉ 2 Aug 16:19
♊ 4 Aug 23:04
♋ 7 Aug 08:57
♌ 9 Aug 21:00
♍ 12 Aug 10:01
♎ 14 Aug 22:44
♏ 17 Aug 09:45
♐ 19 Aug 17:44
♑ 21 Aug 22:08
♒ 23 Aug 23:26
♓ 25 Aug 23:03
♈ 27 Aug 22:49
♉ 30 Aug 00:37
♊ 1 Sep 05:53
♋ 3 Sep 15:01
♌ 6 Sep 03:01
♍ 8 Sep 16:05
♎ 11 Sep 04:34
♏ 13 Sep 15:23
♐ 15 Sep 23:55
♑ 18 Sep 05:42
♒ 20 Sep 08:44
♓ 22 Sep 09:36
♈ 24 Sep 09:40
♉ 26 Sep 10:42
♊ 28 Sep 14:32
♋ 30 Sep 22:20
♌ 3 Oct 09:44
♍ 5 Oct 22:46
♎ 8 Oct 11:04
♏ 10 Oct 21:20
♐ 13 Oct 05:21
♑ 15 Oct 11:24
♒ 17 Oct 15:37
♓ 19 Oct 18:10
♈ 21 Oct 19:36
♉ 23 Oct 21:07
♊ 26 Oct 00:25
♋ 28 Oct 07:03
♌ 30 Oct 17:30
♍ 2 Nov 06:18
♎ 4 Nov 18:43
♏ 7 Nov 04:41
♐ 9 Nov 11:51
♑ 11 Nov 17:00
♒ 13 Nov 21:00
♓ 16 Nov 00:19
♈ 18 Nov 03:11
♉ 20 Nov 06:03
♊ 22 Nov 09:59
♋ 24 Nov 16:21
♌ 27 Nov 02:02
♍ 29 Nov 14:26
♎ 2 Dec 03:08
♏ 4 Dec 13:30
♐ 6 Dec 20:25
♑ 9 Dec 00:31
♒ 11 Dec 03:12
♓ 13 Dec 05:42
♈ 15 Dec 08:45
♉ 17 Dec 12:39
♊ 19 Dec 17:48
♋ 22 Dec 00:50
♌ 24 Dec 10:26
♍ 26 Dec 22:30
♎ 29 Dec 11:27
♏ 31 Dec 22:42

MERCURY
♑ 1 Jan 00:00
♒ 14 Jan 18:59
♓ 1 Feb 21:40
♒ 25 Feb 00:00
♓ 18 Mar 10:16
♈ 10 Apr 09:23
♉ 26 Apr 14:34
♊ 10 May 16:34
♋ 28 May 17:23
♌ 4 Aug 01:16
♍ 18 Aug 20:52
♎ 4 Sep 22:33
♏ 27 Sep 12:16
♎ 22 Oct 02:30
♏ 10 Nov 23:54
♐ 30 Nov 22:55
♑ 20 Dec 01:05

VENUS
♒ 1 Jan 00:00
♓ 5 Jan 03:31
♈ 2 Feb 04:46
♉ 5 Jun 19:25
♊ 7 Jul 04:33
♋ 3 Aug 15:29
♌ 29 Aug 14:19
♍ 23 Sep 15:43
♎ 18 Oct 02:59
♏ 11 Nov 05:33
♐ 5 Dec 03:41
♑ 29 Dec 00:07

MARS
♋ 1 Jan 00:00
♌ 6 May 01:14
♍ 28 Jun 23:48
♎ 17 Aug 00:42
♏ 1 Oct 20:03
♐ 13 Nov 21:51
♑ 24 Dec 17:51

JUPITER
♑ 1 Jan 00:00
♒ 15 Mar 08:02
♑ 12 Aug 08:55
♒ 4 Nov 02:49

SATURN
♑ 1 Jan 00:00

1962

SUN
♑ 1 Jan 00:00
♒ 20 Jan 12:58
♓ 19 Feb 03:15
♈ 21 Mar 02:30
♉ 20 Apr 13:51
♊ 21 May 13:17
♋ 21 Jun 21:25
♌ 23 Jul 08:19
♍ 23 Aug 15:13
♎ 23 Sep 12:36
♏ 23 Oct 21:41
♐ 22 Nov 19:02
♑ 22 Dec 08:16

MOON
♏ 1 Jan 00:00
♐ 3 Jan 06:24
♑ 5 Jan 10:24
♒ 7 Jan 12:00
♓ 9 Jan 12:54
♈ 11 Jan 14:34
♉ 13 Jan 18:02
♊ 15 Jan 23:42
♋ 18 Jan 07:40
♌ 20 Jan 17:50
♍ 23 Jan 05:54
♎ 25 Jan 18:52
♏ 28 Jan 06:55
♐ 30 Jan 16:00
♑ 1 Feb 21:10
♒ 3 Feb 22:57
♓ 5 Feb 22:53
♈ 7 Feb 22:51
♉ 10 Feb 00:35
♊ 12 Feb 05:19
♋ 14 Feb 13:20
♌ 17 Feb 00:04
♍ 19 Feb 12:27
♎ 22 Feb 01:22
♏ 24 Feb 13:37
♐ 26 Feb 23:47
♑ 1 Mar 06:39
♒ 3 Mar 09:52
♓ 5 Mar 10:17
♈ 7 Mar 09:32
♉ 9 Mar 09:40
♊ 11 Mar 12:36
♋ 13 Mar 19:26
♌ 16 Mar 05:56
♍ 18 Mar 18:33
♎ 21 Mar 07:29
♏ 23 Mar 19:29
♐ 26 Mar 05:49
♑ 28 Mar 13:46
♒ 30 Mar 18:44
♓ 1 Apr 20:43
♈ 3 Apr 20:42
♉ 5 Apr 20:26
♊ 7 Apr 22:00
♋ 10 Apr 03:12
♌ 12 Apr 12:37
♍ 15 Apr 00:57
♎ 17 Apr 13:54
♏ 20 Apr 01:37
♐ 22 Apr 11:27
♑ 24 Apr 19:20
♒ 27 Apr 01:08
♓ 29 Apr 04:40
♈ 1 May 06:12
♉ 3 May 06:50
♊ 5 May 08:17
♋ 7 May 12:28
♌ 9 May 20:36
♍ 12 May 08:12
♎ 14 May 21:03
♏ 17 May 08:43
♐ 19 May 18:03
♑ 22 May 01:09
♒ 24 May 06:31
♓ 26 May 10:30
♈ 28 May 13:15
♉ 30 May 15:17
♊ 1 Jun 17:41
♋ 3 Jun 21:57
♌ 6 Jun 05:24
♍ 8 Jun 16:13
♎ 11 Jun 04:51
♏ 13 Jun 16:45
♐ 16 Jun 02:04
♑ 18 Jun 08:30
♒ 20 Jun 12:49
♓ 22 Jun 15:59
♈ 24 Jun 18:43
♉ 26 Jun 21:35
♊ 29 Jun 01:10
♋ 1 Jul 06:19
♌ 3 Jul 13:56
♍ 6 Jul 00:23
♎ 8 Jul 12:48
♏ 11 Jul 01:06
♐ 13 Jul 11:01
♑ 15 Jul 17:32
♒ 17 Jul 21:08
♓ 19 Jul 23:01
♈ 22 Jul 00:34
♉ 24 Jul 02:57
♊ 26 Jul 06:57
♋ 28 Jul 13:01
♌ 30 Jul 21:21
♍ 2 Aug 07:58
♎ 4 Aug 20:18
♏ 7 Aug 08:56
♐ 9 Aug 19:49
♑ 12 Aug 03:18
♒ 14 Aug 07:08
♓ 16 Aug 08:17
♈ 18 Aug 08:26
♉ 20 Aug 09:20
♊ 22 Aug 12:28
♋ 24 Aug 18:34
♌ 27 Aug 03:30
♍ 29 Aug 14:36
♎ 1 Sep 03:01
♏ 3 Sep 15:47
♐ 6 Sep 03:27
♑ 8 Sep 12:20
♒ 10 Sep 17:27
♓ 12 Sep 19:02
♈ 14 Sep 18:33
♉ 16 Sep 18:01
♊ 18 Sep 19:29
♋ 21 Sep 00:26
♌ 23 Sep 09:07
♍ 25 Sep 20:31
♎ 28 Sep 09:08
♏ 30 Sep 21:49
♐ 3 Oct 09:40
♑ 5 Oct 19:35
♒ 8 Oct 02:22
♓ 10 Oct 05:29
♈ 12 Oct 05:41
♉ 14 Oct 04:44
♊ 16 Oct 04:51
♋ 18 Oct 08:05
♌ 20 Oct 15:31
♍ 23 Oct 02:32
♎ 25 Oct 15:14
♏ 28 Oct 03:49
♐ 30 Oct 15:20
♑ 2 Nov 01:18
♒ 4 Nov 09:03
♓ 6 Nov 13:53
♈ 8 Nov 15:46
♉ 10 Nov 15:45
♊ 12 Nov 15:44
♋ 14 Nov 17:49
♌ 16 Nov 23:40
♍ 19 Nov 09:34
♎ 21 Nov 21:58
♏ 24 Nov 10:34
♐ 26 Nov 21:44
♑ 29 Nov 07:01
♒ 1 Dec 14:26
♓ 3 Dec 19:54
♈ 5 Dec 23:18
♉ 8 Dec 01:00
♊ 10 Dec 02:08
♋ 12 Dec 04:22
♌ 14 Dec 09:21
♍ 16 Dec 18:00
♎ 19 Dec 05:42
♏ 21 Dec 18:18
♐ 24 Dec 05:33
♑ 26 Dec 14:19
♒ 28 Dec 20:43
♓ 31 Dec 01:21

MERCURY
♑ 1 Jan 00:00
♒ 7 Jan 15:08
♓ 15 Mar 11:43
♈ 3 Apr 02:32
♉ 18 Apr 04:10
♊ 3 May 06:05
♋ 11 Jul 07:37
♌ 26 Jul 18:50
♍ 10 Aug 19:30
♎ 29 Aug 15:48
♏ 5 Nov 02:21
♐ 23 Nov 17:32
♑ 12 Dec 20:51

VENUS
♑ 1 Jan 00:00
♒ 21 Jan 20:31
♓ 14 Feb 18:09
♈ 10 Mar 18:29
♉ 3 Apr 23:05
♊ 28 Apr 09:23
♋ 23 May 02:47
♌ 17 Jun 05:31
♍ 12 Jul 22:32
♎ 8 Aug 17:14
♏ 7 Sep 00:11

MARS
♑ 1 Jan 00:00
♒ 1 Feb 23:07
♓ 12 Mar 07:59
♈ 19 Apr 16:59
♉ 28 May 23:48
♊ 9 Jul 03:51
♋ 22 Aug 11:38
♌ 11 Oct 23:55

JUPITER
♒ 1 Jan 00:00
♓ 25 Mar 22:06

SATURN
♑ 1 Jan 00:00
♒ 3 Jan 19:02

1963

SUN
♑ 1 Jan 00:00
♒ 20 Jan 18:54
♓ 19 Feb 09:09
♈ 21 Mar 08:20
♉ 20 Apr 19:37
♊ 21 May 18:59
♋ 22 Jun 03:05
♌ 23 Jul 14:00
♍ 23 Aug 20:58
♎ 23 Sep 18:24
♏ 24 Oct 03:29
♐ 23 Nov 00:50
♑ 22 Dec 14:02

MOON
♓ 1 Jan 00:00
♈ 2 Jan 04:48
♉ 4 Jan 07:34
♊ 6 Jan 10:14
♋ 8 Jan 13:42
♌ 10 Jan 19:01
♍ 13 Jan 03:08
♎ 15 Jan 14:05
♏ 18 Jan 02:36
♐ 20 Jan 14:21
♑ 22 Jan 23:24
♒ 25 Jan 05:14
♓ 27 Jan 08:35
♈ 29 Jan 10:44
♉ 31 Jan 12:55
♊ 2 Feb 16:03
♋ 4 Feb 20:41
♌ 7 Feb 03:06
♍ 9 Feb 11:36
♎ 11 Feb 22:19
♏ 14 Feb 10:39
♐ 16 Feb 22:58
♑ 19 Feb 09:01
♒ 21 Feb 15:24
♓ 23 Feb 18:18
♈ 25 Feb 19:06
♉ 27 Feb 19:39
♊ 1 Mar 21:39
♋ 4 Mar 02:08
♌ 6 Mar 09:15
♍ 8 Mar 18:34
♎ 11 Mar 05:35
♏ 13 Mar 17:52
♐ 16 Mar 06:27
♑ 18 Mar 17:35
♒ 21 Mar 01:22
♓ 23 Mar 05:05
♈ 25 Mar 05:38
♉ 27 Mar 04:57
♊ 29 Mar 05:13
♋ 31 Mar 08:14
♌ 2 Apr 14:46
♍ 5 Apr 00:21
♎ 7 Apr 11:50
♏ 10 Apr 00:14
♐ 12 Apr 12:49
♑ 15 Apr 00:27
♒ 17 Apr 09:35
♓ 19 Apr 14:54
♈ 21 Apr 16:30
♉ 23 Apr 15:51
♊ 25 Apr 15:07
♋ 27 Apr 16:28
♌ 29 Apr 21:25
♍ 2 May 06:13
♎ 4 May 17:43
♏ 7 May 06:16
♐ 9 May 18:43
♑ 12 May 06:14
♒ 14 May 15:52
♓ 16 May 22:32
♈ 19 May 01:48
♉ 21 May 02:22
♊ 23 May 01:54
♋ 25 May 02:29
♌ 27 May 05:59
♍ 29 May 13:22
♎ 1 Jun 00:10
♏ 3 Jun 12:39
♐ 6 Jun 01:01
♑ 8 Jun 12:07
♒ 10 Jun 21:22
♓ 13 Jun 04:21
♈ 15 Jun 08:47
♉ 17 Jun 10:55
♊ 19 Jun 11:44
♋ 21 Jun 12:47
♌ 23 Jun 15:45
♍ 25 Jun 21:57
♎ 28 Jun 07:41
♏ 30 Jun 19:48
♐ 3 Jul 08:12
♑ 5 Jul 19:03
♒ 8 Jul 03:37
♓ 10 Jul 09:53
♈ 12 Jul 14:17
♉ 14 Jul 17:15
♊ 16 Jul 19:28
♋ 18 Jul 21:45
♌ 21 Jul 01:16
♍ 23 Jul 07:07
♎ 25 Jul 16:03
♏ 28 Jul 03:39
♐ 30 Jul 16:08
♑ 2 Aug 03:13
♒ 4 Aug 11:26
♓ 6 Aug 16:46
♈ 8 Aug 20:07
♉ 10 Aug 22:38
♊ 13 Aug 01:16
♋ 15 Aug 04:40
♌ 17 Aug 09:17
♍ 19 Aug 15:41
♎ 22 Aug 00:26
♏ 24 Aug 11:39
♐ 27 Aug 00:16
♑ 29 Aug 11:58
♒ 31 Aug 20:38
♓ 3 Sep 01:38
♈ 5 Sep 03:53
♉ 7 Sep 05:03
♊ 9 Sep 06:46
♋ 11 Sep 10:08
♌ 13 Sep 15:30
♍ 15 Sep 22:48
♎ 18 Sep 08:00
♏ 20 Sep 19:11
♐ 23 Sep 07:50
♑ 25 Sep 20:16
♒ 28 Sep 06:04
♓ 30 Sep 11:47
♈ 2 Oct 13:48
♉ 4 Oct 13:50
♊ 6 Oct 13:59
♋ 8 Oct 16:01
♌ 10 Oct 20:55
♍ 13 Oct 04:35
♎ 15 Oct 14:25
♏ 18 Oct 01:53
♐ 20 Oct 14:33
♑ 23 Oct 03:21
♒ 25 Oct 14:21
♓ 27 Oct 21:37
♈ 30 Oct 00:41
♉ 1 Nov 00:43
♊ 2 Nov 23:49
♋ 5 Nov 00:09
♌ 7 Nov 03:24
♍ 9 Nov 10:14
♎ 11 Nov 20:08
♏ 14 Nov 07:57
♐ 16 Nov 20:40
♑ 19 Nov 09:23
♒ 21 Nov 20:52
♓ 24 Nov 05:33
♈ 26 Nov 10:25
♉ 28 Nov 11:50
♊ 30 Nov 11:15
♋ 2 Dec 10:45
♌ 4 Dec 12:20
♍ 6 Dec 17:27
♎ 9 Dec 02:22
♏ 11 Dec 14:05
♐ 14 Dec 02:54
♑ 16 Dec 15:22
♒ 19 Dec 02:29
♓ 21 Dec 11:29
♈ 23 Dec 17:41
♉ 25 Dec 20:58
♊ 27 Dec 21:59
♋ 29 Dec 22:07
♌ 31 Dec 23:09

MERCURY
♑ 1 Jan 00:00
♒ 2 Jan 01:11
♑ 20 Jan 05:00
♒ 15 Feb 10:09
♓ 9 Mar 05:27
♈ 26 Mar 03:53
♉ 9 Apr 22:04
♊ 3 May 04:18
♉ 10 May 20:39
♊ 14 Jun 23:21
♋ 4 Jul 03:00
♌ 18 Jul 06:20
♍ 3 Aug 09:21
♎ 26 Aug 20:34
♍ 16 Sep 20:30
♎ 10 Oct 16:44
♏ 28 Oct 19:55
♐ 16 Nov 11:08
♑ 6 Dec 05:18

VENUS
♏ 1 Jan 00:00
♐ 6 Jan 17:36
♑ 5 Feb 20:36
♒ 4 Mar 11:42
♓ 30 Mar 01:00
♈ 24 Apr 03:40
♉ 19 May 01:22
♊ 12 Jun 19:57
♋ 7 Jul 11:19
♌ 31 Jul 22:39
♍ 25 Aug 05:49
♎ 18 Sep 09:43
♏ 12 Oct 11:50
♐ 5 Nov 13:26
♑ 29 Nov 15:22
♒ 23 Dec 18:54

MARS
♌ 1 Jan 00:00
♍ 3 Jun 06:30

♎	27 Jul	04:15
♏	12 Sep	09:12
♐	25 Oct	17:32
♑	5 Dec	09:04

JUPITER

♓	1 Jan	00:00
♈	4 Apr	03:20

SATURN

♒	1 Jan	00:00

1964

SUN

♑	1 Jan	00:00
♒	21 Jan	00:42
♓	19 Feb	14:58
♈	20 Mar	14:10
♉	20 Apr	01:28
♊	21 May	00:50
♋	21 Jun	08:57
♌	22 Jul	19:53
♍	23 Aug	02:52
♎	23 Sep	00:17
♏	23 Oct	09:21
♐	22 Nov	06:39
♑	21 Dec	19:50

MOON

♌	1 Jan	00:00
♍	3 Jan	02:48
♎	5 Jan	10:10
♏	7 Jan	21:04
♐	10 Jan	09:50
♑	12 Jan	22:14
♒	15 Jan	08:48
♓	17 Jan	17:04
♈	19 Jan	23:11
♉	22 Jan	03:24
♊	24 Jan	06:05
♋	26 Jan	07:52
♌	28 Jan	09:46
♍	30 Jan	13:09
♎	1 Feb	19:26
♏	4 Feb	05:13
♐	6 Feb	17:36
♑	9 Feb	06:11
♒	11 Feb	16:40
♓	14 Feb	00:09
♈	16 Feb	05:10
♉	18 Feb	08:45
♊	20 Feb	11:48
♋	22 Feb	14:50
♌	24 Feb	18:11
♍	26 Feb	22:30
♎	29 Feb	04:47
♏	2 Mar	13:54
♐	5 Mar	01:47
♑	7 Mar	14:36
♒	10 Mar	01:36
♓	12 Mar	09:06
♈	14 Mar	13:16
♉	16 Mar	15:31
♊	18 Mar	17:26
♋	20 Mar	20:12
♌	23 Mar	00:15
♍	25 Mar	05:42
♎	27 Mar	12:48
♏	29 Mar	22:04
♐	1 Apr	09:41
♑	3 Apr	22:37
♒	6 Apr	10:25
♓	8 Apr	18:47
♈	10 Apr	23:09
♉	13 Apr	00:37
♊	15 Apr	01:06
♋	17 Apr	02:24
♌	19 Apr	05:40
♍	21 Apr	11:18
♎	23 Apr	19:09
♏	26 Apr	05:01
♐	28 Apr	16:46
♑	1 May	05:43
♒	3 May	18:07
♓	6 May	03:44
♈	8 May	09:16
♉	10 May	11:09
♊	12 May	11:02
♋	14 May	10:54
♌	16 May	12:32
♍	18 May	17:03
♎	21 May	00:42
♏	23 May	19:58
♐	25 May	23:04
♑	28 May	12:01
♒	31 May	00:33
♓	2 Jun	11:02
♈	4 Jun	18:03
♉	6 Jun	21:20
♊	8 Jun	21:50
♋	10 Jun	21:17
♌	12 Jun	21:35
♍	15 Jun	00:28
♎	17 Jun	06:54
♏	19 Jun	16:50
♐	22 Jun	05:04
♑	24 Jun	18:02
♒	27 Jun	06:22
♓	29 Jun	16:57
♈	2 Jul	00:53
♉	4 Jul	05:43
♊	6 Jul	07:43
♋	8 Jul	07:57
♌	10 Jul	08:01
♍	12 Jul	09:45
♎	14 Jul	14:42
♏	16 Jul	23:33
♐	19 Jul	11:29
♑	22 Jul	00:27
♒	24 Jul	12:31
♓	26 Jul	22:36
♈	29 Jul	06:26
♉	31 Jul	12:01
♊	2 Aug	15:29
♋	4 Aug	17:13
♌	6 Aug	18:11
♍	8 Aug	19:51
♎	10 Aug	23:52
♏	13 Aug	07:32
♐	15 Aug	18:45
♑	18 Aug	07:39
♒	20 Aug	19:40
♓	23 Aug	05:14
♈	25 Aug	12:16
♉	27 Aug	17:24
♊	29 Aug	21:16
♋	1 Sep	00:14
♌	3 Sep	02:37
♍	5 Sep	05:13
♎	7 Sep	09:20
♏	9 Sep	16:20
♐	12 Sep	02:48
♑	14 Sep	15:31
♒	17 Sep	03:48
♓	19 Sep	13:23
♈	21 Sep	19:44
♉	23 Sep	23:47
♊	26 Sep	02:47
♋	28 Sep	05:40
♌	30 Sep	08:53
♍	2 Oct	12:43
♎	4 Oct	17:45
♏	7 Oct	00:57
♐	9 Oct	11:03
♑	11 Oct	23:32
♒	14 Oct	12:16
♓	16 Oct	22:33
♈	19 Oct	05:05
♉	21 Oct	08:25
♊	23 Oct	10:04
♋	25 Oct	11:38
♌	27 Oct	14:14
♍	29 Oct	18:26
♎	1 Nov	00:25
♏	3 Nov	08:25
♐	5 Nov	18:44
♑	8 Nov	07:06
♒	10 Nov	20:09
♓	13 Nov	07:29
♈	15 Nov	15:11
♉	17 Nov	18:57
♊	19 Nov	19:59
♋	21 Nov	20:04
♌	23 Nov	20:59
♍	26 Nov	00:03
♎	28 Nov	05:55
♏	30 Nov	14:31
♐	3 Dec	01:24
♑	5 Dec	13:54
♒	8 Dec	02:58
♓	10 Dec	15:00
♈	13 Dec	00:13
♉	15 Dec	05:33
♊	17 Dec	07:22
♋	19 Dec	07:03
♌	21 Dec	06:31
♍	23 Dec	07:42
♎	25 Dec	12:05
♏	27 Dec	20:12
♐	30 Dec	07:21

MERCURY

♑	1 Jan	00:00
♒	10 Feb	21:31
♓	29 Feb	22:50
♈	16 Mar	23:55
♉	2 Apr	00:58
♊	9 Jun	15:46
♋	24 Jun	17:18
♌	9 Jul	00:39
♍	27 Jul	11:36
♎	3 Oct	00:13
♏	20 Oct	07:12
♐	8 Nov	11:02
♑	30 Nov	19:31
♐	16 Dec	14:31

VENUS

♒	1 Jan	00:00
♓	17 Jan	02:54
♈	10 Feb	21:10
♉	7 Mar	12:39
♊	4 Apr	03:03
♋	9 May	03:16
♊	17 Jun	18:18
♋	5 Aug	08:53
♌	8 Sep	04:54
♍	5 Oct	18:11
♎	31 Oct	08:55
♏	25 Nov	01:26
♐	19 Dec	07:03

MARS

♑	1 Jan	00:00
♒	13 Jan	06:14
♓	20 Feb	07:33
♈	29 Mar	11:25
♉	7 May	14:41
♊	17 Jun	11:43
♋	30 Jul	18:23
♌	15 Sep	05:23
♍	6 Nov	03:20

JUPITER

♈	1 Jan	00:00
♉	12 Apr	06:53

SATURN

♒	1 Jan	00:00
♓	24 Mar	04:18
♒	17 Sep	00:00
♓	16 Dec	05:39

1965

SUN

♑	1 Jan	00:00
♒	20 Jan	06:29
♓	18 Feb	20:48
♈	20 Mar	20:05
♉	20 Apr	07:27
♊	21 May	06:51
♋	21 Jun	14:56
♌	23 Jul	01:49
♍	23 Aug	08:43
♎	23 Sep	06:07
♏	23 Oct	15:11
♐	22 Nov	12:30
♑	22 Dec	01:41

MOON

♐	1 Jan	00:00
♑	1 Jan	20:07
♒	4 Jan	09:05
♓	6 Jan	21:07
♈	9 Jan	07:09
♉	11 Jan	14:11
♊	13 Jan	17:49
♋	15 Jan	18:35
♌	17 Jan	17:58
♍	19 Jan	17:55
♎	21 Jan	20:28
♏	24 Jan	03:01
♐	26 Jan	13:33
♑	29 Jan	02:22
♒	31 Jan	15:18
♓	3 Feb	02:56
♈	5 Feb	12:44
♉	7 Feb	20:24
♊	10 Feb	01:37
♋	12 Feb	04:14
♌	14 Feb	04:55
♍	16 Feb	05:06
♎	18 Feb	06:46
♏	20 Feb	11:46
♐	22 Feb	20:58
♑	25 Feb	09:17
♒	27 Feb	22:15
♓	2 Mar	09:39
♈	4 Mar	18:45
♉	7 Mar	01:50
♊	9 Mar	07:15
♋	11 Mar	11:03
♌	13 Mar	13:23
♍	15 Mar	14:56
♎	17 Mar	17:04
♏	19 Mar	21:33
♐	22 Mar	05:37
♑	24 Mar	17:07
♒	27 Mar	05:59
♓	29 Mar	17:32
♈	1 Apr	02:19
♉	3 Apr	08:29
♊	5 Apr	12:55
♋	7 Apr	16:25
♌	9 Apr	19:24
♍	11 Apr	22:15
♎	14 Apr	01:39
♏	16 Apr	06:42
♐	18 Apr	14:32
♑	21 Apr	01:24
♒	23 Apr	14:05
♓	26 Apr	02:03
♈	28 Apr	11:12
♉	30 Apr	17:04
♊	2 May	20:27
♋	4 May	22:39
♌	7 May	00:50
♍	9 May	03:48
♎	11 May	08:05
♏	13 May	14:10
♐	15 May	22:32
♑	18 May	09:20
♒	20 May	21:51
♓	23 May	10:15
♈	25 May	20:19
♉	28 May	02:49
♊	30 May	05:59
♋	1 Jun	07:06
♌	3 Jun	07:47
♍	5 Jun	09:34
♎	7 Jun	13:30
♏	9 Jun	20:04
♐	12 Jun	05:10
♑	14 Jun	16:21
♒	17 Jun	04:52
♓	19 Jun	17:29
♈	22 Jun	04:30
♉	24 Jun	12:17
♊	26 Jun	16:19
♋	28 Jun	17:20
♌	30 Jun	16:59
♍	2 Jul	17:12
♎	4 Jul	19:43
♏	7 Jul	01:38
♐	9 Jul	10:54
♑	11 Jul	22:29
♒	14 Jul	11:08
♓	16 Jul	23:45
♈	19 Jul	11:13
♉	21 Jul	20:15
♊	24 Jul	01:49
♋	26 Jul	03:54
♌	28 Jul	03:38
♍	30 Jul	02:55
♎	1 Aug	03:55
♏	3 Aug	08:21
♐	5 Aug	16:50
♑	8 Aug	04:23
♒	10 Aug	17:10
♓	13 Aug	05:38
♈	15 Aug	16:57
♉	18 Aug	02:28
♊	20 Aug	09:21
♋	22 Aug	13:05
♌	24 Aug	14:02
♍	26 Aug	13:37
♎	28 Aug	13:53
♏	30 Aug	16:54
♐	2 Sep	00:00
♑	4 Sep	10:52
♒	6 Sep	23:34
♓	9 Sep	11:57
♈	11 Sep	22:50
♉	14 Sep	07:57
♊	16 Sep	15:07
♋	18 Sep	20:01
♌	20 Sep	22:36
♍	22 Sep	23:30
♎	25 Sep	00:16
♏	27 Sep	02:47
♐	29 Sep	08:43
♑	1 Oct	18:29
♒	4 Oct	06:49
♓	6 Oct	19:14
♈	9 Oct	05:54
♉	11 Oct	14:17
♊	13 Oct	20:40
♋	16 Oct	01:27
♌	18 Oct	04:52
♍	20 Oct	07:14
♎	22 Oct	09:21
♏	24 Oct	12:32
♐	26 Oct	18:10
♑	29 Oct	03:05
♒	31 Oct	14:50
♓	3 Nov	03:23
♈	5 Nov	14:22
♉	7 Nov	22:30
♊	10 Nov	03:55
♋	12 Nov	07:30
♌	14 Nov	10:14
♍	16 Nov	12:55
♎	18 Nov	16:11
♏	20 Nov	20:37
♐	23 Nov	02:57
♑	25 Nov	11:46
♒	27 Nov	23:04
♓	30 Nov	11:40
♈	2 Dec	23:23
♉	5 Dec	08:12
♊	7 Dec	13:28
♋	9 Dec	15:57
♌	11 Dec	17:09
♍	13 Dec	18:36
♎	15 Dec	21:34
♏	18 Dec	02:41
♐	20 Dec	10:02
♑	22 Dec	19:27
♒	25 Dec	06:45
♓	27 Dec	19:18
♈	30 Dec	07:40

MERCURY

♐	1 Jan	00:00
♑	13 Jan	03:13
♒	3 Feb	09:03
♓	21 Feb	05:40
♈	9 Mar	02:19
♉	15 May	13:20
♊	2 Jun	03:48
♋	16 Jun	02:05
♌	1 Jul	15:55
♍	31 Jul	11:24
♌	3 Aug	08:09
♍	8 Sep	17:14
♎	25 Sep	05:50
♏	12 Oct	21:16
♐	2 Nov	06:05

VENUS

♐	1 Jan	00:00
♑	12 Jan	08:01
♒	5 Feb	07:42
♓	1 Mar	07:56
♈	25 Mar	09:55
♉	18 Apr	14:31
♊	12 May	22:08
♋	6 Jun	08:39
♌	30 Jun	22:00
♍	25 Jul	14:52
♎	19 Aug	13:07
♏	13 Sep	19:51
♐	9 Oct	16:47
♑	5 Nov	19:36
♒	7 Dec	04:37

MARS

♍	1 Jan	00:00
♎	29 Jun	01:12
♏	20 Aug	12:17
♐	4 Oct	06:47
♑	14 Nov	07:20
♒	23 Dec	05:37

JUPITER

♉	1 Jan	00:00
♊	22 Apr	14:33
♋	21 Sep	04:40
♊	17 Nov	03:09

SATURN

♓	1 Jan	00:00

1966

SUN

♑	1 Jan	00:00
♒	20 Jan	12:20
♓	19 Feb	02:38
♈	21 Mar	01:54
♉	20 Apr	13:12
♊	21 May	12:33
♋	21 Jun	20:34
♌	23 Jul	07:24
♍	23 Aug	14:18
♎	23 Sep	11:44
♏	23 Oct	20:51
♐	22 Nov	18:15
♑	22 Dec	07:29

MOON

♈	1 Jan	00:00
♉	1 Jan	17:47
♊	4 Jan	00:07
♋	6 Jan	02:41
♌	8 Jan	02:50
♍	10 Jan	02:35
♎	12 Jan	03:53
♏	14 Jan	08:09
♐	16 Jan	15:40
♑	19 Jan	01:45
♒	21 Jan	13:27
♓	24 Jan	01:59
♈	26 Jan	14:33
♉	29 Jan	01:43
♊	31 Jan	09:44
♋	2 Feb	13:41
♌	4 Feb	14:14
♍	6 Feb	13:12
♎	8 Feb	12:51
♏	10 Feb	15:15
♐	12 Feb	21:34
♑	15 Feb	07:26
♒	17 Feb	19:26
♓	20 Feb	08:06
♈	22 Feb	20:31
♉	25 Feb	07:54
♊	27 Feb	17:03
♋	1 Mar	22:48
♌	4 Mar	00:57
♍	6 Mar	00:37
♎	7 Mar	23:49
♏	10 Mar	00:47
♐	12 Mar	05:19
♑	14 Mar	13:56
♒	17 Mar	01:35
♓	19 Mar	14:19
♈	22 Mar	02:34
♉	24 Mar	13:32
♊	26 Mar	22:42
♋	29 Mar	05:24
♌	31 Mar	09:12
♍	2 Apr	10:31
♎	4 Apr	10:40
♏	6 Apr	11:31
♐	8 Apr	14:54
♑	10 Apr	22:02
♒	13 Apr	08:43
♓	15 Apr	21:14
♈	18 Apr	09:28
♉	20 Apr	20:01
♊	23 Apr	04:28
♋	25 Apr	10:48
♌	27 Apr	15:10
♍	29 Apr	17:50
♎	1 May	19:31
♏	3 May	21:24
♐	6 May	00:53
♑	8 May	07:13
♒	10 May	16:52
♓	13 May	04:55
♈	15 May	17:16
♉	18 May	03:50
♊	20 May	11:40
♋	22 May	17:01
♌	24 May	20:37
♍	26 May	23:23
♎	29 May	02:00
♏	31 May	05:12
♐	2 Jun	09:39
♑	4 Jun	16:11
♒	7 Jun	01:21
♓	9 Jun	12:57
♈	12 Jun	01:27
♉	14 Jun	12:30
♊	16 Jun	20:27
♋	19 Jun	01:06
♌	21 Jun	03:29
♍	23 Jun	05:08
♎	25 Jun	07:23
♏	27 Jun	11:04
♐	29 Jun	16:32
♑	1 Jul	23:52
♒	4 Jul	09:15
♓	6 Jul	20:40
♈	9 Jul	09:16
♉	11 Jul	21:04
♊	14 Jul	05:52
♋	16 Jul	10:45
♌	18 Jul	12:28
♍	20 Jul	12:47
♎	22 Jul	13:39
♏	24 Jul	16:32
♐	26 Jul	22:05
♑	29 Jul	06:05
♒	31 Jul	16:02
♓	3 Aug	03:36
♈	5 Aug	16:15
♉	8 Aug	04:38
♊	10 Aug	14:39
♋	12 Aug	20:42
♌	14 Aug	22:51
♍	16 Aug	22:35
♎	18 Aug	22:06
♏	20 Aug	23:25
♐	23 Aug	03:51
♑	25 Aug	11:37
♒	27 Aug	21:56
♓	30 Aug	09:49
♈	1 Sep	22:28
♉	4 Sep	11:00
♊	6 Sep	21:53
♋	9 Sep	05:27
♌	11 Sep	09:01
♍	13 Sep	09:26
♎	15 Sep	08:33
♏	17 Sep	08:35
♐	19 Sep	11:22
♑	21 Sep	17:53
♒	24 Sep	03:48
♓	26 Sep	15:49
♈	29 Sep	04:30
♉	1 Oct	16:48
♊	4 Oct	03:44
♋	6 Oct	12:13
♌	8 Oct	17:25
♍	10 Oct	19:27
♎	12 Oct	19:30
♏	14 Oct	19:22
♐	16 Oct	21:00
♑	19 Oct	01:56
♒	21 Oct	10:41
♓	23 Oct	22:21
♈	26 Oct	11:04
♉	28 Oct	23:06
♊	31 Oct	09:28
♋	2 Nov	17:43
♌	4 Nov	23:37
♍	7 Nov	03:10
♎	9 Nov	04:55
♏	11 Nov	05:54
♐	13 Nov	07:37
♑	15 Nov	11:37
♒	17 Nov	19:04
♓	20 Nov	05:53
♈	22 Nov	18:32
♉	25 Nov	06:37
♊	27 Nov	16:31
♋	29 Nov	23:50
♌	2 Dec	05:02
♍	4 Dec	08:49
♎	6 Dec	11:44
♏	8 Dec	14:18
♐	10 Dec	17:14
♑	12 Dec	21:31
♒	15 Dec	04:20
♓	17 Dec	14:18
♈	20 Dec	02:40
♉	22 Dec	15:08
♊	25 Dec	01:14
♋	27 Dec	07:59
♌	29 Dec	11:58
♍	31 Dec	14:34

MERCURY

♐	1 Jan	00:00
♑	7 Jan	18:26
♒	27 Jan	04:10
♓	13 Feb	10:18
♈	3 Mar	02:58
♓	22 Mar	02:34
♈	17 Apr	21:32
♉	9 May	14:49
♊	24 May	18:00
♋	7 Jun	19:12
♌	26 Jun	19:06
♍	1 Sep	10:36
♎	17 Sep	08:20
♏	5 Oct	22:03
♐	30 Oct	07:39
♏	13 Nov	03:26
♐	11 Dec	15:28

VENUS

♒	1 Jan	00:00
♑	6 Feb	12:47
♒	25 Feb	10:55
♓	6 Apr	15:54
♈	5 May	04:34
♉	31 May	18:01
♊	26 Jun	11:41
♋	21 Jul	17:12
♌	15 Aug	12:48
♍	8 Sep	23:41
♎	3 Oct	03:45
♏	27 Oct	03:28
♐	20 Nov	01:07
♑	13 Dec	22:09

MARS

♒	1 Jan	00:00
♓	30 Jan	07:02
♈	9 Mar	12:56
♉	17 Apr	20:35
♊	28 May	22:08
♋	11 Jul	03:15
♌	25 Aug	15:52
♍	12 Oct	18:38
♐	4 Dec	00:55

JUPITER

♊	1 Jan	00:00
♋	5 May	14:52
♌	27 Sep	13:19

SATURN

♓	1 Jan	00:00

1967

SUN

♑	1 Jan	00:00
♒	20 Jan	18:08
♓	19 Feb	08:24
♈	21 Mar	07:37
♉	20 Apr	18:56
♊	21 May	18:19
♋	22 Jun	02:23
♌	23 Jul	13:16
♍	23 Aug	20:13
♎	23 Sep	17:39
♏	24 Oct	02:44
♐	23 Nov	00:05
♑	22 Dec	13:17

MOON

♍	1 Jan	00:00
♎	2 Jan	17:04
♏	4 Jan	20:17
♐	7 Jan	00:28
♑	9 Jan	05:54
♒	11 Jan	13:06
♓	13 Jan	22:45
♈	16 Jan	10:48
♉	18 Jan	23:40
♊	21 Jan	10:39
♋	23 Jan	17:51
♌	25 Jan	21:21
♍	27 Jan	22:37
♎	29 Jan	23:33
♏	1 Feb	01:44
♐	3 Feb	05:56
♑	5 Feb	12:11
♒	7 Feb	20:17
♓	10 Feb	06:19
♈	12 Feb	18:17
♉	15 Feb	07:19
♊	17 Feb	19:16
♋	20 Feb	03:48
♌	22 Feb	08:05
♍	24 Feb	09:04
♎	26 Feb	08:45
♏	28 Feb	09:10
♐	2 Mar	11:53
♑	4 Mar	17:36
♒	7 Mar	02:04
♓	9 Mar	12:42
♈	12 Mar	00:53
♉	14 Mar	13:55
♊	17 Mar	02:20
♋	19 Mar	12:10
♌	21 Mar	18:04
♍	23 Mar	20:09
♎	25 Mar	19:51
♏	27 Mar	19:11
♐	29 Mar	20:09
♑	1 Apr	00:11
♒	3 Apr	07:49
♓	5 Apr	18:29
♈	8 Apr	06:57
♉	10 Apr	19:57
♊	13 Apr	08:15
♋	15 Apr	18:37
♌	18 Apr	01:55
♍	20 Apr	05:43
♎	22 Apr	06:42
♏	24 Apr	06:19
♐	26 Apr	06:27
♑	28 Apr	08:54
♒	30 Apr	14:58
♓	3 May	00:48
♈	5 May	13:10
♉	8 May	02:10
♊	10 May	14:09
♋	13 May	00:11
♌	15 May	07:49
♍	17 May	12:52

♎ 19 May 15:31
♏ 21 May 16:30
♐ 23 May 17:06
♑ 25 May 18:59
♒ 27 May 23:44
♓ 30 May 08:19
♈ 1 Jun 20:07
♉ 4 Jun 09:05
♊ 6 Jun 20:53
♋ 9 Jun 06:18
♌ 11 Jun 13:19
♍ 13 Jun 18:24
♎ 15 Jun 21:59
♏ 18 Jun 00:26
♐ 20 Jun 02:20
♑ 22 Jun 04:47
♒ 24 Jun 09:11
♓ 26 Jun 16:50
♈ 29 Jun 03:53
♉ 1 Jul 16:43
♊ 4 Jul 04:39
♋ 6 Jul 13:48
♌ 8 Jul 19:59
♍ 11 Jul 00:08
♎ 13 Jul 03:20
♏ 15 Jul 06:18
♐ 17 Jul 09:23
♑ 19 Jul 13:00
♒ 21 Jul 18:00
♓ 24 Jul 01:29
♈ 26 Jul 12:01
♉ 29 Jul 00:41
♊ 31 Jul 13:01
♋ 2 Aug 22:32
♌ 5 Aug 04:27
♍ 7 Aug 07:36
♎ 9 Aug 09:35
♏ 11 Aug 11:45
♐ 13 Aug 14:53
♑ 15 Aug 19:19
♒ 18 Aug 01:17
♓ 20 Aug 09:18
♈ 22 Aug 19:48
♉ 25 Aug 08:22
♊ 27 Aug 21:09
♋ 30 Aug 07:35
♌ 1 Sep 14:09
♍ 3 Sep 17:08
♎ 5 Sep 18:04
♏ 7 Sep 18:45
♐ 9 Sep 20:40
♑ 12 Sep 00:43
♒ 14 Sep 07:09
♓ 16 Sep 15:53
♈ 19 Sep 02:47
♉ 21 Sep 15:21
♊ 24 Sep 04:22
♋ 26 Sep 15:46
♌ 28 Sep 23:42
♍ 1 Oct 03:39
♎ 3 Oct 04:35
♏ 5 Oct 04:15
♐ 7 Oct 04:33
♑ 9 Oct 07:04
♒ 11 Oct 12:46
♓ 13 Oct 21:38
♈ 16 Oct 08:58
♉ 18 Oct 21:42
♊ 21 Oct 10:39
♋ 23 Oct 22:28
♌ 26 Oct 07:41
♍ 28 Oct 13:20
♎ 30 Oct 15:32
♏ 1 Nov 15:27
♐ 3 Nov 14:52
♑ 5 Nov 15:45
♒ 7 Nov 19:46
♓ 10 Nov 03:43
♈ 12 Nov 14:59
♉ 15 Nov 03:53
♊ 17 Nov 16:41
♋ 20 Nov 04:13
♌ 22 Nov 13:48
♍ 24 Nov 20:46
♎ 27 Nov 00:49
♏ 29 Nov 02:14
♐ 1 Dec 02:11
♑ 3 Dec 02:25
♒ 5 Dec 04:57
♓ 7 Dec 11:20
♈ 9 Dec 21:44
♉ 12 Dec 10:32
♊ 14 Dec 23:19
♋ 17 Dec 10:23
♌ 19 Dec 19:21
♍ 22 Dec 02:22
♎ 24 Dec 07:27
♏ 26 Dec 10:36
♐ 28 Dec 12:10
♑ 30 Dec 13:11

MERCURY
♐ 1 Jan 00:00
♑ 1 Jan 00:52
♒ 19 Jan 17:06
♓ 6 Feb 00:38
♈ 14 Apr 14:38
♉ 1 May 23:27
♊ 16 May 03:28
♋ 31 May 18:03
♌ 8 Aug 22:10
♍ 24 Aug 06:18
♎ 9 Sep 16:54
♏ 30 Sep 01:47
♐ 5 Dec 13:42
♑ 24 Dec 20:34

VENUS
♑ 1 Jan 00:00
♒ 6 Jan 19:36
♓ 30 Jan 18:54
♈ 23 Feb 22:30
♉ 20 Mar 09:57
♊ 14 Apr 09:55
♋ 10 May 06:06
♌ 6 Jun 16:49
♍ 8 Jul 22:12
♌ 9 Sep 11:58
♍ 1 Oct 18:08
♎ 9 Nov 16:33
♏ 7 Dec 08:48

MARS
♎ 1 Jan 00:00
♏ 12 Feb 12:20
♎ 31 Mar 06:10
♏ 19 Jul 22:57
♐ 10 Sep 01:45
♑ 23 Oct 02:15
♒ 1 Dec 20:12

JUPITER
♌ 1 Jan 00:00
♋ 16 Jan 03:50
♌ 23 May 08:21
♍ 19 Oct 10:52

SATURN
♓ 1 Jan 00:00
♈ 3 Mar 21:32

1968

SUN
♑ 1 Jan 00:00
♒ 20 Jan 23:55
♓ 19 Feb 14:10
♈ 20 Mar 13:23
♉ 20 Apr 00:42
♊ 21 May 00:07
♋ 21 Jun 08:14
♌ 22 Jul 19:08
♍ 23 Aug 02:04
♎ 22 Sep 23:27
♏ 23 Oct 08:30
♐ 22 Nov 05:49
♑ 21 Dec 19:00

MOON
♑ 1 Jan 00:00
♒ 1 Jan 15:24
♓ 3 Jan 20:36
♈ 6 Jan 05:46
♉ 8 Jan 18:03
♊ 11 Jan 06:55
♋ 13 Jan 17:54
♌ 16 Jan 02:10
♍ 18 Jan 08:11
♎ 20 Jan 12:48
♏ 22 Jan 16:28
♐ 24 Jan 19:24
♑ 26 Jan 21:57
♒ 29 Jan 01:06
♓ 31 Jan 06:16
♈ 2 Feb 14:40
♉ 5 Feb 02:16
♊ 7 Feb 15:09
♋ 10 Feb 02:35
♌ 12 Feb 10:50
♍ 14 Feb 16:03
♎ 16 Feb 19:22
♏ 18 Feb 22:00
♐ 21 Feb 00:48
♑ 23 Feb 04:12
♒ 25 Feb 08:37
♓ 27 Feb 14:43
♈ 29 Feb 23:15
♉ 3 Mar 10:28
♊ 5 Mar 23:17
♋ 8 Mar 11:22
♌ 10 Mar 20:28
♍ 13 Mar 01:52
♎ 15 Mar 04:24
♏ 17 Mar 05:34
♐ 19 Mar 06:54
♑ 21 Mar 09:35
♒ 23 Mar 14:17
♓ 25 Mar 21:16
♈ 28 Mar 06:32
♉ 30 Mar 17:55
♊ 2 Apr 06:41
♋ 4 Apr 19:13
♌ 7 Apr 05:29
♍ 9 Apr 12:04
♎ 11 Apr 15:01
♏ 13 Apr 15:32
♐ 15 Apr 15:24
♑ 17 Apr 16:23
♒ 19 Apr 19:58
♓ 22 Apr 02:46
♈ 24 Apr 12:33
♉ 27 Apr 00:23
♊ 29 Apr 13:12
♋ 2 May 01:50
♌ 4 May 12:54
♍ 6 May 20:59
♎ 9 May 01:21
♏ 11 May 02:30
♐ 13 May 01:54
♑ 15 May 01:31
♒ 17 May 03:22
♓ 19 May 08:53
♈ 21 May 18:15
♉ 24 May 06:16
♊ 26 May 19:13
♋ 29 May 07:43
♌ 31 May 18:54
♍ 3 Jun 03:53
♎ 5 Jun 09:50
♏ 7 Jun 12:31
♐ 9 Jun 12:43
♑ 11 Jun 12:06
♒ 13 Jun 12:47
♓ 15 Jun 16:43
♈ 18 Jun 00:50
♉ 20 Jun 12:26
♊ 23 Jun 01:23
♋ 25 Jun 13:43
♌ 28 Jun 00:31
♍ 30 Jun 09:27
♎ 2 Jul 16:10
♏ 4 Jul 20:21
♐ 6 Jul 22:05
♑ 8 Jul 22:24
♒ 10 Jul 23:04
♓ 13 Jul 02:03
♈ 15 Jul 08:52
♉ 17 Jul 19:31
♊ 20 Jul 08:13
♋ 22 Jul 20:32
♌ 25 Jul 06:55
♍ 27 Jul 15:10
♎ 29 Jul 21:33
♏ 1 Aug 02:12
♐ 3 Aug 05:11
♑ 5 Aug 06:58
♒ 7 Aug 08:38
♓ 9 Aug 11:46
♈ 11 Aug 17:54
♉ 14 Aug 03:36
♊ 16 Aug 15:52
♋ 19 Aug 04:16
♌ 21 Aug 14:40
♍ 23 Aug 22:21
♎ 26 Aug 03:45
♏ 28 Aug 07:39
♐ 30 Aug 10:41
♑ 1 Sep 13:22
♒ 3 Sep 16:20
♓ 5 Sep 20:28
♈ 8 Sep 02:50
♉ 10 Sep 12:06
♊ 12 Sep 23:55
♋ 15 Sep 12:29
♌ 17 Sep 23:26
♍ 20 Sep 07:16
♎ 22 Sep 12:00
♏ 24 Sep 14:39
♐ 26 Sep 16:31
♑ 28 Sep 18:45
♒ 30 Sep 22:11
♓ 3 Oct 03:21
♈ 5 Oct 10:36
♉ 7 Oct 20:07
♊ 10 Oct 07:44
♋ 12 Oct 20:24
♌ 15 Oct 08:09
♍ 17 Oct 16:59
♎ 19 Oct 22:06
♏ 22 Oct 00:06
♐ 24 Oct 00:33
♑ 26 Oct 01:14
♒ 28 Oct 03:43
♓ 30 Oct 08:55
♈ 1 Nov 16:51
♉ 4 Nov 03:02
♊ 6 Nov 14:48
♋ 9 Nov 03:27
♌ 11 Nov 15:45
♍ 14 Nov 01:55
♎ 16 Nov 08:27
♏ 18 Nov 11:06
♐ 20 Nov 11:04
♑ 22 Nov 10:20
♒ 24 Nov 11:03
♓ 26 Nov 14:53
♈ 28 Nov 22:26
♉ 1 Dec 08:58
♊ 3 Dec 21:06
♋ 6 Dec 09:44
♌ 8 Dec 22:03
♍ 11 Dec 09:00
♎ 13 Dec 17:09
♏ 15 Dec 21:32
♐ 17 Dec 22:28
♑ 19 Dec 21:33
♒ 21 Dec 21:00
♓ 23 Dec 23:01
♈ 26 Dec 05:03
♉ 28 Dec 14:57
♊ 31 Dec 03:12

MERCURY
♒ 1 Jan 00:00
♓ 12 Jan 07:20
♈ 7 Apr 01:02
♉ 22 Apr 16:19
♊ 6 May 22:56
♋ 29 May 22:44
♊ 13 Jun 22:33
♋ 13 Jul 01:30
♌ 31 Jul 06:11
♍ 15 Aug 00:54
♎ 1 Sep 16:59
♏ 28 Sep 14:41
♎ 7 Oct 22:46
♏ 8 Nov 11:01
♐ 27 Nov 12:48
♑ 16 Dec 14:11

VENUS
♏ 1 Jan 00:00
♐ 1 Jan 22:38
♑ 26 Jan 17:35
♒ 20 Feb 04:56
♓ 15 Mar 13:32
♈ 8 Apr 21:49
♉ 3 May 06:57
♊ 27 May 17:03
♋ 21 Jun 03:21
♌ 15 Jul 13:00
♍ 8 Aug 21:49
♎ 2 Sep 06:40
♏ 26 Sep 16:46
♐ 21 Oct 05:17
♑ 14 Nov 21:48
♒ 9 Dec 22:40

MARS
♒ 1 Jan 00:00
♓ 9 Jan 09:50
♈ 17 Feb 03:18
♉ 27 Mar 23:44
♊ 8 May 14:15
♋ 21 Jun 05:04
♌ 5 Aug 17:08
♍ 21 Sep 18:39
♎ 9 Nov 06:10
♏ 29 Dec 22:08

JUPITER
♍ 1 Jan 00:00
♌ 27 Feb 03:34
♍ 15 Jun 14:44
♎ 15 Nov 22:44

SATURN
♈ 1 Jan 00:00

1969

SUN
♑ 1 Jan 00:00
♒ 20 Jan 05:39
♓ 18 Feb 19:55
♈ 20 Mar 19:09
♉ 20 Apr 06:28
♊ 21 May 05:50
♋ 21 Jun 13:56
♌ 23 Jul 00:49
♍ 23 Aug 07:44
♎ 23 Sep 05:08
♏ 23 Oct 14:12
♐ 22 Nov 11:32
♑ 22 Dec 00:44

MOON
♊ 1 Jan 00:00
♋ 2 Jan 15:53
♌ 5 Jan 03:55
♍ 7 Jan 14:43
♎ 9 Jan 23:33
♏ 12 Jan 05:32
♐ 14 Jan 08:19
♑ 16 Jan 08:40
♒ 18 Jan 08:17
♓ 20 Jan 09:21
♈ 22 Jan 13:44
♉ 24 Jan 22:13
♊ 27 Jan 09:54
♋ 29 Jan 22:37
♌ 1 Feb 10:29
♍ 3 Feb 20:41
♎ 6 Feb 05:01
♏ 8 Feb 11:19
♐ 10 Feb 15:24
♑ 12 Feb 17:29
♒ 14 Feb 18:31
♓ 16 Feb 20:04
♈ 18 Feb 23:49
♉ 21 Feb 07:02
♊ 23 Feb 17:42
♋ 26 Feb 06:12
♌ 28 Feb 18:12
♍ 3 Mar 04:07
♎ 5 Mar 11:34
♏ 7 Mar 16:57
♐ 9 Mar 20:48
♑ 11 Mar 23:41
♒ 14 Mar 02:10
♓ 16 Mar 05:04
♈ 18 Mar 09:27
♉ 20 Mar 16:21
♊ 23 Mar 02:13
♋ 25 Mar 14:19
♌ 28 Mar 02:37
♍ 30 Mar 12:54
♎ 1 Apr 20:04
♏ 4 Apr 00:23
♐ 6 Apr 02:58
♑ 8 Apr 05:05
♒ 10 Apr 07:47
♓ 12 Apr 11:42
♈ 14 Apr 17:14
♉ 17 Apr 00:44
♊ 19 Apr 10:29
♋ 21 Apr 22:18
♌ 24 Apr 10:51
♍ 26 Apr 21:57
♎ 29 Apr 05:44
♏ 1 May 09:50
♐ 3 May 11:19
♑ 5 May 11:57
♒ 7 May 13:28
♓ 9 May 17:05
♈ 11 May 23:09
♉ 14 May 07:29
♊ 16 May 17:42
♋ 19 May 05:31
♌ 21 May 18:13
♍ 24 May 06:07
♎ 26 May 15:08
♏ 28 May 20:06
♐ 30 May 21:31
♑ 1 Jun 21:07
♒ 3 Jun 21:04
♓ 5 Jun 23:14
♈ 8 Jun 04:37
♉ 10 Jun 13:06
♊ 12 Jun 23:49
♋ 15 Jun 11:53
♌ 18 Jun 00:36
♍ 20 Jun 12:54
♎ 22 Jun 23:04
♏ 25 Jun 05:31
♐ 27 Jun 08:00
♑ 29 Jun 07:45
♒ 1 Jul 06:50
♓ 3 Jul 07:27
♈ 5 Jul 11:17
♉ 7 Jul 18:54
♊ 10 Jul 05:32
♋ 12 Jul 17:48
♌ 15 Jul 06:30
♍ 17 Jul 18:43
♎ 20 Jul 05:20
♏ 22 Jul 13:04
♐ 24 Jul 17:11
♑ 26 Jul 18:10
♒ 28 Jul 17:35
♓ 30 Jul 17:31
♈ 1 Aug 19:55
♉ 4 Aug 02:02
♊ 6 Aug 11:50
♋ 8 Aug 23:58
♌ 11 Aug 12:39
♍ 14 Aug 00:33
♎ 16 Aug 10:51
♏ 18 Aug 18:54
♐ 21 Aug 00:13
♑ 23 Aug 02:49
♒ 25 Aug 03:36
♓ 27 Aug 04:04
♈ 29 Aug 05:58
♉ 31 Aug 10:51
♊ 2 Sep 19:24
♋ 5 Sep 06:58
♌ 7 Sep 19:37
♍ 10 Sep 07:21
♎ 12 Sep 17:02
♏ 15 Sep 00:26
♐ 17 Sep 05:43
♑ 19 Sep 09:14
♒ 21 Sep 11:32
♓ 23 Sep 13:23
♈ 25 Sep 15:56
♉ 27 Sep 20:29
♊ 30 Sep 04:06
♋ 2 Oct 14:53
♌ 5 Oct 03:26
♍ 7 Oct 15:22
♎ 10 Oct 00:49
♏ 12 Oct 07:19
♐ 14 Oct 11:34
♑ 16 Oct 14:36
♒ 18 Oct 17:22
♓ 20 Oct 20:26
♈ 23 Oct 00:18
♉ 25 Oct 05:33
♊ 27 Oct 13:01
♋ 29 Oct 23:13
♌ 1 Nov 11:35
♍ 4 Nov 00:01
♎ 6 Nov 09:59
♏ 8 Nov 16:18
♐ 10 Nov 19:31
♑ 12 Nov 21:09
♒ 14 Nov 22:53
♓ 17 Nov 01:53
♈ 19 Nov 06:32
♉ 21 Nov 12:53
♊ 23 Nov 20:59
♋ 26 Nov 07:11
♌ 28 Nov 19:23
♍ 1 Dec 08:14
♎ 3 Dec 19:17
♏ 6 Dec 02:31
♐ 8 Dec 05:43
♑ 10 Dec 06:21
♒ 12 Dec 06:28
♓ 14 Dec 07:57
♈ 16 Dec 11:56
♉ 18 Dec 18:36
♊ 21 Dec 03:28
♋ 23 Dec 14:09
♌ 26 Dec 02:22
♍ 28 Dec 15:21
♎ 31 Dec 03:19

MERCURY
♑ 1 Jan 00:00
♒ 4 Jan 12:19
♓ 12 Mar 15:20
♈ 30 Mar 09:59
♉ 14 Apr 05:55
♊ 30 Apr 15:19
♋ 8 Jul 03:59
♌ 22 Jul 19:12
♍ 7 Aug 04:21
♎ 27 Aug 06:51
♍ 7 Oct 02:58
♎ 9 Oct 16:56
♏ 1 Nov 16:54
♐ 20 Nov 06:01
♑ 9 Dec 13:22

VENUS
♒ 1 Jan 00:00
♓ 4 Jan 20:08
♈ 2 Feb 04:45
♉ 6 Jun 01:49
♊ 6 Jul 22:04
♋ 3 Aug 05:31
♌ 29 Aug 02:48
♍ 23 Sep 03:26
♎ 17 Oct 14:18
♏ 10 Nov 16:40
♐ 4 Dec 14:41
♑ 28 Dec 11:04

MARS
♏ 1 Jan 00:00
♐ 25 Feb 06:21
♑ 21 Sep 06:36
♒ 4 Nov 18:51
♓ 15 Dec 14:23

JUPITER
♎ 1 Jan 00:00
♍ 30 Mar 21:37
♎ 15 Jul 13:30
♏ 16 Dec 15:56

SATURN
♈ 1 Jan 00:00
♉ 29 Apr 22:24

1970

SUN
♑ 1 Jan 00:00
♒ 20 Jan 11:24
♓ 19 Feb 01:42
♈ 21 Mar 00:57
♉ 20 Apr 12:16
♊ 21 May 11:38
♋ 21 Jun 19:43
♌ 23 Jul 06:38
♍ 23 Aug 13:35
♎ 23 Sep 11:00
♏ 23 Oct 20:05
♐ 22 Nov 17:25
♑ 22 Dec 06:36

MOON
♎ 1 Jan 00:00
♏ 2 Jan 12:04
♐ 4 Jan 16:33
♑ 6 Jan 17:30
♒ 8 Jan 16:48
♓ 10 Jan 16:37
♈ 12 Jan 18:48
♉ 15 Jan 00:21
♊ 17 Jan 09:07
♋ 19 Jan 20:14
♌ 22 Jan 08:41
♍ 24 Jan 21:33
♎ 27 Jan 09:43
♏ 29 Jan 19:35
♐ 1 Feb 01:50
♑ 3 Feb 04:22
♒ 5 Feb 04:20
♓ 7 Feb 03:38
♈ 9 Feb 04:18
♉ 11 Feb 08:00
♊ 13 Feb 15:30
♋ 16 Feb 02:17
♌ 18 Feb 14:54
♍ 21 Feb 03:42
♎ 23 Feb 15:30
♏ 26 Feb 01:24
♐ 28 Feb 08:39
♑ 2 Mar 12:55
♒ 4 Mar 14:35
♓ 6 Mar 14:49
♈ 8 Mar 15:17
♉ 10 Mar 17:44
♊ 12 Mar 23:37
♋ 15 Mar 09:19
♌ 17 Mar 21:40
♍ 20 Mar 10:30
♎ 22 Mar 21:57
♏ 25 Mar 07:11
♐ 27 Mar 14:07
♑ 29 Mar 19:01
♒ 31 Mar 22:09
♓ 3 Apr 00:01
♈ 5 Apr 01:32
♉ 7 Apr 04:03
♊ 9 Apr 09:02
♋ 11 Apr 17:34
♌ 14 Apr 05:16
♍ 16 Apr 18:08
♎ 19 Apr 05:35
♏ 21 Apr 14:16
♐ 23 Apr 20:15
♑ 26 Apr 00:27
♒ 28 Apr 03:44
♓ 30 Apr 06:38
♈ 2 May 09:33
♉ 4 May 13:05
♊ 6 May 18:18
♋ 9 May 02:17
♌ 11 May 13:22
♍ 14 May 02:11
♎ 16 May 14:03
♏ 18 May 22:50
♐ 21 May 04:12
♑ 23 May 07:14
♒ 25 May 09:26
♓ 27 May 11:59
♈ 29 May 15:27
♉ 31 May 20:04
♊ 3 Jun 02:10
♋ 5 Jun 10:26
♌ 7 Jun 21:17
♍ 10 Jun 10:02
♎ 12 Jun 22:28
♏ 15 Jun 08:02
♐ 17 Jun 13:39
♑ 19 Jun 16:05
♒ 21 Jun 17:01
♓ 23 Jun 18:12
♈ 25 Jun 20:53
♉ 28 Jun 01:35
♊ 30 Jun 08:25
♋ 2 Jul 17:21
♌ 5 Jul 04:26
♍ 7 Jul 17:12
♎ 10 Jul 06:03
♏ 12 Jul 16:41
♐ 14 Jul 23:26
♑ 17 Jul 02:20
♒ 19 Jul 02:45
♓ 21 Jul 02:37
♈ 23 Jul 03:43
♉ 25 Jul 07:19
♊ 27 Jul 13:53
♋ 29 Jul 23:14
♌ 1 Aug 10:45
♍ 3 Aug 23:35
♎ 6 Aug 12:33
♏ 8 Aug 23:57
♐ 11 Aug 08:08
♑ 13 Aug 12:25
♒ 15 Aug 13:31
♓ 17 Aug 13:02
♈ 19 Aug 12:51
♉ 21 Aug 14:46
♊ 23 Aug 20:04
♋ 26 Aug 04:59
♌ 28 Aug 16:39
♍ 31 Aug 05:36
♎ 2 Sep 18:26
♏ 5 Sep 05:55
♐ 7 Sep 14:59
♑ 9 Sep 20:52
♒ 11 Sep 23:34
♓ 13 Sep 23:58
♈ 15 Sep 23:36
♉ 18 Sep 00:21
♊ 20 Sep 04:02
♋ 22 Sep 11:41
♌ 24 Sep 22:55
♍ 27 Sep 11:54
♎ 30 Sep 00:34
♏ 2 Oct 11:36
♐ 4 Oct 20:32
♑ 7 Oct 03:11
♒ 9 Oct 07:26
♓ 11 Oct 09:31
♈ 13 Oct 10:13
♉ 15 Oct 11:00
♊ 17 Oct 13:44
♋ 19 Oct 19:59
♌ 22 Oct 06:13
♍ 24 Oct 18:58
♎ 27 Oct 07:37
♏ 29 Oct 18:15
♐ 1 Nov 02:25
♑ 3 Nov 08:33
♒ 5 Nov 13:11
♓ 7 Nov 16:33
♈ 9 Nov 18:52
♉ 11 Nov 20:51
♊ 13 Nov 23:49
♋ 16 Nov 05:24
♌ 18 Nov 14:36
♍ 21 Nov 02:50
♎ 23 Nov 15:40
♏ 26 Nov 02:25
♐ 28 Nov 10:03
♑ 30 Nov 15:06
♒ 2 Dec 18:45
♓ 4 Dec 21:56
♈ 7 Dec 01:04
♉ 9 Dec 04:25
♊ 11 Dec 08:34
♋ 13 Dec 14:33

1970 (continued)

MOON (continued)
♌ 15 Dec 23:22
♍ 18 Dec 11:05
♎ 21 Dec 00:02
♏ 23 Dec 11:28
♐ 25 Dec 19:28
♑ 28 Dec 00:02
♒ 30 Dec 02:24

MERCURY
♑ 1 Jan 00:00
♒ 13 Feb 13:09
♓ 8 Mar 20:11
♈ 22 Mar 08:00
♉ 6 Apr 07:41
♊ 13 Jun 12:46
♋ 30 Jun 06:23
♌ 14 Jul 08:07
♍ 31 Jul 05:22
♎ 17 Oct 18:04
♏ 25 Oct 06:17
♐ 13 Nov 01:17
♑ 3 Dec 10:15

VENUS
♑ 1 Jan 00:00
♒ 21 Jan 07:27
♓ 14 Feb 05:05
♈ 10 Mar 05:25
♉ 3 Apr 10:05
♊ 27 Apr 20:34
♋ 22 May 14:20
♌ 16 Jun 17:50
♍ 12 Jul 12:17
♎ 8 Aug 10:00
♏ 7 Sep 01:54

MARS
♓ 1 Jan 00:00
♈ 24 Jan 21:30
♉ 7 Mar 01:29
♊ 18 Apr 18:59
♋ 2 Jun 06:51
♌ 18 Jul 06:44
♍ 3 Sep 04:58
♎ 20 Oct 10:57
♏ 6 Dec 16:35

JUPITER
♏ 1 Jan 00:00
♎ 30 Apr 06:45
♏ 15 Aug 17:58

SATURN
♉ 1 Jan 00:00

1971

SUN
♑ 1 Jan 00:00
♒ 20 Jan 17:13
♓ 19 Feb 07:28
♈ 21 Mar 06:39
♉ 20 Apr 17:55
♊ 21 May 17:16
♋ 22 Jun 01:20
♌ 23 Jul 12:15
♍ 23 Aug 19:16
♎ 23 Sep 16:46
♏ 24 Oct 01:54
♐ 22 Nov 23:15
♑ 22 Dec 12:25

MOON
♑ 1 Jan 00:00
♓ 1 Jan 04:08
♈ 3 Jan 06:27
♉ 5 Jan 10:01
♊ 7 Jan 15:09
♋ 9 Jan 22:09
♌ 12 Jan 07:25
♍ 14 Jan 18:58
♎ 17 Jan 07:54
♏ 19 Jan 20:04
♐ 22 Jan 05:16
♑ 24 Jan 10:33
♒ 26 Jan 12:37
♓ 28 Jan 13:02
♈ 30 Jan 13:37
♉ 1 Feb 15:49
♊ 3 Feb 20:35
♋ 6 Feb 04:07
♌ 8 Feb 14:07
♍ 11 Feb 01:58
♎ 13 Feb 14:51
♏ 16 Feb 03:22
♐ 18 Feb 13:46
♑ 20 Feb 20:37
♒ 22 Feb 23:44
♓ 25 Feb 00:01
♈ 26 Feb 23:30
♉ 28 Feb 23:55
♊ 3 Mar 03:02
♋ 5 Mar 09:48
♌ 7 Mar 19:56
♍ 10 Mar 08:11
♎ 12 Mar 21:06
♏ 15 Mar 09:32
♐ 17 Mar 20:24
♑ 20 Mar 04:38
♒ 22 Mar 09:29
♓ 24 Mar 11:08
♈ 26 Mar 10:46
♉ 28 Mar 10:16
♊ 30 Mar 11:44
♋ 1 Apr 16:51
♌ 4 Apr 02:06
♍ 6 Apr 14:17
♎ 9 Apr 03:17
♏ 11 Apr 15:28
♐ 14 Apr 02:04
♑ 16 Apr 10:39
♒ 18 Apr 16:46
♓ 20 Apr 20:08
♈ 22 Apr 21:09
♉ 24 Apr 21:07
♊ 26 Apr 21:59
♋ 29 Apr 01:44
♌ 1 May 09:35
♍ 3 May 21:04
♎ 6 May 10:00
♏ 8 May 22:04
♐ 11 May 08:08
♑ 13 May 16:10
♒ 15 May 22:20
♓ 18 May 02:40
♈ 20 May 05:12
♉ 22 May 06:32
♊ 24 May 08:02
♋ 26 May 11:27
♌ 28 May 18:17
♍ 31 May 04:49
♎ 2 Jun 17:27
♏ 5 Jun 05:37
♐ 7 Jun 15:29
♑ 9 Jun 22:46
♒ 12 Jun 04:03
♓ 14 Jun 08:02
♈ 16 Jun 11:06
♉ 18 Jun 13:39
♊ 20 Jun 16:24
♋ 22 Jun 20:31
♌ 25 Jun 03:13
♍ 27 Jun 13:07
♎ 30 Jun 01:23
♏ 2 Jul 13:47
♐ 4 Jul 23:59
♑ 7 Jul 07:04
♒ 9 Jul 11:27
♓ 11 Jul 14:15
♈ 13 Jul 16:33
♉ 15 Jul 19:11
♊ 17 Jul 22:47
♋ 20 Jul 03:57
♌ 22 Jul 11:17
♍ 24 Jul 21:10
♎ 27 Jul 09:12
♏ 29 Jul 21:51
♐ 1 Aug 08:50
♑ 3 Aug 16:32
♒ 5 Aug 20:47
♓ 7 Aug 22:35
♈ 9 Aug 23:27
♉ 12 Aug 00:56
♊ 14 Aug 04:11
♋ 16 Aug 09:50
♌ 18 Aug 17:58
♍ 21 Aug 04:19
♎ 23 Aug 16:23
♏ 26 Aug 05:10
♐ 28 Aug 16:57
♑ 31 Aug 01:55
♒ 2 Sep 07:05
♓ 4 Sep 08:51
♈ 6 Sep 08:44
♉ 8 Sep 08:38
♊ 10 Sep 10:26
♋ 12 Sep 15:21
♌ 14 Sep 23:38
♍ 17 Sep 10:29
♎ 19 Sep 22:48
♏ 22 Sep 11:34
♐ 24 Sep 23:44
♑ 27 Sep 09:53
♒ 29 Sep 16:39
♓ 1 Oct 19:37
♈ 3 Oct 19:41
♉ 5 Oct 18:42
♊ 7 Oct 18:54
♋ 9 Oct 22:11
♌ 12 Oct 05:31
♍ 14 Oct 16:17
♎ 17 Oct 04:48
♏ 19 Oct 17:31
♐ 22 Oct 05:32
♑ 24 Oct 16:06
♒ 27 Oct 00:12
♓ 29 Oct 04:57
♈ 31 Oct 06:27
♉ 2 Nov 05:56
♊ 4 Nov 05:28
♋ 6 Nov 07:15
♌ 8 Nov 12:57
♍ 10 Nov 22:45
♎ 13 Nov 11:06
♏ 15 Nov 23:50
♐ 18 Nov 11:30
♑ 20 Nov 21:37
♒ 23 Nov 05:53
♓ 25 Nov 11:48
♈ 27 Nov 15:04
♉ 29 Nov 16:09
♊ 1 Dec 16:26
♋ 3 Dec 17:52
♌ 5 Dec 22:17
♍ 8 Dec 06:41
♎ 10 Dec 18:20
♏ 13 Dec 07:02
♐ 15 Dec 18:38
♑ 18 Dec 04:08
♒ 20 Dec 11:33
♓ 22 Dec 17:10
♈ 24 Dec 21:10
♉ 26 Dec 23:46
♊ 29 Dec 01:39
♋ 31 Dec 04:02

MERCURY
♑ 1 Jan 00:00
♒ 2 Jan 23:37
♑ 14 Jan 02:17
♒ 7 Feb 20:52
♓ 26 Feb 07:58
♈ 14 Mar 04:46
♉ 1 Apr 14:12
♈ 18 Apr 21:52
♉ 17 May 03:33
♊ 7 Jun 06:46
♋ 21 Jun 16:25
♌ 6 Jul 08:54
♍ 26 Jul 17:04
♎ 29 Aug 20:42
♍ 11 Sep 06:45
♎ 30 Sep 09:19
♏ 17 Oct 17:50
♐ 6 Nov 07:00

VENUS
♏ 1 Jan 00:00
♐ 7 Jan 01:01
♑ 5 Feb 14:57
♒ 4 Mar 02:25
♓ 29 Mar 14:02
♈ 23 Apr 15:45
♉ 18 May 12:49
♊ 12 Jun 06:58
♋ 6 Jul 22:03
♌ 31 Jul 09:16
♍ 24 Aug 16:26
♎ 17 Sep 20:26
♏ 11 Oct 22:43
♐ 5 Nov 00:31
♑ 29 Nov 02:42
♒ 23 Dec 06:33

MARS
♏ 1 Jan 00:00
♐ 23 Jan 01:35
♑ 12 Mar 10:12
♒ 3 May 20:58
♓ 6 Nov 12:32
♒ 26 Dec 18:05

JUPITER
♏ 1 Jan 00:00
♐ 14 Jan 08:50
♏ 5 Jun 02:13
♐ 11 Sep 15:33

SATURN
♉ 1 Jan 00:00
♊ 18 Jan 16:10

1972

SUN
♑ 1 Jan 00:00
♒ 20 Jan 23:00
♓ 19 Feb 13:12
♈ 20 Mar 12:22
♉ 19 Apr 23:38
♊ 20 May 23:00
♋ 21 Jun 07:07
♌ 22 Jul 18:03
♍ 23 Aug 01:04
♎ 22 Sep 22:33
♏ 23 Oct 07:42
♐ 22 Nov 05:03
♑ 21 Dec 18:14

MOON
♋ 1 Jan 00:00
♌ 2 Jan 08:22
♍ 4 Jan 15:51
♎ 7 Jan 02:34
♏ 9 Jan 15:04
♐ 12 Jan 02:58
♑ 14 Jan 12:26
♒ 16 Jan 19:04
♓ 18 Jan 23:29
♈ 21 Jan 02:36
♉ 23 Jan 05:18
♊ 25 Jan 08:14
♋ 27 Jan 12:02
♌ 29 Jan 17:22
♍ 1 Feb 00:56
♎ 3 Feb 11:07
♏ 5 Feb 23:18
♐ 8 Feb 11:38
♑ 10 Feb 21:51
♒ 13 Feb 04:37
♓ 15 Feb 08:11
♈ 17 Feb 09:51
♉ 19 Feb 11:12
♊ 21 Feb 13:36
♋ 23 Feb 17:53
♌ 26 Feb 00:15
♍ 28 Feb 08:40
♎ 1 Mar 19:01
♏ 4 Mar 07:01
♐ 6 Mar 19:37
♑ 9 Mar 06:50
♒ 11 Mar 14:43
♓ 13 Mar 18:40
♈ 15 Mar 19:38
♉ 17 Mar 19:28
♊ 19 Mar 20:13
♋ 21 Mar 23:27
♌ 24 Mar 05:47
♍ 26 Mar 14:48
♎ 29 Mar 01:42
♏ 31 Mar 13:49
♐ 3 Apr 02:28
♑ 5 Apr 14:21
♒ 7 Apr 23:38
♓ 10 Apr 04:58
♈ 12 Apr 06:33
♉ 14 Apr 05:55
♊ 16 Apr 05:17
♋ 18 Apr 06:47
♌ 20 Apr 11:47
♍ 22 Apr 20:25
♎ 25 Apr 07:35
♏ 27 Apr 19:56
♐ 30 Apr 08:31
♑ 2 May 20:29
♒ 5 May 06:36
♓ 7 May 13:28
♈ 9 May 16:35
♉ 11 May 16:48
♊ 13 May 15:58
♋ 15 May 16:17
♌ 17 May 19:38
♍ 20 May 02:57
♎ 22 May 13:37
♏ 25 May 02:01
♐ 27 May 14:34
♑ 30 May 02:13
♒ 1 Jun 12:16
♓ 3 Jun 19:53
♈ 6 Jun 00:28
♉ 8 Jun 02:15
♊ 10 Jun 02:25
♋ 12 Jun 02:40
♌ 14 Jun 05:10
♍ 16 Jun 11:04
♎ 18 Jun 20:39
♏ 21 Jun 08:43
♐ 23 Jun 21:15
♑ 26 Jun 08:37
♒ 28 Jun 18:03
♓ 1 Jul 01:19
♈ 3 Jul 06:23
♉ 5 Jul 09:25
♊ 7 Jul 11:05
♋ 9 Jul 12:30
♌ 11 Jul 15:06
♍ 13 Jul 20:17
♎ 16 Jul 04:49
♏ 18 Jul 16:16
♐ 21 Jul 04:47
♑ 23 Jul 16:11
♒ 26 Jul 01:08
♓ 28 Jul 07:29
♈ 30 Jul 11:51
♉ 1 Aug 14:58
♊ 3 Aug 17:34
♋ 5 Aug 20:18
♌ 7 Aug 23:57
♍ 10 Aug 05:23
♎ 12 Aug 13:28
♏ 15 Aug 00:20
♐ 17 Aug 12:50
♑ 20 Aug 00:38
♒ 22 Aug 09:44
♓ 24 Aug 15:29
♈ 26 Aug 18:41
♉ 28 Aug 20:43
♊ 30 Aug 22:56
♋ 2 Sep 02:12
♌ 4 Sep 06:54
♍ 6 Sep 13:16
♎ 8 Sep 21:37
♏ 11 Sep 08:16
♐ 13 Sep 20:43
♑ 16 Sep 09:08
♒ 18 Sep 19:05
♓ 21 Sep 01:10
♈ 23 Sep 03:45
♉ 25 Sep 04:28
♊ 27 Sep 05:15
♋ 29 Sep 07:39
♌ 1 Oct 12:26
♍ 3 Oct 19:31
♎ 6 Oct 04:35
♏ 9 Oct 15:28
♐ 11 Oct 03:53
♑ 13 Oct 16:45
♒ 16 Oct 03:52
♓ 18 Oct 11:13
♈ 20 Oct 14:23
♉ 22 Oct 14:38
♊ 24 Oct 14:03
♋ 26 Oct 14:45
♌ 28 Oct 18:15
♍ 31 Oct 01:00
♎ 2 Nov 10:28
♏ 4 Nov 21:47
♐ 7 Nov 10:17
♑ 9 Nov 23:12
♒ 12 Nov 11:03
♓ 14 Nov 19:57
♈ 17 Nov 00:45
♉ 19 Nov 01:53
♊ 21 Nov 01:06
♋ 23 Nov 00:32
♌ 25 Nov 02:12
♍ 27 Nov 07:25
♎ 29 Nov 16:16
♏ 2 Dec 03:43
♐ 4 Dec 16:23
♑ 7 Dec 05:07
♒ 9 Dec 16:54
♓ 12 Dec 02:33
♈ 14 Dec 09:00
♉ 16 Dec 12:00
♊ 18 Dec 12:25
♋ 20 Dec 11:57
♌ 22 Dec 12:35
♍ 24 Dec 16:03
♎ 26 Dec 23:22
♏ 29 Dec 10:11
♐ 31 Dec 22:52

MERCURY
♑ 1 Jan 00:00
♒ 11 Jan 18:18
♓ 31 Jan 23:47
♒ 18 Feb 12:54
♓ 5 Mar 17:00
♈ 12 May 23:46
♉ 29 May 06:46
♊ 12 Jun 02:56
♋ 28 Jun 16:53
♌ 12 Sep 11:37
♎ 21 Sep 12:12
♏ 9 Oct 11:11
♐ 30 Oct 19:28
♑ 29 Nov 07:09
♐ 12 Dec 23:21

VENUS
♋ 8 Apr 18:05
♌ 10 Apr 21:32
♍ 13 Apr 02:47
♎ 15 Apr 09:51
♏ 17 Apr 18:52
♐ 20 Apr 06:02
♑ 22 Apr 18:50
♒ 25 Apr 07:22
♓ 27 Apr 17:10
♈ 29 Apr 22:54
♉ 2 May 01:02
♊ 4 May 01:16
♋ 6 May 01:36
♌ 8 May 03:37
♍ 10 May 08:13
♎ 12 May 15:31
♏ 15 May 01:10
♐ 17 May 12:42
♑ 20 May 01:31
♒ 22 May 14:18
♓ 25 May 01:06
♈ 27 May 08:15
♉ 29 May 11:28
♊ 31 May 11:53
♋ 2 Jun 11:22
♌ 4 Jun 11:50
♍ 6 Jun 14:52
♎ 8 Jun 21:16
♏ 11 Jun 06:52
♐ 13 Jun 18:43
♑ 16 Jun 07:37
♒ 18 Jun 20:20
♓ 21 Jun 07:29
♈ 23 Jun 15:49
♉ 25 Jun 20:38
♊ 27 Jun 22:18
♋ 29 Jun 22:09
♌ 1 Jul 21:56
♍ 3 Jul 23:31
♎ 6 Jul 04:24
♏ 8 Jul 13:06
♐ 11 Jul 00:48
♑ 13 Jul 13:46
♒ 16 Jul 02:15
♓ 18 Jul 13:08
♈ 20 Jul 21:44
♉ 23 Jul 03:41
♊ 25 Jul 06:59
♋ 27 Jul 08:11
♌ 29 Jul 08:30
♍ 31 Jul 09:35
♎ 2 Aug 13:13
♏ 4 Aug 20:36
♐ 7 Aug 07:37
♑ 9 Aug 20:30
♒ 12 Aug 08:53
♓ 14 Aug 19:15
♈ 17 Aug 03:16
♉ 19 Aug 09:14
♊ 21 Aug 13:27
♋ 23 Aug 16:08
♌ 25 Aug 17:50
♍ 27 Aug 19:34
♎ 29 Aug 22:53
♏ 1 Sep 05:18
♐ 3 Sep 15:25
♑ 6 Sep 04:02
♒ 8 Sep 16:31
♓ 11 Sep 02:41
♈ 13 Sep 09:57
♉ 15 Sep 15:00
♊ 17 Sep 18:48
♋ 19 Sep 22:02
♌ 22 Sep 00:57
♍ 24 Sep 03:59
♎ 26 Sep 08:01
♏ 28 Sep 14:19
♐ 30 Sep 23:48
♑ 3 Oct 12:03
♒ 6 Oct 00:49
♓ 8 Oct 11:24
♈ 10 Oct 18:29
♉ 12 Oct 22:37
♊ 15 Oct 01:09
♋ 17 Oct 03:29
♌ 19 Oct 06:25
♍ 21 Oct 10:19
♎ 23 Oct 15:29
♏ 25 Oct 22:28
♐ 28 Oct 07:58
♑ 31 Oct 19:58
♒ 2 Nov 08:59
♓ 4 Nov 20:27
♈ 7 Nov 04:20
♉ 9 Nov 08:26
♊ 11 Nov 10:00
♋ 13 Nov 10:47
♌ 15 Nov 12:20
♍ 17 Nov 15:42
♎ 19 Nov 21:16
♏ 22 Nov 05:07
♐ 24 Nov 15:11
♑ 27 Nov 03:13
♒ 29 Nov 16:18
♓ 2 Dec 04:33
♈ 4 Dec 13:51
♉ 6 Dec 19:09
♊ 8 Dec 20:58
♋ 10 Dec 20:52
♌ 12 Dec 20:45
♍ 14 Dec 22:21
♎ 17 Dec 02:54
♏ 19 Dec 10:44
♐ 21 Dec 21:20
♑ 24 Dec 09:42
♒ 26 Dec 22:43
♓ 29 Dec 11:10
♈ 31 Dec 21:35

MERCURY
♑ 1 Jan 00:00
♒ 4 Jan 14:42
♓ 23 Jan 15:24
♈ 9 Feb 19:30
♉ 16 Apr 21:18
♊ 6 May 02:55
♋ 20 May 17:24
♌ 4 Jun 04:43
♍ 16 Jul 08:04
♎ 11 Aug 15:22
♏ 28 Aug 15:22
♐ 13 Sep 16:17
♑ 2 Oct 20:13
♐ 7 Dec 21:30
♑ 28 Dec 15:15

VENUS
♒ 1 Jan 00:00
♓ 11 Jan 19:15
♈ 4 Feb 18:46
♉ 28 Feb 18:46
♊ 24 Mar 20:35
♋ 18 Apr 01:06
♌ 12 May 08:43
♍ 5 Jun 19:21
♎ 30 Jun 08:56
♏ 19 Aug 01:11
♐ 13 Sep 09:06
♑ 9 Oct 08:08
♒ 5 Nov 15:40
♓ 7 Dec 21:38

MARS
♈ 1 Jan 00:00
♉ 12 Feb 05:51
♊ 26 Mar 21:00
♋ 8 May 10:10
♌ 20 Jun 20:54
♍ 12 Aug 14:57
♎ 29 Oct 08:10

JUPITER
♑ 1 Jan 00:00
♒ 23 Feb 09:28

SATURN
♊ 1 Jan 00:00
♋ 1 Aug 22:21

1974

SUN
♑ 1 Jan 00:00
♒ 20 Jan 10:46
♓ 19 Feb 00:59
♈ 21 Mar 00:07
♉ 20 Apr 11:20
♊ 21 May 10:37
♋ 21 Jun 18:38
♌ 23 Jul 05:31
♍ 23 Aug 12:29
♎ 23 Sep 09:59
♏ 23 Oct 19:11
♐ 22 Nov 16:39
♑ 22 Dec 05:57

MOON
♈ 1 Jan 00:00
♉ 3 Jan 04:38
♊ 5 Jan 08:00
♋ 7 Jan 08:29
♌ 9 Jan 07:43
♍ 11 Jan 07:42
♎ 13 Jan 10:22

♏	15 Jan	16:55
♐	18 Jan	03:13
♑	20 Jan	15:48
♒	23 Jan	04:50
♓	25 Jan	17:01
♈	28 Jan	03:32
♉	30 Jan	11:42
♊	1 Feb	16:54
♋	3 Feb	19:06
♌	5 Feb	19:12
♍	7 Feb	18:52
♎	9 Feb	20:11
♏	12 Feb	00:58
♐	14 Feb	10:02
♑	16 Feb	22:16
♒	19 Feb	11:21
♓	21 Feb	23:16
♈	24 Feb	09:13
♉	26 Feb	17:12
♊	28 Feb	23:11
♋	3 Mar	03:00
♌	5 Mar	04:49
♍	7 Mar	05:34
♎	9 Mar	06:52
♏	11 Mar	10:40
♐	13 Mar	18:21
♑	16 Mar	05:42
♒	18 Mar	18:39
♓	21 Mar	06:34
♈	23 Mar	16:03
♉	25 Mar	23:10
♊	28 Mar	04:34
♋	30 Mar	08:40
♌	1 Apr	11:41
♍	3 Apr	13:57
♎	5 Apr	16:23
♏	7 Apr	20:26
♐	10 Apr	03:28
♑	12 Apr	13:57
♒	15 Apr	02:35
♓	17 Apr	14:45
♈	20 Apr	00:21
♉	22 Apr	06:54
♊	24 Apr	11:11
♋	26 Apr	14:18
♌	28 Apr	17:04
♍	30 Apr	20:01
♎	2 May	23:40
♏	5 May	04:44
♐	7 May	12:06
♑	9 May	22:16
♒	12 May	10:35
♓	14 May	23:04
♈	17 May	09:20
♉	19 May	16:11
♊	21 May	19:55
♋	23 May	21:46
♌	25 May	23:13
♍	28 May	01:26
♎	30 May	05:17
♏	1 Jun	11:11
♐	3 Jun	19:22
♑	6 Jun	05:49
♒	8 Jun	18:03
♓	11 Jun	06:44
♈	13 Jun	17:53
♉	16 Jun	01:47
♊	18 Jun	05:59
♋	20 Jun	07:22
♌	22 Jun	07:30
♍	24 Jun	08:12
♎	26 Jun	10:58
♏	28 Jun	16:41
♐	1 Jul	01:21
♑	3 Jul	12:20
♒	6 Jul	00:42
♓	8 Jul	13:26
♈	11 Jul	01:11
♉	13 Jul	10:22
♊	15 Jul	15:55
♋	17 Jul	17:57
♌	19 Jul	17:44
♍	21 Jul	17:10
♎	23 Jul	18:20
♏	25 Jul	22:46
♐	28 Jul	07:00
♑	30 Jul	18:11
♒	2 Aug	06:47
♓	4 Aug	19:27
♈	7 Aug	07:16
♉	9 Aug	17:13
♊	12 Aug	00:16
♋	14 Aug	03:49
♌	16 Aug	04:27
♍	18 Aug	03:43
♎	20 Aug	03:45
♏	22 Aug	06:38
♐	24 Aug	13:35
♑	27 Aug	00:16
♒	29 Aug	12:53
♓	1 Sep	01:30
♈	3 Sep	12:59
♉	5 Sep	22:51
♊	8 Sep	06:37
♋	10 Sep	11:40
♌	12 Sep	13:55
♍	14 Sep	14:13
♎	16 Sep	14:18
♏	18 Sep	16:15
♐	20 Sep	21:47
♑	23 Sep	07:22
♒	25 Sep	19:39
♓	28 Sep	08:15
♈	30 Sep	19:26
♉	3 Oct	04:40
♊	5 Oct	12:01
♋	7 Oct	17:31
♌	9 Oct	21:03
♍	11 Oct	22:57
♎	14 Oct	00:11
♏	16 Oct	02:24
♐	18 Oct	07:15
♑	20 Oct	15:45
♒	23 Oct	03:21
♓	25 Oct	15:57
♈	28 Oct	03:14
♉	30 Oct	12:01
♊	1 Nov	18:24
♋	3 Nov	23:02
♌	6 Nov	02:31
♍	8 Nov	05:19
♎	10 Nov	07:59
♏	12 Nov	11:24
♐	14 Nov	16:40
♑	17 Nov	00:42
♒	19 Nov	11:39
♓	22 Nov	00:12
♈	24 Nov	12:00
♉	26 Nov	21:05
♊	29 Nov	02:59
♋	1 Dec	06:22
♌	3 Dec	08:32
♍	5 Dec	10:41
♎	7 Dec	13:43
♏	9 Dec	18:14
♐	12 Dec	00:35
♑	14 Dec	09:04
♒	16 Dec	19:49
♓	19 Dec	08:13
♈	21 Dec	20:36
♉	24 Dec	06:45
♊	26 Dec	13:16
♋	28 Dec	16:16
♌	30 Dec	17:05

MERCURY

♑	1 Jan	00:00
♒	16 Jan	03:57
♓	2 Feb	22:42
♒	3 Mar	00:00
♓	17 Mar	20:11
♈	11 Apr	15:21
♉	28 Apr	03:11
♊	12 May	04:55
♋	29 May	08:04
♌	5 Aug	11:42
♍	20 Aug	09:04
♎	6 Sep	05:49
♏	28 Sep	00:21
♎	26 Oct	23:22
♏	11 Nov	16:06
♐	2 Dec	06:18
♑	21 Dec	09:17

VENUS

♒	1 Jan	00:00
♑	29 Jan	19:52
♒	28 Feb	14:26
♓	6 Apr	14:17
♈	4 May	20:22
♉	31 May	07:19
♊	25 Jun	23:44
♋	21 Jul	04:35
♌	14 Aug	23:47
♍	8 Sep	10:28
♎	2 Oct	14:28
♏	26 Oct	14:13
♐	19 Nov	11:57
♑	13 Dec	09:06

MARS

♉	1 Jan	00:00
♊	27 Feb	10:12
♋	20 Apr	08:19
♌	9 Jun	00:55
♍	27 Jul	14:05
♎	12 Sep	19:09
♏	28 Oct	07:05
♐	10 Dec	22:06

JUPITER

♒	1 Jan	00:00
♓	8 Mar	11:12

SATURN

♋	1 Jan	00:00
♊	7 Jan	20:28
♋	18 Apr	22:34

1975

SUN

♑	1 Jan	00:00
♒	20 Jan	16:37
♓	19 Feb	06:50
♈	21 Mar	05:57
♉	20 Apr	17:08
♊	21 May	16:24
♋	22 Jun	00:27
♌	23 Jul	11:23
♍	23 Aug	18:24
♎	23 Sep	15:56
♏	24 Oct	01:07
♐	22 Nov	22:31
♑	22 Dec	11:46

MOON

♌	1 Jan	00:00
♍	1 Jan	17:33
♎	3 Jan	19:22
♏	5 Jan	23:39
♐	8 Jan	06:40
♑	10 Jan	15:59
♒	13 Jan	03:04
♓	15 Jan	15:24
♈	18 Jan	04:04
♉	20 Jan	15:22
♊	22 Jan	23:23
♋	25 Jan	03:21
♌	27 Jan	04:01
♍	29 Jan	03:14
♎	31 Jan	03:14
♏	2 Feb	05:54
♐	4 Feb	12:11
♑	6 Feb	21:43
♒	9 Feb	09:17
♓	11 Feb	21:46
♈	14 Feb	10:23
♉	16 Feb	22:10
♊	19 Feb	07:35
♋	21 Feb	13:19
♌	23 Feb	15:14
♍	25 Feb	14:38
♎	27 Feb	13:39
♏	1 Mar	14:34
♐	3 Mar	19:06
♑	6 Mar	03:40
♒	8 Mar	15:10
♓	11 Mar	03:50
♈	13 Mar	16:19
♉	16 Mar	03:53
♊	18 Mar	13:44
♋	20 Mar	20:49
♌	23 Mar	00:32
♍	25 Mar	01:22
♎	27 Mar	00:52
♏	29 Mar	01:08
♐	31 Mar	04:10
♑	2 Apr	11:09
♒	4 Apr	21:46
♓	7 Apr	10:17
♈	9 Apr	22:45
♉	12 Apr	09:54
♊	14 Apr	19:15
♋	17 Apr	02:28
♌	19 Apr	07:15
♍	21 Apr	09:43
♎	23 Apr	10:42
♏	25 Apr	11:40
♐	27 Apr	14:20
♑	29 Apr	20:09
♒	2 May	05:34
♓	4 May	17:35
♈	7 May	06:03
♉	9 May	17:04
♊	12 May	01:45
♋	14 May	08:08
♌	16 May	12:39
♍	18 May	15:46
♎	20 May	18:06
♏	22 May	20:26
♐	24 May	23:52
♑	27 May	05:31
♒	29 May	14:10
♓	1 Jun	01:33
♈	3 Jun	14:02
♉	6 Jun	01:19
♊	8 Jun	09:50
♋	10 Jun	15:22
♌	12 Jun	18:46
♍	14 Jun	21:11
♎	16 Jun	23:41
♏	19 Jun	03:00
♐	21 Jun	07:35
♑	23 Jun	13:57
♒	25 Jun	22:34
♓	28 Jun	09:34
♈	30 Jun	22:03
♉	3 Jul	09:55
♊	5 Jul	18:59
♋	8 Jul	00:24
♌	10 Jul	02:51
♍	12 Jul	03:56
♎	14 Jul	05:22
♏	16 Jul	08:24
♐	18 Jul	13:33
♑	20 Jul	20:46
♒	23 Jul	05:56
♓	25 Jul	16:59
♈	28 Jul	05:28
♉	30 Jul	17:54
♊	2 Aug	04:03
♋	4 Aug	10:18
♌	6 Aug	12:44
♍	8 Aug	12:54
♎	10 Aug	12:52
♏	12 Aug	14:31
♐	14 Aug	19:00
♑	17 Aug	02:26
♒	19 Aug	12:10
♓	21 Aug	23:33
♈	24 Aug	12:03
♉	27 Aug	00:45
♊	29 Aug	11:54
♋	31 Aug	19:36
♌	2 Sep	23:09
♍	4 Sep	23:30
♎	6 Sep	22:38
♏	8 Sep	22:46
♐	11 Sep	01:41
♑	13 Sep	08:12
♒	15 Sep	17:52
♓	18 Sep	05:32
♈	20 Sep	18:08
♉	23 Sep	06:44
♊	25 Sep	18:14
♋	28 Sep	03:08
♌	30 Sep	08:21
♍	2 Oct	10:04
♎	4 Oct	09:39
♏	6 Oct	09:09
♐	8 Oct	10:36
♑	10 Oct	15:29
♒	13 Oct	00:10
♓	15 Oct	11:41
♈	18 Oct	00:21
♉	20 Oct	12:44
♊	22 Oct	23:52
♋	25 Oct	08:58
♌	27 Oct	15:20
♍	29 Oct	18:47
♎	31 Oct	19:56
♏	2 Nov	20:08
♐	4 Nov	21:11
♑	7 Nov	00:46
♒	9 Nov	08:00
♓	11 Nov	18:43
♈	14 Nov	07:18
♉	16 Nov	19:38
♊	19 Nov	06:15
♋	21 Nov	14:37
♌	23 Nov	20:49
♍	26 Nov	01:05
♎	28 Nov	03:48
♏	30 Nov	05:37
♐	2 Dec	07:34
♑	4 Dec	10:59
♒	6 Dec	17:13
♓	9 Dec	02:52
♈	11 Dec	15:07
♉	14 Dec	03:40
♊	16 Dec	14:13
♋	18 Dec	21:50
♌	21 Dec	02:54
♍	23 Dec	06:28
♎	25 Dec	09:28
♏	27 Dec	12:29
♐	29 Dec	15:53
♑	31 Dec	20:17

MERCURY

♑	1 Jan	00:00
♒	8 Jan	21:59
♓	16 Mar	11:51
♈	4 Apr	12:28
♉	19 Apr	17:21
♊	4 May	11:55
♋	12 Jul	08:57
♌	28 Jul	08:05
♍	12 Aug	06:13
♎	30 Aug	17:21
♏	6 Nov	08:58
♐	25 Nov	01:45
♑	14 Dec	04:10

VENUS

♑	1 Jan	00:00
♒	6 Jan	06:40
♓	30 Jan	06:05
♈	23 Feb	09:54
♉	19 Mar	21:43
♊	13 Apr	22:26
♋	9 May	20:12
♌	6 Jun	10:55
♍	9 Jul	11:07
♌	2 Sep	15:35
♍	4 Oct	05:20
♎	9 Nov	13:53
♏	7 Dec	00:29

MARS

♐	1 Jan	00:00
♑	21 Jan	18:50
♒	3 Mar	05:32
♓	11 Apr	19:16
♈	21 May	08:14
♉	1 Jul	03:54
♊	14 Aug	20:47
♋	17 Oct	08:44
♊	25 Nov	18:31

JUPITER

♓	1 Jan	00:00
♈	18 Mar	16:48

SATURN

♋	1 Jan	00:00
♌	17 Sep	04:57

1976

SUN

♑	1 Jan	00:00
♒	20 Jan	22:26
♓	19 Feb	12:41
♈	20 Mar	11:50
♉	19 Apr	23:04
♊	20 May	22:22
♋	21 Jun	06:25
♌	22 Jul	17:19
♍	23 Aug	00:19
♎	22 Sep	21:49
♏	23 Oct	06:59
♐	22 Nov	04:22
♑	21 Dec	17:36

MOON

♑	1 Jan	00:00
♒	3 Jan	02:34
♓	5 Jan	11:36
♈	7 Jan	23:22
♉	10 Jan	12:10
♊	12 Jan	23:20
♋	15 Jan	07:01
♌	17 Jan	11:16
♍	19 Jan	13:26
♎	21 Jan	15:11
♏	23 Jan	17:49
♐	25 Jan	21:52
♑	28 Jan	03:25
♒	30 Jan	10:35
♓	1 Feb	19:47
♈	4 Feb	07:18
♉	6 Feb	20:14
♊	9 Feb	08:17
♋	11 Feb	16:59
♌	13 Feb	21:33
♍	15 Feb	23:00
♎	17 Feb	23:15
♏	20 Feb	00:14
♐	22 Feb	03:19
♑	24 Feb	08:55
♒	26 Feb	16:49
♓	29 Feb	02:42
♈	2 Mar	14:23
♉	5 Mar	03:19
♊	7 Mar	15:56
♋	10 Mar	01:59
♌	12 Mar	07:56
♍	14 Mar	09:59
♎	16 Mar	09:45
♏	18 Mar	09:18
♐	20 Mar	10:34
♑	22 Mar	14:49
♒	24 Mar	22:20
♓	27 Mar	08:34
♈	29 Mar	20:38
♉	1 Apr	09:35
♊	3 Apr	22:16
♋	6 Apr	09:07
♌	8 Apr	16:37
♍	10 Apr	20:16
♎	12 Apr	20:55
♏	14 Apr	20:15
♐	16 Apr	20:16
♑	18 Apr	22:44
♒	21 Apr	04:48
♓	23 Apr	14:28
♈	26 Apr	02:37
♉	28 Apr	15:38
♊	1 May	04:06
♋	3 May	14:54
♌	5 May	23:10
♍	8 May	04:22
♎	10 May	06:40
♏	12 May	07:03
♐	14 May	07:05
♑	16 May	08:32
♒	18 May	13:03
♓	20 May	21:27
♈	23 May	09:08
♉	25 May	22:08
♊	28 May	10:23
♋	30 May	20:40
♌	2 Jun	04:38
♍	4 Jun	10:22
♎	6 Jun	14:00
♏	8 Jun	15:59
♐	10 Jun	17:07
♑	12 Jun	18:46
♒	14 Jun	22:32
♓	17 Jun	05:44
♈	19 Jun	16:33
♉	22 Jun	05:22
♊	24 Jun	17:37
♋	27 Jun	03:30
♌	29 Jun	10:40
♍	1 Jul	15:47
♎	3 Jul	19:35
♏	5 Jul	22:34
♐	8 Jul	01:06
♑	10 Jul	03:50
♒	12 Jul	07:54
♓	14 Jul	14:37
♈	17 Jul	00:40
♉	19 Jul	13:12
♊	22 Jul	01:41
♋	24 Jul	11:40
♌	26 Jul	18:19
♍	28 Jul	22:24
♎	31 Jul	01:14
♏	2 Aug	03:56
♐	4 Aug	07:04
♑	6 Aug	10:55
♒	8 Aug	15:58
♓	10 Aug	23:01
♈	13 Aug	08:50
♉	15 Aug	21:06
♊	18 Aug	09:55
♋	20 Aug	20:34
♌	23 Aug	03:31
♍	25 Aug	07:04
♎	27 Aug	08:42
♏	29 Aug	10:06
♐	31 Aug	12:29
♑	2 Sep	16:30
♒	4 Sep	22:21
♓	7 Sep	06:12
♈	9 Sep	16:19
♉	12 Sep	04:31
♊	14 Sep	17:33
♋	17 Sep	05:07
♌	19 Sep	13:11
♍	21 Sep	17:17
♎	23 Sep	18:28
♏	25 Sep	18:34
♐	27 Sep	19:22
♑	29 Sep	22:14
♒	2 Oct	03:50
♓	4 Oct	12:10
♈	6 Oct	22:50
♉	9 Oct	11:12
♊	12 Oct	00:15
♋	14 Oct	12:25
♌	16 Oct	21:50
♍	19 Oct	03:25
♎	21 Oct	05:27
♏	23 Oct	05:18
♐	25 Oct	04:49
♑	27 Oct	05:56
♒	29 Oct	10:06
♓	31 Oct	17:54
♈	3 Nov	04:46
♉	5 Nov	17:24
♊	8 Nov	06:22
♋	10 Nov	18:29
♌	13 Nov	04:37
♍	15 Nov	11:47
♎	17 Nov	15:35
♏	19 Nov	16:32
♐	21 Nov	16:04
♑	23 Nov	16:04
♒	25 Nov	18:31
♓	28 Nov	00:48
♈	30 Nov	11:02
♉	2 Dec	23:42
♊	5 Dec	12:39
♋	8 Dec	00:22
♌	10 Dec	10:13
♍	12 Dec	17:56
♎	14 Dec	23:14
♏	17 Dec	02:02
♐	19 Dec	02:55
♑	21 Dec	03:12
♒	23 Dec	04:49
♓	25 Dec	09:37
♈	27 Dec	18:32
♉	30 Dec	06:44

MERCURY

♑	1 Jan	00:00
♒	2 Jan	20:23
♑	25 Jan	01:31
♒	15 Feb	19:03
♓	9 Mar	12:03
♈	26 Mar	15:37
♉	10 Apr	09:30
♊	29 Apr	23:12
♉	19 May	19:22
♊	13 Jun	19:20
♋	4 Jul	14:19
♌	18 Jul	19:36
♍	3 Aug	16:42
♎	25 Aug	20:53
♍	21 Sep	07:15
♎	10 Oct	14:48
♏	29 Oct	04:56
♐	16 Nov	19:03
♑	6 Dec	09:25

VENUS

♏	1 Jan	00:00
♐	1 Jan	12:15
♑	26 Jan	06:09
♒	19 Feb	16:51
♓	15 Mar	01:00
♈	8 Apr	08:57
♉	2 May	17:49
♊	27 May	03:44
♋	20 Jun	13:57
♌	14 Jul	23:37
♍	8 Aug	08:36
♎	1 Sep	17:45
♏	26 Sep	04:18
♐	20 Oct	17:23
♑	14 Nov	10:43
♒	9 Dec	12:54

MARS

♊	1 Jan	00:00
♋	18 Mar	13:15
♌	16 May	11:11
♍	6 Jul	23:28
♎	24 Aug	05:55
♏	8 Oct	20:24

JUPITER

♈	1 Jan	00:00
♉	26 Mar	10:25
♊	23 Aug	10:25
♉	16 Oct	20:25

SATURN

♌	1 Jan	00:00
♋	14 Jan	13:17
♌	5 Jun	05:09

1977

SUN

♑	1 Jan	00:00
♒	20 Jan	04:15
♓	18 Feb	18:31
♈	20 Mar	17:43
♉	20 Apr	04:58
♊	21 May	04:15
♋	21 Jun	12:15
♌	22 Jul	23:04
♍	23 Aug	06:01
♎	23 Sep	03:30
♏	23 Oct	12:41
♐	22 Nov	10:08
♑	21 Dec	23:24

MOON

♉	1 Jan	00:00
♊	1 Jan	19:43
♋	4 Jan	07:13
♌	6 Jan	16:21
♍	8 Jan	23:24
♎	11 Jan	04:48
♏	13 Jan	08:45
♐	15 Jan	11:19
♑	17 Jan	13:03
♒	19 Jan	15:13
♓	21 Jan	19:31
♈	24 Jan	03:20
♉	26 Jan	14:42
♊	29 Jan	03:38
♋	31 Jan	15:21
♌	3 Feb	00:12
♍	5 Feb	06:18
♎	7 Feb	10:37
♏	9 Feb	14:05
♐	11 Feb	17:12
♑	13 Feb	20:14
♒	15 Feb	23:46
♓	18 Feb	04:45
♈	20 Feb	12:23
♉	22 Feb	23:07
♊	25 Feb	11:51
♋	28 Feb	00:03
♌	2 Mar	09:26
♍	4 Mar	15:19
♎	6 Mar	18:35
♏	8 Mar	20:38
♐	10 Mar	22:42
♑	13 Mar	01:40
♒	15 Mar	06:01
♓	17 Mar	12:06
♈	19 Mar	20:24
♉	22 Mar	07:06
♊	24 Mar	19:39
♋	27 Mar	08:17
♌	29 Mar	18:41
♍	1 Apr	01:26
♎	3 Apr	04:40
♏	5 Apr	05:40
♐	7 Apr	06:09
♑	9 Apr	07:41
♒	11 Apr	11:24
♓	13 Apr	17:50
♈	16 Apr	02:53
♉	18 Apr	14:03
♊	21 Apr	02:38
♋	23 Apr	15:26
♌	26 Apr	02:44
♍	28 Apr	10:53
♎	30 Apr	15:13
♏	2 May	16:24
♐	4 May	15:59
♑	6 May	15:55
♒	8 May	18:00
♓	10 May	23:30
♈	13 May	08:30
♉	15 May	20:05
♊	18 May	08:51
♋	20 May	21:36
♌	23 May	09:14
♍	25 May	18:32
♎	28 May	00:29
♏	30 May	02:57
♐	1 Jun	02:55
♑	3 Jun	02:08
♒	5 Jun	02:44
♓	7 Jun	06:36
♈	9 Jun	14:35
♉	12 Jun	01:57
♊	14 Jun	14:50
♋	17 Jun	03:29
♌	19 Jun	14:54
♍	22 Jun	00:30
♎	24 Jun	07:36
♏	26 Jun	11:43
♐	28 Jun	13:03
♑	30 Jun	12:49
♒	2 Jul	12:57
♓	4 Jul	15:32
♈	6 Jul	22:04
♉	9 Jul	08:34
♊	11 Jul	21:16
♋	14 Jul	09:50
♌	16 Jul	20:52
♍	19 Jul	05:59
♎	21 Jul	13:10
♏	23 Jul	18:14
♐	25 Jul	21:05
♑	27 Jul	22:15
♒	29 Jul	23:05

MOON (cont.)

♓ 1 Aug 01:24
♈ 3 Aug 06:55
♉ 5 Aug 16:19
♊ 8 Aug 04:30
♋ 10 Aug 17:05
♌ 13 Aug 03:57
♍ 15 Aug 12:26
♎ 17 Aug 18:50
♏ 19 Aug 23:36
♐ 22 Aug 03:03
♑ 24 Aug 05:31
♒ 26 Aug 07:41
♓ 28 Aug 10:47
♈ 30 Aug 16:12
♉ 2 Sep 00:52
♊ 4 Sep 12:28
♋ 7 Sep 01:04
♌ 9 Sep 12:14
♍ 11 Sep 20:35
♎ 14 Sep 02:08
♏ 16 Sep 05:46
♐ 18 Sep 08:29
♑ 20 Sep 11:05
♒ 22 Sep 14:13
♓ 24 Sep 18:30
♈ 27 Sep 00:41
♉ 29 Sep 09:22
♊ 1 Oct 20:34
♋ 4 Oct 09:10
♌ 6 Oct 20:58
♍ 9 Oct 05:59
♎ 11 Oct 11:30
♏ 13 Oct 14:11
♐ 15 Oct 15:28
♑ 17 Oct 16:51
♒ 19 Oct 19:37
♓ 22 Oct 00:27
♈ 24 Oct 07:35
♉ 26 Oct 16:54
♊ 29 Oct 04:09
♋ 31 Oct 16:41
♌ 3 Nov 05:04
♍ 5 Nov 15:17
♎ 7 Nov 21:52
♏ 10 Nov 00:43
♐ 12 Nov 01:04
♑ 14 Nov 00:51
♒ 16 Nov 02:01
♓ 18 Nov 05:59
♈ 20 Nov 13:14
♉ 22 Nov 23:10
♊ 25 Nov 10:49
♋ 27 Nov 23:23
♌ 30 Nov 11:54
♍ 2 Dec 23:06
♎ 5 Dec 07:18
♏ 7 Dec 11:34
♐ 9 Dec 12:22
♑ 11 Dec 11:27
♒ 13 Dec 11:00
♓ 15 Dec 13:10
♈ 17 Dec 19:12
♉ 20 Dec 04:55
♊ 22 Dec 16:52
♋ 25 Dec 05:31
♌ 27 Dec 17:52
♍ 30 Dec 05:14

MERCURY

♑ 1 Jan 00:00
♒ 10 Feb 23:56
♓ 2 Mar 08:09
♈ 18 Mar 11:57
♉ 3 Apr 02:46
♊ 10 Jun 21:07
♋ 26 Jun 07:08
♌ 10 Jul 12:01
♍ 28 Jul 10:16
♎ 4 Oct 09:17
♏ 21 Oct 16:24
♐ 9 Nov 17:21
♑ 1 Dec 06:44
♒ 21 Dec 07:19

VENUS

♒ 1 Jan 00:00
♓ 4 Jan 13:02
♈ 2 Feb 05:55
♉ 6 Mar 06:11
♊ 6 Jun 15:10
♋ 2 Aug 19:19
♌ 28 Aug 15:10
♍ 22 Sep 15:06
♎ 17 Oct 01:38
♏ 10 Nov 03:52
♐ 4 Dec 01:50
♑ 27 Dec 22:10

MARS

♐ 1 Jan 00:00
♐ 1 Jan 00:42
♑ 9 Feb 11:58
♓ 20 Mar 02:20
♈ 27 Apr 15:46
♉ 6 Jun 03:00
♊ 17 Jul 15:13
♋ 1 Sep 00:21
♌ 26 Oct 18:57

JUPITER

♉ 1 Jan 00:00
♊ 3 Apr 15:43
♊ 20 Aug 12:43

SATURN

♌ 1 Jan 00:00
♌ 17 Nov 02:42

1978

SUN

♑ 1 Jan 00:00
♒ 20 Jan 10:05
♓ 19 Feb 00:22
♈ 20 Mar 23:34
♉ 20 Apr 10:50
♊ 21 May 10:09
♋ 21 Jun 18:10
♌ 23 Jul 05:01
♍ 23 Aug 11:58
♎ 23 Sep 09:26
♏ 23 Oct 18:38
♐ 22 Nov 16:05
♑ 22 Dec 05:22

MOON

♎ 1 Jan 00:00
♏ 1 Jan 14:32
♐ 3 Jan 20:36
♑ 5 Jan 23:04
♒ 7 Jan 22:55
♓ 9 Jan 22:06
♈ 11 Jan 22:51
♉ 14 Jan 03:06
♊ 16 Jan 11:31
♋ 18 Jan 23:07
♌ 21 Jan 11:51
♍ 24 Jan 00:03
♎ 26 Jan 10:57
♏ 28 Jan 20:08
♐ 31 Jan 03:04
♑ 2 Feb 07:14
♒ 4 Feb 08:51
♓ 6 Feb 09:05
♈ 8 Feb 09:48
♉ 10 Feb 12:57
♊ 12 Feb 19:51
♋ 15 Feb 06:25
♌ 17 Feb 18:56
♍ 20 Feb 07:10
♎ 22 Feb 17:40
♏ 25 Feb 02:04
♐ 27 Feb 08:29
♑ 1 Mar 13:03
♒ 3 Mar 15:59
♓ 5 Mar 17:51
♈ 7 Mar 19:46
♉ 9 Mar 23:09
♊ 12 Mar 05:19
♋ 14 Mar 14:49
♌ 17 Mar 02:50
♍ 19 Mar 15:13
♎ 22 Mar 01:50
♏ 24 Mar 09:42
♐ 26 Mar 15:02
♑ 28 Mar 18:38
♒ 30 Mar 21:24
♓ 2 Apr 00:06
♈ 4 Apr 03:21
♉ 6 Apr 07:52
♊ 8 Apr 14:22
♋ 10 Apr 23:28
♌ 13 Apr 11:00
♍ 15 Apr 23:31
♎ 18 Apr 10:45
♏ 20 Apr 18:54
♐ 22 Apr 23:40
♑ 25 Apr 02:01
♒ 27 Apr 03:28
♓ 29 Apr 05:29
♈ 1 May 09:01
♉ 3 May 14:28
♊ 5 May 21:53
♋ 8 May 07:19
♌ 10 May 18:42
♍ 13 May 07:18
♎ 15 May 19:16
♏ 20 May 09:39
♐ 22 May 11:32
♑ 24 May 11:42
♒ 26 May 12:11
♓ 28 May 14:37
♈ 30 May 19:53
♉ 2 Jun 03:51
♊ 4 Jun 13:54
♋ 7 Jun 01:31
♌ 9 Jun 14:08
♍ 12 Jun 02:35
♎ 14 Jun 12:56
♏ 16 Jun 19:29
♐ 18 Jun 22:02
♑ 20 Jun 21:53
♒ 22 Jun 21:08
♓ 24 Jun 21:58
♈ 27 Jun 01:54
♉ 29 Jun 09:22
♊ 1 Jul 19:38
♋ 4 Jul 07:34
♌ 6 Jul 20:14
♍ 9 Jul 08:45
♎ 11 Jul 19:49
♏ 14 Jul 03:48
♐ 16 Jul 07:50
♑ 18 Jul 08:34
♒ 20 Jul 07:42
♓ 22 Jul 07:27
♈ 24 Jul 09:47
♉ 26 Jul 15:51
♊ 29 Jul 01:31
♋ 31 Jul 13:39
♌ 3 Aug 02:11
♍ 5 Aug 14:30
♎ 8 Aug 01:30
♏ 10 Aug 10:12
♐ 12 Aug 15:43
♑ 14 Aug 18:04
♒ 16 Aug 18:16
♓ 18 Aug 18:05
♈ 20 Aug 19:30
♉ 23 Aug 00:06
♊ 25 Aug 08:32
♋ 27 Aug 20:00
♌ 30 Aug 08:40
♍ 1 Sep 20:47
♎ 4 Sep 07:16
♏ 6 Sep 15:39
♐ 8 Sep 21:40
♑ 11 Sep 01:20
♒ 13 Sep 03:09
♓ 15 Sep 04:10
♈ 17 Sep 05:51
♉ 19 Sep 09:44
♊ 21 Sep 16:57
♋ 24 Sep 03:32
♌ 26 Sep 16:02
♍ 29 Sep 04:12
♎ 1 Oct 14:17
♏ 3 Oct 21:49
♐ 6 Oct 03:07
♑ 8 Oct 06:53
♒ 10 Oct 09:43
♓ 12 Oct 12:13
♈ 14 Oct 15:07
♉ 16 Oct 19:23
♊ 19 Oct 02:06
♋ 21 Oct 11:53
♌ 24 Oct 00:05
♍ 26 Oct 12:33
♎ 28 Oct 22:52
♏ 31 Oct 05:53
♐ 2 Nov 10:04
♑ 4 Nov 12:41
♒ 6 Nov 15:04
♓ 8 Nov 18:07
♈ 10 Nov 22:12
♉ 13 Nov 03:36
♊ 15 Nov 10:45
♋ 17 Nov 20:17
♌ 20 Nov 08:10
♍ 22 Nov 20:58
♎ 25 Nov 08:08
♏ 27 Nov 15:39
♐ 29 Nov 19:24
♑ 1 Dec 20:45
♒ 3 Dec 21:36
♓ 5 Dec 23:37
♈ 8 Dec 03:40
♉ 10 Dec 09:51
♊ 12 Dec 17:55
♋ 15 Dec 04:35
♌ 17 Dec 15:38
♍ 20 Dec 04:35
♎ 22 Dec 16:41
♏ 25 Dec 01:33
♐ 27 Dec 06:08
♑ 29 Dec 07:16
♒ 31 Dec 06:54

MERCURY

♐ 1 Jan 00:00
♑ 1 Jan 20:08
♒ 4 Feb 15:55
♓ 26 Feb 16:11
♈ 10 Mar 12:11
♉ 16 Mar 08:21
♊ 3 Jun 15:27
♋ 17 Jun 15:49
♌ 2 Jul 22:29
♍ 27 Jul 06:11
♎ 13 Aug 07:06
♍ 9 Sep 19:24
♎ 14 Oct 05:30
♐ 3 Nov 07:49

VENUS

♑ 1 Jan 00:00
♒ 20 Jan 18:30
♓ 13 Feb 16:07
♈ 9 Mar 16:30
♉ 2 Apr 21:14
♊ 27 Apr 07:54
♋ 22 May 02:04
♌ 16 Jun 06:20
♍ 12 Jul 02:15
♎ 8 Aug 03:09
♏ 7 Sep 05:08

MARS

♑ 1 Jan 00:00
♒ 26 Jan 02:00
♓ 10 Apr 18:51
♈ 14 Jun 02:39
♉ 4 Aug 09:08
♊ 19 Sep 20:58
♋ 2 Nov 01:21
♋ 12 Dec 17:40

JUPITER

♊ 1 Jan 00:00
♋ 12 Apr 00:12
♌ 5 Sep 08:31

SATURN

♌ 1 Jan 00:00
♌ 5 Jan 00:48
♍ 26 Jul 12:02

1979

SUN

♑ 1 Jan 00:00
♒ 20 Jan 16:01
♓ 19 Feb 06:14
♈ 21 Mar 05:23
♉ 20 Apr 16:36
♊ 21 May 15:55
♋ 21 Jun 23:57
♌ 23 Jul 10:49
♍ 23 Aug 17:48
♎ 23 Sep 15:17
♏ 24 Oct 00:29
♐ 22 Nov 21:55
♑ 22 Dec 11:11

MOON

♒ 1 Jan 00:00
♓ 2 Jan 07:09
♈ 4 Jan 09:42
♉ 6 Jan 15:18
♊ 8 Jan 23:43
♋ 11 Jan 10:15
♌ 13 Jan 22:17
♍ 16 Jan 11:11
♎ 18 Jan 23:41
♏ 21 Jan 09:51
♐ 23 Jan 16:09
♑ 25 Jan 18:28
♒ 27 Jan 18:13
♓ 29 Jan 17:26
♈ 31 Jan 18:12
♉ 2 Feb 22:04
♊ 5 Feb 05:34
♋ 7 Feb 16:06
♌ 10 Feb 04:26
♍ 12 Feb 17:18
♎ 15 Feb 05:38
♏ 17 Feb 16:13
♐ 19 Feb 23:52
♑ 22 Feb 04:01
♒ 24 Feb 05:13
♓ 26 Feb 04:53
♈ 28 Feb 04:55
♉ 2 Mar 07:10
♊ 4 Mar 12:59
♋ 6 Mar 22:35
♌ 9 Mar 10:48
♍ 11 Mar 23:43
♎ 14 Mar 11:42
♏ 16 Mar 21:50
♐ 19 Mar 05:39
♑ 21 Mar 10:57
♒ 23 Mar 13:53
♓ 25 Mar 15:05
♈ 27 Mar 15:48
♉ 29 Mar 17:37
♊ 31 Mar 22:09
♋ 3 Apr 06:24
♌ 5 Apr 17:58
♍ 8 Apr 06:53
♎ 10 Apr 18:46
♏ 13 Apr 04:16
♐ 15 Apr 11:19
♑ 17 Apr 16:24
♒ 19 Apr 20:03
♓ 21 Apr 22:42
♈ 24 Apr 00:52
♉ 26 Apr 03:28
♊ 28 Apr 07:49
♋ 30 Apr 15:12
♌ 3 May 01:57
♍ 5 May 14:42
♎ 8 May 02:48
♏ 10 May 12:11
♐ 12 May 18:25
♑ 14 May 22:26
♒ 17 May 01:26
♓ 19 May 04:19
♈ 21 May 07:31
♉ 23 May 11:21
♊ 25 May 16:29
♋ 27 May 23:51
♌ 30 May 10:09
♍ 1 Jun 22:41
♎ 4 Jun 11:12
♏ 6 Jun 21:06
♐ 9 Jun 03:15
♑ 11 Jun 06:24
♒ 13 Jun 08:07
♓ 15 Jun 09:57
♈ 17 Jun 12:53
♉ 19 Jun 17:19
♊ 21 Jun 23:23
♋ 24 Jun 07:25
♌ 26 Jun 17:48
♍ 29 Jun 06:15
♎ 1 Jul 19:09
♏ 4 Jul 05:58
♐ 6 Jul 12:56
♑ 8 Jul 16:08
♒ 10 Jul 17:00
♓ 12 Jul 17:23
♈ 14 Jul 18:58
♉ 16 Jul 22:44
♊ 19 Jul 05:00
♋ 21 Jul 13:41
♌ 24 Jul 00:31
♍ 26 Jul 13:02
♎ 29 Jul 02:07
♏ 31 Jul 13:47
♐ 2 Aug 22:06
♑ 5 Aug 02:23
♒ 7 Aug 03:29
♓ 9 Aug 03:06
♈ 11 Aug 03:11
♉ 13 Aug 05:22
♊ 15 Aug 10:42
♋ 17 Aug 19:18
♌ 20 Aug 06:29
♍ 22 Aug 19:12
♎ 25 Aug 08:14
♏ 27 Aug 20:13
♐ 30 Aug 05:40
♑ 1 Sep 11:34
♒ 3 Sep 14:00
♓ 5 Sep 14:04
♈ 7 Sep 13:30
♉ 9 Sep 14:13
♊ 11 Sep 17:55
♋ 14 Sep 01:28
♌ 16 Sep 12:26
♍ 19 Sep 01:16
♎ 21 Sep 14:11
♏ 24 Sep 01:55
♐ 26 Sep 11:36
♑ 28 Sep 18:41
♒ 30 Sep 22:50
♓ 3 Oct 00:24
♈ 5 Oct 00:29
♉ 7 Oct 00:45
♊ 9 Oct 03:08
♋ 11 Oct 09:10
♌ 13 Oct 19:12
♍ 16 Oct 07:52
♎ 18 Oct 20:45
♏ 21 Oct 08:03
♐ 23 Oct 17:10
♑ 26 Oct 00:12
♒ 28 Oct 05:17
♓ 30 Oct 08:30
♈ 1 Nov 10:10
♉ 3 Nov 11:17
♊ 5 Nov 13:26
♋ 7 Nov 18:24
♌ 10 Nov 03:15
♍ 12 Nov 15:21
♎ 15 Nov 04:17
♏ 17 Nov 15:30
♐ 19 Nov 23:57
♑ 22 Nov 06:02
♒ 24 Nov 10:37
♓ 26 Nov 14:18
♈ 28 Nov 17:17
♉ 30 Nov 19:55
♊ 2 Dec 23:03
♋ 5 Dec 04:02
♌ 7 Dec 12:10
♍ 9 Dec 23:33
♎ 12 Dec 12:30
♏ 15 Dec 00:09
♐ 17 Dec 08:37
♑ 19 Dec 13:55
♒ 21 Dec 17:13
♓ 23 Dec 19:51
♈ 25 Dec 22:41
♉ 28 Dec 02:08
♊ 30 Dec 06:33

MERCURY

♐ 1 Jan 00:00
♑ 8 Jan 22:34
♒ 28 Jan 12:50
♓ 14 Feb 20:39
♈ 3 Mar 21:33
♉ 28 Mar 10:40
♊ 17 Apr 12:49
♋ 10 May 22:04
♌ 26 May 07:45
♋ 9 Jun 06:33
♌ 27 Jun 09:52
♍ 2 Aug 21:39
♎ 18 Sep 19:00
♏ 7 Oct 03:55
♐ 30 Oct 09:06
♏ 18 Nov 03:09
♐ 12 Dec 13:35

VENUS

♏ 1 Jan 00:00
♐ 7 Jan 06:39
♑ 5 Feb 09:16
♒ 3 Mar 17:19
♓ 29 Mar 03:19
♈ 23 Apr 04:03
♉ 18 May 00:30
♊ 11 Jun 18:14
♋ 6 Jul 09:03
♌ 30 Jul 20:08
♍ 24 Aug 03:17
♎ 17 Sep 07:22
♏ 11 Oct 09:49
♐ 4 Nov 11:51
♑ 28 Nov 14:20
♒ 22 Dec 18:35

MARS

♋ 1 Jan 00:00
♋ 20 Jan 17:08
♊ 27 Feb 20:26
♋ 7 Apr 01:09
♌ 16 May 04:26
♍ 26 Jun 01:56
♎ 8 Aug 13:29
♏ 24 Sep 21:22
♐ 19 Nov 21:37

JUPITER

♌ 1 Jan 00:00
♋ 28 Feb 23:36
♌ 20 Apr 08:30
♍ 29 Sep 10:24

SATURN

♍ 1 Jan 00:00

1980

SUN

♑ 1 Jan 00:00
♒ 20 Jan 21:49
♓ 19 Feb 12:03
♈ 20 Mar 11:11
♉ 19 Apr 22:24
♊ 20 May 21:43
♋ 21 Jun 05:48
♌ 22 Jul 16:43
♍ 22 Aug 23:42
♎ 22 Sep 21:10
♏ 23 Oct 06:18
♐ 22 Nov 03:42
♑ 21 Dec 16:57

MOON

♊ 1 Jan 00:00
♋ 1 Jan 12:30
♌ 3 Jan 20:48
♍ 6 Jan 07:49
♎ 8 Jan 20:39
♏ 11 Jan 08:56
♐ 13 Jan 18:18
♑ 15 Jan 23:52
♒ 18 Jan 02:26
♓ 20 Jan 03:34
♈ 22 Jan 04:52
♉ 24 Jan 07:32
♊ 26 Jan 12:12
♋ 28 Jan 19:03
♌ 31 Jan 04:09
♍ 2 Feb 15:22
♎ 5 Feb 03:53
♏ 7 Feb 16:47
♐ 10 Feb 03:20
♑ 12 Feb 10:13
♒ 14 Feb 13:20
♓ 16 Feb 13:55
♈ 18 Feb 13:43
♉ 20 Feb 14:36
♊ 22 Feb 17:59
♋ 25 Feb 00:35
♌ 27 Feb 10:11
♍ 29 Feb 21:54
♎ 3 Mar 10:41
♏ 5 Mar 23:23
♐ 8 Mar 10:39
♑ 10 Mar 19:03
♒ 12 Mar 23:46
♓ 15 Mar 01:11
♈ 17 Mar 00:42
♉ 19 Mar 00:14
♊ 21 Mar 01:48
♋ 23 Mar 06:56
♌ 25 Mar 15:59
♍ 28 Mar 03:53
♎ 30 Mar 16:50
♏ 2 Apr 05:22
♐ 4 Apr 16:35
♑ 7 Apr 01:43
♒ 9 Apr 08:00
♓ 11 Apr 11:07
♈ 13 Apr 11:41
♉ 15 Apr 11:11
♊ 17 Apr 11:42
♋ 19 Apr 15:12
♌ 21 Apr 22:53
♍ 24 Apr 10:19
♎ 26 Apr 23:10
♏ 29 Apr 11:36
♐ 1 May 22:22
♑ 4 May 06:40
♒ 6 May 14:04
♓ 8 May 18:34
♈ 10 May 20:45
♉ 12 May 21:25
♊ 14 May 22:08
♋ 17 May 00:53
♌ 19 May 07:15
♍ 21 May 17:33
♎ 24 May 06:12
♏ 26 May 18:37
♐ 29 May 05:05
♑ 31 May 13:15
♒ 2 Jun 19:30
♓ 5 Jun 00:11
♈ 7 Jun 03:24
♉ 9 Jun 05:30
♊ 11 Jun 07:23
♋ 13 Jun 10:30
♌ 15 Jun 16:23
♍ 18 Jun 01:48
♎ 20 Jun 13:56
♏ 23 Jun 02:27
♐ 25 Jun 13:02
♑ 27 Jun 20:47
♒ 30 Jun 02:04
♓ 2 Jul 05:49
♈ 4 Jul 08:47
♉ 6 Jul 11:31
♊ 8 Jul 14:34
♋ 10 Jul 18:45
♌ 13 Jul 01:03
♍ 15 Jul 10:12
♎ 17 Jul 21:56
♏ 20 Jul 10:34
♐ 22 Jul 21:43
♑ 25 Jul 05:45
♒ 27 Jul 10:35
♓ 29 Jul 13:11
♈ 31 Jul 14:54
♉ 2 Aug 16:56
♊ 4 Aug 20:10
♋ 7 Aug 01:13
♌ 9 Aug 08:24
♍ 11 Aug 17:55
♎ 14 Aug 05:33
♏ 16 Aug 18:16
♐ 19 Aug 06:08
♑ 21 Aug 15:12
♒ 23 Aug 20:33
♓ 25 Aug 22:44
♈ 27 Aug 23:12
♉ 29 Aug 23:42
♊ 1 Sep 01:51
♋ 3 Sep 06:40
♌ 5 Sep 14:23
♍ 8 Sep 00:32
♎ 10 Sep 12:23
♏ 13 Sep 01:07
♐ 15 Sep 13:29
♑ 17 Sep 23:46
♒ 20 Sep 06:31
♓ 22 Sep 09:28
♈ 24 Sep 09:38
♉ 26 Sep 08:54
♊ 28 Sep 09:22
♋ 30 Sep 12:47
♌ 2 Oct 19:58
♍ 5 Oct 06:20
♎ 7 Oct 18:31
♏ 10 Oct 07:16
♐ 12 Oct 19:38
♑ 15 Oct 06:37
♒ 17 Oct 14:54
♓ 19 Oct 19:32
♈ 21 Oct 20:44
♉ 23 Oct 19:56
♊ 25 Oct 19:18
♋ 27 Oct 21:01
♌ 30 Oct 02:39
♍ 1 Nov 12:19
♎ 4 Nov 00:32
♏ 6 Nov 13:20
♐ 9 Nov 01:26
♑ 11 Nov 12:16
♒ 13 Nov 21:11
♓ 16 Nov 03:22
♈ 18 Nov 06:22
♉ 20 Nov 06:52
♊ 22 Nov 06:28
♋ 24 Nov 07:19
♌ 26 Nov 11:24
♍ 28 Nov 19:38
♎ 1 Dec 07:14
♏ 3 Dec 20:01
♐ 6 Dec 07:58
♑ 8 Dec 18:13
♒ 11 Dec 02:37
♓ 13 Dec 09:04
♈ 15 Dec 13:22
♉ 17 Dec 15:37
♊ 19 Dec 16:40
♋ 21 Dec 18:04
♌ 23 Dec 21:34
♍ 26 Dec 04:33
♎ 28 Dec 15:06
♏ 31 Dec 03:37

MERCURY

♐ 1 Jan 00:00
♑ 2 Jan 08:03
♒ 21 Jan 02:19
♓ 7 Feb 08:08
♈ 14 Apr 15:59
♉ 2 May 10:56
♊ 16 May 17:07
♋ 31 May 22:06
♌ 9 Aug 03:31
♍ 24 Aug 18:48
♎ 10 Sep 02:01
♏ 30 Sep 01:17
♐ 5 Dec 19:46
♑ 25 Dec 04:47

VENUS
♒ 1 Jan 00:00
♓ 16 Jan 03:37
♈ 9 Feb 23:40
♉ 6 Mar 18:55
♊ 3 Apr 19:47
♋ 12 May 20:53
♊ 5 Jun 05:45
♋ 6 Aug 14:26
♌ 7 Sep 17:58
♍ 4 Oct 23:08
♎ 30 Oct 10:39
♏ 24 Nov 01:36
♐ 18 Dec 06:22

MARS
♍ 1 Jan 00:00
♌ 11 Mar 20:47
♍ 4 May 02:27
♎ 10 Jul 18:00
♏ 29 Aug 05:51
♐ 12 Oct 06:27
♑ 22 Nov 01:43
♒ 30 Dec 22:31

JUPITER
♍ 1 Jan 00:00
♎ 27 Oct 10:11

SATURN
♍ 1 Jan 00:00
♎ 21 Sep 10:48

1981

SUN
♑ 1 Jan 00:00
♒ 20 Jan 03:37
♓ 18 Feb 17:53
♈ 20 Mar 17:04
♉ 20 Apr 04:19
♊ 21 May 03:40
♋ 21 Jun 11:46
♌ 22 Jul 22:41
♍ 23 Aug 05:39
♎ 23 Sep 03:06
♏ 23 Oct 12:14
♐ 22 Nov 09:37
♑ 21 Dec 22:51

MOON
♏ 1 Jan 00:00
♐ 2 Jan 15:43
♑ 5 Jan 01:42
♒ 7 Jan 09:13
♓ 9 Jan 14:43
♈ 11 Jan 18:44
♉ 13 Jan 21:46
♊ 16 Jan 00:18
♋ 18 Jan 03:08
♌ 20 Jan 07:22
♍ 22 Jan 14:03
♎ 24 Jan 23:46
♏ 27 Jan 11:49
♐ 30 Jan 00:12
♑ 1 Feb 10:38
♒ 3 Feb 17:56
♓ 5 Feb 22:22
♈ 8 Feb 01:02
♉ 10 Feb 03:11
♊ 12 Feb 05:52
♋ 14 Feb 09:43
♌ 16 Feb 15:11
♍ 18 Feb 22:35
♎ 21 Feb 08:13
♏ 23 Feb 19:55
♐ 26 Feb 08:30
♑ 28 Feb 19:47
♒ 3 Mar 03:51
♓ 5 Mar 08:13
♈ 7 Mar 09:49
♉ 9 Mar 10:23
♊ 11 Mar 11:43
♋ 13 Mar 15:06
♌ 15 Mar 21:03
♍ 18 Mar 05:20
♎ 20 Mar 15:31
♏ 23 Mar 03:15
♐ 25 Mar 15:52
♑ 28 Mar 03:53
♒ 30 Mar 13:16
♓ 1 Apr 18:42
♈ 3 Apr 20:26
♉ 5 Apr 20:05
♊ 7 Apr 19:48
♋ 9 Apr 21:34
♌ 12 Apr 02:37
♍ 14 Apr 10:57
♎ 16 Apr 21:39
♏ 19 Apr 09:40
♐ 21 Apr 22:16
♑ 24 Apr 10:32
♒ 26 Apr 20:58
♓ 29 Apr 03:57
♈ 1 May 06:58
♉ 3 May 07:00
♊ 5 May 06:02
♋ 7 May 06:18
♌ 9 May 09:41
♍ 11 May 16:56
♎ 14 May 03:25
♏ 16 May 15:38
♐ 19 May 04:15
♑ 21 May 16:21
♒ 24 May 03:01
♓ 26 May 11:06
♈ 28 May 15:44
♉ 30 May 17:11
♊ 1 Jun 16:49
♋ 3 Jun 16:39
♌ 5 Jun 18:44
♍ 8 Jun 00:26
♎ 10 Jun 09:56
♏ 12 Jun 21:55
♐ 15 Jun 10:32
♑ 17 Jun 22:22
♒ 20 Jun 08:37
♓ 22 Jun 16:45
♈ 24 Jun 22:19
♉ 27 Jun 01:17
♊ 29 Jun 02:22
♋ 1 Jul 02:58
♌ 3 Jul 04:48
♍ 5 Jul 09:27
♎ 7 Jul 17:43
♏ 10 Jul 05:03
♐ 12 Jul 17:36
♑ 15 Jul 05:20
♒ 17 Jul 15:03
♓ 19 Jul 22:26
♈ 22 Jul 03:44
♉ 24 Jul 07:19
♊ 26 Jul 09:42
♋ 28 Jul 11:42
♌ 30 Jul 14:21
♍ 1 Aug 18:55
♎ 4 Aug 02:25
♏ 6 Aug 12:59
♐ 9 Aug 01:23
♑ 11 Aug 13:21
♒ 13 Aug 22:57
♓ 16 Aug 05:35
♈ 18 Aug 09:50
♉ 20 Aug 12:44
♊ 22 Aug 15:19
♋ 24 Aug 18:17
♌ 26 Aug 22:11
♍ 29 Aug 03:32
♎ 31 Aug 11:03
♏ 2 Sep 21:11
♐ 5 Sep 09:24
♑ 7 Sep 21:49
♒ 10 Sep 07:59
♓ 12 Sep 14:35
♈ 14 Sep 17:56
♉ 16 Sep 19:31
♊ 18 Sep 21:00
♋ 20 Sep 23:40
♌ 23 Sep 04:09
♍ 25 Sep 10:29
♎ 27 Sep 18:41
♏ 30 Sep 04:54
♐ 2 Oct 17:00
♑ 5 Oct 05:50
♒ 7 Oct 17:02
♓ 10 Oct 00:33
♈ 12 Oct 04:02
♉ 14 Oct 04:44
♊ 16 Oct 04:42
♋ 18 Oct 05:53
♌ 20 Oct 09:35
♍ 22 Oct 16:06
♎ 25 Oct 00:57
♏ 27 Oct 11:39
♐ 29 Oct 23:49
♑ 1 Nov 12:47
♒ 4 Nov 00:52
♓ 6 Nov 09:53
♈ 8 Nov 14:39
♉ 10 Nov 15:45
♊ 12 Nov 15:00
♋ 14 Nov 14:38
♌ 16 Nov 16:33
♍ 18 Nov 21:54
♎ 21 Nov 06:34
♏ 23 Nov 17:37
♐ 26 Nov 06:01
♑ 28 Nov 18:54
♒ 1 Dec 07:10
♓ 3 Dec 17:17
♈ 5 Dec 23:50
♉ 8 Dec 02:32
♊ 10 Dec 02:31
♋ 12 Dec 01:41
♌ 14 Dec 02:09
♍ 16 Dec 05:39
♎ 18 Dec 12:59
♏ 20 Dec 23:40
♐ 23 Dec 12:12
♑ 26 Dec 01:00
♒ 28 Dec 12:54
♓ 30 Dec 23:02

MERCURY
♑ 1 Jan 00:00
♒ 12 Jan 15:48
♓ 31 Jan 17:36
♒ 17 Feb 00:00
♓ 18 Mar 04:34
♈ 8 Apr 09:12
♉ 24 Apr 05:32
♊ 8 May 09:43
♋ 28 May 17:05
♊ 22 Jun 22:52
♋ 12 Jul 21:09
♌ 1 Aug 18:31
♍ 16 Aug 12:48
♎ 2 Sep 22:41
♏ 27 Sep 11:03
♎ 14 Oct 02:09
♏ 9 Nov 13:15
♐ 28 Nov 20:53
♑ 17 Dec 22:21

VENUS
♐ 1 Jan 00:00
♑ 11 Jan 06:49
♒ 4 Feb 06:08
♓ 28 Feb 06:02
♈ 24 Mar 07:44
♉ 17 Apr 12:09
♊ 11 May 19:46
♋ 5 Jun 06:30
♌ 29 Jun 20:21
♍ 24 Jul 14:05
♎ 18 Aug 13:45
♏ 12 Sep 22:51
♐ 9 Oct 00:05
♑ 5 Nov 12:40
♒ 8 Dec 20:53

MARS
♒ 1 Jan 00:00
♓ 6 Feb 22:49
♈ 17 Mar 02:40
♉ 25 Apr 07:18
♊ 5 Jun 05:27
♋ 18 Jul 08:55
♌ 2 Sep 01:53
♍ 21 Oct 01:57
♎ 16 Dec 00:15

JUPITER
♎ 1 Jan 00:00
♏ 27 Nov 02:20

SATURN
♎ 1 Jan 00:00

1982

SUN
♑ 1 Jan 00:00
♒ 20 Jan 09:32
♓ 18 Feb 23:47
♈ 20 Mar 22:57
♉ 20 Apr 10:08
♊ 21 May 09:24
♋ 21 Jun 17:24
♌ 23 Jul 04:16
♍ 23 Aug 11:16
♎ 23 Sep 08:47
♏ 23 Oct 17:59
♐ 22 Nov 15:24
♑ 22 Dec 04:39

MOON
♓ 1 Jan 00:00
♈ 2 Jan 06:34
♉ 4 Jan 11:03
♊ 6 Jan 12:49
♋ 8 Jan 13:02
♌ 10 Jan 13:22
♍ 12 Jan 15:38
♎ 14 Jan 21:18
♏ 17 Jan 06:47
♐ 19 Jan 19:01
♑ 22 Jan 07:51
♒ 24 Jan 19:26
♓ 27 Jan 04:50
♈ 29 Jan 11:59
♉ 31 Jan 17:04
♊ 2 Feb 20:21
♋ 4 Feb 22:19
♌ 6 Feb 23:51
♍ 9 Feb 02:16
♎ 11 Feb 07:03
♏ 13 Feb 15:17
♐ 16 Feb 02:46
♑ 18 Feb 15:37
♒ 21 Feb 03:16
♓ 23 Feb 12:10
♈ 25 Feb 18:18
♉ 27 Feb 22:33
♊ 2 Mar 01:51
♋ 4 Mar 04:49
♌ 6 Mar 07:51
♍ 8 Mar 11:28
♎ 10 Mar 16:35
♏ 13 Mar 00:17
♐ 15 Mar 11:04
♑ 17 Mar 23:48
♒ 20 Mar 11:54
♓ 22 Mar 21:02
♈ 25 Mar 02:38
♉ 27 Mar 05:40
♊ 29 Mar 07:45
♋ 31 Mar 10:10
♌ 2 Apr 13:37
♍ 4 Apr 18:19
♎ 7 Apr 00:27
♏ 9 Apr 08:34
♐ 11 Apr 19:08
♑ 14 Apr 07:42
♒ 16 Apr 20:19
♓ 19 Apr 06:20
♈ 21 Apr 12:24
♉ 23 Apr 14:59
♊ 25 Apr 15:49
♋ 27 Apr 16:44
♌ 29 Apr 19:10
♍ 1 May 23:46
♎ 4 May 06:33
♏ 6 May 15:25
♐ 9 May 02:17
♑ 11 May 14:50
♒ 14 May 03:45
♓ 16 May 14:47
♈ 18 May 22:05
♉ 21 May 01:23
♊ 23 May 01:55
♋ 25 May 01:39
♌ 27 May 02:28
♍ 29 May 05:44
♎ 31 May 12:03
♏ 2 Jun 21:13
♐ 5 Jun 08:32
♑ 7 Jun 21:13
♒ 10 Jun 10:09
♓ 12 Jun 21:45
♈ 15 Jun 06:21
♉ 17 Jun 11:07
♊ 19 Jun 12:35
♋ 21 Jun 12:13
♌ 23 Jun 11:58
♍ 25 Jun 13:37
♎ 27 Jun 18:31
♏ 30 Jun 03:02
♐ 2 Jul 14:26
♑ 5 Jul 03:16
♒ 7 Jul 16:04
♓ 10 Jul 03:36
♈ 12 Jul 12:50
♉ 14 Jul 19:01
♊ 16 Jul 22:04
♋ 18 Jul 22:47
♌ 20 Jul 22:36
♍ 22 Jul 23:21
♎ 25 Jul 02:46
♏ 27 Jul 09:59
♐ 29 Jul 20:48
♑ 1 Aug 09:37
♒ 3 Aug 22:18
♓ 6 Aug 09:24
♈ 8 Aug 18:21
♉ 11 Aug 01:01
♊ 13 Aug 05:23
♋ 15 Aug 07:41
♌ 17 Aug 08:41
♍ 19 Aug 09:41
♎ 21 Aug 12:23
♏ 23 Aug 18:22
♐ 26 Aug 04:12
♑ 28 Aug 16:42
♒ 31 Aug 05:24
♓ 2 Sep 16:11
♈ 5 Sep 00:25
♉ 7 Sep 06:28
♊ 9 Sep 10:58
♋ 11 Sep 14:19
♌ 13 Sep 16:47
♍ 15 Sep 18:58
♎ 17 Sep 22:04
♏ 20 Sep 03:33
♐ 22 Sep 12:31
♑ 25 Sep 00:32
♒ 27 Sep 13:22
♓ 30 Sep 00:19
♈ 2 Oct 08:07
♉ 4 Oct 13:10
♊ 6 Oct 16:40
♋ 8 Oct 19:40
♌ 10 Oct 22:45
♍ 13 Oct 02:10
♎ 15 Oct 06:23
♏ 17 Oct 12:21
♐ 19 Oct 21:03
♑ 22 Oct 08:39
♒ 24 Oct 21:37
♓ 27 Oct 09:13
♈ 29 Oct 17:26
♉ 31 Oct 22:04
♊ 3 Nov 00:23
♋ 5 Nov 02:00
♌ 7 Nov 04:11
♍ 9 Nov 07:41
♎ 11 Nov 12:46
♏ 13 Nov 19:43
♐ 16 Nov 04:52
♑ 18 Nov 16:22
♒ 21 Nov 05:21
♓ 23 Nov 17:43
♈ 26 Nov 03:08
♉ 28 Nov 08:32
♊ 30 Nov 10:36
♋ 2 Dec 10:58
♌ 4 Dec 11:27
♍ 6 Dec 13:33
♎ 8 Dec 18:11
♏ 11 Dec 01:35
♐ 13 Dec 11:28
♑ 15 Dec 23:16
♒ 18 Dec 12:13
♓ 21 Dec 00:57
♈ 23 Dec 11:35
♉ 25 Dec 18:37
♊ 27 Dec 21:49
♋ 29 Dec 22:13
♌ 31 Dec 21:34

MERCURY
♑ 1 Jan 00:00
♒ 5 Jan 16:50
♓ 13 Mar 19:12
♈ 31 Mar 21:00
♉ 15 Apr 18:55
♊ 1 May 13:30
♋ 9 Jul 11:27
♌ 24 Jul 08:49
♍ 8 Aug 14:07
♎ 28 Aug 03:23
♏ 3 Nov 01:11
♐ 21 Nov 14:28
♑ 10 Dec 20:05

VENUS
♒ 1 Jan 00:00
♑ 23 Jan 02:57
♒ 2 Mar 11:26
♓ 6 Apr 12:21
♈ 4 May 12:27
♉ 30 May 21:03
♊ 25 Jun 12:14
♋ 20 Jul 16:22
♌ 14 Aug 11:10
♍ 7 Sep 21:38
♎ 2 Oct 01:33
♏ 26 Oct 01:20
♐ 18 Nov 23:07
♑ 12 Dec 20:21

MARS
♎ 1 Jan 00:00
♏ 3 Aug 11:46
♐ 20 Sep 01:21
♑ 31 Oct 23:06
♒ 10 Dec 06:18

JUPITER
♏ 1 Jan 00:00
♐ 26 Dec 01:58

SATURN
♎ 1 Jan 00:00

1983

SUN
♑ 1 Jan 00:00
♒ 20 Jan 15:18
♓ 19 Feb 05:31
♈ 21 Mar 04:40
♉ 20 Apr 15:51
♊ 21 May 15:07
♋ 21 Jun 23:10
♌ 23 Jul 10:05
♍ 23 Aug 17:08
♎ 23 Sep 14:43
♏ 23 Oct 23:55
♐ 22 Nov 21:19
♑ 22 Dec 10:31

MOON
♌ 1 Jan 00:00
♍ 2 Jan 21:50
♎ 5 Jan 00:45
♏ 7 Jan 07:17
♐ 9 Jan 17:14
♑ 12 Jan 05:27
♒ 14 Jan 18:27
♓ 17 Jan 07:03
♈ 19 Jan 18:09
♉ 22 Jan 02:37
♊ 24 Jan 07:41
♋ 26 Jan 09:29
♌ 28 Jan 09:11
♍ 30 Jan 08:35
♎ 1 Feb 09:48
♏ 3 Feb 14:33
♐ 5 Feb 23:29
♑ 8 Feb 11:34
♒ 11 Feb 00:41
♓ 13 Feb 13:02
♈ 15 Feb 23:47
♉ 18 Feb 08:31
♊ 20 Feb 14:53
♋ 22 Feb 18:32
♌ 24 Feb 19:47
♍ 26 Feb 19:50
♎ 28 Feb 20:31
♏ 2 Mar 23:51
♐ 5 Mar 07:16
♑ 7 Mar 18:30
♒ 10 Mar 07:31
♓ 12 Mar 19:48
♈ 15 Mar 06:01
♉ 17 Mar 14:05
♊ 19 Mar 20:21
♋ 22 Mar 00:53
♌ 24 Mar 03:44
♍ 26 Mar 05:19
♎ 28 Mar 06:49
♏ 30 Mar 09:58
♐ 1 Apr 16:21
♑ 4 Apr 02:30
♒ 6 Apr 15:07
♓ 9 Apr 03:31
♈ 11 Apr 13:38
♉ 13 Apr 21:00
♊ 16 Apr 02:16
♋ 18 Apr 06:15
♌ 20 Apr 09:27
♍ 22 Apr 12:12
♎ 24 Apr 15:05
♏ 26 Apr 19:05
♐ 29 Apr 01:29
♑ 1 May 11:02
♒ 3 May 23:10
♓ 6 May 11:44
♈ 8 May 22:17
♉ 11 May 05:37
♊ 13 May 10:04
♋ 15 May 12:49
♌ 17 May 15:02
♍ 19 May 17:37
♎ 21 May 21:12
♏ 24 May 02:18
♐ 26 May 09:28
♑ 28 May 19:08
♒ 31 May 07:00
♓ 2 Jun 19:43
♈ 5 Jun 07:00
♉ 7 Jun 15:06
♊ 9 Jun 19:38
♋ 11 Jun 21:33
♌ 13 Jun 22:22
♍ 15 Jun 23:39
♎ 18 Jun 02:37
♏ 20 Jun 08:00
♐ 22 Jun 15:56
♑ 25 Jun 02:09
♒ 27 Jun 14:07
♓ 30 Jun 02:52
♈ 2 Jul 14:48
♉ 5 Jul 00:06
♊ 7 Jul 05:42
♋ 9 Jul 07:51
♌ 11 Jul 07:54
♍ 13 Jul 07:44
♎ 15 Jul 09:11
♏ 17 Jul 13:39
♐ 19 Jul 21:32
♑ 22 Jul 08:12
♒ 24 Jul 20:27
♓ 27 Jul 09:12
♈ 29 Jul 21:22
♉ 1 Aug 07:38
♊ 3 Aug 14:44
♋ 5 Aug 18:10
♌ 7 Aug 18:38
♍ 9 Aug 17:50
♎ 11 Aug 17:52
♏ 13 Aug 20:45
♐ 16 Aug 03:34
♑ 18 Aug 14:00
♒ 21 Aug 02:26
♓ 23 Aug 15:11
♈ 26 Aug 03:09
♉ 28 Aug 13:39
♊ 30 Aug 21:50
♋ 2 Sep 02:54
♌ 4 Sep 04:48
♍ 6 Sep 04:37
♎ 8 Sep 04:14
♏ 10 Sep 05:50
♐ 12 Sep 11:09
♑ 14 Sep 20:34
♒ 17 Sep 08:46
♓ 19 Sep 21:31
♈ 22 Sep 09:11
♉ 24 Sep 19:13
♊ 27 Sep 03:25
♋ 29 Sep 09:25
♌ 1 Oct 12:55
♍ 3 Oct 14:16
♎ 5 Oct 14:43
♏ 7 Oct 16:07
♐ 9 Oct 20:21
♑ 12 Oct 04:31
♒ 14 Oct 16:01
♓ 17 Oct 04:42
♈ 19 Oct 16:19
♉ 22 Oct 01:48
♊ 24 Oct 09:11
♋ 26 Oct 14:48
♌ 28 Oct 18:51
♍ 30 Oct 21:34
♎ 1 Nov 23:32
♏ 4 Nov 01:54
♐ 6 Nov 06:10
♑ 8 Nov 13:32
♒ 11 Nov 00:11
♓ 13 Nov 12:42
♈ 16 Nov 00:37
♉ 18 Nov 10:07
♊ 20 Nov 16:46
♋ 22 Nov 21:11
♌ 25 Nov 00:20
♍ 27 Nov 03:03
♎ 29 Nov 05:58
♏ 1 Dec 09:41
♐ 3 Dec 14:57
♑ 5 Dec 22:29
♒ 8 Dec 08:40
♓ 10 Dec 20:54
♈ 13 Dec 09:17
♉ 15 Dec 19:34
♊ 18 Dec 02:24
♋ 20 Dec 06:03
♌ 22 Dec 07:45
♍ 24 Dec 09:02
♎ 26 Dec 11:19
♏ 28 Dec 15:27
♐ 30 Dec 21:45

MERCURY
♑ 1 Jan 00:00
♒ 1 Jan 13:32
♑ 12 Jan 06:56
♒ 14 Feb 09:37
♓ 7 Mar 04:24
♈ 23 Mar 20:10
♉ 7 Apr 17:04
♊ 14 Jun 08:07
♋ 1 Jul 19:19
♌ 15 Jul 20:57
♍ 1 Aug 10:23
♎ 29 Aug 06:08
♍ 6 Sep 02:31
♎ 8 Oct 23:45
♏ 26 Oct 15:48
♐ 14 Nov 08:57
♑ 4 Dec 11:23

VENUS
♑ 1 Jan 00:00
♒ 5 Jan 17:59
♓ 29 Jan 17:32
♈ 22 Feb 21:35
♉ 19 Mar 09:52
♊ 13 Apr 11:27
♋ 9 May 10:57
♌ 6 Jun 06:05
♍ 10 Jul 05:26
♌ 27 Aug 11:44
♍ 5 Oct 19:36
♎ 9 Nov 10:53
♏ 6 Dec 16:15

MARS
♒ 1 Jan 00:00
♓ 17 Jan 13:11
♈ 25 Feb 00:20
♉ 5 Apr 14:04
♊ 16 May 21:44
♋ 29 Jun 06:55
♌ 13 Aug 16:55
♍ 30 Sep 00:13
♎ 18 Nov 10:27

JUPITER
♐ 1 Jan 00:00

SATURN
♏ 1 Jan 00:00
♎ 6 May 19:32
♏ 24 Aug 11:53

1984

SUN
♑ 1 Jan 00:00
♒ 20 Jan 21:06
♓ 19 Feb 11:17
♈ 20 Mar 10:25
♉ 19 Apr 21:39
♊ 20 May 20:59
♋ 21 Jun 05:03
♌ 22 Jul 15:59
♍ 22 Aug 23:01
♎ 22 Sep 20:34
♏ 23 Oct 05:47
♐ 22 Nov 03:12
♑ 21 Dec 16:24

MOON
♐ 1 Jan 00:00
♑ 2 Jan 06:08
♒ 4 Jan 16:31
♓ 7 Jan 04:35
♈ 9 Jan 17:16
♉ 12 Jan 04:37
♊ 14 Jan 12:41
♋ 16 Jan 16:48
♌ 18 Jan 17:50
♍ 20 Jan 17:36
♎ 22 Jan 18:08
♏ 24 Jan 21:05
♐ 27 Jan 03:13
♑ 29 Jan 12:13
♒ 31 Jan 23:12
♓ 3 Feb 11:23
♈ 6 Feb 00:05
♉ 8 Feb 12:06
♊ 10 Feb 21:40
♋ 13 Feb 03:21
♌ 15 Feb 05:10
♍ 17 Feb 04:33
♎ 19 Feb 03:40
♏ 21 Feb 04:45
♐ 23 Feb 09:23
♑ 25 Feb 17:50
♒ 28 Feb 05:03
♓ 1 Mar 17:30
♈ 4 Mar 06:08
♉ 6 Mar 18:10
♊ 9 Mar 04:30
♋ 11 Mar 11:49
♌ 13 Mar 15:22
♍ 15 Mar 15:48
♎ 17 Mar 14:52
♏ 19 Mar 14:50
♐ 21 Mar 17:42
♑ 24 Mar 00:37
♒ 26 Mar 11:10
♓ 28 Mar 23:38
♈ 31 Mar 12:15

MOON (1984, continued)

♉ 2 Apr 23:56
♊ 5 Apr 10:05
♋ 7 Apr 18:00
♌ 9 Apr 23:02
♍ 12 Apr 01:12
♎ 14 Apr 01:30
♏ 16 Apr 01:42
♐ 18 Apr 03:45
♑ 20 Apr 09:11
♒ 22 Apr 18:28
♓ 25 Apr 06:27
♈ 27 Apr 19:03
♉ 30 Apr 06:31
♊ 2 May 16:03
♋ 4 May 23:27
♌ 7 May 04:44
♍ 9 May 08:03
♎ 11 May 09:55
♏ 13 May 11:23
♐ 15 May 13:51
♑ 17 May 18:44
♒ 20 May 02:56
♓ 22 May 14:09
♈ 25 May 02:40
♉ 27 May 14:14
♊ 29 May 23:24
♋ 1 Jun 05:54
♌ 3 Jun 10:20
♍ 5 Jun 13:28
♎ 7 Jun 16:04
♏ 9 Jun 18:49
♐ 11 Jun 22:27
♑ 14 Jun 03:49
♒ 16 Jun 11:42
♓ 18 Jun 22:19
♈ 21 Jun 10:41
♉ 23 Jun 22:39
♊ 26 Jun 08:05
♋ 28 Jun 14:10
♌ 30 Jun 17:31
♍ 2 Jul 19:28
♎ 4 Jul 21:28
♏ 6 Jul 00:29
♐ 9 Jul 05:04
♑ 11 Jul 11:24
♒ 13 Jul 19:42
♓ 16 Jul 06:11
♈ 18 Jul 18:27
♉ 21 Jul 06:53
♊ 23 Jul 17:11
♋ 25 Jul 23:45
♌ 28 Jul 02:42
♍ 30 Jul 03:30
♎ 1 Aug 04:04
♏ 3 Aug 06:05
♐ 5 Aug 10:30
♑ 7 Aug 17:25
♒ 10 Aug 02:26
♓ 12 Aug 13:14
♈ 15 Aug 01:29
♉ 17 Aug 14:14
♊ 20 Aug 01:32
♋ 22 Aug 09:21
♌ 24 Aug 13:01
♍ 26 Aug 13:33
♎ 28 Aug 12:58
♏ 30 Aug 12:58
♐ 1 Sep 16:30
♑ 3 Sep 22:56
♒ 6 Sep 08:12
♓ 8 Sep 19:25
♈ 11 Sep 07:47
♉ 13 Sep 20:34
♊ 16 Sep 08:26
♋ 18 Sep 17:37
♌ 20 Sep 22:50
♍ 23 Sep 00:20
♎ 24 Sep 23:42
♏ 26 Sep 23:05
♐ 29 Sep 00:33
♑ 1 Oct 05:29
♒ 3 Oct 14:04
♓ 6 Oct 01:20
♈ 8 Oct 13:52
♉ 11 Oct 02:29
♊ 13 Oct 14:15
♋ 16 Oct 00:01
♌ 18 Oct 06:42
♍ 20 Oct 09:57
♎ 22 Oct 10:32
♏ 24 Oct 10:09
♐ 26 Oct 10:44
♑ 28 Oct 14:06
♒ 30 Oct 21:14
♓ 2 Nov 07:50
♈ 4 Nov 20:21
♉ 7 Nov 08:54
♊ 9 Nov 20:11
♋ 12 Nov 05:32
♌ 14 Nov 12:34
♍ 16 Nov 17:09
♎ 18 Nov 19:30
♏ 20 Nov 20:31
♐ 22 Nov 21:35
♑ 25 Nov 00:18
♒ 27 Nov 06:07
♓ 29 Nov 15:34
♈ 2 Dec 03:43
♉ 4 Dec 16:21
♊ 7 Dec 03:25
♋ 9 Dec 11:57
♌ 11 Dec 18:09
♍ 13 Dec 22:36
♎ 16 Dec 01:53
♏ 18 Dec 04:28
♐ 20 Dec 06:59
♑ 22 Dec 10:22
♒ 24 Dec 15:48
♓ 27 Dec 00:19
♈ 29 Dec 11:50

MERCURY (1984)

♑ 1 Jan 00:00
♒ 9 Feb 01:51
♓ 27 Feb 18:08
♈ 14 Mar 16:28
♉ 31 Mar 20:26
♈ 25 Apr 11:50
♉ 15 May 12:34
♊ 7 Jun 15:45
♋ 22 Jun 06:40
♌ 6 Jul 18:57
♍ 26 Jul 06:50
♎ 30 Sep 19:45
♏ 18 Oct 03:02
♐ 6 Nov 12:10
♑ 1 Dec 16:30
♐ 7 Dec 21:46

VENUS (1984)

♏ 1 Jan 00:00
♐ 1 Jan 02:01
♑ 25 Jan 18:52
♒ 19 Feb 04:53
♓ 14 Mar 12:36
♈ 7 Apr 20:14
♉ 2 May 04:54
♊ 26 May 14:41
♋ 20 Jun 00:49
♌ 14 Jul 10:31
♍ 7 Aug 19:41
♎ 1 Sep 05:08
♏ 25 Sep 16:06
♐ 20 Oct 05:46
♑ 13 Nov 23:55
♒ 9 Dec 03:27

MARS (1984)

♎ 1 Jan 01:29
♏ 11 Jan 03:21
♐ 17 Aug 19:51
♑ 5 Oct 06:03
♒ 15 Nov 18:09
♓ 25 Dec 06:39

JUPITER (1984)

♑ 1 Jan 00:00
♒ 19 Jan 15:05

SATURN (1984)

♏ 1 Jan 00:00

1985

SUN

♑ 1 Jan 00:00
♒ 20 Jan 02:58
♓ 18 Feb 17:08
♈ 20 Mar 16:15
♉ 20 Apr 03:27
♊ 21 May 02:44
♋ 21 Jun 10:45
♌ 22 Jul 21:37
♍ 23 Aug 04:37
♎ 23 Sep 02:08
♏ 23 Oct 11:23
♐ 22 Nov 08:52
♑ 22 Dec 22:09

MOON

♓ 1 Jan 00:00
♈ 1 Jan 00:37
♉ 3 Jan 12:01
♊ 5 Jan 20:18
♋ 8 Jan 01:29
♌ 10 Jan 04:40
♍ 12 Jan 07:14
♎ 14 Jan 10:08
♏ 16 Jan 13:49
♐ 18 Jan 18:30
♑ 21 Jan 00:39
♒ 23 Jan 09:03
♓ 25 Jan 20:06
♈ 28 Jan 08:54
♉ 30 Jan 21:01
♊ 2 Feb 06:00
♋ 4 Feb 11:03
♌ 6 Feb 13:10
♍ 8 Feb 14:11
♎ 10 Feb 15:50
♏ 12 Feb 19:10
♐ 15 Feb 00:08
♑ 17 Feb 07:37
♒ 19 Feb 16:39
♓ 22 Feb 03:43
♈ 24 Feb 16:28
♉ 27 Feb 05:12
♊ 1 Mar 15:24
♋ 3 Mar 23:43
♌ 5 Mar 23:48
♍ 7 Mar 23:48
♎ 9 Mar 23:48
♏ 12 Mar 01:30
♐ 14 Mar 05:55
♑ 16 Mar 13:12
♒ 18 Mar 22:51
♓ 21 Mar 10:21
♈ 23 Mar 23:07
♉ 26 Mar 12:03
♊ 28 Mar 23:14
♋ 31 Mar 06:52
♌ 2 Apr 10:26
♍ 4 Apr 10:54
♎ 6 Apr 10:11
♏ 8 Apr 10:18
♐ 10 Apr 12:58
♑ 12 Apr 19:05
♒ 15 Apr 04:31
♓ 17 Apr 16:19
♈ 20 Apr 05:13
♉ 22 Apr 18:01
♊ 25 Apr 05:27
♋ 27 Apr 14:11
♌ 29 Apr 19:25
♍ 1 May 21:23
♎ 3 May 21:18
♏ 5 May 20:57
♐ 7 May 22:12
♑ 10 May 02:39
♒ 12 May 10:57
♓ 14 May 22:26
♈ 17 May 11:24
♉ 20 May 00:02
♊ 22 May 11:06
♋ 24 May 19:55
♌ 27 May 02:07
♍ 29 May 05:41
♎ 31 May 07:08
♏ 2 Jun 07:34
♐ 4 Jun 08:35
♑ 6 Jun 11:53
♒ 8 Jun 18:47
♓ 11 Jun 05:25
♈ 13 Jun 18:12
♉ 16 Jun 06:46
♊ 18 Jun 17:23
♋ 21 Jun 01:33
♌ 23 Jun 07:33
♍ 25 Jun 11:48
♎ 27 Jun 14:38
♏ 29 Jun 16:31
♐ 1 Jul 18:23
♑ 3 Jul 21:37
♒ 6 Jul 03:41
♓ 8 Jul 13:21
♈ 11 Jul 01:45
♉ 13 Jul 14:24
♊ 16 Jul 00:55
♋ 18 Jul 08:26
♌ 20 Jul 13:30
♍ 22 Jul 17:11
♎ 24 Jul 20:17
♏ 26 Jul 23:13
♐ 29 Jul 02:22
♑ 31 Jul 06:26
♒ 2 Aug 12:34
♓ 4 Aug 21:44
♈ 7 Aug 09:42
♉ 9 Aug 22:32
♊ 12 Aug 09:29
♋ 14 Aug 16:58
♌ 16 Aug 21:16
♍ 18 Aug 23:45
♎ 21 Aug 01:52
♏ 23 Aug 04:37
♐ 25 Aug 08:25
♑ 27 Aug 13:32
♒ 29 Aug 20:26
♓ 1 Sep 05:43
♈ 3 Sep 17:29
♉ 6 Sep 06:28
♊ 8 Sep 18:11
♋ 11 Sep 02:28
♌ 13 Sep 06:53
♍ 15 Sep 08:35
♎ 17 Sep 09:18
♏ 19 Sep 10:41
♐ 21 Sep 13:50
♑ 23 Sep 19:12
♒ 26 Sep 02:51
♓ 28 Sep 12:43
♈ 1 Oct 00:36
♉ 3 Oct 13:37
♊ 6 Oct 02:00
♋ 8 Oct 11:34
♌ 10 Oct 17:10
♍ 12 Oct 19:13
♎ 14 Oct 19:14
♏ 16 Oct 19:06
♐ 18 Oct 20:36
♑ 21 Oct 00:55
♒ 23 Oct 08:28
♓ 25 Oct 18:48
♈ 28 Oct 07:00
♉ 30 Oct 20:00
♊ 2 Nov 08:32
♋ 4 Nov 19:04
♌ 7 Nov 02:19
♍ 9 Nov 05:53
♎ 11 Nov 06:32
♏ 13 Nov 05:53
♐ 15 Nov 05:54
♑ 17 Nov 08:26
♒ 19 Nov 14:43
♓ 22 Nov 00:43
♈ 24 Nov 13:08
♉ 27 Nov 02:09
♊ 29 Nov 14:24
♋ 2 Dec 01:00
♌ 4 Dec 09:15
♍ 6 Dec 14:34
♎ 8 Dec 16:57
♏ 10 Dec 17:14
♐ 12 Dec 17:00
♑ 14 Dec 18:16
♒ 16 Dec 22:51
♓ 19 Dec 07:37
♈ 21 Dec 19:41
♉ 24 Dec 08:46
♊ 26 Dec 20:45
♋ 29 Dec 06:45
♌ 31 Dec 14:44

MERCURY

♐ 1 Jan 00:00
♑ 11 Jan 18:25
♒ 1 Feb 07:44
♓ 18 Feb 23:42
♈ 7 Mar 00:08
♉ 14 May 02:11
♊ 30 May 19:45
♋ 13 Jun 16:12
♌ 29 Jun 19:35
♍ 6 Sep 19:40
♎ 10 Oct 18:51
♏ 31 Oct 16:45
♐ 4 Dec 19:24
♑ 12 Dec 11:06

VENUS

♒ 1 Jan 00:00
♓ 4 Jan 06:24
♈ 2 Feb 08:30
♉ 6 Jun 08:54
♊ 6 Jul 08:02
♋ 2 Aug 09:11
♌ 28 Aug 03:39
♍ 22 Sep 02:54
♎ 16 Oct 13:04
♏ 9 Nov 15:09
♐ 3 Dec 13:01
♑ 27 Dec 09:18

MARS

♓ 1 Jan 00:00
♈ 2 Feb 17:20
♉ 26 Apr 09:14
♊ 9 Jun 10:41
♋ 25 Jul 04:05
♌ 10 Sep 01:32
♍ 27 Oct 15:16
♎ 14 Dec 19:00

JUPITER

♑ 1 Jan 00:00
♒ 6 Feb 15:36

SATURN

♏ 1 Jan 00:00
♐ 17 Nov 02:10

1986

SUN

♑ 1 Jan 00:00
♒ 20 Jan 08:47
♓ 18 Feb 22:58
♈ 20 Mar 22:04
♉ 20 Apr 09:13
♊ 21 May 08:29
♋ 21 Jun 16:31
♌ 23 Jul 03:25
♍ 23 Aug 10:27
♎ 23 Sep 08:00
♏ 23 Oct 17:15
♐ 22 Nov 14:45
♑ 22 Dec 04:03

MOON

♏ 1 Jan 00:00
♐ 2 Jan 20:46
♑ 5 Jan 00:45
♒ 7 Jan 02:48
♓ 9 Jan 03:43
♈ 11 Jan 05:02
♉ 13 Jan 08:40
♊ 15 Jan 16:04
♋ 18 Jan 03:14
♌ 20 Jan 16:13
♍ 23 Jan 04:15
♎ 25 Jan 13:48
♏ 27 Jan 20:52
♐ 30 Jan 02:11
♑ 1 Feb 06:20
♒ 3 Feb 09:32
♓ 5 Feb 12:02
♈ 7 Feb 14:36
♉ 9 Feb 18:33
♊ 12 Feb 01:22
♋ 14 Feb 11:39
♌ 17 Feb 00:18
♍ 19 Feb 12:40
♎ 21 Feb 22:26
♏ 24 Feb 04:59
♐ 26 Feb 09:08
♑ 28 Feb 12:07
♒ 2 Mar 14:52
♓ 4 Mar 17:57
♈ 6 Mar 21:43
♉ 9 Mar 02:49
♊ 11 Mar 10:04
♋ 13 Mar 20:05
♌ 16 Mar 08:24
♍ 18 Mar 21:05
♎ 21 Mar 07:39
♏ 23 Mar 14:40
♐ 25 Mar 18:23
♑ 27 Mar 20:06
♒ 29 Mar 21:21
♓ 31 Mar 23:26
♈ 3 Apr 03:12
♉ 5 Apr 09:04
♊ 7 Apr 17:13
♋ 10 Apr 03:37
♌ 12 Apr 15:52
♍ 15 Apr 04:43
♎ 17 Apr 16:11
♏ 20 Apr 00:25
♐ 22 Apr 04:51
♑ 24 Apr 06:16
♒ 26 Apr 06:17
♓ 28 Apr 06:42
♈ 30 Apr 09:07
♉ 2 May 14:31
♊ 4 May 23:02
♋ 7 May 10:00
♌ 9 May 22:27
♍ 12 May 11:19
♎ 14 May 23:16
♏ 17 May 08:46
♐ 19 May 14:42
♑ 21 May 17:03
♒ 23 May 16:58
♓ 25 May 16:16
♈ 27 May 17:01
♉ 29 May 20:55
♊ 1 Jun 04:44
♋ 3 Jun 15:46
♌ 6 Jun 04:27
♍ 8 Jun 17:17
♎ 11 Jun 05:12
♏ 13 Jun 15:19
♐ 15 Jun 22:39
♑ 18 Jun 02:37
♒ 20 Jun 03:37
♓ 22 Jun 03:01
♈ 24 Jun 02:51
♉ 26 Jun 05:13
♊ 28 Jun 11:35
♋ 30 Jun 21:55
♌ 3 Jul 10:33
♍ 5 Jul 23:20
♎ 8 Jul 10:57
♏ 10 Jul 20:51
♐ 13 Jul 04:41
♑ 15 Jul 09:59
♒ 17 Jul 12:35
♓ 19 Jul 13:11
♈ 21 Jul 13:18
♉ 23 Jul 15:00
♊ 25 Jul 20:03
♋ 28 Jul 05:12
♌ 30 Jul 17:20
♍ 2 Aug 06:05
♎ 4 Aug 17:27
♏ 7 Aug 02:45
♐ 9 Aug 10:05
♑ 11 Aug 15:37
♒ 13 Aug 19:18
♓ 15 Aug 21:23
♈ 17 Aug 22:45
♉ 20 Aug 00:53
♊ 22 Aug 05:38
♋ 24 Aug 13:37
♌ 27 Aug 01:07
♍ 29 Aug 13:41
♎ 1 Sep 01:09
♏ 3 Sep 10:07
♐ 5 Sep 16:34
♑ 7 Sep 21:13
♒ 10 Sep 00:41
♓ 12 Sep 03:29
♈ 14 Sep 06:08
♉ 16 Sep 09:28
♊ 18 Sep 14:34
♋ 20 Sep 22:26
♌ 23 Sep 09:14
♍ 25 Sep 21:45
♎ 28 Sep 09:40
♏ 30 Sep 18:58
♐ 3 Oct 01:04
♑ 5 Oct 04:36
♒ 7 Oct 06:49
♓ 9 Oct 08:53
♈ 11 Oct 11:46
♉ 13 Oct 16:04
♊ 15 Oct 22:14
♋ 18 Oct 06:36
♌ 20 Oct 17:16
♍ 23 Oct 05:38
♎ 25 Oct 18:03
♏ 28 Oct 04:21
♐ 30 Oct 11:05
♑ 1 Nov 14:20
♒ 3 Nov 15:20
♓ 5 Nov 15:49
♈ 7 Nov 17:29
♉ 9 Nov 21:30
♊ 12 Nov 04:15
♋ 14 Nov 13:25
♌ 17 Nov 00:27
♍ 19 Nov 12:47
♎ 22 Nov 01:26
♏ 24 Nov 12:47
♐ 27 Nov 21:00
♑ 29 Nov 01:14
♒ 1 Dec 02:09
♓ 3 Dec 01:29
♈ 5 Dec 01:24
♉ 7 Dec 03:49
♊ 9 Dec 09:50
♋ 11 Dec 19:11
♌ 14 Dec 06:42
♍ 16 Dec 19:10
♎ 19 Dec 07:45
♏ 21 Dec 19:31
♐ 24 Dec 05:06
♑ 26 Dec 11:07
♒ 28 Dec 13:20
♓ 30 Dec 12:55

MERCURY

♐ 1 Jan 00:00
♑ 5 Jan 20:43
♒ 25 Jan 00:34
♓ 11 Feb 05:22
♈ 3 Mar 07:23
♉ 17 Mar 17:37
♊ 22 May 07:27
♋ 5 Jun 14:07
♌ 26 Jun 14:16
♋ 23 Jul 21:51
♌ 11 Aug 21:10
♍ 30 Aug 03:29
♎ 15 Sep 02:29
♏ 4 Oct 00:20
♐ 23 Oct 00:35
♑ 29 Dec 23:10

VENUS

♑ 1 Jan 00:00
♒ 20 Jan 05:36
♓ 13 Feb 03:12
♈ 9 Mar 03:33
♉ 2 Apr 08:20
♊ 26 Apr 19:11
♋ 21 May 13:47
♌ 15 Jun 18:53
♍ 11 Jul 16:24
♎ 7 Aug 20:47
♏ 7 Sep 10:16

MARS

♏ 1 Jan 00:00
♐ 2 Feb 06:28
♑ 28 Mar 03:48
♒ 9 Oct 01:02
♓ 26 Nov 02:36

JUPITER

♒ 1 Jan 00:00
♓ 20 Feb 16:06

SATURN

♐ 1 Jan 00:00

1987

SUN

♑ 1 Jan 00:00
♒ 20 Jan 14:41
♓ 19 Feb 04:51
♈ 21 Mar 03:53
♉ 20 Apr 14:58
♊ 21 May 14:11
♋ 21 Jun 22:12
♌ 23 Jul 09:07
♍ 23 Aug 16:11
♎ 23 Sep 13:46
♏ 24 Oct 00:01
♐ 22 Nov 20:30
♑ 22 Dec 09:47

MOON

♑ 1 Jan 00:00
♒ 1 Jan 11:54
♓ 3 Jan 12:37
♈ 5 Jan 16:52
♉ 8 Jan 01:14
♊ 10 Jan 12:40
♋ 13 Jan 01:19
♌ 15 Jan 13:46
♍ 18 Jan 01:16
♎ 20 Jan 11:10
♏ 22 Jan 18:31
♐ 24 Jan 22:36
♑ 26 Jan 23:43
♒ 28 Jan 23:18
♓ 30 Jan 23:25
♈ 2 Feb 02:10
♉ 4 Feb 08:54
♊ 6 Feb 19:24
♋ 9 Feb 07:56
♌ 11 Feb 20:22
♍ 14 Feb 07:27
♎ 16 Feb 16:45
♏ 19 Feb 00:05
♐ 21 Feb 05:10
♑ 23 Feb 07:58
♒ 25 Feb 09:09
♓ 27 Feb 10:08
♈ 1 Mar 12:05
♉ 3 Mar 18:12
♊ 6 Mar 03:27
♋ 8 Mar 15:25
♌ 11 Mar 03:55
♍ 13 Mar 14:56
♎ 15 Mar 23:35
♏ 18 Mar 05:58
♐ 20 Mar 10:33
♑ 22 Mar 13:49
♒ 24 Mar 16:19
♓ 26 Mar 18:46
♈ 28 Mar 22:13
♉ 31 Mar 03:47
♊ 2 Apr 12:17
♋ 4 Apr 23:34
♌ 7 Apr 12:05
♍ 9 Apr 23:29
♎ 12 Apr 08:06
♏ 14 Apr 13:41
♐ 16 Apr 17:02
♑ 18 Apr 19:22
♒ 20 Apr 21:46
♓ 23 Apr 01:03
♈ 25 Apr 05:41
♉ 27 Apr 12:07
♊ 29 Apr 20:44
♋ 2 May 07:40
♌ 4 May 20:07
♍ 7 May 08:08
♎ 9 May 17:30
♏ 11 May 23:10
♐ 14 May 01:42
♑ 16 May 02:37
♒ 18 May 03:43
♓ 20 May 06:25
♈ 22 May 11:24
♉ 24 May 18:40
♊ 27 May 03:56
♋ 29 May 15:00
♌ 1 Jun 03:26
♍ 3 Jun 15:57
♎ 6 Jun 02:25
♏ 8 Jun 09:07
♐ 10 Jun 11:54
♑ 12 Jun 12:06
♒ 14 Jun 11:46
♓ 16 Jun 12:55
♈ 18 Jun 16:57
♉ 21 Jun 00:10
♊ 23 Jun 09:55
♋ 25 Jun 21:23
♌ 28 Jun 09:53
♍ 30 Jun 22:35
♎ 3 Jul 09:56
♏ 5 Jul 18:04
♐ 7 Jul 22:06
♑ 9 Jul 22:44
♒ 11 Jul 21:50
♓ 13 Jul 21:37
♈ 16 Jul 00:01
♉ 18 Jul 06:05
♊ 20 Jul 15:33
♋ 23 Jul 03:14
♌ 25 Jul 15:51
♍ 28 Jul 04:27
♎ 30 Jul 16:00
♏ 2 Aug 01:10
♐ 4 Aug 06:48
♑ 6 Aug 08:52
♒ 8 Aug 08:38
♓ 10 Aug 08:02
♈ 12 Aug 09:10
♉ 14 Aug 13:39
♊ 16 Aug 22:00
♋ 19 Aug 09:20
♌ 21 Aug 21:59
♍ 24 Aug 10:24
♎ 26 Aug 21:36
♏ 29 Aug 06:50
♐ 31 Aug 13:25
♑ 2 Sep 17:05
♒ 4 Sep 18:22
♓ 6 Sep 18:38
♈ 8 Sep 19:35
♉ 10 Sep 22:58
♊ 13 Sep 05:55
♋ 15 Sep 16:23
♌ 18 Sep 04:51
♍ 20 Sep 17:14
♎ 23 Sep 03:59
♏ 25 Sep 12:31
♐ 27 Sep 18:50
♑ 29 Sep 23:09
♒ 2 Oct 01:52
♓ 4 Oct 03:40
♈ 6 Oct 05:36
♉ 8 Oct 08:58
♊ 10 Oct 15:04
♋ 13 Oct 00:32
♌ 15 Oct 12:35
♍ 18 Oct 01:07
♎ 20 Oct 11:51
♏ 22 Oct 19:42
♐ 25 Oct 00:58
♑ 27 Oct 04:34
♒ 29 Oct 07:28
♓ 31 Oct 10:20
♈ 2 Nov 13:41
♉ 4 Nov 18:03
♊ 7 Nov 00:17
♋ 9 Nov 09:11
♌ 11 Nov 20:46
♍ 14 Nov 09:30

(MOON, continued)

♎ 16 Nov 20:49
♏ 19 Nov 04:48
♐ 21 Nov 09:17
♑ 23 Nov 11:33
♒ 25 Nov 13:14
♓ 27 Nov 15:41
♈ 29 Nov 19:37
♉ 2 Dec 01:06
♊ 4 Dec 08:14
♋ 6 Dec 17:21
♌ 9 Dec 04:41
♍ 11 Dec 17:31
♎ 14 Dec 05:41
♏ 16 Dec 14:42
♐ 18 Dec 19:34
♑ 20 Dec 21:08
♒ 22 Dec 21:21
♓ 24 Dec 22:11
♈ 27 Dec 01:06
♉ 29 Dec 06:37
♊ 31 Dec 14:30

MERCURY
♑ 1 Jan 00:00
♒ 17 Jan 13:09
♓ 4 Feb 02:32
♒ 12 Mar 00:00
♓ 13 Mar 21:10
♈ 12 Apr 20:24
♉ 29 Apr 15:40
♊ 13 May 17:51
♋ 30 May 04:22
♌ 6 Aug 21:21
♍ 21 Aug 21:36
♎ 7 Sep 13:53
♏ 28 Sep 17:22
♐ 1 Nov 01:58
♏ 11 Nov 21:58
♐ 3 Dec 13:34
♑ 22 Dec 17:41

VENUS
♏ 1 Jan 00:00
♐ 7 Jan 10:21
♑ 5 Feb 03:04
♒ 3 Mar 07:56
♓ 28 Mar 16:21
♈ 22 Apr 14:04
♉ 17 May 11:56
♊ 11 Jun 05:16
♋ 5 Jul 19:51
♌ 30 Jul 06:50
♍ 23 Aug 14:01
♎ 16 Sep 18:13
♏ 10 Oct 20:49
♐ 3 Nov 23:05
♑ 28 Nov 01:52
♒ 22 Dec 06:30

MARS
♓ 1 Jan 00:00
♈ 8 Jan 12:21
♉ 20 Feb 14:45
♊ 5 Apr 16:38
♋ 21 May 04:02
♌ 6 Jul 16:47
♍ 22 Aug 19:52
♎ 8 Oct 19:28
♏ 24 Nov 03:20

JUPITER
♓ 1 Jan 00:00
♈ 2 Mar 18:42

SATURN
♐ 1 Jan 00:00

1988

SUN
♑ 1 Jan 00:00
♒ 20 Jan 20:25
♓ 19 Feb 10:36
♈ 20 Mar 09:40
♉ 19 Apr 20:46
♊ 20 May 19:58
♋ 21 Jun 03:57
♌ 22 Jul 14:52
♍ 22 Aug 21:55
♎ 22 Sep 19:30
♏ 23 Oct 04:45
♐ 22 Nov 02:13
♑ 21 Dec 15:29

MOON
♊ 1 Jan 00:00
♋ 3 Jan 00:17
♌ 5 Jan 11:48
♍ 8 Jan 00:36
♎ 10 Jan 13:18
♏ 12 Jan 23:40
♐ 15 Jan 05:59
♑ 17 Jan 08:16
♒ 19 Jan 08:03
♓ 21 Jan 07:28
♈ 23 Jan 08:32
♉ 25 Jan 12:37
♊ 27 Jan 20:03
♋ 30 Jan 06:12
♌ 1 Feb 18:07
♍ 4 Feb 06:55
♎ 6 Feb 19:37
♏ 9 Feb 06:43
♐ 11 Feb 14:37
♑ 13 Feb 18:37
♒ 15 Feb 19:26
♓ 17 Feb 18:45
♈ 19 Feb 18:36
♉ 21 Feb 20:51
♊ 24 Feb 02:43
♋ 26 Feb 12:13
♌ 29 Feb 00:13
♍ 2 Mar 13:07
♎ 5 Mar 01:33
♏ 7 Mar 12:28
♐ 9 Mar 21:00
♑ 12 Mar 02:32
♒ 14 Mar 05:09
♓ 16 Mar 05:43
♈ 18 Mar 05:46
♉ 20 Mar 07:06
♊ 22 Mar 11:22
♋ 24 Mar 19:28
♌ 27 Mar 06:55
♍ 29 Mar 19:50
♎ 1 Apr 08:06
♏ 3 Apr 18:27
♐ 6 Apr 02:30
♑ 8 Apr 08:20
♒ 10 Apr 12:11
♓ 12 Apr 14:25
♈ 14 Apr 15:48
♉ 16 Apr 17:32
♊ 18 Apr 21:11
♋ 21 Apr 04:05
♌ 23 Apr 14:35
♍ 26 Apr 03:17
♎ 28 Apr 15:38
♏ 1 May 01:40
♐ 3 May 08:53
♑ 5 May 13:55
♒ 7 May 17:38
♓ 9 May 20:40
♈ 11 May 23:24
♉ 14 May 02:23
♊ 16 May 06:32
♋ 18 May 13:06
♌ 20 May 22:52
♍ 23 May 11:13
♎ 25 May 23:50
♏ 28 May 10:07
♐ 30 May 16:58
♑ 1 Jun 20:59
♒ 3 Jun 23:35
♓ 6 Jun 02:01
♈ 8 Jun 05:05
♉ 10 Jun 09:03
♊ 12 Jun 14:15
♋ 14 Jun 21:20
♌ 17 Jun 06:58
♍ 19 Jun 19:04
♎ 22 Jun 07:58
♏ 24 Jun 18:59
♐ 27 Jun 02:19
♑ 29 Jun 06:01
♒ 1 Jul 07:30
♓ 3 Jul 08:34
♈ 5 Jul 10:38
♉ 7 Jul 14:28
♊ 9 Jul 20:17
♋ 12 Jul 04:09
♌ 14 Jul 14:12
♍ 17 Jul 02:18
♎ 19 Jul 15:23
♏ 22 Jul 03:14
♐ 24 Jul 11:43
♑ 26 Jul 16:08
♒ 28 Jul 17:26
♓ 30 Jul 17:24

MARS
♏ 1 Jan 00:00
♐ 8 Jan 15:25
♑ 22 Feb 10:16
♒ 6 Apr 01:44
♓ 22 May 07:43
♈ 13 Jul 20:01
♉ 1 Nov 12:58

(MOON, continued)
♐ 20 Aug 19:56
♑ 23 Aug 04:06
♒ 25 Aug 04:06
♓ 27 Aug 04:02
♈ 29 Aug 03:30
♉ 31 Aug 04:23
♊ 2 Sep 08:12
♋ 4 Sep 15:38
♌ 7 Sep 02:15
♍ 9 Sep 14:49
♎ 12 Sep 03:52
♏ 14 Sep 16:08
♐ 17 Sep 02:26
♑ 19 Sep 09:46
♒ 21 Sep 13:44
♓ 23 Sep 14:52
♈ 25 Sep 14:30
♉ 27 Sep 14:30
♊ 29 Sep 16:44
♋ 1 Oct 22:39
♌ 4 Oct 08:32
♍ 6 Oct 21:02
♎ 9 Oct 10:04
♏ 11 Oct 21:59
♐ 14 Oct 07:59
♑ 16 Oct 15:45
♒ 18 Oct 21:06
♓ 20 Oct 23:59
♈ 23 Oct 01:00
♉ 25 Oct 01:23
♊ 27 Oct 02:56
♋ 29 Oct 07:29
♌ 31 Oct 16:04
♍ 3 Nov 04:03
♎ 5 Nov 17:05
♏ 8 Nov 04:47
♐ 10 Nov 14:07
♑ 12 Nov 21:13
♒ 15 Nov 02:37
♓ 17 Nov 06:35
♈ 19 Nov 09:13
♉ 21 Nov 11:03
♊ 23 Nov 13:13
♋ 25 Nov 17:20
♌ 28 Nov 00:53
♍ 30 Nov 12:00
♎ 3 Dec 00:57
♏ 5 Dec 12:52
♐ 7 Dec 21:56
♑ 10 Dec 04:08
♒ 12 Dec 08:26
♓ 14 Dec 11:54
♈ 16 Dec 15:04
♉ 18 Dec 18:12
♊ 20 Dec 21:44
♋ 23 Dec 02:36
♌ 25 Dec 09:58
♍ 27 Dec 20:28
♎ 30 Dec 09:10

JUPITER
♈ 1 Jan 00:00
♉ 8 Mar 15:45
♊ 22 Jul 00:00
♉ 30 Nov 20:55

SATURN
♐ 1 Jan 00:00
♑ 13 Feb 23:51
♐ 10 Jun 05:24
♑ 12 Nov 09:26

1989

SUN
♑ 1 Jan 00:00
♒ 20 Jan 02:08
♓ 18 Feb 16:21
♈ 20 Mar 15:29
♉ 20 Apr 02:40
♊ 21 May 01:54
♋ 21 Jun 09:54
♌ 22 Jul 20:46
♍ 23 Aug 03:47
♎ 23 Sep 01:21
♏ 23 Oct 10:36
♐ 22 Nov 08:06
♑ 21 Dec 21:23

MOON
♎ 1 Jan 00:00
♏ 1 Jan 21:35
♐ 4 Jan 07:12
♑ 6 Jan 13:15
♒ 8 Jan 16:31
♓ 10 Jan 18:32
♈ 12 Jan 20:37
♉ 14 Jan 23:37
♊ 17 Jan 03:58
♋ 19 Jan 09:06
♌ 21 Jan 18:03
♍ 24 Jan 04:33
♎ 26 Jan 17:02
♏ 29 Jan 05:50
♐ 31 Jan 16:31
♑ 2 Feb 23:31
♒ 5 Feb 02:52
♓ 7 Feb 03:53
♈ 9 Feb 04:19
♉ 11 Feb 05:46
♊ 13 Feb 09:23
♋ 15 Feb 15:41
♌ 18 Feb 00:34
♍ 20 Feb 11:35
♎ 23 Feb 00:06
♏ 25 Feb 12:58
♐ 28 Feb 00:30
♑ 2 Mar 08:59
♒ 4 Mar 13:37
♓ 6 Mar 15:00
♈ 8 Mar 14:37
♉ 10 Mar 14:26
♊ 12 Mar 16:17
♋ 14 Mar 21:28
♌ 17 Mar 06:14
♍ 19 Mar 17:40
♎ 22 Mar 06:25
♏ 24 Mar 19:11
♐ 27 Mar 06:55
♑ 29 Mar 16:26
♒ 31 Mar 22:46
♓ 3 Apr 01:38
♈ 5 Apr 01:52
♉ 7 Apr 01:08
♊ 9 Apr 01:32
♋ 11 Apr 04:59
♌ 13 Apr 12:32
♍ 15 Apr 23:40
♎ 18 Apr 12:32
♏ 21 Apr 01:14
♐ 23 Apr 12:39
♑ 26 Apr 22:16
♒ 28 Apr 05:34
♓ 30 Apr 10:04
♈ 2 May 11:51
♉ 4 May 11:56
♊ 6 May 12:04
♋ 8 May 14:20
♌ 10 May 20:24
♍ 13 May 06:31
♎ 15 May 19:08
♏ 18 May 07:48
♐ 20 May 18:53
♑ 23 May 03:55
♒ 25 May 11:02
♓ 27 May 16:14
♈ 29 May 19:26
♉ 31 May 21:00
♊ 2 Jun 22:03
♋ 5 Jun 00:18
♌ 7 Jun 05:29
♍ 9 Jun 14:30
♎ 12 Jun 02:32
♏ 14 Jun 15:12
♐ 17 Jun 02:13
♑ 19 Jun 10:42
♒ 21 Jun 16:58
♓ 23 Jun 21:37
♈ 26 Jun 01:07
♉ 28 Jun 03:46
♊ 30 Jun 06:09
♋ 2 Jul 09:20
♌ 4 Jul 14:38
♍ 6 Jul 23:05
♎ 9 Jul 10:31
♏ 11 Jul 23:10
♐ 14 Jul 10:32
♑ 16 Jul 19:02
♒ 19 Jul 00:36
♓ 21 Jul 04:08
♈ 23 Jul 06:41
♉ 25 Jul 09:11
♊ 27 Jul 12:18
♋ 29 Jul 16:33
♌ 31 Jul 22:42
♍ 3 Aug 07:20
♎ 5 Aug 18:29
♏ 8 Aug 07:06
♐ 10 Aug 19:03
♑ 13 Aug 04:17
♒ 15 Aug 10:00
♓ 17 Aug 12:46
♈ 19 Aug 14:00
♉ 21 Aug 15:11
♊ 23 Aug 17:40
♋ 25 Aug 22:14
♌ 28 Aug 05:41
♍ 30 Aug 14:30
♎ 2 Sep 01:48
♏ 4 Sep 14:24
♐ 7 Sep 02:52
♑ 9 Sep 13:14
♒ 11 Sep 20:03
♓ 13 Sep 23:08
♈ 15 Sep 23:39
♉ 17 Sep 23:23
♊ 20 Sep 00:17
♋ 22 Sep 03:51
♌ 24 Sep 10:45
♍ 26 Sep 20:33
♎ 29 Sep 08:16
♏ 1 Oct 20:54
♐ 4 Oct 09:30
♑ 6 Oct 20:46
♒ 9 Oct 05:07
♓ 11 Oct 09:38
♈ 13 Oct 10:42
♉ 15 Oct 09:53
♊ 17 Oct 09:20
♋ 19 Oct 11:10
♌ 21 Oct 16:48
♍ 24 Oct 02:16
♎ 26 Oct 14:12
♏ 29 Oct 02:57
♐ 31 Oct 15:24
♑ 3 Nov 02:47
♒ 5 Nov 12:10
♓ 7 Nov 18:25
♈ 9 Nov 21:09
♉ 11 Nov 21:10
♊ 13 Nov 20:20
♋ 15 Nov 20:52
♌ 18 Nov 00:46
♍ 20 Nov 08:55
♎ 22 Nov 20:26
♏ 25 Nov 09:14
♐ 27 Nov 21:31
♑ 30 Nov 08:27
♒ 2 Dec 17:43
♓ 5 Dec 00:49
♈ 7 Dec 05:12
♉ 9 Dec 07:00
♊ 11 Dec 07:16
♋ 13 Dec 07:20
♌ 15 Dec 10:42
♍ 17 Dec 17:20
♎ 20 Dec 03:46
♏ 22 Dec 16:19
♐ 25 Dec 04:38
♑ 27 Dec 15:11
♒ 29 Dec 23:39

MERCURY
♐ 1 Jan 00:00
♑ 2 Jan 19:42
♒ 29 Jan 04:07
♓ 14 Feb 18:12
♈ 10 Mar 18:08
♉ 28 Mar 03:17
♊ 11 Apr 21:37
♋ 29 Apr 19:54
♌ 28 May 22:54
♊ 12 Jun 08:57
♋ 6 Jul 00:56
♌ 20 Jul 09:05
♍ 5 Aug 00:55
♎ 26 Aug 06:15
♏ 26 Sep 15:29
♎ 11 Oct 06:12
♏ 30 Oct 13:54
♐ 18 Nov 03:11
♑ 7 Dec 14:31

VENUS
♐ 1 Jan 00:00
♑ 10 Jan 18:09
♒ 3 Feb 17:16
♓ 27 Feb 17:00
♈ 23 Mar 18:33
♉ 16 Apr 22:53
♊ 11 May 06:29
♋ 4 Jun 17:18
♌ 29 Jun 07:22
♍ 24 Jul 01:32
♎ 18 Aug 01:59
♏ 12 Sep 12:23
♐ 8 Oct 16:01
♑ 5 Nov 10:14
♒ 10 Dec 04:55

MARS
♈ 1 Jan 00:00
♉ 19 Jan 08:12
♊ 11 Mar 08:52
♋ 29 Apr 04:38
♌ 16 Jun 14:11
♍ 3 Aug 13:36
♎ 19 Sep 14:39
♏ 4 Nov 05:30
♐ 18 Dec 04:58

JUPITER
♉ 1 Jan 00:00
♊ 11 Mar 03:27
♋ 30 Jul 23:51

SATURN
♑ 1 Jan 00:00

1990

SUN
♑ 1 Jan 00:00
♒ 20 Jan 08:03
♓ 18 Feb 22:15
♈ 20 Mar 21:20
♉ 20 Apr 08:28
♊ 21 May 07:38
♋ 21 Jun 15:34
♌ 23 Jul 02:22
♍ 23 Aug 09:22
♎ 23 Sep 06:56
♏ 23 Oct 16:15
♐ 22 Nov 13:48
♑ 22 Dec 03:08

MOON
♒ 1 Jan 00:00
♓ 1 Jan 06:11
♈ 3 Jan 10:57
♉ 5 Jan 14:05
♊ 7 Jan 16:02
♋ 9 Jan 17:53
♌ 11 Jan 21:03
♍ 14 Jan 02:58
♎ 16 Jan 12:18
♏ 19 Jan 00:17
♐ 21 Jan 12:45
♑ 23 Jan 23:28
♒ 26 Jan 07:26
♓ 28 Jan 12:52
♈ 30 Jan 16:35
♉ 1 Feb 19:28
♊ 3 Feb 22:13
♋ 6 Feb 01:28
♌ 8 Feb 05:52
♍ 10 Feb 12:14
♎ 12 Feb 21:10
♏ 15 Feb 08:35
♐ 17 Feb 21:08
♑ 20 Feb 08:31
♒ 22 Feb 16:53
♓ 24 Feb 21:50
♈ 27 Feb 00:17
♉ 1 Mar 01:44
♊ 3 Mar 03:38
♋ 5 Mar 07:03
♌ 7 Mar 12:25
♍ 9 Mar 19:48
♎ 12 Mar 05:10
♏ 14 Mar 16:26
♐ 17 Mar 04:57
♑ 19 Mar 17:02
♒ 22 Mar 02:32
♓ 24 Mar 08:09
♈ 26 Mar 10:16
♉ 28 Mar 10:27
♊ 30 Mar 10:43
♋ 1 Apr 12:51
♌ 3 Apr 17:51
♍ 6 Apr 01:43
♎ 8 Apr 11:45
♏ 10 Apr 23:19
♐ 13 Apr 11:49
♑ 16 Apr 00:16
♒ 18 Apr 10:53
♓ 20 Apr 17:58
♈ 22 Apr 20:59
♉ 24 Apr 21:04
♊ 26 Apr 20:13
♋ 28 Apr 20:40
♌ 1 May 00:09
♍ 3 May 07:19
♎ 5 May 17:29
♏ 8 May 05:23
♐ 10 May 17:57
♑ 13 May 06:22
♒ 15 May 17:31
♓ 18 May 01:55
♈ 20 May 06:32
♉ 22 May 07:43
♊ 24 May 07:01
♋ 26 May 06:35
♌ 28 May 08:30
♍ 30 May 14:09
♎ 1 Jun 23:32
♏ 4 Jun 11:22
♐ 7 Jun 00:00
♑ 9 Jun 12:13
♒ 11 Jun 23:10
♓ 14 Jun 08:01
♈ 16 Jun 13:56
♉ 18 Jun 16:44
♊ 20 Jun 17:15
♋ 22 Jun 17:10
♌ 24 Jun 18:26
♍ 26 Jun 22:43
♎ 29 Jun 06:48
♏ 1 Jul 18:02
♐ 4 Jul 06:40
♑ 6 Jul 18:40
♒ 9 Jul 05:07
♓ 11 Jul 13:30
♈ 13 Jul 19:37
♉ 15 Jul 23:30
♊ 18 Jul 01:33
♋ 20 Jul 02:45
♌ 22 Jul 04:30
♍ 24 Jul 08:18
♎ 26 Jul 15:19
♏ 29 Jul 01:40
♐ 31 Jul 14:01
♑ 3 Aug 02:09
♒ 5 Aug 12:09
♓ 7 Aug 19:55
♈ 10 Aug 01:14
♉ 12 Aug 04:56
♊ 14 Aug 07:42
♋ 16 Aug 10:13
♌ 18 Aug 13:12
♍ 20 Aug 17:34
♎ 23 Aug 00:18
♏ 25 Aug 09:57
♐ 27 Aug 21:58
♑ 30 Aug 10:24
♒ 1 Sep 20:52
♓ 4 Sep 04:06
♈ 6 Sep 08:24
♉ 8 Sep 10:56
♊ 10 Sep 13:06
♋ 12 Sep 15:54
♌ 14 Sep 19:53
♍ 17 Sep 01:19
♎ 19 Sep 08:35
♏ 21 Sep 18:07
♐ 24 Sep 05:53
♑ 26 Sep 18:37
♒ 29 Sep 06:35
♓ 1 Oct 15:43
♍ 14 Oct 07:21
♎ 16 Oct 01:25
♏ 19 Oct 01:25
♐ 21 Oct 13:10
♑ 24 Oct 02:04
♒ 26 Oct 14:15
♓ 28 Oct 23:23
♈ 31 Oct 04:15
♉ 2 Nov 05:32
♊ 4 Nov 05:07
♋ 6 Nov 05:08
♌ 8 Nov 07:25
♍ 10 Nov 12:49
♎ 12 Nov 21:09
♏ 15 Nov 07:40
♐ 17 Nov 19:40
♑ 20 Nov 08:32
♒ 22 Nov 21:08
♓ 25 Nov 07:33
♈ 27 Nov 14:07
♉ 29 Nov 16:38
♊ 1 Dec 16:23
♋ 3 Dec 15:28
♌ 5 Dec 16:01
♍ 7 Dec 19:40
♎ 10 Dec 03:01
♏ 12 Dec 13:29
♐ 15 Dec 01:45
♑ 17 Dec 14:36
♒ 20 Dec 03:00
♓ 22 Dec 13:49
♈ 24 Dec 21:46
♉ 27 Dec 02:10
♊ 29 Dec 03:27
♋ 31 Dec 03:03

MERCURY
♑ 1 Jan 00:00
♒ 12 Feb 01:12
♓ 3 Mar 17:15
♈ 4 Apr 07:36
♉ 16 Apr 00:30
♊ 27 Jun 20:47
♋ 11 Jul 23:49
♌ 29 Jul 11:11
♍ 5 Oct 01:47
♎ 11 Nov 00:07
♏ 2 Dec 00:14
♐ 25 Dec 22:58

VENUS
♒ 1 Jan 00:00
♓ 16 Jan 15:24
♈ 3 Mar 17:53
♉ 6 Apr 09:14
♊ 4 May 03:53
♋ 30 May 10:14
♌ 25 Jun 00:15
♍ 20 Jul 03:42
♎ 13 Aug 22:06
♏ 7 Sep 08:22
♐ 1 Oct 12:14
♑ 25 Oct 12:04
♒ 18 Nov 09:59
♓ 12 Dec 07:19

MARS
♐ 1 Jan 00:00
♑ 29 Jan 14:11
♒ 11 Mar 15:55
♓ 20 Apr 22:10
♈ 31 May 07:12
♉ 12 Jul 14:45
♊ 31 Aug 11:40
♋ 14 Dec 07:47

JUPITER
♋ 1 Jan 00:00
♌ 18 Aug 07:31

SATURN
♑ 1 Jan 00:00

1991

SUN
♑ 1 Jan 00:00
♒ 20 Jan 13:48
♓ 19 Feb 03:59
♈ 20 Mar 03:03
♉ 20 Apr 14:09
♊ 21 May 13:21
♋ 21 Jun 21:20
♌ 23 Jul 08:12
♍ 23 Aug 15:14
♎ 23 Sep 12:49

♏ 23 Oct 22:06
♐ 22 Nov 19:37
♑ 22 Dec 08:55

MOON
♋ 1 Jan 00:00
♌ 2 Jan 02:55
♍ 4 Jan 04:58
♎ 6 Jan 10:34
♏ 8 Jan 20:00
♐ 11 Jan 08:07
♑ 13 Jan 21:01
♒ 16 Jan 09:05
♓ 18 Jan 19:24
♈ 21 Jan 03:28
♉ 23 Jan 09:02
♊ 25 Jan 12:07
♋ 27 Jan 13:24
♌ 29 Jan 14:04
♍ 31 Jan 15:45
♎ 2 Feb 20:03
♏ 5 Feb 04:02
♐ 7 Feb 15:24
♑ 10 Feb 04:17
♒ 12 Feb 16:17
♓ 15 Feb 02:00
♈ 17 Feb 09:12
♉ 19 Feb 14:25
♊ 21 Feb 18:11
♋ 23 Feb 20:57
♌ 25 Feb 23:14
♍ 28 Feb 01:51
♎ 2 Mar 06:04
♏ 4 Mar 13:09
♐ 6 Mar 23:36
♑ 9 Mar 12:15
♒ 12 Mar 00:32
♓ 14 Mar 10:12
♈ 16 Mar 16:38
♉ 18 Mar 20:41
♊ 20 Mar 23:38
♋ 23 Mar 02:28
♌ 25 Mar 05:44
♍ 27 Mar 09:42
♎ 29 Mar 14:50
♏ 31 Mar 22:02
♐ 3 Apr 08:00
♑ 5 Apr 20:20
♒ 8 Apr 09:00
♓ 10 Apr 19:18
♈ 13 Apr 01:50
♉ 15 Apr 05:06
♊ 17 Apr 06:42
♋ 19 Apr 08:18
♌ 21 Apr 11:05
♍ 23 Apr 15:30
♎ 25 Apr 21:37
♏ 28 Apr 05:35
♐ 30 Apr 15:43
♑ 3 May 03:55
♒ 5 May 16:52
♓ 8 May 04:05
♈ 10 May 11:35
♉ 12 May 15:08
♊ 14 May 16:03
♋ 16 May 16:15
♌ 18 May 17:31
♍ 20 May 21:01
♎ 23 May 03:09
♏ 25 May 11:42
♐ 27 May 22:22
♑ 30 May 10:41
♒ 1 Jun 23:42
♓ 4 Jun 11:37
♈ 6 Jun 20:26
♉ 9 Jun 01:14
♊ 11 Jun 02:37
♋ 13 Jun 02:17
♌ 15 Jun 02:11
♍ 17 Jun 04:04
♎ 19 Jun 09:02
♏ 21 Jun 17:19
♐ 24 Jun 04:17
♑ 26 Jun 16:50
♒ 29 Jun 05:48
♓ 1 Jul 17:52
♈ 4 Jul 03:34
♉ 6 Jul 09:53
♊ 8 Jul 12:43
♋ 10 Jul 13:04
♌ 12 Jul 12:36
♍ 14 Jul 13:13
♎ 16 Jul 16:35
♏ 18 Jul 23:42
♐ 21 Jul 10:17
♑ 23 Jul 22:56
♒ 26 Jul 11:50
♓ 28 Jul 23:36
♈ 31 Jul 09:21
♉ 2 Aug 16:33
♊ 4 Aug 20:55
♋ 6 Aug 22:48
♌ 8 Aug 23:10
♍ 10 Aug 23:36
♎ 13 Aug 01:53
♏ 15 Aug 07:35
♐ 17 Aug 17:12
♑ 20 Aug 05:35
♒ 22 Aug 18:28
♓ 25 Aug 05:52
♈ 27 Aug 15:02
♉ 29 Aug 22:01
♊ 1 Sep 03:03
♋ 3 Sep 06:20
♌ 5 Sep 08:14
♍ 7 Sep 09:36
♎ 9 Sep 11:52
♏ 11 Sep 16:43
♐ 14 Sep 01:15
♑ 16 Sep 13:05
♒ 19 Sep 01:59
♓ 21 Sep 13:21
♈ 23 Sep 21:57
♉ 26 Sep 04:00
♊ 28 Sep 08:26
♋ 30 Sep 11:59
♌ 2 Oct 14:59
♍ 4 Oct 17:46
♎ 6 Oct 21:01
♏ 9 Oct 02:01
♐ 11 Oct 09:59
♑ 13 Oct 21:11
♒ 16 Oct 10:05
♓ 18 Oct 21:54
♈ 21 Oct 06:34
♉ 23 Oct 11:56
♊ 25 Oct 15:10
♋ 27 Oct 17:38
♌ 29 Oct 20:21
♍ 31 Oct 23:48
♎ 3 Nov 04:13
♏ 5 Nov 10:10
♐ 7 Nov 18:22
♑ 10 Nov 05:17
♒ 12 Nov 18:07
♓ 15 Nov 06:34
♈ 17 Nov 16:08
♉ 19 Nov 21:50
♊ 22 Nov 00:23
♋ 24 Nov 01:26
♌ 26 Nov 02:38
♍ 28 Nov 05:13
♎ 30 Nov 09:48
♏ 2 Dec 16:34
♐ 5 Dec 01:33
♑ 7 Dec 12:42
♒ 10 Dec 01:28
♓ 12 Dec 14:20
♈ 15 Dec 01:07
♉ 17 Dec 08:11
♊ 19 Dec 11:22
♋ 21 Dec 11:55
♌ 23 Dec 11:39
♍ 25 Dec 12:25
♎ 27 Dec 15:38
♏ 29 Dec 22:04

MERCURY
♐ 1 Jan 00:00
♑ 14 Jan 08:03
♒ 5 Feb 22:21
♓ 24 Feb 21:46
♈ 11 Mar 22:41
♉ 16 May 22:46
♊ 5 Jun 02:25
♋ 19 Jun 05:41
♌ 4 Jul 06:06
♍ 26 Jul 13:01
♌ 19 Aug 21:41
♍ 10 Sep 17:15
♎ 28 Sep 03:27
♏ 15 Oct 14:02
♐ 4 Nov 10:42

VENUS
♑ 1 Jan 00:00
♒ 5 Jan 05:04
♓ 29 Jan 04:45
♈ 22 Feb 09:03
♉ 18 Mar 21:46
♊ 13 Apr 00:11
♋ 9 May 01:29
♌ 6 Jun 01:17
♍ 11 Jul 05:07
♌ 21 Aug 15:07
♍ 6 Oct 21:16
♎ 9 Nov 06:37
♏ 6 Dec 07:22

MARS
♉ 1 Jan 00:00
♊ 21 Jan 01:16
♋ 3 Apr 00:50
♌ 26 May 12:20
♍ 15 Jul 12:37
♎ 1 Sep 06:39
♏ 16 Oct 19:06
♐ 29 Nov 02:20

JUPITER
♌ 1 Jan 00:00
♍ 12 Sep 06:01

SATURN
♑ 1 Jan 00:00
♒ 6 Feb 18:52

1992

SUN
♑ 1 Jan 00:00
♒ 20 Jan 19:33
♓ 19 Feb 09:44
♈ 20 Mar 08:49
♉ 19 Apr 19:58
♊ 20 May 19:13
♋ 21 Jun 03:15
♌ 22 Jul 14:10
♍ 22 Aug 21:11
♎ 22 Sep 18:44
♏ 23 Oct 03:58
♐ 22 Nov 01:27
♑ 21 Dec 14:44

MOON
♏ 1 Jan 00:00
♐ 1 Jan 07:31
♑ 3 Jan 19:10
♒ 6 Jan 08:00
♓ 8 Jan 20:53
♈ 11 Jan 08:23
♉ 13 Jan 17:01
♊ 15 Jan 21:56
♋ 17 Jan 23:27
♌ 19 Jan 22:58
♍ 21 Jan 22:23
♎ 23 Jan 23:43
♏ 26 Jan 04:33
♐ 28 Jan 13:21
♑ 31 Jan 01:06
♒ 2 Feb 14:10
♓ 5 Feb 02:52
♈ 7 Feb 14:16
♉ 9 Feb 23:37
♊ 12 Feb 06:09
♋ 14 Feb 09:32
♌ 16 Feb 10:16
♍ 18 Feb 09:48
♎ 20 Feb 10:06
♏ 22 Feb 13:12
♐ 24 Feb 20:27
♑ 27 Feb 07:34
♒ 29 Feb 20:35
♓ 3 Mar 09:12
♈ 5 Mar 20:08
♉ 8 Mar 05:06
♊ 10 Mar 12:04
♋ 12 Mar 16:51
♌ 14 Mar 19:21
♍ 16 Mar 20:14
♎ 18 Mar 20:56
♏ 20 Mar 23:21
♐ 23 Mar 05:14
♑ 25 Mar 15:09
♒ 28 Mar 03:45
♓ 30 Mar 16:24
♈ 2 Apr 03:05
♉ 4 Apr 11:19
♊ 6 Apr 17:34
♋ 8 Apr 22:19
♌ 11 Apr 01:47
♍ 13 Apr 04:10
♎ 15 Apr 06:11
♏ 17 Apr 09:11
♐ 19 Apr 14:41
♑ 21 Apr 23:41
♒ 24 Apr 11:39
♓ 27 Apr 00:21
♈ 29 Apr 11:14
♉ 1 May 19:10
♊ 4 May 00:29
♋ 6 May 04:10
♌ 8 May 07:08
♍ 10 May 09:57
♎ 12 May 13:06
♏ 14 May 17:16
♐ 16 May 23:23
♑ 19 May 08:14
♒ 21 May 19:44
♓ 24 May 08:26
♈ 26 May 19:53
♉ 29 May 04:17
♊ 31 May 09:20
♋ 2 Jun 11:58
♌ 4 Jun 13:36
♍ 6 Jun 15:29
♎ 8 Jun 18:34
♏ 10 Jun 23:28
♐ 13 Jun 06:30
♑ 15 Jun 15:51
♒ 18 Jun 03:20
♓ 20 Jun 16:01
♈ 23 Jun 04:04
♉ 25 Jun 13:29
♊ 27 Jun 19:15
♋ 29 Jun 21:43
♌ 1 Jul 22:16
♍ 3 Jul 22:38
♎ 6 Jul 00:28
♏ 8 Jul 04:54
♐ 10 Jul 12:18
♑ 12 Jul 22:16
♒ 15 Jul 10:04
♓ 17 Jul 22:45
♈ 20 Jul 11:08
♉ 22 Jul 21:37
♊ 25 Jul 04:45
♋ 27 Jul 08:09
♌ 29 Jul 08:40
♍ 31 Jul 08:02
♎ 2 Aug 08:18
♏ 4 Aug 11:17
♐ 6 Aug 17:58
♑ 9 Aug 04:01
♒ 11 Aug 16:07
♓ 14 Aug 04:52
♈ 16 Aug 17:12
♉ 19 Aug 04:11
♊ 21 Aug 12:37
♋ 23 Aug 17:37
♌ 25 Aug 19:16
♍ 27 Aug 18:47
♎ 29 Aug 18:12
♏ 31 Aug 19:39
♐ 3 Sep 00:51
♑ 5 Sep 10:07
♒ 7 Sep 22:09
♓ 10 Sep 10:57
♈ 12 Sep 23:03
♉ 15 Sep 09:48
♊ 17 Sep 18:41
♋ 20 Sep 01:00
♌ 22 Sep 04:20
♍ 24 Sep 05:09
♎ 26 Sep 04:56
♏ 28 Sep 05:45
♐ 30 Sep 09:34
♑ 2 Oct 17:30
♒ 5 Oct 04:54
♓ 7 Oct 17:39
♈ 10 Oct 05:37
♉ 12 Oct 15:49
♊ 15 Oct 00:09
♋ 17 Oct 06:37
♌ 19 Oct 11:02
♍ 21 Oct 13:28
♎ 23 Oct 14:40
♏ 25 Oct 16:05
♐ 27 Oct 19:30
♑ 30 Oct 02:19
♒ 1 Nov 12:44
♓ 4 Nov 01:14
♈ 6 Nov 13:20
♉ 8 Nov 23:20
♊ 11 Nov 06:50
♋ 13 Nov 12:20
♌ 15 Nov 16:24
♍ 17 Nov 19:29
♎ 19 Nov 22:04
♏ 22 Nov 00:53
♐ 24 Nov 05:02
♑ 26 Nov 11:39
♒ 28 Nov 21:20
♓ 1 Dec 09:24
♈ 3 Dec 21:50
♉ 6 Dec 08:17
♊ 8 Dec 15:38
♋ 10 Dec 20:06
♌ 12 Dec 22:48
♍ 15 Dec 00:57
♎ 17 Dec 03:34
♏ 19 Dec 07:21
♐ 21 Dec 12:43
♑ 23 Dec 20:05
♒ 26 Dec 05:44
♓ 28 Dec 17:29
♈ 31 Dec 06:08

MERCURY
♐ 1 Jan 00:00
♑ 10 Jan 01:47
♒ 29 Jan 21:16
♓ 16 Feb 07:05
♈ 3 Mar 21:46
♓ 3 Apr 23:53
♈ 14 Apr 17:36
♉ 11 May 04:11
♊ 26 May 21:17
♋ 9 Jun 18:28
♌ 27 Jun 05:12
♍ 3 Sep 08:04
♎ 19 Sep 05:42
♏ 7 Oct 10:14
♐ 29 Oct 17:03
♏ 21 Nov 19:45
♐ 12 Dec 08:06

VENUS
♐ 1 Jan 00:00
♑ 25 Jan 07:15
♒ 18 Feb 16:41
♓ 13 Mar 23:58
♈ 7 Apr 07:17
♉ 1 May 15:42
♊ 26 May 01:19
♋ 19 Jun 11:23
♌ 13 Jul 21:08
♍ 7 Aug 06:26
♎ 31 Aug 16:10
♏ 25 Sep 03:32
♐ 19 Oct 17:48
♑ 13 Nov 12:49
♒ 8 Dec 17:50

MARS
♐ 1 Jan 00:00
♑ 9 Jan 09:48
♒ 18 Feb 04:39
♓ 28 Mar 02:05
♈ 5 May 21:37
♉ 14 Jun 15:57
♊ 26 Jul 19:00
♋ 12 Sep 06:06

JUPITER
♍ 1 Jan 00:00
♎ 10 Oct 13:27

SATURN
♒ 1 Jan 00:00

1993

SUN
♑ 1 Jan 00:00
♒ 20 Jan 01:24
♓ 18 Feb 15:36
♈ 20 Mar 14:42
♉ 20 Apr 01:50
♊ 21 May 01:03
♋ 21 Jun 09:01
♌ 22 Jul 19:52
♍ 23 Aug 02:51
♎ 23 Sep 00:23
♏ 23 Oct 09:38
♐ 22 Nov 07:08
♑ 21 Dec 20:27

MOON
♈ 1 Jan 00:00
♉ 2 Jan 17:31
♊ 5 Jan 01:43
♋ 7 Jan 06:11
♌ 9 Jan 07:50
♍ 11 Jan 08:21
♎ 13 Jan 09:31
♏ 15 Jan 12:43
♐ 17 Jan 18:31
♑ 20 Jan 02:47
♒ 22 Jan 13:01
♓ 25 Jan 00:48
♈ 27 Jan 13:29
♉ 30 Jan 01:38
♊ 1 Feb 11:15
♋ 3 Feb 16:57
♌ 5 Feb 18:52
♍ 7 Feb 18:30
♎ 9 Feb 17:59
♏ 11 Feb 19:24
♐ 14 Feb 00:09
♑ 16 Feb 08:21
♒ 18 Feb 19:06
♓ 21 Feb 07:13
♈ 23 Feb 19:51
♉ 26 Feb 08:12
♊ 28 Feb 18:53
♋ 3 Mar 02:17
♌ 5 Mar 05:41
♍ 7 Mar 05:53
♎ 9 Mar 04:47
♏ 11 Mar 04:41
♐ 13 Mar 07:34
♑ 15 Mar 14:29
♒ 18 Mar 00:53
♓ 20 Mar 13:12
♈ 23 Mar 01:52
♉ 25 Mar 14:00
♊ 28 Mar 00:49
♋ 30 Mar 09:15
♌ 1 Apr 14:22
♍ 3 Apr 16:11
♎ 5 Apr 15:55
♏ 7 Apr 15:33
♐ 9 Apr 17:11
♑ 11 Apr 22:25
♒ 14 Apr 07:37
♓ 16 Apr 19:33
♈ 19 Apr 08:15
♉ 21 Apr 20:09
♊ 24 Apr 06:28
♋ 26 Apr 14:46
♌ 28 Apr 20:40
♍ 1 May 00:01
♎ 3 May 01:21
♏ 5 May 01:58
♐ 7 May 03:35
♑ 9 May 07:52
♒ 11 May 15:45
♓ 14 May 02:51
♈ 16 May 15:25
♉ 19 May 03:17
♊ 21 May 13:08
♋ 23 May 20:39
♌ 26 May 02:04
♍ 28 May 05:47
♎ 30 May 08:19
♏ 1 Jun 10:23
♐ 3 Jun 13:02
♑ 5 Jun 17:27
♒ 8 Jun 00:40
♓ 10 Jun 10:58
♈ 12 Jun 23:15
♉ 15 Jun 11:20
♊ 17 Jun 21:13
♋ 20 Jun 04:06
♌ 22 Jun 08:27
♍ 24 Jun 11:19
♎ 26 Jun 13:46
♏ 28 Jun 16:38
♐ 30 Jun 20:29
♑ 3 Jul 01:49
♒ 5 Jul 09:15
♓ 7 Jul 19:11
♈ 10 Jul 07:12
♉ 12 Jul 19:38
♊ 15 Jul 06:08
♋ 17 Jul 13:09
♌ 19 Jul 16:48
♍ 21 Jul 18:25
♎ 23 Jul 19:40
♏ 25 Jul 22:01
♐ 28 Jul 02:14
♑ 30 Jul 08:28
♒ 1 Aug 16:37
♓ 4 Aug 02:45
♈ 6 Aug 14:40
♉ 9 Aug 03:23
♊ 11 Aug 14:48
♋ 13 Aug 22:47
♌ 16 Aug 02:44
♍ 18 Aug 03:42
♎ 20 Aug 03:36
♏ 22 Aug 04:28
♐ 24 Aug 07:46
♑ 26 Aug 13:59
♒ 28 Aug 22:43
♓ 31 Aug 09:19
♈ 2 Sep 21:22
♉ 5 Sep 10:10
♊ 7 Sep 22:17
♋ 10 Sep 07:38
♌ 12 Sep 12:52
♍ 14 Sep 14:21
♎ 16 Sep 13:45
♏ 18 Sep 13:16
♐ 20 Sep 14:54
♑ 22 Sep 19:55
♒ 25 Sep 04:20
♓ 27 Sep 15:14
♈ 30 Sep 03:30
♉ 2 Oct 16:14
♊ 5 Oct 04:28
♋ 7 Oct 14:43
♌ 9 Oct 21:35
♍ 12 Oct 00:37
♎ 14 Oct 00:48
♏ 16 Oct 00:02
♐ 18 Oct 00:24
♑ 20 Oct 03:43
♒ 22 Oct 10:50
♓ 24 Oct 21:18
♈ 27 Oct 09:40
♉ 29 Oct 22:21
♊ 1 Nov 10:14
♋ 3 Nov 20:26
♌ 6 Nov 04:07
♍ 8 Nov 08:48
♎ 10 Nov 10:43
♏ 12 Nov 11:01
♐ 14 Nov 11:21
♑ 16 Nov 13:35
♒ 18 Nov 19:09
♓ 21 Nov 04:28
♈ 23 Nov 16:31
♉ 26 Nov 05:15
♊ 28 Nov 16:49
♋ 1 Dec 02:18
♌ 3 Dec 09:34
♍ 5 Dec 14:44
♎ 7 Dec 18:04
♏ 9 Dec 20:05
♐ 11 Dec 21:40
♑ 14 Dec 00:07
♒ 16 Dec 04:52
♓ 18 Dec 13:00
♈ 21 Dec 00:20
♉ 23 Dec 13:06
♊ 26 Dec 00:47
♋ 28 Dec 09:47
♌ 30 Dec 16:00

MERCURY
♐ 1 Jan 00:00
♑ 2 Jan 14:48
♒ 21 Jan 11:26
♓ 7 Feb 16:20
♈ 15 Apr 15:19
♉ 3 May 21:55
♊ 18 May 06:54
♋ 2 Jun 03:55
♌ 10 Aug 05:52
♍ 26 Aug 07:07
♎ 11 Sep 11:19
♏ 1 Oct 02:10
♐ 7 Dec 01:05
♑ 26 Dec 12:48

VENUS
♒ 1 Jan 00:00
♓ 3 Jan 23:55
♈ 2 Feb 12:38
♉ 6 Jun 10:04
♊ 6 Jul 00:22
♋ 1 Aug 22:39
♌ 27 Aug 15:49
♍ 21 Sep 14:23
♎ 16 Oct 00:14
♏ 9 Nov 02:08
♐ 2 Dec 23:55
♑ 26 Dec 20:10

MARS
♋ 1 Jan 00:00
♌ 27 Apr 23:41
♍ 23 Jun 07:43
♎ 12 Aug 01:11
♏ 27 Sep 02:16
♐ 9 Nov 05:30
♑ 20 Dec 00:35

JUPITER
♎ 1 Jan 00:00
♏ 10 Nov 08:16

SATURN
♒ 1 Jan 00:00
♓ 21 May 04:58
♒ 1 Jul 00:00

1994

SUN
♑ 1 Jan 00:00
♒ 20 Jan 07:08
♓ 18 Feb 21:23
♈ 20 Mar 20:29
♉ 20 Apr 07:37
♊ 21 May 06:49
♋ 21 Jun 14:49
♌ 23 Jul 01:42
♍ 23 Aug 08:45
♎ 23 Sep 06:20
♏ 23 Oct 15:37
♐ 22 Nov 13:07
♑ 22 Dec 02:24

MOON
♌ 1 Jan 00:00
♍ 1 Jan 20:16
♎ 3 Jan 23:32
♏ 6 Jan 02:30
♐ 8 Jan 05:35
♑ 10 Jan 09:17
♒ 12 Jan 14:26
♓ 14 Jan 22:05
♈ 17 Jan 08:43
♉ 19 Jan 21:23
♊ 22 Jan 09:35
♋ 24 Jan 18:56
♌ 27 Jan 00:39
♍ 29 Jan 03:40
♎ 31 Jan 05:35
♏ 2 Feb 07:50
♐ 4 Feb 11:15
♑ 6 Feb 16:03
♒ 8 Feb 22:17
♓ 11 Feb 06:24
♈ 13 Feb 16:50
♉ 16 Feb 05:21
♊ 18 Feb 18:06
♋ 21 Feb 04:28
♌ 23 Feb 10:48
♍ 25 Feb 13:28
♎ 27 Feb 14:07
♏ 1 Mar 14:44
♐ 3 Mar 16:55
♑ 5 Mar 21:55
♒ 8 Mar 04:16
♓ 10 Mar 13:10
♈ 13 Mar 00:00
♉ 15 Mar 12:28
♊ 18 Mar 01:30
♋ 20 Mar 12:55
♌ 22 Mar 20:40
♍ 25 Mar 00:15
♎ 27 Mar 00:47
♏ 29 Mar 00:16
♐ 31 Mar 00:42
♑ 2 Apr 03:39
♒ 4 Apr 09:46
♓ 6 Apr 18:52
♈ 9 Apr 06:10
♉ 11 Apr 18:49
♊ 14 Apr 07:49
♋ 16 Apr 19:42
♌ 19 Apr 04:46
♍ 21 Apr 09:59
♎ 23 Apr 11:41
♏ 25 Apr 11:19
♐ 27 Apr 10:49
♑ 29 Apr 12:06
♒ 1 May 16:35
♓ 4 May 00:48
♈ 6 May 12:02
♉ 9 May 00:51
♊ 11 May 13:44
♋ 14 May 01:28
♌ 16 May 10:59
♍ 18 May 17:32
♎ 20 May 20:55
♏ 22 May 21:52
♐ 24 May 21:44
♑ 26 May 22:18
♒ 29 May 01:20
♓ 31 May 08:04
♈ 2 Jun 18:32
♉ 5 Jun 07:15
♊ 7 Jun 20:04
♋ 10 Jun 07:23
♌ 12 Jun 16:30
♍ 14 Jun 23:17
♎ 17 Jun 03:49
♏ 19 Jun 06:21
♐ 21 Jun 07:33
♑ 23 Jun 08:38
♒ 25 Jun 11:11
♓ 27 Jun 16:45
♈ 30 Jun 02:08
♉ 2 Jul 14:24
♊ 5 Jul 03:13
♋ 7 Jul 14:18
♌ 9 Jul 22:44
♍ 12 Jul 04:49
♎ 14 Jul 09:16
♏ 16 Jul 12:36
♐ 18 Jul 15:10
♑ 20 Jul 17:31
♒ 22 Jul 20:39
♓ 25 Jul 01:57
♈ 27 Jul 10:32

MOON (continued)

♉ 29 Jul 22:14
♊ 1 Aug 11:06
♊ 3 Aug 22:23
♌ 6 Aug 06:32
♍ 8 Aug 11:43
♎ 10 Aug 15:08
♐ 12 Aug 17:57
♐ 14 Aug 20:54
♑ 17 Aug 00:19
♒ 19 Aug 04:35
♓ 21 Aug 10:28
♈ 23 Aug 18:56
♉ 26 Aug 06:14
♊ 28 Aug 19:08
♋ 31 Aug 07:01
♌ 2 Sep 15:38
♍ 4 Sep 20:34
♎ 6 Sep 22:58
♏ 9 Sep 00:27
♐ 11 Sep 02:26
♑ 13 Sep 05:45
♒ 15 Sep 10:43
♈ 17 Sep 17:32
♈ 20 Sep 02:31
♉ 22 Sep 13:48
♊ 25 Sep 02:42
♋ 27 Sep 15:13
♌ 30 Sep 00:56
♍ 2 Oct 06:40
♎ 4 Oct 08:57
♏ 6 Oct 09:23
♐ 8 Oct 09:48
♑ 10 Oct 11:45
♒ 12 Oct 16:10
♈ 14 Oct 23:19
♈ 17 Oct 08:57
♉ 19 Oct 20:35
♊ 22 Oct 09:29
♋ 24 Oct 22:16
♌ 27 Oct 09:06
♍ 29 Oct 16:22
♎ 31 Oct 19:47
♏ 2 Nov 20:20
♐ 4 Nov 19:47
♑ 6 Nov 20:03
♒ 8 Nov 22:49
♈ 11 Nov 05:05
♈ 13 Nov 14:45
♉ 16 Nov 02:45
♊ 18 Nov 15:42
♋ 21 Nov 04:22
♌ 23 Nov 15:34
♍ 26 Nov 00:10
♎ 28 Nov 05:23
♏ 30 Nov 07:22
♐ 2 Dec 07:14
♑ 4 Dec 06:43
♒ 6 Dec 07:53
♓ 8 Dec 12:25
♈ 10 Dec 21:04
♉ 13 Dec 08:57
♊ 15 Dec 22:01
♋ 18 Dec 10:26
♌ 20 Dec 21:14
♍ 23 Dec 06:02
♎ 25 Dec 12:28
♏ 27 Dec 16:18
♐ 29 Dec 17:46
♑ 31 Dec 17:58

MERCURY
♑ 1 Jan 00:00
♑ 14 Jan 00:26
♓ 1 Feb 10:29
♓ 22 Feb 10:00
♓ 18 Mar 12:05
♈ 9 Apr 16:31
♉ 25 Apr 18:28
♊ 9 May 14:53
♋ 2 Jul 12:42
♌ 10 Jul 12:42
♌ 3 Aug 06:10
♍ 18 Aug 00:45
♎ 4 Sep 04:56
♏ 27 Sep 08:52
♐ 19 Oct 06:20
♐ 10 Nov 04:39
♑ 30 Nov 04:39
♑ 19 Dec 06:27

VENUS
♑ 1 Jan 00:00
♑ 19 Jan 16:29
♓ 12 Feb 14:29
♓ 8 Mar 14:29
♈ 1 Apr 19:21
♉ 26 Apr 06:25
♊ 21 May 01:27

♌ 15 Jun 07:24
♎ 11 Jul 06:34
♎ 7 Aug 14:37
♏ 7 Sep 17:13

MARS
♑ 1 Jan 00:00
♒ 28 Jan 04:06
♈ 7 Mar 11:02
♈ 14 Apr 18:03
♉ 23 May 22:38
♊ 3 Jul 22:31
♋ 16 Aug 19:16
♌ 4 Oct 15:49
♍ 12 Dec 11:33

JUPITER
♏ 1 Jan 00:00
♐ 9 Dec 10:55

SATURN
♓ 1 Jan 00:00
♓ 28 Jan 23:44

1995

SUN
♑ 1 Jan 00:00
♒ 20 Jan 13:01
♓ 19 Feb 03:12
♈ 21 Mar 02:15
♉ 20 Apr 13:22
♊ 21 May 12:35
♋ 21 Jun 20:35
♌ 23 Jul 07:31
♍ 23 Aug 14:36
♎ 23 Sep 12:14
♏ 23 Oct 21:33
♐ 22 Nov 19:02
♑ 22 Dec 08:18

MOON
♑ 1 Jan 00:00
♒ 2 Jan 18:40
♓ 4 Jan 21:50
♈ 7 Jan 04:57
♉ 9 Jan 15:59
♊ 12 Jan 04:58
♋ 14 Jan 17:21
♌ 17 Jan 03:37
♍ 19 Jan 11:40
♎ 21 Jan 17:55
♏ 23 Jan 22:33
♐ 26 Jan 01:38
♑ 28 Jan 03:27
♒ 30 Jan 05:04
♓ 1 Feb 08:06
♈ 3 Feb 14:13
♉ 6 Feb 00:10
♊ 8 Feb 12:45
♋ 11 Feb 01:18
♌ 13 Feb 11:32
♍ 15 Feb 18:53
♎ 18 Feb 00:01
♏ 20 Feb 03:56
♐ 22 Feb 07:14
♑ 24 Feb 10:12
♒ 26 Feb 13:15
♓ 28 Feb 17:17
♈ 2 Mar 23:31
♉ 5 Mar 08:51
♊ 7 Mar 20:56
♋ 10 Mar 09:41
♌ 12 Mar 20:29
♍ 15 Mar 03:55
♎ 17 Mar 08:19
♏ 19 Mar 10:53
♐ 21 Mar 12:58
♑ 23 Mar 15:32
♒ 25 Mar 19:11
♓ 28 Mar 00:19
♈ 30 Mar 07:27
♉ 1 Apr 17:00
♊ 4 Apr 04:50
♋ 6 Apr 17:41
♌ 9 Apr 05:16
♍ 11 Apr 13:40
♎ 13 Apr 18:21
♏ 15 Apr 20:14
♐ 17 Apr 20:52
♑ 19 Apr 21:55
♒ 22 Apr 00:39
♓ 24 Apr 05:52
♈ 26 Apr 13:42
♉ 28 Apr 23:54
♊ 1 May 11:54
♋ 4 May 00:46
♌ 6 May 12:56

♍ 8 May 22:34
♎ 11 May 04:31
♏ 13 May 06:54
♐ 15 May 06:59
♑ 17 May 06:37
♒ 19 May 07:40
♓ 21 May 11:41
♈ 23 May 19:14
♉ 26 May 05:47
♊ 28 May 18:08
♋ 31 May 07:00
♌ 2 Jun 19:18
♍ 5 Jun 05:47
♎ 7 Jun 13:14
♏ 9 Jun 17:04
♐ 11 Jun 17:51
♑ 13 Jun 17:06
♒ 15 Jun 16:53
♓ 17 Jun 19:14
♈ 20 Jun 01:30
♉ 22 Jun 11:36
♊ 25 Jun 00:03
♋ 27 Jun 12:57
♌ 30 Jun 01:03
♍ 2 Jul 11:36
♎ 4 Jul 19:56
♏ 7 Jul 01:20
♐ 9 Jul 03:38
♑ 11 Jul 03:44
♒ 13 Jul 03:22
♓ 15 Jul 04:48
♈ 17 Jul 09:24
♉ 19 Jul 18:21
♊ 22 Jul 06:24
♋ 24 Jul 19:17
♌ 27 Jul 07:08
♍ 29 Jul 17:13
♎ 1 Aug 01:24
♏ 3 Aug 07:30
♐ 5 Aug 11:15
♑ 7 Aug 12:53
♒ 9 Aug 13:29
♓ 11 Aug 14:47
♈ 13 Aug 18:42
♉ 16 Aug 02:26
♊ 18 Aug 13:41
♋ 21 Aug 02:25
♌ 23 Aug 14:14
♍ 25 Aug 23:51
♎ 28 Aug 07:16
♏ 30 Aug 12:52
♐ 1 Sep 16:58
♑ 3 Sep 19:46
♒ 5 Sep 21:48
♓ 8 Sep 00:09
♈ 10 Sep 04:15
♉ 12 Sep 11:22
♊ 14 Sep 21:49
♋ 17 Sep 10:17
♌ 19 Sep 22:20
♍ 22 Sep 08:02
♎ 24 Sep 14:51
♏ 26 Sep 19:21
♐ 28 Sep 22:31
♑ 1 Oct 01:11
♒ 3 Oct 04:00
♓ 5 Oct 07:36
♈ 7 Oct 12:42
♉ 9 Oct 20:06
♊ 12 Oct 06:11
♋ 14 Oct 18:21
♌ 17 Oct 07:12
♍ 19 Oct 17:12
♎ 22 Oct 00:16
♏ 24 Oct 04:07
♐ 26 Oct 05:57
♑ 28 Oct 07:16
♒ 30 Oct 09:24
♓ 1 Nov 13:18
♈ 3 Nov 19:22
♉ 6 Nov 03:36
♊ 8 Nov 13:56
♋ 11 Nov 01:58
♌ 13 Nov 14:38
♍ 16 Nov 02:03
♎ 18 Nov 10:19
♏ 20 Nov 14:41
♐ 22 Nov 15:57
♑ 24 Nov 15:49
♒ 26 Nov 16:16
♓ 28 Nov 16:59
♈ 1 Dec 00:52
♉ 3 Dec 09:13
♊ 5 Dec 20:36
♋ 8 Dec 08:45
♌ 10 Dec 21:25
♍ 13 Dec 09:27
♎ 15 Dec 19:10
♏ 18 Dec 01:08

♐ 20 Dec 03:14
♑ 22 Dec 02:47
♒ 24 Dec 01:53
♓ 26 Dec 02:46
♈ 28 Dec 07:07
♉ 30 Dec 15:22

MERCURY
♑ 1 Jan 00:00
♑ 6 Jan 22:18
♒ 14 Mar 21:36
♓ 2 Apr 07:30
♈ 17 Apr 07:55
♉ 2 May 15:19
♊ 10 Jul 16:59
♋ 25 Jul 22:20
♌ 10 Aug 00:14
♍ 29 Aug 02:08
♎ 4 Nov 08:51
♏ 22 Nov 22:47
♐ 12 Dec 02:58

VENUS
♏ 1 Jan 00:00
♐ 7 Jan 12:08
♑ 4 Feb 20:13
♒ 2 Mar 22:12
♓ 28 Mar 05:11
♈ 22 Apr 04:08
♉ 16 May 23:23
♊ 10 Jun 16:19
♋ 5 Jul 06:40
♌ 29 Jul 17:33
♍ 23 Aug 00:44
♎ 16 Sep 05:02
♏ 10 Oct 07:49
♐ 3 Nov 10:19
♑ 27 Nov 13:24
♒ 21 Dec 18:24

MARS
♌ 1 Jan 00:00
♌ 22 Jan 23:49
♍ 25 May 16:10
♍ 21 Jul 09:22
♎ 7 Sep 07:01
♏ 20 Oct 21:03
♐ 30 Nov 13:59

JUPITER
♐ 1 Jan 00:00

SATURN
♓ 1 Jan 00:00

1996

SUN
♑ 1 Jan 00:00
♒ 20 Jan 18:54
♓ 19 Feb 09:02
♈ 20 Mar 08:04
♉ 19 Apr 19:11
♊ 20 May 18:24
♋ 21 Jun 02:25
♌ 22 Jul 13:20
♍ 22 Aug 20:24
♎ 22 Sep 18:01
♏ 23 Oct 03:20
♐ 22 Nov 00:50
♑ 21 Dec 14:07

MOON
♑ 1 Jan 00:00
♒ 2 Jan 02:30
♓ 4 Jan 14:57
♈ 7 Jan 03:31
♉ 9 Jan 15:30
♊ 12 Jan 01:56
♋ 14 Jan 09:31
♌ 16 Jan 13:26
♍ 18 Jan 14:08
♎ 20 Jan 13:16
♏ 22 Jan 13:03
♐ 24 Jan 15:38
♑ 26 Jan 22:17
♒ 29 Jan 08:43
♓ 31 Jan 21:12
♈ 3 Feb 09:47
♉ 5 Feb 21:23
♊ 8 Feb 07:31
♋ 10 Feb 15:36
♌ 12 Feb 20:59
♍ 14 Feb 23:30
♎ 17 Feb 00:01
♏ 19 Feb 00:10
♐ 21 Feb 01:59
♉ 23 Feb 07:09

♊ 25 Feb 16:15
♋ 28 Feb 04:11
♌ 1 Mar 16:48
♍ 4 Mar 04:14
♎ 6 Mar 13:41
♏ 8 Mar 21:06
♐ 11 Mar 02:33
♑ 13 Mar 06:09
♒ 15 Mar 08:16
♓ 17 Mar 09:51
♈ 19 Mar 12:16
♉ 21 Mar 17:00
♊ 24 Mar 01:00
♋ 26 Mar 12:07
♌ 29 Mar 00:38
♍ 31 Mar 12:16
♎ 2 Apr 21:27
♏ 5 Apr 03:58
♐ 7 Apr 08:22
♑ 9 Apr 11:31
♒ 11 Apr 14:10
♓ 13 Apr 17:01
♈ 15 Apr 20:44
♉ 18 Apr 02:06
♊ 20 Apr 09:55
♋ 22 Apr 20:26
♌ 25 Apr 08:45
♍ 27 Apr 20:50
♎ 30 Apr 06:38
♏ 2 May 12:43
♐ 4 May 16:06
♑ 6 May 17:55
♒ 8 May 19:40
♓ 10 May 22:30
♈ 13 May 03:01
♉ 15 May 09:26
♊ 17 May 17:49
♋ 20 May 04:17
♌ 22 May 16:29
♍ 25 May 04:59
♎ 27 May 15:34
♏ 29 May 22:31
♐ 1 Jun 01:44
♑ 3 Jun 02:30
♒ 5 Jun 02:46
♓ 7 Jun 04:20
♈ 9 Jun 08:24
♉ 11 Jun 15:12
♊ 14 Jun 00:17
♋ 16 Jun 11:09
♌ 18 Jun 23:23
♍ 21 Jun 12:08
♎ 23 Jun 23:38
♏ 26 Jun 07:54
♐ 28 Jun 12:02
♑ 30 Jun 12:48
♒ 2 Jul 12:06
♓ 4 Jul 12:08
♈ 6 Jul 14:43
♉ 8 Jul 20:44
♊ 11 Jul 05:53
♋ 13 Jul 17:09
♌ 16 Jul 05:32
♍ 18 Jul 18:17
♎ 21 Jul 06:15
♏ 23 Jul 15:44
♐ 25 Jul 21:25
♑ 27 Jul 23:18
♒ 29 Jul 22:48
♓ 31 Jul 22:02
♈ 2 Aug 23:06
♉ 5 Aug 03:34
♊ 7 Aug 11:50
♋ 9 Aug 23:11
♌ 12 Aug 11:30
♍ 15 Aug 00:08
♎ 17 Aug 11:56
♏ 19 Aug 21:51
♐ 22 Aug 04:49
♑ 24 Aug 08:23
♒ 26 Aug 09:31
♓ 28 Aug 08:50
♈ 30 Aug 09:16
♉ 1 Sep 12:11
♊ 3 Sep 19:09
♋ 6 Sep 05:30
♌ 8 Sep 17:55
♍ 11 Sep 06:29
♎ 13 Sep 17:52
♏ 16 Sep 03:21
♐ 18 Sep 10:32
♑ 20 Sep 15:13
♒ 22 Sep 17:40
♓ 24 Sep 18:44
♈ 26 Sep 19:55
♉ 28 Sep 22:25
♊ 1 Oct 04:02
♋ 3 Oct 13:15

♍ 8 Oct 13:50
♎ 11 Oct 01:01
♏ 13 Oct 09:47
♐ 15 Oct 16:08
♑ 17 Oct 20:38
♒ 19 Oct 23:52
♓ 22 Oct 02:23
♈ 24 Oct 04:51
♉ 26 Oct 08:12
♊ 28 Oct 13:36
♋ 30 Oct 21:57
♌ 2 Nov 09:17
♍ 4 Nov 21:58
♎ 7 Nov 09:30
♏ 9 Nov 18:03
♐ 11 Nov 23:27
♑ 14 Nov 02:45
♒ 16 Nov 05:15
♓ 18 Nov 08:01
♈ 20 Nov 11:35
♉ 22 Nov 16:13
♊ 24 Nov 22:21
♋ 27 Nov 06:38
♌ 29 Nov 17:31
♍ 2 Dec 06:12
♎ 4 Dec 18:24
♏ 7 Dec 03:40
♐ 9 Dec 08:59
♑ 11 Dec 11:15
♒ 13 Dec 12:15
♓ 15 Dec 13:45
♈ 17 Dec 16:56
♉ 19 Dec 22:11
♊ 22 Dec 05:18
♋ 24 Dec 14:15
♌ 27 Dec 01:10
♍ 29 Dec 13:46

MERCURY
♑ 1 Jan 00:00
♑ 1 Jan 18:07
♒ 17 Jan 09:38
♓ 15 Feb 02:45
♈ 7 Mar 11:54
♈ 24 Mar 08:04
♉ 8 Apr 03:17
♊ 13 Jun 21:46
♋ 2 Jul 07:38
♌ 16 Jul 09:57
♍ 1 Aug 16:18
♎ 26 Aug 05:18
♍ 9 Sep 09:33
♎ 9 Oct 03:14
♏ 27 Oct 01:02
♐ 14 Nov 16:37
♐ 3 Dec 13:49

VENUS
♑ 1 Jan 00:00
♓ 15 Jan 04:31
♒ 9 Feb 02:32
♓ 6 Mar 02:02
♈ 3 Apr 15:27
♉ 7 Aug 06:16
♊ 7 Sep 05:08
♋ 4 Oct 03:23
♌ 29 Oct 12:03
♍ 23 Nov 01:35
♎ 17 Dec 05:35

MARS
♑ 1 Jan 00:00
♒ 8 Jan 11:03
♓ 15 Feb 11:51
♈ 24 Mar 15:13
♉ 2 May 18:17
♊ 12 Jun 14:43
♋ 25 Jul 18:33
♌ 9 Sep 20:03
♍ 30 Oct 07:14

JUPITER
♐ 1 Jan 00:00
♑ 3 Jan 07:23

SATURN
♓ 1 Jan 00:00
♈ 7 Apr 08:50

1997

SUN
♑ 1 Jan 00:00
♒ 20 Jan 00:44
♓ 18 Feb 14:53
♈ 20 Mar 13:56
♉ 20 Apr 01:04

♊ 21 May 00:19
♋ 22 Jun 08:21
♌ 22 Jul 19:16
♍ 23 Aug 02:20
♎ 23 Sep 23:57
♏ 22 Oct 09:16
♐ 22 Nov 06:49
♑ 21 Dec 20:08

MOON
♍ 1 Jan 00:00
♎ 1 Jan 02:33
♏ 3 Jan 13:03
♐ 5 Jan 19:28
♑ 7 Jan 21:56
♒ 9 Jan 22:01
♓ 11 Jan 21:52
♈ 13 Jan 23:23
♉ 16 Jan 03:41
♊ 18 Jan 10:54
♋ 20 Jan 20:30
♌ 23 Jan 07:51
♍ 25 Jan 20:27
♎ 28 Jan 09:22
♏ 30 Jan 20:49
♐ 2 Feb 04:52
♑ 4 Feb 08:45
♒ 6 Feb 09:22
♓ 8 Feb 08:35
♈ 10 Feb 08:30
♉ 12 Feb 10:57
♊ 14 Feb 16:54
♋ 17 Feb 02:14
♌ 19 Feb 13:53
♍ 22 Feb 02:39
♎ 24 Feb 15:24
♏ 27 Feb 02:58
♐ 1 Mar 12:02
♑ 3 Mar 17:39
♒ 5 Mar 19:55
♓ 7 Mar 19:58
♈ 9 Mar 19:34
♉ 11 Mar 20:38
♊ 14 Mar 00:49
♋ 16 Mar 08:52
♌ 18 Mar 20:09
♍ 21 Mar 09:00
♎ 23 Mar 21:36
♏ 26 Mar 08:43
♐ 28 Mar 17:41
♑ 31 Mar 00:08
♒ 2 Apr 04:00
♓ 4 Apr 06:20
♈ 6 Apr 07:21
♉ 8 Apr 08:43
♊ 10 Apr 12:17
♋ 12 Apr 19:04
♌ 15 Apr 05:23
♍ 17 Apr 16:01
♎ 20 Apr 04:37
♏ 22 Apr 15:20
♐ 24 Apr 23:33
♑ 27 Apr 05:33
♒ 29 Apr 09:51
♓ 1 May 12:51
♈ 3 May 15:00
♉ 5 May 17:05
♊ 7 May 20:22
♋ 10 May 02:14
♌ 12 May 11:34
♍ 14 May 23:44
♎ 17 May 12:23
♏ 19 May 23:13
♐ 22 May 06:52
♑ 24 May 11:52
♒ 26 May 15:21
♓ 28 May 18:19
♈ 30 May 21:19
♉ 2 Jun 00:40
♊ 4 Jun 04:56
♋ 6 Jun 11:03
♌ 8 Jun 19:59
♍ 11 Jun 07:44
♎ 13 Jun 20:36
♏ 16 Jun 07:52
♐ 18 Jun 15:40
♑ 20 Jun 20:03
♒ 22 Jun 22:21
♓ 25 Jun 00:10
♈ 27 Jun 02:40
♉ 29 Jun 06:24
♊ 1 Jul 11:36
♋ 3 Jul 18:34
♌ 6 Jul 03:46
♍ 8 Jul 15:23
♎ 11 Jul 04:22
♏ 13 Jul 16:21
♐ 16 Jul 01:03
♑ 18 Jul 05:46

MERCURY
♑ 1 Jan 00:00
♒ 5 Jan 05:54
♓ 28 Feb 03:55
♈ 16 Mar 04:14
♈ 1 Apr 13:46
♉ 5 May 01:49
♊ 12 May 10:26
♋ 8 Jun 23:26
♌ 23 Jun 20:42
♍ 8 Jul 05:29
♎ 2 Oct 05:39
♏ 19 Oct 12:09
♐ 7 Nov 17:43
♐ 30 Nov 19:12
♑ 18 Dec 18:07

VENUS
♑ 1 Jan 00:00
♒ 10 Jan 05:33
♓ 3 Feb 04:29
♈ 27 Feb 04:02
♉ 23 Mar 05:27
♊ 16 Apr 09:44

♊ 10 May 17:21
♋ 4 Jun 04:19
♌ 28 Jun 18:39
♍ 23 Jul 13:18
♎ 17 Aug 14:32
♏ 12 Sep 02:18
♐ 8 Oct 08:26
♑ 5 Nov 08:51
♒ 12 Dec 04:40

MARS
♍ 1 Jan 00:00
♎ 3 Jan 08:11
♍ 8 Mar 19:51
♎ 19 Jun 08:31
♏ 14 Aug 08:43
♐ 28 Sep 22:23
♑ 9 Nov 05:34
♒ 18 Dec 06:38

JUPITER
♑ 1 Jan 00:00
♒ 21 Jan 15:14

SATURN
♈ 1 Jan 00:00

1998

SUN
♑ 1 Jan 00:00
♒ 20 Jan 06:47
♓ 18 Feb 20:56
♈ 20 Mar 19:56
♉ 20 Apr 06:58
♊ 21 May 06:06
♋ 21 Jun 14:04
♌ 23 Jul 00:56
♍ 23 Aug 08:00
♎ 23 Sep 05:38
♏ 23 Oct 15:00
♐ 22 Nov 12:35
♑ 22 Dec 01:58

MOON
♒ 1 Jan 00:00
♓ 2 Jan 09:57
♈ 4 Jan 12:44
♉ 6 Jan 15:53
♊ 8 Jan 19:43
♋ 11 Jan 00:44
♌ 13 Jan 07:46
♍ 15 Jan 17:32
♎ 18 Jan 05:45
♏ 20 Jan 18:35
♐ 23 Jan 05:26
♑ 25 Jan 12:40
♒ 27 Jan 16:28
♓ 29 Jan 18:09
♈ 31 Jan 19:22
♉ 2 Feb 21:26
♊ 5 Feb 01:10
♋ 7 Feb 06:58
♌ 9 Feb 14:58
♍ 12 Feb 01:10
♎ 14 Feb 13:18
♏ 17 Feb 02:14
♐ 19 Feb 13:57
♑ 21 Feb 22:31
♒ 24 Feb 03:11
♓ 26 Feb 04:43
♈ 28 Feb 04:43
♉ 2 Mar 05:01
♊ 4 Mar 07:16
♋ 6 Mar 12:28
♌ 8 Mar 20:47
♍ 11 Mar 07:36
♎ 13 Mar 19:59
♏ 16 Mar 08:52
♐ 18 Mar 20:57
♑ 21 Mar 06:44
♒ 23 Mar 13:02
♓ 25 Mar 15:44
♈ 27 Mar 15:50
♉ 29 Mar 15:05
♊ 31 Mar 15:39
♋ 2 Apr 19:11
♌ 5 Apr 02:37
♍ 7 Apr 13:26
♎ 10 Apr 02:05
♏ 12 Apr 14:57
♐ 15 Apr 02:53
♑ 17 Apr 13:06
♒ 19 Apr 20:42
♓ 22 Apr 01:07
♈ 24 Apr 02:31
♉ 26 Apr 02:10
♊ 28 Apr 01:56
♋ 30 Apr 03:58
♌ 2 May 09:50
♍ 4 May 19:48
♎ 7 May 08:20
♏ 9 May 21:11
♐ 12 May 08:49
♑ 14 May 18:40
♒ 17 May 02:31
♓ 19 May 08:04
♈ 21 May 11:07
♉ 23 May 12:07
♊ 25 May 12:26
♋ 27 May 13:59
♌ 29 May 18:39
♍ 1 Jun 03:22
♎ 3 Jun 15:18
♏ 6 Jun 04:07
♐ 8 Jun 15:35
♑ 11 Jun 00:51
♒ 13 Jun 08:04
♓ 15 Jun 13:32
♈ 17 Jun 17:24
♉ 19 Jun 19:48
♊ 21 Jun 21:27
♋ 23 Jun 23:40
♌ 26 Jun 04:05
♍ 28 Jun 11:55
♎ 30 Jun 23:06
♏ 3 Jul 11:46
♐ 5 Jul 23:25
♑ 8 Jul 08:28
♒ 10 Jul 14:53
♓ 12 Jul 19:23
♈ 14 Jul 22:46
♉ 17 Jul 01:34
♊ 19 Jul 04:19
♋ 21 Jul 07:44
♌ 23 Jul 12:50
♍ 25 Jul 20:35
♎ 28 Jul 07:15
♏ 30 Jul 19:45
♐ 2 Aug 07:49
♑ 4 Aug 17:19
♒ 6 Aug 23:32
♓ 9 Aug 03:05
♈ 11 Aug 05:11
♉ 13 Aug 07:05
♊ 15 Aug 09:47
♋ 17 Aug 13:56
♌ 19 Aug 20:02
♍ 22 Aug 04:22
♎ 24 Aug 15:03
♏ 27 Aug 03:26
♐ 29 Aug 15:56
♑ 1 Sep 02:24
♒ 3 Sep 09:22
♓ 5 Sep 12:49
♈ 7 Sep 13:53
♉ 9 Sep 14:17
♊ 11 Sep 15:41
♋ 13 Sep 19:21
♌ 16 Sep 01:49
♍ 18 Sep 10:53
♎ 20 Sep 21:58
♏ 23 Sep 10:23
♐ 25 Sep 23:06
♑ 28 Sep 10:31
♒ 30 Sep 18:54
♓ 2 Oct 23:24
♈ 5 Oct 00:33
♉ 6 Oct 23:58
♊ 8 Oct 23:45
♋ 11 Oct 01:49
♌ 13 Oct 07:26
♍ 15 Oct 16:33
♎ 18 Oct 04:03
♏ 20 Oct 16:37
♐ 23 Oct 05:17
♑ 25 Oct 17:06
♒ 28 Oct 02:45
♓ 30 Oct 08:59
♈ 1 Nov 11:28
♉ 3 Nov 11:13
♊ 5 Nov 10:12
♋ 7 Nov 10:40
♌ 9 Nov 14:34
♍ 11 Nov 22:38
♎ 14 Nov 09:59
♏ 16 Nov 22:42
♐ 19 Nov 11:14
♑ 21 Nov 22:46
♒ 24 Nov 08:44
♓ 26 Nov 16:15
♈ 28 Nov 20:35
♉ 30 Nov 21:54
♊ 2 Dec 21:31
♋ 4 Dec 21:29
♌ 6 Dec 23:56
♍ 9 Dec 06:22
♎ 11 Dec 16:44
♏ 14 Dec 05:17
♐ 16 Dec 17:48
♑ 19 Dec 04:56
♒ 21 Dec 14:18
♓ 23 Dec 21:46
♈ 26 Dec 03:05
♉ 28 Dec 06:06
♊ 30 Dec 07:23

MERCURY
♐ 1 Jan 00:00
♑ 12 Jan 16:21
♒ 2 Feb 15:16
♓ 20 Feb 10:23
♈ 8 Mar 08:29
♉ 15 May 02:11
♊ 1 Jun 08:08
♋ 15 Jun 05:34
♌ 30 Jun 23:53
♍ 8 Sep 01:59
♎ 24 Sep 10:14
♏ 12 Oct 02:46
♐ 1 Nov 16:04

VENUS
♒ 1 Jan 00:00
♑ 9 Jan 21:04
♒ 4 Mar 16:15
♓ 6 Apr 05:39
♈ 3 May 19:17
♉ 29 May 23:33
♊ 24 Jun 12:28
♋ 19 Jul 15:18
♌ 13 Aug 09:21
♍ 6 Sep 19:26
♎ 30 Sep 23:14
♏ 24 Oct 23:07
♐ 17 Nov 21:07
♑ 11 Dec 18:34

MARS
♒ 1 Jan 00:00
♓ 25 Jan 09:27
♈ 4 Mar 16:19
♉ 13 Apr 01:06
♊ 24 May 03:43
♋ 6 Jul 09:01
♌ 20 Aug 19:17
♍ 7 Oct 12:29
♎ 27 Nov 10:11

JUPITER
♒ 1 Jan 00:00
♓ 4 Feb 10:53

SATURN
♈ 1 Jan 00:00
♉ 9 Jun 06:08
♈ 25 Oct 18:42

1999

SUN
♑ 1 Jan 00:00
♒ 20 Jan 12:38
♓ 19 Feb 02:48
♈ 21 Mar 01:47
♉ 20 Apr 12:47
♊ 21 May 11:53
♋ 21 Jun 19:50
♌ 23 Jul 06:45
♍ 23 Aug 13:52
♎ 23 Sep 11:33
♏ 23 Oct 20:53
♐ 22 Nov 18:26
♑ 22 Dec 07:45

MOON
♊ 1 Jan 00:00
♋ 1 Jan 08:16
♌ 3 Jan 10:32
♍ 5 Jan 15:50
♎ 8 Jan 00:54
♏ 10 Jan 12:50
♐ 13 Jan 01:24
♑ 15 Jan 12:30
♒ 17 Jan 21:12
♓ 20 Jan 03:41
♈ 22 Jan 08:26
♉ 24 Jan 11:53
♊ 26 Jan 14:30
♋ 28 Jan 16:58
♌ 30 Jan 20:17
♍ 2 Feb 01:38
♎ 4 Feb 09:57
♏ 6 Feb 21:07
♐ 9 Feb 09:39
♑ 11 Feb 21:11
♒ 14 Feb 05:58
♓ 16 Feb 11:41
♈ 18 Feb 15:07
♉ 20 Feb 17:30
♊ 22 Feb 19:55
♋ 24 Feb 23:10
♌ 27 Feb 03:45
♍ 1 Mar 10:06
♎ 3 Mar 18:35
♏ 6 Mar 05:23
♐ 8 Mar 17:47
♑ 11 Mar 05:55
♒ 13 Mar 15:33
♓ 15 Mar 21:31
♈ 18 Mar 00:14
♉ 20 Mar 01:10
♊ 22 Mar 02:06
♋ 24 Mar 04:34
♌ 26 Mar 09:23
♍ 28 Mar 16:35
♎ 31 Mar 01:50
♏ 2 Apr 12:50
♐ 5 Apr 01:08
♑ 7 Apr 13:40
♒ 10 Apr 00:25
♓ 12 Apr 07:36
♈ 14 Apr 10:47
♉ 16 Apr 11:08
♊ 18 Apr 10:40
♋ 20 Apr 11:28
♌ 22 Apr 15:07
♍ 24 Apr 22:05
♎ 27 Apr 07:47
♏ 29 Apr 19:14
♐ 2 May 07:37
♑ 4 May 20:13
♒ 7 May 07:41
♓ 9 May 16:17
♈ 11 May 20:54
♉ 13 May 21:57
♊ 15 May 21:08
♋ 17 May 20:40
♌ 19 May 22:38
♍ 22 May 04:16
♎ 24 May 13:30
♏ 27 May 01:06
♐ 29 May 13:38
♑ 1 Jun 02:07
♒ 3 Jun 13:38
♓ 5 Jun 23:02
♈ 8 Jun 05:09
♉ 10 Jun 07:44
♊ 12 Jun 07:49
♋ 14 Jun 07:15
♌ 16 Jun 08:08
♍ 18 Jun 12:13
♎ 20 Jun 20:11
♏ 23 Jun 07:19
♐ 25 Jun 19:52
♑ 28 Jun 08:13
♒ 30 Jun 19:20
♓ 3 Jul 04:35
♈ 5 Jul 11:22
♉ 7 Jul 15:23
♊ 9 Jul 17:01
♋ 11 Jul 17:28
♌ 13 Jul 18:27
♍ 15 Jul 21:40
♎ 18 Jul 04:20
♏ 20 Jul 14:31
♐ 23 Jul 02:49
♑ 25 Jul 15:09
♒ 28 Jul 01:55
♓ 30 Jul 10:28
♈ 1 Aug 16:48
♉ 3 Aug 21:10
♊ 5 Aug 23:58
♋ 8 Aug 01:54
♌ 10 Aug 03:57
♍ 12 Aug 07:23
♎ 14 Aug 13:25
♏ 16 Aug 22:41
♐ 19 Aug 10:33
♑ 21 Aug 23:00
♒ 24 Aug 09:50
♓ 26 Aug 17:51
♈ 28 Aug 23:10
♉ 31 Aug 02:42
♊ 2 Sep 05:26
♋ 4 Sep 08:11
♌ 6 Sep 11:30
♍ 8 Sep 15:58
♎ 10 Sep 22:17
♏ 13 Sep 07:09
♐ 15 Sep 18:36
♑ 18 Sep 07:14
♒ 20 Sep 18:39
♓ 23 Sep 02:52
♈ 25 Sep 07:35
♉ 27 Sep 09:52
♊ 29 Sep 11:22
♋ 1 Oct 13:32
♌ 3 Oct 17:14
♍ 5 Oct 22:41
♎ 8 Oct 05:53
♏ 10 Oct 15:02
♐ 13 Oct 02:20
♑ 15 Oct 15:05
♒ 18 Oct 03:18
♓ 20 Oct 12:34
♈ 22 Oct 17:42
♉ 24 Oct 19:26
♊ 26 Oct 19:34
♋ 28 Oct 20:10
♌ 30 Oct 22:48
♍ 2 Nov 04:08
♎ 4 Nov 11:58
♏ 6 Nov 21:47
♐ 9 Nov 09:16
♑ 11 Nov 22:01
♒ 14 Nov 10:47
♓ 16 Nov 21:22
♈ 19 Nov 03:58
♉ 21 Nov 06:27
♊ 23 Nov 06:15
♋ 25 Nov 05:30
♌ 27 Nov 06:20
♍ 29 Nov 10:12
♎ 1 Dec 17:30
♏ 4 Dec 03:36
♐ 6 Dec 15:28
♑ 9 Dec 04:15
♒ 11 Dec 17:00
♓ 14 Dec 04:19
♈ 16 Dec 12:31
♉ 18 Dec 16:46
♊ 20 Dec 17:40
♋ 22 Dec 16:53
♌ 24 Dec 16:33
♍ 26 Dec 18:35
♎ 29 Dec 00:15
♏ 31 Dec 09:37

MERCURY
♐ 1 Jan 00:00
♑ 7 Jan 02:05
♒ 26 Jan 09:33
♓ 12 Feb 15:29
♈ 2 Mar 22:51
♓ 18 Mar 09:24
♈ 17 Apr 22:10
♉ 8 May 21:23
♊ 23 May 21:23
♋ 7 Jun 00:19
♌ 26 Jun 15:40
♋ 31 Jul 18:45
♌ 11 Aug 04:26
♍ 31 Aug 15:16
♎ 16 Sep 12:54
♏ 5 Oct 05:13
♐ 30 Oct 20:09
♏ 9 Nov 20:14
♐ 11 Dec 02:10
♑ 31 Dec 06:49

VENUS
♑ 1 Jan 00:00
♒ 4 Jan 16:26
♓ 28 Jan 16:18
♈ 21 Feb 20:50
♉ 18 Mar 10:00
♊ 12 Apr 13:18
♋ 8 May 16:30
♌ 5 Jun 21:26
♍ 12 Jul 15:19
♌ 15 Aug 14:13
♍ 7 Oct 16:52
♎ 9 Nov 20:27
♏ 5 Dec 22:42
♐ 31 Dec 04:55

MARS
♎ 1 Jan 00:00
♏ 26 Jan 12:00
♎ 5 May 21:33
♏ 5 Jul 04:00
♐ 2 Sep 19:30
♑ 17 Oct 01:36
♒ 26 Nov 06:57

JUPITER
♓ 1 Jan 00:00
♈ 13 Feb 01:23
♉ 28 Jun 09:30
♈ 23 Oct 05:50

SATURN
♈ 1 Jan 00:00
♉ 1 Mar 01:26

2000

SUN
♑ 1 Jan 00:00
♒ 20 Jan 18:24
♓ 19 Feb 08:34
♈ 20 Mar 07:36
♉ 19 Apr 18:41
♊ 20 May 17:50
♋ 21 Jun 01:49
♌ 22 Jul 12:44
♍ 22 Aug 19:50
♎ 22 Sep 17:29
♏ 23 Oct 02:49
♐ 22 Nov 00:20
♑ 21 Dec 13:38

MOON
♏ 1 Jan 00:00
♐ 2 Jan 21:33
♑ 5 Jan 10:25
♒ 7 Jan 22:54
♓ 10 Jan 10:00
♈ 12 Jan 18:49
♉ 15 Jan 00:39
♊ 17 Jan 03:26
♋ 19 Jan 04:02
♌ 21 Jan 03:59
♍ 23 Jan 05:08
♎ 25 Jan 09:10
♏ 27 Jan 17:02
♐ 30 Jan 04:19
♑ 1 Feb 17:11
♒ 4 Feb 05:32
♓ 6 Feb 16:03
♈ 9 Feb 00:18
♉ 11 Feb 06:22
♊ 13 Feb 10:24
♋ 15 Feb 12:46
♌ 17 Feb 14:12
♍ 19 Feb 15:54
♎ 21 Feb 19:22
♏ 24 Feb 01:59
♐ 26 Feb 12:11
♑ 29 Feb 00:46
♒ 2 Mar 13:15
♓ 4 Mar 23:31
♈ 7 Mar 06:55
♉ 9 Mar 12:02
♊ 11 Mar 15:47
♋ 13 Mar 18:52
♌ 15 Mar 21:44
♍ 18 Mar 00:49
♎ 20 Mar 04:58
♏ 22 Mar 11:19
♐ 24 Mar 20:44
♑ 27 Mar 08:52
♒ 29 Mar 21:35
♓ 1 Apr 08:13
♈ 3 Apr 15:23
♉ 5 Apr 19:30
♊ 7 Apr 21:59
♋ 10 Apr 00:17
♌ 12 Apr 03:17
♍ 14 Apr 07:20
♎ 16 Apr 12:37
♏ 18 Apr 19:36
♐ 21 Apr 04:59
♑ 23 Apr 16:48
♒ 26 Apr 05:43
♓ 28 Apr 17:07
♈ 1 May 00:56
♉ 3 May 04:55
♊ 5 May 06:24
♋ 7 May 07:15
♌ 9 May 09:02
♍ 11 May 12:42
♎ 13 May 18:28
♏ 16 May 02:17
♐ 18 May 12:10
♑ 21 May 00:02
♒ 23 May 13:01
♓ 26 May 01:08
♈ 28 May 10:09
♉ 30 May 15:03
♊ 1 Jun 16:35
♋ 3 Jun 16:31
♌ 5 Jun 16:47
♍ 7 Jun 18:58
♎ 10 Jun 00:00
♏ 12 Jun 07:56
♐ 14 Jun 18:19
♑ 17 Jun 06:28
♒ 19 Jun 19:27
♓ 22 Jun 07:53
♈ 24 Jun 17:56
♉ 27 Jun 00:20
♊ 29 Jun 03:00
♋ 1 Jul 03:10
♌ 3 Jul 02:39
♍ 5 Jul 03:20
♎ 7 Jul 06:48
♏ 9 Jul 13:49
♐ 12 Jul 00:07
♑ 14 Jul 12:29
♒ 17 Jul 01:28
♓ 19 Jul 13:45
♈ 22 Jul 00:10
♉ 24 Jul 07:45
♊ 26 Jul 12:02
♋ 28 Jul 13:31
♌ 30 Jul 13:25
♍ 1 Aug 13:28
♎ 3 Aug 15:32
♏ 5 Aug 21:05
♐ 8 Aug 06:31
♑ 10 Aug 18:45
♒ 13 Aug 07:44
♓ 15 Aug 19:42
♈ 18 Aug 05:45
♉ 20 Aug 13:32
♊ 22 Aug 18:56
♋ 24 Aug 22:01
♌ 26 Aug 23:18
♍ 28 Aug 23:56
♎ 31 Aug 01:34
♏ 2 Sep 05:56
♐ 4 Sep 14:09
♑ 7 Sep 01:48
♒ 9 Sep 14:45
♓ 12 Sep 02:35
♈ 14 Sep 12:01
♉ 16 Sep 19:06
♊ 19 Sep 00:23
♋ 21 Sep 04:17
♌ 23 Sep 07:01
♍ 25 Sep 09:03
♎ 27 Sep 11:23
♏ 29 Sep 15:31
♐ 1 Oct 22:51
♑ 4 Oct 09:43
♒ 6 Oct 22:34
♓ 9 Oct 10:37
♈ 11 Oct 19:52
♉ 14 Oct 02:07
♊ 16 Oct 06:20
♋ 18 Oct 09:38
♌ 20 Oct 12:43
♍ 22 Oct 15:53
♎ 24 Oct 19:31
♏ 27 Oct 00:24
♐ 29 Oct 07:41
♑ 31 Oct 18:03
♒ 3 Nov 06:42
♓ 5 Nov 19:14
♈ 8 Nov 05:03
♉ 10 Nov 11:13
♊ 12 Nov 14:28
♋ 14 Nov 16:22
♌ 16 Nov 18:20
♍ 18 Nov 21:16
♎ 21 Nov 01:36
♏ 23 Nov 07:34
♐ 25 Nov 15:34
♑ 28 Nov 01:58
♒ 30 Nov 14:28
♓ 3 Dec 03:24
♈ 5 Dec 14:18
♉ 7 Dec 21:28
♊ 10 Dec 00:51
♋ 12 Dec 01:50
♌ 14 Dec 02:10
♍ 16 Dec 03:31
♎ 18 Dec 07:02
♏ 20 Dec 13:13
♐ 22 Dec 21:58
♑ 25 Dec 08:55
♒ 27 Dec 21:26
♓ 30 Dec 10:28

MERCURY
♑ 1 Jan 00:00
♒ 18 Jan 22:21
♓ 5 Feb 08:10
♈ 13 Apr 00:18
♉ 30 Apr 03:54
♊ 14 May 07:11
♋ 30 May 04:28
♌ 7 Aug 05:43
♍ 22 Aug 10:12
♎ 7 Sep 22:23
♏ 28 Sep 13:29
♎ 7 Nov 07:29
♏ 8 Nov 21:43
♐ 3 Dec 20:27
♑ 23 Dec 02:04

VENUS
♐ 1 Jan 00:00
♑ 24 Jan 19:54
♒ 18 Feb 04:44
♓ 13 Mar 11:37
♈ 6 Apr 18:38
♉ 1 May 02:50
♊ 25 May 12:16
♋ 18 Jun 22:16
♌ 13 Jul 08:03
♍ 6 Aug 17:33
♎ 31 Aug 03:36
♏ 24 Sep 15:27
♐ 19 Oct 06:19
♑ 13 Nov 02:15
♒ 8 Dec 08:49

MARS
♒ 1 Jan 00:00
♓ 4 Jan 03:02
♈ 12 Feb 01:05
♉ 23 Mar 01:26
♊ 3 May 19:19
♋ 16 Jun 12:31
♌ 1 Aug 01:22
♍ 17 Sep 00:20
♎ 4 Nov 02:01
♏ 23 Dec 14:38

JUPITER
♈ 1 Jan 00:00
♉ 14 Feb 21:40
♊ 30 Jun 07:36

SATURN
♉ 1 Jan 00:00
♊ 10 Aug 02:26
♉ 16 Oct 00:47

2001

SUN
♑ 1 Jan 00:00
♒ 20 Jan 00:17
♓ 18 Feb 14:28
♈ 20 Mar 13:32
♉ 20 Apr 00:37
♊ 20 May 23:45
♋ 21 Jun 07:39
♌ 22 Jul 18:27
♍ 23 Aug 01:28
♎ 22 Sep 23:06
♏ 23 Oct 08:27
♐ 22 Nov 06:02
♑ 21 Dec 19:23

MOON
♓ 1 Jan 00:00
♈ 1 Jan 22:15
♉ 4 Jan 06:58
♊ 6 Jan 11:45
♋ 8 Jan 13:10
♌ 10 Jan 12:45
♍ 12 Jan 12:27
♎ 14 Jan 14:06
♏ 16 Jan 19:03
♐ 19 Jan 03:37
♑ 21 Jan 14:58
♒ 24 Jan 03:44
♓ 26 Jan 16:40
♈ 29 Jan 04:36
♉ 31 Jan 14:22
♊ 2 Feb 20:57
♋ 5 Feb 00:01
♌ 7 Feb 00:22
♍ 8 Feb 23:36
♎ 10 Feb 23:47
♏ 13 Feb 02:52
♐ 15 Feb 10:03
♑ 17 Feb 21:00
♒ 20 Feb 09:55
♓ 22 Feb 22:46
♈ 25 Feb 10:21
♉ 27 Feb 20:07
♊ 2 Mar 03:37
♋ 4 Mar 08:25
♌ 6 Mar 10:31
♍ 8 Mar 10:45
♎ 10 Mar 10:48
♏ 12 Mar 12:44
♐ 14 Mar 18:18
♑ 17 Mar 04:03
♒ 19 Mar 16:37
♓ 22 Mar 05:29

♈ 24 Mar 16:45
♉ 27 Mar 01:52
♊ 29 Mar 09:02
♋ 31 Mar 14:24
♌ 2 Apr 17:55
♍ 4 Apr 19:48
♎ 6 Apr 20:58
♏ 8 Apr 23:02
♐ 11 Apr 03:48
♑ 13 Apr 12:22
♒ 16 Apr 00:12
♓ 18 Apr 13:01
♈ 21 Apr 00:19
♉ 23 Apr 08:57
♊ 25 Apr 15:12
♋ 27 Apr 19:50
♌ 29 Apr 23:26
♍ 2 May 02:17
♎ 4 May 04:51
♏ 6 May 08:02
♐ 8 May 13:06
♑ 10 May 21:11
♒ 13 May 08:21
♓ 15 May 21:02
♈ 18 May 08:42
♉ 20 May 17:30
♊ 22 May 23:13
♋ 25 May 02:43
♌ 27 May 05:13
♍ 29 May 07:39
♎ 31 May 10:42
♏ 2 Jun 14:57
♐ 4 Jun 20:59
♑ 7 Jun 05:24
♒ 9 Jun 16:21
♓ 12 Jun 04:54
♈ 14 Jun 17:04
♉ 17 Jun 02:40
♊ 19 Jun 08:43
♋ 21 Jun 11:42
♌ 23 Jun 12:56
♍ 25 Jun 13:59
♎ 27 Jun 16:12
♏ 29 Jun 20:30
♐ 2 Jul 03:14
♑ 4 Jul 12:23
♒ 6 Jul 23:34
♓ 9 Jul 12:06
♈ 12 Jul 00:37
♉ 14 Jul 11:14
♊ 16 Jul 18:27
♋ 18 Jul 21:57
♌ 20 Jul 22:44
♍ 22 Jul 22:30
♎ 24 Jul 23:09
♏ 27 Jul 02:18
♐ 29 Jul 08:45
♑ 31 Jul 18:17
♒ 3 Aug 05:54
♓ 5 Aug 18:31
♈ 8 Aug 07:06
♉ 10 Aug 18:24
♊ 13 Aug 03:00
♋ 15 Aug 07:56
♌ 17 Aug 09:26
♍ 19 Aug 08:54
♎ 21 Aug 08:20
♏ 23 Aug 09:51
♐ 25 Aug 15:00
♑ 28 Aug 00:03
♒ 30 Aug 11:49
♓ 2 Sep 00:33
♈ 4 Sep 12:59
♉ 7 Sep 00:19
♊ 9 Sep 09:42
♋ 11 Sep 16:10
♌ 13 Sep 19:17
♍ 15 Sep 19:40
♎ 17 Sep 19:01
♏ 19 Sep 19:28
♐ 21 Sep 23:03
♑ 24 Sep 06:49
♒ 26 Sep 18:06
♓ 29 Sep 06:51
♈ 1 Oct 19:09
♉ 4 Oct 06:02
♊ 6 Oct 15:13
♋ 8 Oct 22:20
♌ 11 Oct 02:55
♍ 13 Oct 04:59
♎ 15 Oct 05:27
♏ 17 Oct 06:04
♐ 19 Oct 08:48
♑ 21 Oct 15:12
♒ 24 Oct 01:27
♓ 26 Oct 13:57
♈ 29 Oct 02:16
♉ 31 Oct 12:49
♊ 2 Nov 21:14
♋ 5 Nov 03:45
♌ 7 Nov 08:35
♍ 9 Nov 11:50
♎ 11 Nov 13:54
♏ 13 Nov 15:46
♐ 15 Nov 18:52
♑ 18 Nov 00:41
♒ 20 Nov 09:56
♓ 22 Nov 21:53
♈ 25 Nov 10:22
♉ 27 Nov 21:07
♊ 30 Nov 05:05
♋ 2 Dec 10:31
♌ 4 Dec 14:17
♍ 6 Dec 17:12
♎ 8 Dec 19:58
♏ 10 Dec 23:10
♐ 13 Dec 03:31
♑ 15 Dec 09:49
♒ 17 Dec 18:44
♓ 20 Dec 06:10
♈ 22 Dec 18:46
♉ 25 Dec 06:13
♊ 27 Dec 14:40
♋ 29 Dec 19:41
♌ 31 Dec 22:10

MERCURY
♑ 1 Jan 00:00
♒ 10 Jan 13:27
♓ 1 Feb 07:14
♒ 6 Feb 19:58
♓ 17 Mar 06:06
♈ 6 Apr 07:15
♉ 21 Apr 20:09
♊ 6 May 04:54
♋ 12 Jul 22:48
♌ 30 Jul 10:19
♍ 14 Aug 05:05
♎ 1 Sep 00:38
♏ 7 Nov 19:54
♐ 26 Nov 18:25
♑ 15 Dec 19:56

VENUS
♒ 1 Jan 00:00
♓ 3 Jan 18:15
♈ 2 Feb 19:15
♉ 6 Jun 10:26
♊ 5 Jul 16:45
♋ 1 Aug 12:19
♌ 27 Aug 04:13
♍ 21 Sep 02:10
♎ 15 Oct 11:43
♏ 8 Nov 13:29
♐ 2 Dec 11:13
♑ 26 Dec 07:26

MARS
♏ 1 Jan 00:00
♐ 14 Feb 20:07
♑ 8 Sep 17:52
♒ 27 Oct 17:20
♓ 8 Dec 21:53

JUPITER
♊ 1 Jan 00:00
♋ 13 Jul 00:04

SATURN
♉ 1 Jan 00:00
♊ 20 Apr 22:00

2002

SUN
♑ 1 Jan 00:00
♒ 20 Jan 06:03
♓ 18 Feb 20:14
♈ 20 Mar 19:17
♉ 20 Apr 06:22
♊ 21 May 05:30
♋ 21 Jun 13:25
♌ 23 Jul 00:16
♍ 23 Aug 07:18
♎ 23 Sep 04:56
♏ 23 Oct 14:19
♐ 22 Nov 11:55
♑ 22 Dec 01:15

MOON
♌ 1 Jan 00:00
♍ 2 Jan 23:35
♎ 5 Jan 01:25
♏ 7 Jan 04:42
♐ 9 Jan 09:58
♑ 11 Jan 17:19
♒ 14 Jan 02:42
♓ 16 Jan 14:01
♈ 19 Jan 02:36
♉ 21 Jan 14:46
♊ 24 Jan 00:29
♋ 26 Jan 06:18
♌ 28 Jan 08:32
♍ 30 Jan 08:41
♎ 1 Feb 08:45
♏ 3 Feb 10:36
♐ 5 Feb 15:22
♑ 7 Feb 23:09
♒ 10 Feb 09:16
♓ 12 Feb 20:54
♈ 15 Feb 09:27
♉ 17 Feb 21:59
♊ 20 Feb 08:51
♋ 22 Feb 16:17
♌ 24 Feb 19:37
♍ 26 Feb 19:48
♎ 28 Feb 18:48
♏ 2 Mar 18:52
♐ 4 Mar 21:56
♑ 7 Mar 04:49
♒ 9 Mar 14:57
♓ 12 Mar 02:57
♈ 14 Mar 15:35
♉ 17 Mar 04:02
♊ 19 Mar 15:21
♋ 22 Mar 00:07
♌ 24 Mar 05:14
♍ 26 Mar 06:45
♎ 28 Mar 06:05
♏ 30 Mar 05:22
♐ 1 Apr 06:49
♑ 3 Apr 11:59
♒ 5 Apr 21:08
♓ 8 Apr 08:59
♈ 10 Apr 21:42
♉ 13 Apr 09:56
♊ 15 Apr 20:57
♋ 18 Apr 06:02
♌ 20 Apr 12:22
♍ 22 Apr 15:36
♎ 24 Apr 16:23
♏ 26 Apr 16:16
♐ 28 Apr 17:14
♑ 30 Apr 21:04
♒ 3 May 04:45
♓ 5 May 15:47
♈ 8 May 04:23
♉ 10 May 16:33
♊ 13 May 03:05
♋ 15 May 11:34
♌ 17 May 17:53
♍ 19 May 22:02
♎ 22 May 00:20
♏ 24 May 01:39
♐ 26 May 03:21
♑ 28 May 06:55
♒ 30 May 13:36
♓ 1 Jun 23:38
♈ 4 Jun 11:52
♉ 7 Jun 00:08
♊ 9 Jun 10:30
♋ 11 Jun 18:16
♌ 13 Jun 23:40
♍ 16 Jun 03:25
♎ 18 Jun 06:12
♏ 20 Jun 08:43
♐ 22 Jun 11:43
♑ 24 Jun 16:02
♒ 26 Jun 22:37
♓ 29 Jun 08:02
♈ 1 Jul 19:50
♉ 4 Jul 08:17
♊ 6 Jul 19:02
♋ 9 Jul 02:38
♌ 11 Jul 07:09
♍ 13 Jul 09:42
♎ 15 Jul 11:40
♏ 17 Jul 14:14
♐ 19 Jul 18:03
♑ 21 Jul 23:27
♒ 24 Jul 06:41
♓ 26 Jul 16:05
♈ 29 Jul 03:40
♉ 31 Jul 16:18
♊ 3 Aug 03:48
♋ 5 Aug 12:03
♌ 7 Aug 16:28
♍ 9 Aug 18:04
♎ 11 Aug 18:39
♏ 13 Aug 20:02
♐ 15 Aug 23:26
♑ 18 Aug 05:16
♒ 20 Aug 13:18
♓ 22 Aug 23:12
♈ 25 Aug 10:49
♉ 27 Aug 23:33
♊ 30 Aug 11:46
♋ 1 Sep 21:15
♌ 4 Sep 02:38
♍ 6 Sep 04:17
♎ 8 Sep 03:58
♏ 10 Sep 03:49
♐ 12 Sep 05:45
♑ 14 Sep 10:49
♒ 16 Sep 18:55
♓ 19 Sep 05:19
♈ 21 Sep 17:12
♉ 24 Sep 05:56
♊ 26 Sep 18:28
♋ 29 Sep 05:03
♌ 1 Oct 11:59
♍ 3 Oct 14:53
♎ 5 Oct 14:52
♏ 7 Oct 13:58
♐ 9 Oct 14:22
♑ 11 Oct 17:46
♒ 14 Oct 00:52
♓ 16 Oct 11:08
♈ 18 Oct 23:15
♉ 21 Oct 11:58
♊ 24 Oct 00:18
♋ 26 Oct 11:11
♌ 28 Oct 19:21
♍ 31 Oct 00:00
♎ 2 Nov 01:29
♏ 4 Nov 01:11
♐ 6 Nov 01:02
♑ 8 Nov 03:00
♒ 10 Nov 08:26
♓ 12 Nov 17:43
♈ 15 Nov 05:39
♉ 17 Nov 18:25
♊ 20 Nov 06:26
♋ 22 Nov 16:49
♌ 25 Nov 01:01
♍ 27 Nov 06:43
♎ 29 Nov 09:55
♏ 1 Dec 11:18
♐ 3 Dec 11:59
♑ 5 Dec 13:40
♒ 7 Dec 17:55
♓ 10 Dec 01:47
♈ 12 Dec 12:59
♉ 15 Dec 01:44
♊ 17 Dec 13:44
♋ 19 Dec 23:31
♌ 22 Dec 06:49
♍ 24 Dec 12:06
♎ 26 Dec 15:54
♏ 28 Dec 18:42
♐ 30 Dec 21:02

MERCURY
♑ 1 Jan 00:00
♒ 3 Jan 21:39
♑ 4 Feb 04:20
♒ 13 Feb 17:21
♓ 11 Mar 23:35
♈ 29 Mar 14:45
♉ 13 Apr 10:12
♊ 30 Apr 07:17
♋ 7 Jul 10:37
♌ 21 Jul 22:42
♍ 6 Aug 09:52
♎ 26 Aug 21:11
♍ 2 Oct 09:27
♎ 11 Oct 05:57
♏ 31 Oct 22:44
♐ 19 Nov 11:30
♑ 8 Dec 20:22

VENUS
♑ 1 Jan 00:00
♒ 19 Jan 03:43
♓ 12 Feb 01:19
♈ 8 Mar 01:43
♉ 1 Apr 06:41
♊ 25 Apr 17:58
♋ 20 May 13:28
♌ 14 Jun 20:17
♍ 10 Jul 21:10
♎ 7 Aug 09:10
♏ 8 Sep 03:06

MARS
♓ 1 Jan 00:00
♈ 18 Jan 22:54
♉ 1 Mar 15:06
♊ 13 Apr 17:37
♋ 28 May 11:44
♌ 13 Jul 15:24
♍ 29 Aug 14:39
♎ 15 Oct 17:39
♏ 1 Dec 14:27

JUPITER
♋ 1 Jan 00:00
♌ 1 Aug 17:21

SATURN
♊ 1 Jan 00:00

2003

SUN
♑ 1 Jan 00:00
♒ 20 Jan 11:54
♓ 19 Feb 02:01
♈ 21 Mar 01:01
♉ 20 Apr 12:04
♊ 21 May 11:13
♋ 21 Jun 19:12
♌ 23 Jul 06:05
♍ 23 Aug 13:09
♎ 23 Sep 10:48
♏ 23 Oct 20:10
♐ 22 Nov 17:44
♑ 22 Dec 07:05

MOON
♐ 1 Jan 00:00
♑ 1 Jan 23:44
♒ 4 Jan 03:58
♓ 6 Jan 10:58
♈ 8 Jan 21:16
♉ 11 Jan 09:49
♊ 13 Jan 22:09
♋ 16 Jan 07:57
♌ 18 Jan 14:30
♍ 20 Jan 18:33
♎ 22 Jan 21:24
♏ 25 Jan 00:10
♐ 27 Jan 03:27
♑ 29 Jan 07:31
♒ 31 Jan 12:45
♓ 2 Feb 19:56
♈ 5 Feb 05:45
♉ 7 Feb 18:00
♊ 10 Feb 06:46
♋ 12 Feb 17:20
♌ 15 Feb 00:05
♍ 17 Feb 03:24
♎ 19 Feb 04:49
♏ 21 Feb 06:10
♐ 23 Feb 08:47
♑ 25 Feb 13:12
♒ 27 Feb 19:26
♓ 2 Mar 03:27
♈ 4 Mar 13:31
♉ 7 Mar 01:37
♊ 9 Mar 14:39
♋ 12 Mar 02:13
♌ 14 Mar 10:07
♍ 16 Mar 13:54
♎ 18 Mar 14:44
♏ 20 Mar 14:39
♐ 22 Mar 15:34
♑ 24 Mar 18:49
♒ 27 Mar 00:52
♓ 29 Mar 09:27
♈ 31 Mar 20:06
♉ 3 Apr 08:21
♊ 5 Apr 21:25
♋ 8 Apr 09:37
♌ 10 Apr 18:55
♍ 13 Apr 00:08
♎ 15 Apr 01:43
♏ 17 Apr 01:17
♐ 19 Apr 00:53
♑ 21 Apr 02:21
♒ 23 Apr 06:59
♓ 25 Apr 15:03
♈ 28 Apr 01:55
♉ 30 Apr 14:27
♊ 3 May 03:28
♋ 5 May 15:43
♌ 8 May 01:47
♍ 10 May 08:32
♎ 12 May 11:43
♏ 14 May 12:15
♐ 16 May 11:44
♑ 18 May 12:04
♒ 20 May 15:02
♓ 22 May 21:42
♈ 25 May 08:00
♉ 27 May 20:33
♊ 30 May 09:33
♋ 1 Jun 21:28
♌ 4 Jun 07:28
♍ 6 Jun 14:52
♎ 8 Jun 19:31
♏ 10 Jun 21:40
♐ 12 Jun 22:13
♑ 14 Jun 22:39
♒ 17 Jun 00:42
♓ 19 Jun 05:58
♈ 21 Jun 15:07
♉ 24 Jun 03:16
♊ 26 Jun 16:14
♋ 29 Jun 03:53
♌ 1 Jul 13:14
♍ 3 Jul 20:17
♎ 6 Jul 01:21
♏ 8 Jul 04:45
♐ 10 Jul 06:49
♑ 12 Jul 08:22
♒ 14 Jul 10:39
♓ 16 Jul 15:15
♈ 18 Jul 23:21
♉ 21 Jul 10:49
♊ 23 Jul 23:43
♋ 26 Jul 11:24
♌ 28 Jul 20:18
♍ 31 Jul 02:28
♎ 2 Aug 06:49
♏ 4 Aug 10:13
♐ 6 Aug 13:12
♑ 8 Aug 16:03
♒ 10 Aug 19:25
♓ 13 Aug 00:20
♈ 15 Aug 08:01
♉ 17 Aug 18:53
♊ 20 Aug 07:42
♋ 22 Aug 19:45
♌ 25 Aug 04:49
♍ 27 Aug 10:28
♎ 29 Aug 13:42
♏ 31 Aug 16:01
♐ 2 Sep 18:33
♑ 4 Sep 21:52
♒ 7 Sep 02:16
♓ 9 Sep 08:08
♈ 11 Sep 16:10
♉ 14 Sep 02:51
♊ 16 Sep 15:33
♋ 19 Sep 04:08
♌ 21 Sep 14:04
♍ 23 Sep 20:06
♎ 25 Sep 22:50
♏ 27 Sep 23:53
♐ 30 Sep 00:58
♑ 2 Oct 03:22
♒ 4 Oct 07:46
♓ 6 Oct 14:21
♈ 8 Oct 23:09
♉ 11 Oct 10:06
♊ 13 Oct 22:46
♋ 16 Oct 11:42
♌ 18 Oct 22:42
♍ 21 Oct 06:02
♎ 23 Oct 09:28
♏ 25 Oct 10:10
♐ 27 Oct 09:56
♑ 29 Oct 10:38
♒ 31 Oct 13:42
♓ 2 Nov 19:53
♈ 5 Nov 05:04
♉ 7 Nov 16:30
♊ 10 Nov 05:15
♋ 12 Nov 18:11
♌ 15 Nov 05:49
♍ 17 Nov 14:37
♎ 19 Nov 19:43
♏ 21 Nov 21:25
♐ 23 Nov 21:04
♑ 25 Nov 20:32
♒ 27 Nov 21:49
♓ 30 Nov 02:26
♈ 2 Dec 10:57
♉ 4 Dec 22:31
♊ 7 Dec 11:27
♋ 10 Dec 00:12
♌ 12 Dec 11:41
♍ 14 Dec 21:08
♎ 17 Dec 03:48
♏ 19 Dec 07:21
♐ 21 Dec 08:17
♑ 23 Dec 07:56
♒ 25 Dec 08:14
♓ 27 Dec 11:11
♈ 29 Dec 18:09

MERCURY
♑ 1 Jan 00:00
♒ 13 Feb 01:01
♓ 5 Mar 02:05
♈ 21 Mar 12:17
♉ 5 Apr 14:38
♊ 13 Jun 01:35
♋ 29 Jun 10:16
♌ 13 Jul 12:11
♍ 30 Jul 14:06
♎ 7 Oct 01:29
♏ 24 Oct 11:21
♐ 12 Nov 07:20
♑ 2 Dec 21:35
♐ 30 Dec 19:53

VENUS
♏ 1 Jan 00:00
♐ 7 Jan 13:08
♑ 4 Feb 13:28
♒ 2 Mar 12:41
♓ 27 Mar 18:15
♈ 21 Apr 16:19
♉ 16 May 10:59
♊ 10 Jun 03:33
♋ 4 Jul 17:40
♌ 29 Jul 04:26
♍ 22 Aug 11:37
♎ 15 Sep 15:59
♏ 9 Oct 18:57
♐ 2 Nov 21:43
♑ 27 Nov 01:08
♒ 21 Dec 06:34

MARS
♏ 1 Jan 00:00
♐ 17 Jan 04:23
♑ 4 Mar 21:18
♒ 21 Apr 23:49
♓ 17 Jun 02:27
♈ 16 Dec 13:25

JUPITER
♌ 1 Jan 00:00
♍ 27 Aug 09:27

SATURN
♊ 1 Jan 00:00
♋ 4 Jun 01:28

2004

SUN
♑ 1 Jan 00:00
♒ 20 Jan 17:43
♓ 19 Feb 07:51
♈ 20 Mar 06:50
♉ 19 Apr 17:51
♊ 20 May 17:00
♋ 21 Jun 00:58
♌ 22 Jul 11:51
♍ 22 Aug 18:54
♎ 22 Sep 16:31
♏ 23 Oct 01:50
♐ 21 Nov 23:23
♑ 21 Dec 12:43

MOON
♈ 1 Jan 00:00
♉ 1 Jan 05:03
♊ 3 Jan 17:59
♋ 6 Jan 06:40
♌ 8 Jan 17:39
♍ 11 Jan 02:39
♎ 13 Jan 09:39
♏ 15 Jan 14:34
♐ 17 Jan 17:19
♑ 19 Jan 18:25
♒ 21 Jan 19:12
♓ 23 Jan 21:30
♈ 26 Jan 03:07
♉ 28 Jan 12:47
♊ 31 Jan 01:19
♋ 2 Feb 14:04
♌ 5 Feb 00:51
♍ 7 Feb 09:04
♎ 9 Feb 15:14
♏ 11 Feb 19:59
♐ 13 Feb 23:36
♑ 16 Feb 02:15
♒ 18 Feb 04:28
♓ 20 Feb 07:28
♈ 22 Feb 12:46
♉ 24 Feb 21:31
♊ 27 Feb 09:23
♋ 29 Feb 22:13
♌ 3 Mar 09:19
♍ 5 Mar 17:19
♎ 7 Mar 22:32
♏ 10 Mar 02:04
♐ 12 Mar 04:58
♑ 14 Mar 07:53
♒ 16 Mar 11:11
♓ 18 Mar 15:27
♈ 20 Mar 21:30
♉ 23 Mar 06:11
♊ 25 Mar 17:36
♋ 28 Mar 06:24
♌ 30 Mar 18:08
♍ 2 Apr 02:46
♎ 4 Apr 07:53
♏ 6 Apr 10:25
♐ 8 Apr 11:51
♑ 10 Apr 13:34
♒ 12 Apr 16:34
♓ 14 Apr 21:25
♈ 17 Apr 04:25
♉ 19 Apr 13:44
♊ 22 Apr 01:11
♋ 24 Apr 13:57
♌ 27 Apr 02:15
♍ 29 Apr 12:01
♎ 1 May 18:04
♏ 3 May 20:40
♐ 5 May 21:09
♑ 7 May 21:18
♒ 9 May 22:47
♓ 12 May 02:53
♈ 14 May 10:03
♉ 16 May 19:58
♊ 19 May 07:48
♋ 21 May 20:36
♌ 24 May 09:08
♍ 26 May 19:53
♎ 29 May 03:24
♏ 31 May 07:09
♐ 2 Jun 07:53
♑ 4 Jun 07:13
♒ 6 Jun 07:11
♓ 8 Jun 09:39
♈ 10 Jun 15:30
♉ 13 Jun 01:38
♊ 15 Jun 13:45
♋ 18 Jun 02:38
♌ 20 Jun 15:06
♍ 23 Jun 02:11
♎ 25 Jun 10:51
♏ 27 Jun 16:14
♐ 29 Jun 18:17
♑ 1 Jul 18:02
♒ 3 Jul 17:23
♓ 5 Jul 18:27
♈ 7 Jul 23:04
♉ 10 Jul 07:52
♊ 12 Jul 19:46
♋ 15 Jul 08:41
♌ 17 Jul 20:57
♍ 20 Jul 07:45
♎ 22 Jul 16:40
♏ 24 Jul 23:09
♐ 27 Jul 02:49
♑ 29 Jul 03:59
♒ 31 Jul 03:55
♓ 2 Aug 04:35
♈ 4 Aug 08:00
♉ 6 Aug 15:27
♊ 9 Aug 02:34
♋ 11 Aug 15:21
♌ 14 Aug 03:31
♍ 16 Aug 13:50
♎ 18 Aug 22:10
♏ 21 Aug 04:38
♐ 23 Aug 09:10
♑ 25 Aug 11:48
♒ 27 Aug 13:09
♓ 29 Aug 14:34
♈ 31 Aug 17:47
♉ 3 Sep 00:17
♊ 5 Sep 10:26
♋ 7 Sep 22:51
♌ 10 Sep 11:07
♍ 12 Sep 21:17
♎ 15 Sep 04:55
♏ 17 Sep 10:26
♐ 19 Sep 14:31
♑ 21 Sep 17:36
♒ 23 Sep 20:11
♓ 25 Sep 22:56
♈ 28 Sep 02:58
♉ 30 Sep 09:25
♊ 2 Oct 18:56
♋ 5 Oct 06:55
♌ 7 Oct 19:24
♍ 10 Oct 06:01
♎ 12 Oct 13:33
♏ 14 Oct 18:11
♐ 16 Oct 20:59
♑ 18 Oct 23:08
♒ 21 Oct 01:39
♓ 23 Oct 05:14
♈ 25 Oct 10:25
♉ 27 Oct 17:28
♊ 30 Oct 03:12
♋ 1 Nov 14:54
♌ 4 Nov 03:33
♍ 6 Nov 15:01
♎ 8 Nov 23:24

♏	11 Nov	04:06
♐	13 Nov	05:57
♑	15 Nov	06:34
♒	17 Nov	07:40
♓	19 Nov	10:39
♈	21 Nov	16:12
♉	24 Nov	00:17
♊	26 Nov	10:26
♋	28 Nov	22:12
♌	1 Dec	10:51
♍	3 Dec	23:01
♎	6 Dec	08:47
♏	8 Dec	14:45
♐	10 Dec	16:55
♑	12 Dec	16:43
♒	14 Dec	16:11
♓	16 Dec	17:25
♈	18 Dec	21:53
♉	21 Dec	05:53
♊	23 Dec	16:33
♋	26 Dec	04:39
♌	28 Dec	17:15
♍	31 Dec	05:34

MERCURY

♐	1 Jan	00:00
♑	14 Jan	11:03
♒	7 Feb	04:21
♓	25 Feb	12:59
♈	12 Mar	09:45
♉	1 Apr	02:29
♈	13 Apr	01:24
♉	16 May	06:55
♊	5 Jun	12:49
♋	19 Jun	19:51
♌	4 Jul	14:53
♍	25 Jul	13:59
♌	25 Aug	01:34
♍	10 Sep	07:39
♎	28 Sep	14:14
♏	15 Oct	22:58
♐	4 Nov	14:41

VENUS

♒	1 Jan	00:00
♓	14 Jan	17:17
♈	8 Feb	16:22
♉	5 Mar	18:13
♊	3 Apr	14:58
♋	7 Aug	11:03
♌	6 Sep	22:17
♍	3 Oct	17:21
♎	29 Oct	00:40
♏	22 Nov	13:32
♐	16 Dec	17:11

MARS

♈	1 Jan	00:00
♉	3 Feb	10:05
♊	21 Mar	07:40
♋	7 May	08:47
♌	23 Jun	20:52
♍	10 Aug	10:15
♎	26 Sep	09:17
♏	11 Nov	05:12
♐	25 Dec	16:05

JUPITER

♍	1 Jan	00:00
♎	25 Sep	03:24

SATURN

♋	1 Jan	00:00

2005

SUN

♑	1 Jan	00:00
♒	19 Jan	23:23
♓	18 Feb	13:33
♈	20 Mar	12:34
♉	19 Apr	23:38
♊	20 May	22:48
♋	21 Jun	06:47
♌	22 Jul	17:42
♍	23 Aug	00:47
♎	22 Sep	22:24
♏	23 Oct	07:43
♐	22 Nov	05:16
♑	21 Dec	18:36

MOON

♍	1 Jan	00:00
♎	2 Jan	16:21
♏	5 Jan	00:01
♐	7 Jan	03:45
♑	9 Jan	04:12
♒	11 Jan	03:08
♓	13 Jan	02:51
♈	15 Jan	05:28
♉	17 Jan	12:07
♊	19 Jan	22:25
♋	22 Jan	10:43
♌	24 Jan	23:22
♍	27 Jan	11:25
♎	29 Jan	22:14
♏	1 Feb	06:52
♐	3 Feb	12:22
♑	5 Feb	14:33
♒	7 Feb	14:27
♓	9 Feb	14:00
♈	11 Feb	15:22
♉	13 Feb	20:19
♊	16 Feb	05:19
♋	18 Feb	17:14
♌	21 Feb	05:56
♍	23 Feb	17:45
♎	26 Feb	04:00
♏	28 Feb	12:22
♐	2 Mar	18:31
♑	4 Mar	22:13
♒	6 Mar	23:50
♓	9 Mar	00:33
♈	11 Mar	02:04
♉	13 Mar	06:06
♊	15 Mar	13:45
♋	18 Mar	00:45
♌	20 Mar	13:18
♍	23 Mar	01:11
♎	25 Mar	11:01
♏	27 Mar	18:30
♐	29 Mar	23:58
♑	1 Apr	03:49
♒	3 Apr	06:32
♓	5 Apr	08:46
♈	7 Apr	11:29
♉	9 Apr	15:51
♊	11 Apr	22:56
♋	14 Apr	09:04
♌	16 Apr	21:18
♍	19 Apr	09:28
♎	21 Apr	19:28
♏	24 Apr	02:26
♐	26 Apr	06:47
♑	28 Apr	09:34
♒	30 Apr	11:55
♓	2 May	14:44
♈	4 May	18:37
♉	7 May	00:02
♊	9 May	07:30
♋	11 May	17:21
♌	14 May	05:18
♍	16 May	17:47
♎	19 May	04:31
♏	21 May	11:50
♐	23 May	15:39
♑	25 May	17:12
♒	27 May	18:11
♓	29 May	20:10
♈	1 Jun	00:09
♉	3 Jun	06:21
♊	5 Jun	14:37
♋	8 Jun	00:47
♌	10 Jun	12:41
♍	13 Jun	01:23
♎	15 Jun	13:00
♏	17 Jun	21:25
♐	20 Jun	01:46
♑	22 Jun	02:53
♒	24 Jun	02:37
♓	26 Jun	03:04
♈	28 Jun	05:52
♉	30 Jun	11:46
♊	2 Jul	20:27
♋	5 Jul	07:08
♌	7 Jul	19:12
♍	10 Jul	07:58
♎	12 Jul	20:10
♏	15 Jul	05:52
♐	17 Jul	11:36
♑	19 Jul	13:27
♒	21 Jul	12:56
♓	23 Jul	12:13
♈	25 Jul	13:24
♉	27 Jul	17:55
♊	30 Jul	02:03
♋	1 Aug	12:53
♌	4 Aug	01:11
♍	6 Aug	13:55
♎	9 Aug	02:10
♏	11 Aug	12:36
♐	13 Aug	19:48
♑	15 Aug	23:14
♒	17 Aug	23:40
♓	19 Aug	22:53
♈	21 Aug	23:02
♉	24 Aug	01:59
♊	26 Aug	08:44
♋	28 Aug	18:58
♌	31 Aug	07:15
♍	2 Sep	19:57
♎	5 Sep	07:53
♏	7 Sep	18:11
♐	10 Sep	02:04
♑	12 Sep	06:58
♒	14 Sep	09:03
♓	16 Sep	09:25
♈	18 Sep	09:44
♉	20 Sep	11:48
♊	22 Sep	17:08
♋	25 Sep	02:11
♌	27 Sep	14:04
♍	30 Sep	02:45
♎	2 Oct	14:25
♏	5 Oct	00:04
♐	7 Oct	07:29
♑	9 Oct	12:45
♒	11 Oct	16:06
♓	13 Oct	18:06
♈	15 Oct	19:40
♉	17 Oct	22:05
♊	20 Oct	02:45
♋	22 Oct	10:42
♌	24 Oct	21:50
♍	27 Oct	10:29
♎	29 Oct	22:16
♏	1 Nov	07:30
♐	3 Nov	13:56
♑	5 Nov	18:18
♒	7 Nov	21:32
♓	10 Nov	00:24
♈	12 Nov	03:23
♉	14 Nov	07:03
♊	16 Nov	12:11
♋	18 Nov	19:43
♌	21 Nov	06:11
♍	23 Nov	18:33
♎	26 Nov	06:59
♏	28 Nov	16:34
♐	30 Nov	22:33
♑	3 Dec	01:43
♒	5 Dec	03:37
♓	7 Dec	05:45
♈	9 Dec	09:03
♉	11 Dec	13:47
♊	13 Dec	20:00
♋	16 Dec	04:02
♌	18 Dec	14:19
♍	21 Dec	02:40
♎	23 Dec	15:27
♏	26 Dec	02:05
♐	28 Dec	08:45
♑	30 Dec	11:36

MERCURY

♐	1 Jan	00:00
♑	10 Jan	04:10
♒	30 Jan	05:38
♓	16 Feb	17:47
♈	5 Mar	01:35
♉	12 May	09:15
♊	28 May	10:45
♋	11 Jun	07:04
♌	28 Jun	04:02
♍	4 Sep	17:54
♎	20 Sep	16:41
♏	8 Oct	17:16
♐	30 Oct	09:03
♏	26 Nov	11:54
♐	12 Dec	21:20

VENUS

♐	1 Jan	00:00
♑	9 Jan	16:57
♒	2 Feb	15:43
♓	26 Feb	15:08
♈	22 Mar	16:26
♉	15 Apr	20:38
♊	10 May	04:15
♋	3 Jun	15:19
♌	28 Jun	05:54
♍	23 Jul	01:02
♎	17 Aug	03:06
♏	11 Sep	16:15
♐	8 Oct	01:01
♑	5 Nov	08:12
♒	15 Dec	15:59

MARS

♐	1 Jan	00:00
♑	6 Feb	18:33
♒	20 Mar	18:03
♓	1 May	02:59
♈	12 Jun	02:31
♉	28 Jul	05:13

JUPITER

♎	1 Jan	00:00
♏	26 Oct	02:52

SATURN

♋	1 Jan	00:00
♌	16 Jul	12:31

2006

SUN

♑	1 Jan	00:00
♒	20 Jan	05:16
♓	18 Feb	19:27
♈	20 Mar	18:27
♉	20 Apr	05:27
♊	21 May	04:33
♋	21 Jun	12:27
♌	22 Jul	23:19
♍	23 Aug	06:24
♎	23 Sep	04:04
♏	23 Oct	13:28
♐	22 Nov	11:03
♑	22 Dec	00:23

MOON

♑	1 Jan	00:00
♒	1 Jan	12:15
♓	3 Jan	12:45
♈	5 Jan	14:45
♉	7 Jan	19:10
♊	10 Jan	02:00
♋	12 Jan	10:51
♌	14 Jan	21:32
♍	17 Jan	09:50
♎	19 Jan	22:50
♏	22 Jan	10:30
♐	24 Jan	18:39
♑	26 Jan	22:32
♒	28 Jan	23:10
♓	30 Jan	22:33
♈	1 Feb	22:47
♉	4 Feb	01:32
♊	6 Feb	07:33
♋	8 Feb	16:34
♌	11 Feb	03:45
♍	13 Feb	16:14
♎	16 Feb	05:10
♏	18 Feb	17:12
♐	21 Feb	02:39
♑	23 Feb	08:17
♒	25 Feb	10:16
♓	27 Feb	09:57
♈	1 Mar	09:20
♉	3 Mar	10:23
♊	5 Mar	14:39
♋	7 Mar	22:39
♌	10 Mar	09:43
♍	12 Mar	22:25
♎	15 Mar	11:14
♏	17 Mar	23:00
♐	20 Mar	08:44
♑	22 Mar	15:37
♒	24 Mar	19:22
♓	26 Mar	20:34
♈	28 Mar	20:32
♉	30 Mar	21:02
♊	1 Apr	23:50
♋	4 Apr	06:16
♌	6 Apr	16:26
♍	9 Apr	05:00
♎	11 Apr	17:48
♏	14 Apr	05:09
♐	16 Apr	14:21
♑	18 Apr	21:14
♒	21 Apr	01:57
♓	23 Apr	04:44
♈	25 Apr	06:13
♉	27 Apr	07:28
♊	29 Apr	09:59
♋	1 May	15:18
♌	4 May	00:19
♍	6 May	12:21
♎	9 May	01:11
♏	11 May	12:26
♐	13 May	20:57
♑	16 May	03:00
♒	18 May	07:20
♓	20 May	10:40
♈	22 May	13:25
♉	24 May	16:02
♊	26 May	19:20
♋	29 May	00:35
♌	31 May	08:53
♍	2 Jun	20:18
♎	5 Jun	09:10
♏	7 Jun	20:42
♐	10 Jun	05:06
♑	12 Jun	10:20
♒	14 Jun	13:33
♓	16 Jun	16:06
♈	18 Jun	18:55
♉	20 Jun	22:24
♊	23 Jun	02:50
♋	25 Jun	08:49
♌	27 Jun	17:10
♍	30 Jun	04:16
♎	2 Jul	17:07
♏	5 Jul	05:14
♐	7 Jul	14:15
♑	9 Jul	19:26
♒	11 Jul	21:47
♓	13 Jul	23:01
♈	16 Jul	00:40
♉	18 Jul	03:45
♊	20 Jul	08:39
♋	22 Jul	15:29
♌	25 Jul	00:26
♍	27 Jul	11:37
♎	30 Jul	00:28
♏	1 Aug	13:09
♐	3 Aug	23:14
♑	6 Aug	05:21
♒	8 Aug	07:49
♓	10 Aug	08:11
♈	12 Aug	08:23
♉	14 Aug	10:01
♊	16 Aug	14:08
♋	18 Aug	21:04
♌	21 Aug	06:34
♍	23 Aug	18:09
♎	26 Aug	07:02
♏	28 Aug	19:57
♐	31 Aug	07:01
♑	2 Sep	14:36
♒	4 Sep	18:16
♓	6 Sep	18:56
♈	8 Sep	18:24
♉	10 Sep	18:31
♊	12 Sep	21:00
♋	15 Sep	02:55
♌	17 Sep	12:16
♍	20 Sep	00:08
♎	22 Sep	13:07
♏	25 Sep	01:55
♐	27 Sep	13:17
♑	29 Sep	22:02
♒	2 Oct	03:25
♓	4 Oct	05:34
♈	6 Oct	05:33
♉	8 Oct	05:05
♊	10 Oct	06:07
♋	12 Oct	10:22
♌	14 Oct	18:39
♍	17 Oct	06:17
♎	19 Oct	19:20
♏	22 Oct	07:55
♐	24 Oct	18:54
♑	27 Oct	03:48
♒	29 Oct	10:18
♓	31 Oct	14:12
♈	2 Nov	15:47
♉	4 Nov	16:06
♊	6 Nov	16:47
♋	8 Nov	19:47
♌	11 Nov	02:35
♍	13 Nov	13:20
♎	16 Nov	02:15
♏	18 Nov	14:48
♐	21 Nov	01:16
♑	23 Nov	09:26
♒	25 Nov	15:42
♓	27 Nov	20:22
♈	29 Nov	23:31
♉	2 Dec	01:27
♊	4 Dec	03:06
♋	6 Dec	06:02
♌	8 Dec	11:53
♍	10 Dec	21:32
♎	13 Dec	10:02
♏	15 Dec	22:44
♐	18 Dec	09:11
♑	20 Dec	16:40
♒	22 Dec	20:39
♓	25 Dec	01:44
♈	27 Dec	05:05
♉	29 Dec	08:09
♊	31 Dec	11:17

MERCURY

♐	1 Jan	00:00
♑	3 Jan	21:27
♒	22 Jan	20:43
♓	9 Feb	01:23
♈	16 Apr	12:21
♉	5 May	08:29
♊	19 May	20:53
♋	3 Jun	11:22
♌	28 Jun	19:58
♋	10 Jul	20:19
♌	11 Aug	04:11
♍	27 Aug	19:32
♎	12 Sep	21:09
♏	2 Oct	04:39
♐	8 Dec	05:53
♑	27 Dec	20:56

VENUS

♒	1 Jan	00:00
♑	1 Jan	20:19
♒	5 Mar	08:40
♓	6 Apr	01:22
♈	3 May	10:26
♉	29 May	12:42
♊	24 Jun	00:32
♋	19 Jul	02:42
♌	12 Aug	20:22
♍	6 Sep	06:16
♎	30 Sep	10:03
♏	24 Oct	09:59
♐	17 Nov	08:03
♑	11 Dec	05:34

MARS

♉	1 Jan	00:00
♊	17 Feb	22:45
♋	14 Apr	01:00
♌	3 Jun	18:44
♍	22 Jul	18:54
♎	8 Sep	04:19
♏	23 Oct	16:39
♐	6 Dec	04:59

JUPITER

♏	1 Jan	00:00
♐	24 Nov	04:44

SATURN

♌	1 Jan	00:00

2007

SUN

♑	1 Jan	00:00
♒	20 Jan	11:02
♓	19 Feb	01:10
♈	21 Mar	00:09
♉	20 Apr	11:08
♊	21 May	10:13
♋	21 Jun	18:08
♌	23 Jul	05:01
♍	23 Aug	12:09
♎	23 Sep	09:52
♏	23 Oct	19:16
♐	22 Nov	16:51
♑	22 Dec	06:09

MOON

♊	1 Jan	00:00
♋	2 Jan	15:15
♌	4 Jan	21:15
♍	7 Jan	06:19
♎	9 Jan	18:16
♏	12 Jan	07:09
♐	14 Jan	18:12
♑	17 Jan	01:50
♒	19 Jan	06:17
♓	21 Jan	08:49
♈	23 Jan	10:53
♉	25 Jan	13:30
♊	27 Jan	17:11
♋	29 Jan	22:17
♌	1 Feb	05:16
♍	3 Feb	14:35
♎	6 Feb	02:16
♏	8 Feb	15:11
♐	11 Feb	03:02
♑	13 Feb	11:43
♒	15 Feb	16:36
♓	17 Feb	18:31
♈	19 Feb	19:07
♉	21 Feb	20:04
♊	23 Feb	22:43
♋	26 Feb	03:49
♌	28 Feb	11:31
♍	2 Mar	21:33
♎	5 Mar	09:26
♏	7 Mar	22:18
♐	10 Mar	10:38
♑	12 Mar	20:36
♒	15 Mar	02:53
♓	17 Mar	05:31
♈	19 Mar	05:43
♉	21 Mar	05:16
♊	23 Mar	06:07
♋	25 Mar	09:50
♌	27 Mar	17:05
♍	30 Mar	03:28
♎	1 Apr	15:44
♏	4 Apr	04:37
♐	6 Apr	16:58
♑	9 Apr	03:37
♒	11 Apr	11:24
♓	13 Apr	15:40
♈	15 Apr	16:48
♉	17 Apr	16:12
♊	19 Apr	15:52
♋	21 Apr	17:51
♌	23 Apr	23:39
♍	26 Apr	09:25
♎	28 Apr	21:46
♏	1 May	10:42
♐	3 May	22:49
♑	6 May	09:22
♒	8 May	17:49
♓	10 May	23:33
♈	13 May	02:20
♉	15 May	02:49
♊	17 May	02:35
♋	19 May	03:39
♌	21 May	07:58
♍	23 May	16:27
♎	26 May	04:17
♏	28 May	17:12
♐	31 May	05:08
♑	2 Jun	15:10
♒	4 Jun	23:16
♓	7 Jun	05:25
♈	9 Jun	09:27
♉	11 Jun	11:30
♊	13 Jun	12:25
♋	15 Jun	13:46
♌	17 Jun	17:26
♍	20 Jun	00:47
♎	22 Jun	11:45
♏	25 Jun	00:28
♐	27 Jun	12:25
♑	29 Jun	22:06
♒	2 Jul	05:25
♓	4 Jul	10:53
♈	6 Jul	14:58
♉	8 Jul	17:55
♊	10 Jul	20:11
♋	12 Jul	22:40
♌	15 Jul	02:44
♍	17 Jul	09:40
♎	19 Jul	19:54
♏	22 Jul	08:19
♐	24 Jul	20:31
♑	27 Jul	06:22
♒	29 Jul	13:15
♓	31 Jul	17:42
♈	2 Aug	20:44
♉	4 Aug	23:17
♊	7 Aug	02:02
♋	9 Aug	05:37
♌	11 Aug	10:43
♍	13 Aug	18:04
♎	16 Aug	04:05
♏	18 Aug	16:14
♐	21 Aug	04:45
♑	23 Aug	15:21
♒	25 Aug	22:36
♓	28 Aug	02:35
♈	30 Aug	04:26
♉	1 Sep	05:36
♊	3 Sep	07:31
♋	5 Sep	11:09
♌	7 Sep	17:00
♍	10 Sep	01:11
♎	12 Sep	11:32
♏	14 Sep	23:38
♐	17 Sep	12:22
♑	19 Sep	23:53
♒	22 Sep	08:19
♓	24 Sep	12:56
♈	26 Sep	14:24
♉	28 Sep	14:18
♊	30 Sep	14:35
♋	2 Oct	16:58
♌	4 Oct	22:28
♍	7 Oct	07:04
♎	9 Oct	17:59
♏	12 Oct	06:14
♐	14 Oct	18:59
♑	17 Oct	07:04
♒	19 Oct	16:53
♓	21 Oct	23:03
♈	24 Oct	01:25
♉	26 Oct	01:08
♊	28 Oct	00:12
♋	30 Oct	00:51
♌	1 Nov	04:49
♍	3 Nov	12:46
♎	5 Nov	23:48
♏	8 Nov	12:19
♐	11 Nov	01:00
♑	13 Nov	13:02
♒	15 Nov	23:31
♓	18 Nov	07:16
♈	20 Nov	11:25
♉	22 Nov	12:20
♊	24 Nov	11:30
♋	26 Nov	11:08
♌	28 Nov	13:24
♍	30 Nov	19:45
♎	3 Dec	06:02
♏	5 Dec	18:32
♐	8 Dec	07:12
♑	10 Dec	18:52
♒	13 Dec	05:02
♓	15 Dec	13:16
♈	17 Dec	18:54
♉	19 Dec	21:39
♊	21 Dec	22:15
♋	23 Dec	22:19
♌	25 Dec	23:53
♍	28 Dec	04:45
♎	30 Dec	13:38

MERCURY

♑	1 Jan	00:00
♒	15 Jan	09:26
♓	2 Feb	09:21
♒	27 Feb	03:02
♓	18 Mar	09:36
♈	10 Apr	23:08
♉	27 Apr	07:17
♊	11 May	09:18
♋	29 May	00:57
♌	4 Aug	17:16
♍	19 Aug	13:02
♎	5 Sep	12:03
♏	27 Sep	17:19
♎	24 Oct	03:38
♏	11 Nov	08:42
♐	1 Dec	12:22
♑	20 Dec	14:44

VENUS

♑	1 Jan	00:00
♒	4 Jan	03:32
♓	28 Jan	03:33
♈	21 Feb	08:22
♉	17 Mar	22:02
♊	12 Apr	02:16
♋	8 May	07:29
♌	5 Jun	18:00
♍	14 Jul	18:25
♌	9 Aug	01:11
♍	8 Oct	06:54
♎	8 Nov	21:06
♏	5 Dec	13:30
♐	30 Dec	18:03

MARS

♐	1 Jan	00:00
♑	16 Jan	20:55
♒	26 Feb	01:33
♓	6 Apr	08:51
♈	15 May	14:07
♉	24 Jun	21:28
♊	7 Aug	06:02
♋	28 Sep	23:56

JUPITER

♐	1 Jan	00:00
♑	18 Dec	20:12

SATURN

♌	1 Jan	00:00
♍	2 Sep	13:49

2008

SUN

♑	1 Jan	00:00
♒	20 Jan	16:45
♓	19 Feb	06:51
♈	20 Mar	05:49
♉	19 Apr	16:52
♊	20 May	16:02
♋	21 Jun	00:00
♌	22 Jul	10:56
♍	22 Aug	18:03
♎	22 Sep	15:46
♏	23 Oct	01:10
♐	21 Nov	22:45
♑	21 Dec	12:05

MOON

♎ 1 Jan 00:00 | ♏ 2 Jan 01:33 | ♐ 4 Jan 14:14 | ♑ 7 Jan 01:44 | ♒ 9 Jan 11:14 | ♓ 11 Jan 18:45
♈ 14 Jan 00:24 | ♉ 16 Jan 04:14 | ♊ 18 Jan 06:31 | ♋ 20 Jan 08:06 | ♌ 22 Jan 10:21 | ♍ 24 Jan 14:49
♎ 26 Jan 22:36 | ♏ 29 Jan 09:36 | ♐ 31 Jan 22:09 | ♑ 3 Feb 09:53 | ♒ 5 Feb 19:11 | ♓ 8 Feb 01:47
♈ 10 Feb 06:18 | ♉ 12 Feb 09:35 | ♊ 14 Feb 12:20 | ♋ 16 Feb 15:13 | ♌ 18 Feb 18:52 | ♍ 21 Feb 00:07
♎ 23 Feb 07:46 | ♏ 25 Feb 18:07 | ♐ 28 Feb 06:23 | ♑ 1 Mar 18:34 | ♒ 4 Mar 04:26 | ♓ 6 Mar 10:54
♈ 8 Mar 14:24 | ♉ 10 Mar 16:15 | ♊ 12 Mar 17:55 | ♋ 14 Mar 20:39 | ♌ 17 Mar 01:05 | ♍ 19 Mar 07:26
♎ 21 Mar 15:46 | ♏ 24 Mar 02:07 | ♐ 26 Mar 14:12 | ♑ 29 Mar 02:44 | ♒ 31 Mar 13:35 | ♓ 2 Apr 20:56
♈ 5 Apr 00:28 | ♉ 7 Apr 01:21 | ♊ 9 Apr 01:28 | ♋ 11 Apr 02:44 | ♌ 13 Apr 06:30 | ♍ 15 Apr 13:08
♎ 17 Apr 22:11 | ♏ 20 Apr 09:01 | ♐ 22 Apr 21:08 | ♑ 25 Apr 09:48 | ♒ 27 Apr 21:28 | ♓ 30 Apr 06:12
♈ 2 May 10:52 | ♉ 4 May 11:59 | ♊ 6 May 11:18 | ♋ 8 May 11:03 | ♌ 10 May 13:11 | ♍ 12 May 18:49
♎ 15 May 03:47 | ♏ 17 May 15:00 | ♐ 20 May 03:20 | ♑ 22 May 15:56 | ♒ 25 May 03:53 | ♓ 27 May 13:39
♈ 29 May 19:54 | ♉ 31 May 22:20 | ♊ 2 Jun 21:17 | ♋ 4 Jun 21:17 | ♌ 6 Jun 22:01 | ♍ 9 Jun 02:02
♎ 11 Jun 09:56 | ♏ 13 Jun 20:54 | ♐ 16 Jun 09:21 | ♑ 18 Jun 21:53 | ♒ 21 Jun 09:35 | ♓ 23 Jun 19:33
♈ 26 Jun 02:50 | ♉ 28 Jun 06:51 | ♊ 30 Jun 08:04 | ♋ 2 Jul 07:54 | ♌ 4 Jul 08:16 | ♍ 6 Jul 11:05
♎ 8 Jul 17:32 | ♏ 11 Jul 03:36 | ♐ 13 Jul 15:51 | ♑ 16 Jul 04:21 | ♒ 18 Jul 15:41 | ♓ 21 Jul 01:09
♈ 23 Jul 08:23 | ♉ 25 Jul 13:15 | ♊ 27 Jul 15:56 | ♋ 29 Jul 17:13 | ♌ 31 Jul 18:23 | ♍ 2 Aug 21:00
♎ 5 Aug 02:29 | ♏ 7 Aug 11:27 | ♐ 9 Aug 23:11 | ♑ 12 Aug 11:43 | ♒ 14 Aug 22:57 | ♓ 17 Aug 07:47
♈ 19 Aug 14:11 | ♉ 21 Aug 18:39 | ♊ 23 Aug 21:49 | ♋ 26 Aug 00:20 | ♌ 28 Aug 02:52 | ♍ 30 Aug 08:19
♎ 1 Sep 11:46 | ♏ 3 Sep 20:03 | ♐ 6 Sep 07:12 | ♑ 8 Sep 19:46 | ♒ 11 Sep 07:21 | ♓ 13 Sep 16:06
♈ 15 Sep 21:40 | ♉ 18 Sep 00:58 | ♊ 20 Sep 03:18 | ♋ 22 Sep 05:50 | ♌ 24 Sep 09:15 | ♍ 26 Sep 13:53
♎ 28 Sep 20:07 | ♏ 1 Oct 04:27 | ♐ 3 Oct 15:15 | ♑ 6 Oct 03:50 | ♒ 8 Oct 16:04 | ♓ 11 Oct 01:32
♈ 13 Oct 07:08 | ♉ 15 Oct 09:32 | ♊ 17 Oct 10:26 | ♋ 19 Oct 11:41 | ♌ 21 Oct 14:36 | ♍ 23 Oct 19:41
♎ 26 Oct 02:49 | ♏ 28 Oct 11:48 | ♐ 30 Oct 22:42 | ♑ 2 Nov 11:14 | ♒ 5 Nov 00:03 | ♓ 7 Nov 10:44
♈ 9 Nov 17:27 | ♉ 11 Nov 20:06 | ♊ 13 Nov 20:12 | ♋ 15 Nov 19:53 | ♌ 17 Nov 21:09 | ♍ 20 Nov 01:14
♎ 22 Nov 08:21 | ♏ 24 Nov 17:55 | ♐ 27 Nov 05:15 | ♑ 29 Nov 17:49 | ♒ 2 Dec 06:46 | ♓ 4 Dec 18:24
♈ 7 Dec 02:45 | ♉ 9 Dec 06:53 | ♊ 11 Dec 07:34 | ♋ 13 Dec 06:41 | ♌ 15 Dec 06:24 | ♍ 17 Dec 08:37
♎ 19 Dec 14:24 | ♏ 22 Dec 23:38 | ♐ 24 Dec 11:14 | ♑ 26 Dec 23:57 | ♒ 29 Dec 12:44

VENUS

♎ 1 Jan 00:00 | ♑ 24 Jan 08:07 | ♒ 17 Feb 16:23 | ♓ 12 Mar 22:52 | ♈ 6 Apr 05:36 | ♉ 30 Apr 13:35
♊ 24 May 22:53 | ♋ 18 Jun 08:50 | ♌ 12 Jul 18:40 | ♍ 6 Aug 04:40 | ♎ 30 Aug 14:42 | ♏ 24 Sep 03:00
♐ 18 Oct 18:32 | ♑ 12 Nov 15:26 | ♒ 7 Dec 23:38

MARS

♊ 1 Jan 00:00 | ♋ 4 Mar 10:02 | ♌ 9 May 20:21 | ♍ 1 Jul 16:22 | ♎ 19 Aug 10:04 | ♏ 4 Oct 04:35
♐ 16 Nov 16:50 | ♑ 27 Dec 07:31

JUPITER

♑ 1 Jan 00:00

SATURN

♍ 1 Jan 00:00

MERCURY (2008)

♑ 1 Jan 00:00 | ♓ 14 Mar 22:47 | ♈ 2 Apr 17:46 | ♉ 17 Apr 21:08 | ♊ 2 May 20:01
♋ 10 Jul 20:18 | ♌ 26 Jul 11:49 | ♍ 10 Aug 10:52 | ♎ 29 Aug 02:51 | ♐ 4 Nov 16:01 | ♏ 23 Nov 07:10 | ♑ 12 Dec 10:14

2009

SUN

♑ 1 Jan 00:00 | ♒ 19 Jan 22:41 | ♓ 18 Feb 12:47 | ♈ 20 Mar 11:45 | ♉ 19 Apr 22:45 | ♊ 20 May 21:52
♋ 21 Jun 05:47 | ♌ 22 Jul 16:37 | ♍ 22 Aug 23:40 | ♎ 22 Sep 21:20 | ♏ 23 Oct 06:45 | ♐ 22 Nov 04:24
♑ 21 Dec 17:48

MOON

♈ 1 Jan 00:00 | ♈ 1 Jan 00:28 | ♉ 3 Jan 09:51 | ♊ 5 Jan 15:47 | ♋ 7 Jan 18:13 | ♌ 9 Jan 18:15
♍ 11 Jan 17:42 | ♎ 13 Jan 18:34 | ♏ 15 Jan 22:31 | ♐ 18 Jan 06:21 | ♑ 20 Jan 17:31 | ♒ 23 Jan 06:19
♓ 25 Jan 18:58 | ♈ 28 Jan 06:13 | ♉ 30 Jan 15:26 | ♊ 1 Feb 22:10 | ♋ 4 Feb 02:16 | ♌ 6 Feb 04:07
♍ 8 Feb 04:44 | ♎ 10 Feb 05:39 | ♏ 12 Feb 08:34 | ♐ 14 Feb 14:52 | ♑ 17 Feb 00:54 | ♒ 19 Feb 13:26
♓ 22 Feb 02:07 | ♈ 24 Feb 13:01 | ♉ 26 Feb 21:25 | ♊ 1 Mar 03:34 | ♋ 3 Mar 08:00 | ♌ 5 Mar 11:08
♍ 7 Mar 13:25 | ♎ 9 Mar 15:35 | ♏ 11 Mar 18:47 | ♐ 14 Mar 00:24 | ♑ 16 Mar 09:23 | ♒ 18 Mar 21:20
♓ 21 Mar 10:08 | ♈ 23 Mar 21:09 | ♉ 26 Mar 05:04 | ♊ 28 Mar 10:10 | ♋ 30 Mar 13:37 | ♌ 1 Apr 16:31
♍ 3 Apr 19:34 | ♎ 5 Apr 23:02 | ♏ 8 Apr 03:23 | ♐ 10 Apr 09:24 | ♑ 12 Apr 18:02 | ♒ 15 Apr 05:28
♓ 17 Apr 18:20 | ♈ 20 Apr 05:56 | ♉ 22 Apr 14:10 | ♊ 24 Apr 18:47 | ♋ 26 Apr 21:03 | ♌ 28 Apr 22:39
♍ 1 May 00:57 | ♎ 3 May 04:38 | ♏ 5 May 09:52 | ♐ 7 May 16:49 | ♑ 10 May 01:50 | ♒ 12 May 13:10
♓ 15 May 02:02 | ♈ 17 May 14:18 | ♉ 19 May 23:31 | ♊ 22 May 04:41 | ♋ 24 May 06:35 | ♌ 26 May 06:59
♍ 28 May 07:45 | ♎ 30 May 10:19 | ♏ 1 Jun 15:18 | ♐ 3 Jun 22:45 | ♑ 6 Jun 08:25 | ♒ 8 Jun 20:01
♓ 11 Jun 08:54 | ♈ 13 Jun 21:33 | ♉ 16 Jun 07:53 | ♊ 18 Jun 14:21 | ♋ 20 Jun 17:01 | ♌ 22 Jun 17:13
♍ 24 Jun 16:51 | ♎ 26 Jun 17:48 | ♏ 28 Jun 21:26 | ♐ 1 Jul 04:20 | ♑ 3 Jul 14:12 | ♒ 6 Jul 02:09
♓ 8 Jul 15:04 | ♈ 11 Jul 03:45 | ♉ 13 Jul 14:41 | ♊ 16 Jul 22:31 | ♋ 18 Jul 02:42 | ♌ 20 Jul 03:52
♍ 22 Jul 03:29 | ♎ 24 Jul 03:24 | ♏ 26 Jul 05:27 | ♐ 28 Jul 10:57 | ♑ 30 Jul 20:11 | ♒ 2 Aug 08:09
♓ 4 Aug 21:09 | ♈ 7 Aug 09:35 | ♉ 9 Aug 20:24 | ♊ 12 Aug 04:51 | ♋ 14 Aug 10:27 | ♌ 16 Aug 13:14
♍ 18 Aug 13:58 | ♎ 20 Aug 14:02 | ♏ 22 Aug 15:13 | ♐ 24 Aug 19:17 | ♑ 27 Aug 03:17 | ♒ 29 Aug 14:45
♓ 1 Sep 03:44 | ♈ 3 Sep 15:59 | ♉ 6 Sep 02:15 | ♊ 8 Sep 10:19 | ♋ 10 Sep 16:18 | ♌ 12 Sep 20:21
♍ 14 Sep 22:40 | ♎ 16 Sep 23:57 | ♏ 19 Sep 01:27 | ♐ 21 Sep 04:53 | ♑ 23 Sep 11:44 | ♒ 25 Sep 22:20
♓ 28 Sep 11:08 | ♈ 30 Sep 23:27 | ♉ 3 Oct 09:22 | ♊ 5 Oct 16:34 | ♋ 7 Oct 21:48 | ♌ 10 Oct 01:49
♍ 12 Oct 05:04 | ♎ 14 Oct 07:46 | ♏ 16 Oct 10:31 | ♐ 18 Oct 14:24 | ♑ 20 Oct 20:50 | ♒ 23 Oct 06:40
♓ 25 Oct 19:09 | ♈ 28 Oct 07:46 | ♉ 30 Oct 17:58 | ♊ 2 Nov 00:46 | ♋ 4 Nov 04:54 | ♌ 6 Nov 07:44
♍ 8 Nov 10:24 | ♎ 10 Nov 13:31 | ♏ 12 Nov 17:23 | ♐ 14 Nov 22:25 | ♑ 17 Nov 05:23 | ♒ 19 Nov 15:02
♓ 22 Nov 03:12 | ♈ 24 Nov 16:09 | ♉ 27 Nov 03:12 | ♊ 29 Nov 10:35 | ♋ 1 Dec 14:25 | ♌ 3 Dec 16:02
♍ 5 Dec 17:08 | ♎ 7 Dec 19:07 | ♏ 9 Dec 22:48 | ♐ 12 Dec 04:33 | ♑ 14 Dec 12:26 | ♒ 16 Dec 22:33
♓ 19 Dec 10:40 | ♈ 21 Dec 23:43 | ♉ 24 Dec 11:41 | ♊ 26 Dec 20:27 | ♋ 29 Dec 01:14 | ♌ 31 Dec 02:46

MERCURY

♑ 1 Jan 00:00 | ♒ 1 Jan 09:52 | ♑ 21 Jan 05:37 | ♒ 14 Feb 15:40 | ♓ 8 Mar 18:57 | ♈ 25 Mar 19:56
♉ 9 Apr 14:22 | ♊ 30 Apr 22:30 | ♋ 13 May 23:54 | ♊ 14 Jun 02:48 | ♋ 3 Jul 19:21 | ♌ 17 Jul 23:09
♍ 2 Aug 23:08 | ♎ 25 Aug 20:19 | ♍ 18 Sep 03:27 | ♎ 10 Oct 03:47 | ♏ 28 Oct 10:10 | ♐ 6 Nov 00:29
♑ 5 Dec 17:25

VENUS

♒ 1 Jan 00:00 | ♓ 3 Jan 12:37 | ♈ 3 Feb 03:42 | ♉ 11 Apr 12:48 | ♈ 24 Apr 07:19 | ♉ 6 Jun 00:46
♊ 5 Jul 08:24 | ♋ 1 Aug 01:29 | ♌ 26 Aug 16:13 | ♍ 20 Sep 13:33

MARS

♐ 1 Jan 00:00 | ♑ 4 Feb 15:56 | ♒ 15 Mar 03:21 | ♓ 22 Apr 13:45 | ♈ 31 May 21:19 | ♉ 2 Jul 02:57
♊ 25 Aug 17:17 | ♋ 16 Oct 15:33

JUPITER

♑ 1 Jan 00:00 | ♒ 5 Jan 15:42

SATURN

♍ 1 Jan 00:00 | ♎ 29 Oct 17:09

2010

SUN

♑ 1 Jan 00:00 | ♒ 20 Jan 04:29 | ♓ 18 Feb 18:37 | ♈ 20 Mar 17:33 | ♉ 20 Apr 04:31 | ♊ 21 May 03:35
♋ 21 Jun 11:30 | ♌ 22 Jul 22:22 | ♍ 23 Aug 05:28 | ♎ 23 Sep 03:10 | ♏ 23 Oct 12:36 | ♐ 22 Nov 10:16
♑ 21 Dec 23:40

MOON

♍ 1 Jan 00:00 | ♎ 2 Jan 02:42 | ♏ 4 Jan 02:54 | ♐ 6 Jan 04:59 | ♑ 8 Jan 10:01 | ♒ 10 Jan 18:11
♓ 13 Jan 04:55 | ♈ 15 Jan 17:18 | ♉ 18 Jan 06:18 | ♊ 20 Jan 18:37 | ♋ 23 Jan 04:41 | ♌ 25 Jan 11:12
♍ 27 Jan 14:02 | ♎ 29 Jan 14:11 | ♏ 31 Jan 13:24 | ♐ 2 Feb 13:43 | ♑ 4 Feb 16:57 | ♒ 7 Feb 00:05
♓ 9 Feb 10:45 | ♈ 11 Feb 23:25 | ♉ 14 Feb 12:24 | ♊ 17 Feb 00:31 | ♋ 19 Feb 10:56 | ♌ 21 Feb 18:48
♍ 23 Feb 23:30 | ♎ 26 Feb 01:09 | ♏ 28 Feb 00:53 | ♐ 2 Mar 00:32 | ♑ 4 Mar 02:12 | ♒ 6 Mar 07:37
♓ 8 Mar 17:14 | ♈ 11 Mar 05:43 | ♉ 13 Mar 18:45 | ♊ 16 Mar 06:33 | ♋ 18 Mar 16:30 | ♌ 21 Mar 00:29
♍ 23 Mar 06:17 | ♎ 25 Mar 09:40 | ♏ 27 Mar 10:58 | ♐ 29 Mar 11:22 | ♑ 31 Mar 12:42 | ♒ 2 Apr 16:54
♓ 5 Apr 01:08 | ♈ 7 Apr 12:52 | ♉ 10 Apr 01:49 | ♊ 12 Apr 13:32 | ♋ 14 Apr 22:56 | ♌ 17 Apr 06:09
♍ 19 Apr 11:40 | ♎ 21 Apr 18:25 | ♏ 23 Apr 18:25 | ♐ 27 Apr 22:30 | ♑ 30 Apr 02:37 | ♒ 2 May 10:01
♓ 4 May 20:53 | ♈ 7 May 09:21 | ♉ 9 May 21:30 | ♊ 12 May 06:49 | ♋ 14 May 13:19 | ♌ 16 May 17:47
♍ 18 May 21:07 | ♎ 20 May 23:59 | ♏ 23 May 02:51 | ♐ 25 May 06:18 | ♑ 27 May 11:17 | ♒ 29 May 18:45
♓ 1 Jun 05:09 | ♈ 3 Jun 17:35 | ♉ 6 Jun 05:51 | ♊ 8 Jun 15:42 | ♋ 10 Jun 22:12 | ♌ 13 Jun 01:51
♍ 15 Jun 03:55 | ♎ 17 Jun 05:42 | ♏ 19 Jun 08:14 | ♐ 21 Jun 11:17 | ♑ 23 Jun 18:11 | ♒ 26 Jun 02:22
♓ 28 Jun 13:53 | ♈ 1 Jul 01:11 | ♉ 3 Jul 13:45 | ♊ 6 Jul 00:30 | ♋ 8 Jul 07:52 | ♌ 10 Jul 11:39
♍ 12 Jul 12:55 | ♎ 14 Jul 13:16 | ♏ 16 Jul 14:25 | ♐ 18 Jul 17:43 | ♑ 20 Jul 23:50 | ♒ 23 Jul 08:40
♓ 25 Jul 19:39 | ♈ 28 Jul 08:01 | ♉ 30 Jul 20:43 | ♊ 2 Aug 08:14 | ♋ 4 Aug 16:55 | ♌ 6 Aug 21:51
♍ 8 Aug 23:24 | ♎ 10 Aug 23:02 | ♏ 12 Aug 22:44 | ♐ 14 Aug 00:27 | ♑ 17 Aug 05:35 | ♒ 19 Aug 14:16
♓ 22 Aug 01:38 | ♈ 24 Aug 14:12 | ♉ 27 Aug 02:50 | ♊ 29 Aug 14:36 | ♋ 1 Sep 00:20 | ♌ 3 Sep 06:52
♍ 5 Sep 09:46 | ♎ 7 Sep 09:54 | ♏ 9 Sep 09:02 | ♐ 11 Sep 09:22 | ♑ 13 Sep 12:53 | ♒ 15 Sep 20:31
♓ 18 Sep 07:36 | ♈ 20 Sep 20:16 | ♉ 23 Sep 08:48 | ♊ 25 Sep 20:18 | ♋ 28 Sep 06:12 | ♌ 30 Sep 13:47
♍ 2 Oct 18:21 | ♎ 4 Oct 20:01 | ♏ 6 Oct 19:53 | ♐ 8 Oct 19:53 | ♑ 10 Oct 22:10 | ♒ 13 Oct 04:18
♓ 15 Oct 14:25 | ♈ 18 Oct 02:53 | ♉ 20 Oct 15:24 | ♊ 23 Oct 02:31 | ♋ 25 Oct 11:49 | ♌ 27 Oct 19:15
♍ 30 Oct 00:40 | ♎ 1 Nov 03:52 | ♏ 3 Nov 05:20 | ♐ 5 Nov 08:17 | ♑ 7 Nov 08:29 | ♒ 9 Nov 13:38
♓ 11 Nov 22:33 | ♈ 14 Nov 10:25 | ♉ 17 Nov 23:00 | ♊ 19 Nov 10:05 | ♋ 21 Nov 18:47 | ♌ 24 Nov 01:15
♍ 26 Nov 06:02 | ♎ 28 Nov 09:35 | ♏ 30 Nov 12:16 | ♐ 2 Dec 14:45 | ♑ 4 Dec 18:00 | ♒ 6 Dec 23:17
♓ 9 Dec 07:32 | ♈ 11 Dec 18:42 | ♉ 14 Dec 07:16 | ♊ 16 Dec 18:50 | ♋ 19 Dec 03:38 | ♌ 21 Dec 09:23
♍ 23 Dec 12:52 | ♎ 25 Dec 15:15 | ♏ 27 Dec 17:39 | ♐ 29 Dec 20:51

MERCURY

♑ 1 Jan 00:00 | ♒ 10 Feb 09:07 | ♓ 1 Mar 13:29 | ♈ 17 Mar 16:13 | ♉ 2 Apr 13:07 | ♊ 10 Jun 05:42
♋ 9 Jul 16:30 | ♌ 27 Jul 21:44 | ♍ 3 Oct 15:05 | ♎ 20 Oct 21:20 | ♏ 8 Nov 23:44 | ♐ 1 Dec 00:12
♑ 18 Dec 14:55

VENUS

♒ 1 Jan 00:00 | ♓ 18 Jan 14:36 | ♈ 11 Feb 12:11 | ♉ 7 Mar 12:34 | ♊ 31 Mar 17:36 | ♋ 25 Apr 05:06
♌ 20 May 01:06 | ♍ 14 Jun 08:51 | ♎ 10 Jul 11:33 | ♏ 7 Aug 03:49 | ♐ 8 Sep 15:46 | ♏ 8 Nov 03:07
♐ 30 Nov 00:34

MARS

♌ 1 Jan 00:00 | ♍ 7 Jun 06:12 | ♎ 29 Jul 23:47 | ♏ 14 Sep 22:39 | ♐ 28 Oct 06:49 | ♑ 7 Dec 23:50

JUPITER

♓ 1 Jan 00:00 | ♈ 18 Jan 02:11 | ♓ 6 Jun 02:28 | ♈ 9 Sep 04:51

SATURN

♍ 1 Jan 00:00 | ♎ 7 Apr 18:55 | ♍ 21 Jul 15:09

YOUR BIRTH CHART

So that you can draw up planetary pictures for your-self, your family and your friends, a blank chart is included here for you to photocopy. Use it to record the planetary positions each time you draw up a chart *(see example on page 9)*. You can then refer to it as you look through the book to discover what it all means! (NOTE: If you wish to write in the information as well as the symbols, enlarge the chart when you copy it!)

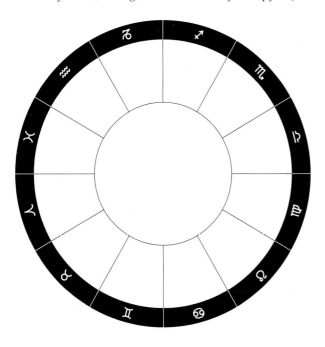

FURTHER READING

If you want to learn more about astrology, there are hundreds of books to choose from, including books telling you how to calculate your own birth chart in great detail. The following list is a selection of books that describe the actions of individual planets and therefore complement the information in this book.

Exploring Jupiter, Stephen Arroyo. CRCS
    Publications, Sebastapol, 1995
Love and Sexuality, Babs Kirby and Janey Stubbs.
    Element Books, Shaftesbury, 1992
Moon Signs: The Key to your Inner Life, Donna
    Cunningham. Ballantine Books, New York, 1988
The Moon in your Life, Donna Cunningham.
    Samuel Weiser, York Beach, 1996
Saturn: A New Look at an Old Devil, Liz Greene.
    Samuel Weiser, York Beach, 1976
Sun Sign, Moon Sign, Charles and Suzi Harvey.
    Thorsons, London, 1994
The Twelve Faces of Saturn, Bil Tierney.
    Llewellyn Publications, 1997

There are some marvellous astrology sites on the inter-net, some of which will calculate a birth chart for you (you should be able to find these sites by doing a search). There are also many excellent astrology magazines now available, catering for every level of knowledge.

ACKNOWLEDGEMENTS

AUTHOR'S ACKNOWLEDGEMENTS

Many people have helped me to write this book. First of all, I would like to say a huge thank you to the team at Eddison Sadd. I have really enjoyed working with them, especially Tessa Monina, Ian Jackson and Nick Eddison. I should also like to thank Brazzle Atkins for making the book look so good, and Mike Shepherd for his marvellous metal artworks that formed the illus-trations. And thanks to my friend, Maggie Genthner, for her pertinent questions; to my agent, Chelsey Fox, for her help; and especially to my husband, Bill Martin, for his love and patient understanding.

EDDISON•SADD EDITIONS

Editorial Director Ian Jackson
Senior Editor Tessa Monina
Proofreader Nikky Twyman

Creative Director Nick Eddison
Art Director Elaine Partington
Senior Art Editor Pritty Ramjee
Mac Designer Brazzle Atkins

Production Karyn Claridge and Charles James